A.L. ~

and Cc

A.L. Rowse frequently expressed ambivalence towards Cornwall and the Cornish people, and yet his sense of his own 'Cornishness' was central to his entire being; neither the man nor his works can be properly understood without taking this fact into account. His books *A Cornish Childhood* and *Tudor Cornwall* remain in strong demand, known and read by the general reader and historian alike, and by those who know and love Cornwall.

Philip Payton's award-winning biographical study sheds new light on this complex character and invites a greater understanding of the broader issues of Cornish identity.

Philip Payton edits the series *Cornish Studies*, published by University of Exeter Press, and is the author of numerous books including *The Making of Modern Cornwall* (1992), *Cornwall: A History* (1996, new edition 2004), *The Cornish Overseas: A History of Cornwall's Great Emigration* (1999, new edition, 2005) and *A Vision of Cornwall* (2002).

His other new book for University of Exeter Press—on Cornish miners in Australia—is called *Making Moonta: The Invention of 'Australia's Little Cornwall'*.

A.L. Rowse and Cornwall was winner of the Adult Non-Fiction section of the *Holyer an Gof* Awards 2006 awarded by the Cornish Gorseth for making a significant contribution to Cornish culture and research, and Overall Winner of the *Holyer an Gof* Trophy.

'. . . The latest and most insightful of biographies of Rowse. . . essential reading for anyone who wants to understand a great Cornishman and the nuances of Cornish and Cornish-American identities.'

Cornish World

'This is A.L. Rowse as we have never seen him before: it provides us with the key—in so far as such a key can ever be found—to Rowse's notoriously contradictory personality.'

Mark Stoyle, University of Southampton

'Professor Payton is to be congratulated on producing such an intriguing, lively and informed volume. . . . I enjoyed the book immensely and found it difficult to put the book down. . .'

Colin H. Williams, Cardiff University

'This is an excellent biography which is highly readable and well worth the effort. It does throw new light on the man and his place amongst Cornish letters and, despite all the negatives and contradictions, recognises Rowse's claim to be, if not necessarily the greatest, certainly a very great Cornishman.'

Cornwall Association of Local Historians Journal

'This probing but affectionate look at a very complex character is not only of interest to those who have followed Rowse, it is also a fascinating insight into both how that character related to Cornwall and how his homeland reacted to him.'

The West Briton

A.L. Rowse

and Cornwall

A Paradoxical Patriot

PHILIP PAYTON

UNIVERSITY
of
EXETER
PRESS

COVER ILLUSTRATIONS: *Front cover:* Rowse at Polmear Mine; *Back cover:* Rowse at Trenarren (courtesy of Special Collections, University of Exeter Library).

First published in 2005 by
University of Exeter Press
Reed Hall, Streatham Drive
Exeter EX4 4QR
UK
www.exeterpress.co.uk

This paperback edition published 2007

British Library Cataloguing in Publication Data
A catalogue record for this book is available
from the British Library.

ISBN 978 0 85989 798 3

Typeset in Plantin Light
by XL Publishing Services, Tiverton

Printed in Great Britain by Antony Rowe Ltd, Chippenham

For James

'Not keen about people writing about me—they are simply not up to the subject—too difficult for them'

(Letter from A.L Rowse to D.R. Rawe of Padstow, Cornwall, 7 February 1972, Llyfrgell Genedlaethol Cymru/ National Library of Wales, Legonna Papers, 33/7)

Contents

Illustrations

Preface

As a teenager I fell under the spell of *Tudor Cornwall*. My first contacts with A.L. Rowse, however, were as a young postgraduate student at the University of Adelaide when I wrote to him to seek advice on writing about the Cornish in Australia. Already aware of his reputation, I was braced for the likely rebuff. But instead of the scornful dismissal of my efforts as the misguided idiocy of an ignorant third-rater, I was pleasantly surprised— or rather astonished—by a return-of-post reply brimming over with encouragement and stuffed full with ideas of sources I might tap and people I might approach. Thereafter, encouragement was constant, not least after my return to the United Kingdom, when I was able to visit Rowse at Trenarren. He was genuinely delighted by my appointment in 1991 as Director of the Institute of Cornish Studies, part of the University of Exeter but situated in Cornwall and part-funded by Cornwall County Council. Enthusiasm and encouragement were matched by generosity, with Rowse donating important volumes and whole runs of journals to the Institute library, which is now subsumed in the Combined Universities in Cornwall library at the new Tremough campus at Penryn.

A.L. Rowse's death in 1997 prompted the first signs of what he had himself long prophesied would be a 'Rowse industry' in the twenty-first century. Richard Ollard's sympathetic biography *A Man of Contradictions: A Life of A.L. Rowse* appeared swiftly, published in 1999, an impressive volume and an indication of the continuing high level of public interest in Rowse's long career. But it was also quickly apparent that Rowse's tortured and tortuous relationship with his native Cornwall would require extended treatment in a separate study of its own if the full complexity of his life was to be grasped. That is the purpose of this present volume.

Happily, Rowse's personal papers—vast and chaotic as they are—were deposited in the University of Exeter Special Collections Library shortly before his death. This immensely rich archive is the basis from which much of the research for this book has been conducted. I am indebted to Alasdair Paterson, the University Librarian, for making this important collection available to me. I am especially indebted to Jessica Gardner, the Special Collections Librarian, for her great enthusiasm for my project and for her constant encouragement and support. Her staff were unfailingly helpful, and Ian Mortimer's exhaustive attempts to place some archival order upon the formidable mass of the Rowse papers helped me enormously in finding my way through box after box of disparate material.

The copyright for the personal papers, as Rowse himself directed, lies with the Royal Institution of Cornwall in Truro, and I am grateful for permission to reproduce material from the archive. Similarly, I am grateful to the wide range of publishers and authors who have allowed me to draw upon their works and to the estate of A.L. Rowse for permission to reproduce extracts from his work.

The Royal Institution of Cornwall assisted with other aspects of the research, and here I should especially liked to thank Angela Broome for her kindness and diligence in searching out books and papers, and Robert Cook for assistance in locating and reproducing photographs in the Institution's collection. Likewise, Terry Knight's staff at the Cornish Studies Library in the Cornwall Centre at Redruth were as friendly and co-operative as ever in hunting out books, pamphlets and journals. Further afield, the Lyfrgell Genedlaethol Cymru/National Library of Wales at Aberystwyth assisted in the identification of important Rowse-related material, and the staffs of the South Australian State Archives in Adelaide and the University of Melbourne Library were likewise helpful in locating relevant papers and volumes. Gage McKinney, historian of the California Cornish Cousins, and Ilka Weber guided me towards important American sources, and introduced me to Grass Valley, Nevada City and other places visited by Rowse during his sojourns in the United States.

At home, colleagues at the Institute of Cornish Studies offered a wide range of assistance. Rachel Cardew provided excellent secretarial and IT support throughout the project. Garry Tregidga and Bernard Deacon—both specialists in the history of modern Cornwall—read my draft manuscript in its entirety, making numerous suggestions and correcting errors. Treve Crago was generous in offering insights and material from his own work on the cultural politics of inter-war Cornwall. Sharron Schwartz, leading Cornish emigration historian, was similarly helpful—as were Lucy Ellis, Madeleine Midgley and Kayleigh Milden, who in their collective enthusiasm for Cornish Studies provided exactly the right intellectual environment in which to undertake this study. Elsewhere in Cornwall and at Exeter, I am similarly indebted to Bert Biscoe, Derek Giles, Philip Hunt, John Hurst, Valerie Jacob, Alan M. Kent, Nicholas Orme, Joanna Mattingly, Donald R. Rawe, James Whetter and Harry Woodhouse for a variety of assistance and encouragement. My thanks too to Sydney Cauveren in Australia for his help and encouragement.

The University of Exeter Press, in particular, deserves my heartfelt thanks for taking on this book so enthusiastically, and Simon Baker and Anna Henderson showed their customary tact, patience and skill in steering the book from raw first draft through to publication. Mark Stoyle, leading proponent of the new British historiography and accomplished historian of early modern Cornwall, read the manuscript for the University of Exeter Press and made numerous, detailed suggestions. As a result of his meticulous attention, the text has been improved immeasurably and I have been saved from various errors. A further, anonymous referee also read the text for the Press, and has been likewise helpful in offering comments and suggestions.

My greatest thanks, however, are due to my wife Deidre, who had to listen to every word in this book at least twice as I read out early drafts, and who suggested numerous alterations and additions. And together we have spent many happy hours tramping across Cornwall to seek out Rowse's 'Naboth's vineyards'. She also took the photograph of Rowse's memorial stone on Black Head, near Trenarren.

Alas, my mother, who was so intrigued by this project, did not live to see it come to fruition. But her ashes rest in Constantine churchyard: favourite spot of Charles Henderson and A.L. Rowse.

Philip Payton
Bodmin, Cornwall
24 July 2004

Memorial Stone, Black Head

1

'This Was the Land of My Content'

A Fitting Epitaph?

On a chilly, drizzling, wind-swept morning in October 1997, mourners gathered at the Glynn Valley crematorium, near Bodmin in Cornwall, for the funeral of Alfred Leslie Rowse. Inside, as the congregation gazed silently through a vast plate-glass window to the characteristic Cornish countryside beyond, the organist played the familiar, gentle, reflective music appropriate on such occasions. Then from behind, the coffin entered, quietly and unnoticed at first, draped with the black and white cross of St Piran, the Cornish flag, together with the hood from Rowse's academic gown. And all at once in a sudden change of mood and tempo, shaking the mourners from their inner thoughts, the organist struck-up 'Trelawny', Parson Hawker's stirring 'Song of the Western Men', the coffin processing now in triumph as it passed the rows of pews.

As those present mused on the old refrain, 'And shall Trelawny live? / And shall Trelawny die? / Here's twenty-thousand Cornishmen / Will know the reason why!', there could be no doubt that they were there to say their last farewells not only to A.L. Rowse the scholar but most especially to A.L. Rowse the Cornishman. At the age of 93 Rowse died in the parish in which he was born, having retired years before to his beloved Trenarren, his house near St Austell, and he was now making his final journey to the accompaniment of the Cornish national anthem, as he called it, draped in Cornwall's national flag. The imagery and the message were unmistakable, these powerful icons of Cornish sentiment impressing upon those there gathered that A.L. Rowse wished to be remembered principally as a Cornish patriot, someone who had for the greater part of the twentieth century celebrated Cornish 'difference' in prose and poem, and who had defended that 'difference', and Cornwall's right to be considered a Celtic realm apart from England, in the face of all-comers.

Indeed, in the final years of his retirement at Trenarren, Rowse had

1 The sylvan delight of Trenarren, the country house which Rowse coveted from his earliest days, into which he moved as tenant in 1953 and where he died in 1997. *Courtesy Charles Woolf.*

2 The austere china-clay country—or Higher Quarter—into which A.L. Rowse was born. In his short-story 'The Curse upon the Clavertons' Rowse described the clay country's 'extraordinary landscape. . . empty shells of ruined engine-houses. . . pits gradually filling with malevolent green water'. (Denys Val Baker [ed.], *Cornish Short Stories*, London, 1979, pp.71–72.) *Courtesy Charles Woolf.*

expressed—as we shall see later in this book—more than a passing sympathy with the aims of Cornish nationalism, and he had affected a happy picture of relaxation and contentment in which he pottered amongst the rhododendrons, azaleas and camellias of his Cornish garden, or sat at his writing-desk and gazed smilingly at the great Cornish headland beyond his window. But such a portrait was inherently misleading, for it obscured the series of paradoxes that complicated Rowse's long relationship with Cornwall, ensuring that for him that relationship would never be easy or comfortable, and, for the external observer, that it would be ever difficult to comprehend or unravel. That is the task of this book, to examine the nature of Rowse's complex relationship with Cornwall and to lay bare at last 'the paradoxical patriot'. This chapter is the first step, and looks beyond the myth of 'contentment' to try to identify not only some of those paradoxes that acted upon him, confusing as they are, but also something of the mass of assumptions, misapprehensions, prejudices, loyalties and enmities that they have conspired to engender. Specifically, it argues that, just as Rowse's relationship with Cornwall was not straightforward, so those who have sought to offer explanations for Rowse's enigmatic life and career have generally understood neither the significance nor the complexity of that relationship, not least the baffling diversity of devotees and detractors that Rowse managed to acquire in his equally enigmatic homeland.

Hawker's inheritance?

In the very choice of Hawker's 'Trelawny' there was a hint of the complexity that hid beneath the apparently straightforward surface. Rowse had admired Robert Stephen Hawker, vicar of Morwenstow in North Cornwall from 1835 until 1875, as 'the patron-saint of the endearing community of eccentric Cornish clerics, with their good lives and their good deeds', and in 1975 he had written that '[i]t is good that Hawker of Morwenstow should be remembered by centenary celebrations—"I would not be forgotten in this land", he wrote. And, in fact, he has never been forgotten in Cornwall.'[1]

But, as Rowse also observed, Hawker 'is no less interesting to study as a figure in complete reaction to all the dominant trends of the nineteenth century'. Indeed, in his own time Hawker was misunderstood and liable to be passed over, his literary work unappreciated, full recognition not achieved until after his death, while 'Trelawny' itself was popularly supposed—even by Macaulay in his *The History of England*—to be a seventeenth-century Cornish folk-ballad and not the work of Hawker's pen.[2] Rowse sympathized with Hawker: 'the history of the ballad and its reception was suggestive of his whole life: his sense of neglect in later years was summed up by what had happened over it. . . its author remained "unnoted and unknown"'.[3]

It would be going too far to suggest that Rowse saw himself as a latter-day Hawker, fiercely attached to his patch of Cornwall but out of sympathy with the norms and mores of the modern world, his work as yet unrewarded (though he had, belatedly, been appointed Companion of Honour in the New Year's Honours for 1997), its significance not yet understood. But Rowse in his later years was cut-off on his Cornish headland as assuredly as Hawker was in his remote cliff-top rectory, his isolation coloured by a shrill academic hostility that (in the words of one commentator) saw him as '[o]utrageous and wounding in controversy, he finished up being regarded as an eccentric'.[4] Like Hawker, Rowse was insistent that he 'would not be forgotten in this land', and just as Hawker eyed with ambivalent suspicion the Bible Christians and Wesleyans who farmed and laboured in the countryside roundabout in Morwenstow parish, so Rowse viewed with disdain those 'idiot people' (not least the Nonconformists) who lived, worked and took holidays around him in St Austell Bay. 'Bugger them!', he would explode, even in the last months of his life.[5]

So when the organ thundered out the strains of 'Trelawny', as Rowse had directed, it was in part expressing Rowse's perceived affinity with Hawker and his predicament, the choice of the 'Cornish national anthem' symbolic not only of a deep patriotic commitment to the land of Cornwall but also of a paradoxical ambiguity shared by both men in which their relationships with Cornwall and its people brought uncertainty, angst and sometimes pain. To that extent, 'Trelawny', the defiant cry of a Cornish rebellion that (paradoxically) had never actually happened, was also emblematic of Rowse's life—or at least of the complex relationship with his native Cornwall that underpinned, and for us explains, so much of his behaviour. In those final moments before Rowse was consumed by flame, his mourners at Glynn Valley paused to consider his life. For some 'Trelawny' was as poignant as it was apt as a choice for his funeral day, an unashamedly nationalistic anthem, fitting for the strident and unbending Cornish pride that Rowse could sometimes express, but tempered by an understanding of the insecurities, frustrations and even loneliness that Rowse shared with Parson Hawker in their sometimes uncomprehending, unsupportive Cornwall.

Holy Trinity and Black Head

Barely two months had passed after the funeral before there was a memorial service for Rowse, held in Holy Trinity, the parish church of St Austell, where as a boy during the Great War Rowse had sung soprano in the choir.

The date was 4 December, Rowse's birthday, and in contrast to his very private cremation in October this was a public, indeed civic event. An affectionate Appreciation by his old friend, Raleigh Trevelyan, and Prayers led by the Bishop of Truro, set the tone for this remembrance. But it was Rowse's own poem, simply entitled 'Home' and read by Margaret Wolfit, that most affected the congregation, revealing not the impossible and irascible Rowse of popular fancy but a humbler, quieter man deep in serene contemplation in the closing years of his life. It was, in effect, a prayer, a fervent hope that when he was gone from this world, his Cornwall would endure:

> Christ keep the cliffs and coves,
> The land that gave me birth,
> And let no harm come to them
> When I am gone to earth.

But the poem was also confessional, or tried to be, for while it drew a veil over earlier trials and traumas, including those dreadful days in the Second World War and after when (as we shall see at length in this book) he had felt rejected and betrayed by Cornwall, forcing him to turn his back on his homeland and its people, it now depicted—unequivocally and without question—Rowse finally at peace with the land of his birth:

> This was the land of my content,
> Blue sea and feathered sky,
> Where, after years away, at last
> I came home to die.[6]

The first line of this stanza, 'This was the land of my content', was engraved on his granite memorial stone erected in July 1999 at Black Head, St Austell Bay, close to Trenarren. There it remains, its large, bold words unambiguously driving home its simple message for those passers-by who care to stop and read. But while it would be unfair to doubt the sincerity of Rowse's poem, there is a sense that, even from the grave, as it were, Rowse is protesting too much, that the simple message of peace and contentment in his native land obscures the reality of a turbulent relationship that, even in old age, was never quite subdued or resolved. To be sure, while the poem's sentiment might evidence the quiet reflection of later years, it is not an epitaph that begins to capture all the subtleties and contradictions of A.L. Rowse and Cornwall.

Earlier compositions tell a different story, revealing torment and equivocation. In the 'Road to Roche', for example, Rowse offers an alternative epitaph, in many respects more apt: 'Here is the hard-bitten country of my birth', he writes. [7] A third, 'Approaching Cornwall: Easter, 1948', penned in that fateful decade, provides another, equally applicable and as deeply felt: 'O country of my humiliation', he cries.[8]

A fourth poem, 'Leaving Cornwall: Autumn 1944', tells us even more, a revelation that borders on the shocking:

> And I have come
> Out of Cornwall, out of the kingdom of *cliché*,
> Out of the region of misunderstanding, out
> Of the dark realm of suspicion and misapprehension,
> The nerves held taut as if for a blow, from the eyes
> That watch for an opportunity, away,
> From it all into the broad Devon day,
> And I am free.

But even as Rowse celebrates this sweet release and sudden sense of freedom, as he crosses the Tamar bridge that physically and metaphorically 'divides me from my people', so he voices the paradox that underscores his life—this *is* his country, to which he is wedded irrevocably, for all time, despite everything:

> Yet each step that takes me away
> I see these evidences that I am bound,
> Bone of my bone, flesh of my flesh, eye
> Of my eye, one with the land that has denied me:
> I am the stone the builders have rejected,
> I am the son the people would not have.
> Yet the roots of the tree are rooted in my heart,
> The little declivities and streams that run,
> Run in my veins and in my blood. This earth
> I breathe in my nostrils and that gave me birth
> Will one day stop my ears and mouth, the stones
> With their vivid orange stains are my very bones,
> The wires along the loved familiar roads
> The fibres of my body, the nerves of my eye.[9]

At Glynn Valley, with 'Trelawny' and its intimations of comparisons with the troubled Parson Hawker, there was room for contemplation of this darker, more contrary, more self-revelatory Rowse, but not so at Holy Trinity and certainly not on Black Head. Indeed, the contrasting experiences of Glynn Valley, Holy Trinity and Black Head somehow exemplified the many paradoxes of Rowse and Cornwall, inviting those present at these profound acts of remembrance to ponder them afresh and to try to grasp their extent and their meaning. This was not, of course, the first time that the complexity of Rowse's relationship with Cornwall and the Cornish had been raised as an issue or considered by commentators. But for many it was the first time that such a powerful combination of circumstances had prompted them to confront head-on the real depth and the enduring consequences—for Rowse and for so many others—of this complexity, encouraging them to look back over Rowse's long life, now that it was at an end, with a completeness of vision that had inevitably eluded earlier, more partial observers.

'Rowse is made up of many paradoxes. . . but then so are the Cornish'

Amongst these earlier observers, Denys Val Baker (whose own relation-ship with Rowse was never easy) stands out. Already established as an author and editor of note in the Cornish literary scene, he was keen to probe the relationship between Cornwall the place and the creative impulse of those who lived and worked there. As early as December 1953, in his article 'Writers of Cornwall' in the *Publishers' Circular and Booksellers' Record* (a book-trade magazine), he had begun to tackle what he saw as the especially complex relationship between Cornwall and Rowse. He noted, correctly, that 'Rowse has written very critically of his native county on many occasions—and his life as a don at Oxford has taken him away from home. . . Yet he loves Cornwall dearly and. . . expresses his feeling tenderly.' But more than this:

> A working-class child who now admires the aristocracy, a one-time Labour candidate who has recently out-Toried the Tories, an emotional Celt who set out to suppress his emotions in favour of intellectual rationalism—Rowse is made up of many paradoxes. But then so are the Cornish, about whom he has written so pene-tratingly.[10]

As Val Baker intimated, with an insight that remains central to an under-standing of Rowse and Cornwall, if Rowse was an enigma, difficult to categorize and dissect, then so too was Cornwall itself. Often overlooked by those seeking easier explanations located within the complexity of his own personality and psychological make-up, the changing nature of twen-tieth-century Cornwall was in fact a powerful determinant of Rowse's behaviour, and indeed of his fortunes. Put another way, to begin to under-stand Rowse we must first try to understand Cornwall, not least the profound changes that overtook it during Rowse's lifetime.

To this day, Cornwall remains enigmatic. Ostensibly 'in' England it is plainly not 'of' England, a contradiction that has engendered perpetual confusion, debate, even conflict. As Michael Williams once put it, 'Cornwall is different things to different people. . . [it] defies neat easy classification'.[11] Competing cultural constructions of Cornwall are likely to defeat even the most shrewd of commentators, and caused Ella Westland to conclude in her own study of the subject that 'Cornwall. . . turns out to be many places'.[12] Even in Rowse's childhood the tourist stereotypes of sunny coves and majestic headlands (to which even he was exposed) contrasted with the sterile mining landscapes and industrial dereliction that for many Cornish typified their homeland, and into which Rowse himself was born. Moreover, after a century and more at the forefront of technological advance, Cornwall was by the time of Rowse's birth in 1903 already slipping into the 'great paralysis' that was to characterize much of the twentieth century, a hitherto assertive Cornish identity built on industrial prowess giving way to an introspective culture of 'making do'.

At the same time, a newly emergent Celtic Revivalism was determined to look back over the debris of the industrial period to an earlier, pre-Reformation, Cornish-speaking, 'Celtic-Catholic' Cornwall. Indeed, Henry Jenner's all-important Revivalist manifesto *A Handbook of the Cornish Language* had appeared in 1904, less than a year after Rowse's birth, testament to this intent and evidence of the commitment that lay behind it.[13] Meanwhile, Cornwall's transformation into England's playground, the 'Cornish Riviera' as the Great Western Railway dubbed it in 1904 (again, just after Rowse's birth), was by now well advanced. The tourist industry was keen to adopt the longstanding stereotypical depiction of the Cornish as 'other' but was quick to invest it with a languid picturesque rusticity that saw the Cornish (as one travelogue writer put it in 1898) as a harmless, likeable peasant folk who were 'very excitable and very kind-hearted' and whose carefree Cornish lives exhibited a 'happy laziness truly Irish'.[14] Although the tourists thus enticed might not have noticed, this romantic picture contrasted strongly with the reality of hard-working, highly-skilled mining families (including Rowse's) who, through a century of sustained emigration, had created the international Cornish identity that was so important to Cornish estimations of who they were, yet was recognized only dimly east of the Tamar.

A.L. Rowse was born—at Tregonissey on the edge of the austere china clay country but not far from idyllic St Austell Bay—into the midst of these competing constructions of Cornwall and, as Val Baker understood, each was to affect him deeply, the paradox of Rowse the Cornishman reflecting the complexities of Cornwall itself. To these environmental influences were added the facts and experiences of his own life, in Cornwall and out of it: his family circumstances, his working-class origins, his education, his friendships, his sexual orientations, his ill-health, his activities and preoccupations as politician, historian, and man of letters. Acutely aware that the Cornish were 'Celtic' and 'not English', his relationship with England and Englishness was nonetheless of vital importance (as we shall see), his glowing, uncritical acclaim for all that England stood for (expressed most clearly during the Second World War) giving way in later years to disappointment, even disgust. And in asserting his Cornishness, not least in the loftily Anglocentric world of scholarly Oxford, he sometimes found himself in the deeply uncomfortable position that has always affected Cornish men and women (before and since), the experience of being regarded as 'other', not quite 'one of us', yet simultaneously denied the right to express separate identity or to have it taken seriously. In December 1944, for example, the *Times Literary Supplement* infuriated Rowse when, in the condescending tones typical of such a response, it observed with patronizing disdain:

> Mr Rowse writes avowedly as one who is himself not English, but a Cornishman, though history itself may without discourtesy remind him that Cornwall by now is no more than what it was in Henry VIII's time, and that it is part of the secret of the greatness of England which Mr Rowse appreciates, that she has absorbed and reconciled so many local patriotisms, to her own permanent enrichment.[15]

This was a decidedly Anglocentric—not to say arrogant—view of British (English) history, of a type which Rowse would later seek to modify. But he was already growing accustomed to the treatment that the Cornish were liable to receive in such circles, and was ready to express annoyance and irritation at the way in which the Cornish were routinely regarded (or disregarded): both the blanket dismissal of the sort expressed by the *TLS* and the ludicrously fantastic theories that were sometimes put forward to explain Cornish 'difference' or to construct the veneer of exotic 'otherness' that tourists sought. As he complained in the *Oxford Magazine* in June 1932:

> So many astonishing ideas seem to prevail in parts outside Cornwall with regard to them [the Cornish]: whether all Cornishmen are not Phoenicians; whether they are not half Spanish. . . I myself have been asked two or three times by different old ladies on a train coming out of Cornwall whether I was Spanish; to which I now have a stereotyped reply:
>
> He reads, but does not speak Spanish.
> He cannot abide ginger-beer.[16]

'His anguished relationship with his own Cornish people'

This nonsensical response was lighthearted enough, but, as Rowse was already discovering, the advocacy of Cornwall and things Cornish was rarely easy, not only because of the misapprehensions that lay beyond the Tamar but as a result of confronting the contradictions and complexities within Cornwall itself. As we shall discover, this was especially true of Rowse's experiences as a Labour candidate in Cornwall in the 1930s, but it was exhibited across a range of other activities, not least in the reaction in Cornwall (at best lukewarm and often hostile) to his autobiographical book *A Cornish Childhood*, first published in 1942.[17] This we shall deal with in greater detail in Chapter 6, but it is important here to note the extent of the disquiet in Cornwall, not only amongst the easily-targeted Nonconformists, whom Rowse regularly pilloried, but in other areas of Cornish society too. Edwin Chirgwin, an Anglican, a leading light in the Cornish-Celtic Revival, one-time secretary of the Cornish Gorsedd (the Revivalist college of bards) and a Cornish-language poet, expressed what many Cornish people felt then:

> knowing Mr Rowse I could almost have anticipated the material in 'A Cornish Childhood'. The book is a faithful picture of the author with all his likes and aversions, but it is not a faithful picture of Cornwall, and although it may read suavely enough to a foreigner be he Englishman or Greek it cannot but leave a nasty taste in the mouth of all those who not only know Cornwall better than the author, and love her as we love our friends for her failings as well as her virtues.[18]

Today, *A Cornish Childhood* (still in print, thanks to the efforts of the Cornish publisher Truran) seems mild and uncontroversial, cosy in places and certainly nostalgic, and for the average early twenty-first-century reader it is hard to see what all the fuss was about. Nonetheless, Chirgwin's strong objections typified Cornish reactions at the time, many of which found their way into the press for all to see. For Rowse, this was another unbearable 'rejection' by his own people, compounding the political 'rejections' he had already suffered at their hands. As ever, Rowse resorted to verse to express his innermost emotions, for, as Keith Brace, one-time literary editor of the *Birmingham Post*, was to note in 1981, he used poetry as his principal vehicle to 'record his anguished relationship with his own Cornish people'.[19]

In this particular case, the verse in question was Rowse's plainly titled 'Cornish Poem', which in calculating manner he arranged to appear in the *Cornish Review* (in the spring 1949 edition) where Chirgwin and friends would surely find it. First, there was in his 'Cornish Poem' the now familiar theme of his inability to escape the bonds that shackled him to Cornwall. Using Trenarren, the deliciously placed country house that he covets but cannot (yet) have, as a metaphor for a Cornwall that similarly eludes him, he tells us with brutal honesty that 'This place [Cornwall/Trenarren] I have excluded from my heart: / Yet it steals back along the secret channels/ Of memory'. But although he sees no end to this agony, he insists defiantly with Hawker-like resilience that he will not be forgotten in this land:

> Yet whenever two or three of them shall be
> Gathered together, they shall remember me:
> I shall always be the one who is present
> Behind their eyelids though always away, a thought
> Impossible to conjure, a shadow that lurks
> Within their conscience: they need not wonder why.
> Nothing that anyone can do or say
> Now can change anything or make
> Any difference. We shall grow old:
> You a closed acre in my mind,
> Shut and walled up, while I shall haunt yours
> Until the years have an end, the heart break.[20]

This was a far cry from 'the land of my content', and although forty years and more separated 'Cornish Poem' from 'Home', the contrast is astonishing. Moreover, the contrast is not merely temporal, for behind the veneer of latter-day 'contentment', the posthumous public face of Rowse that we were now invited to ponder at Black Head, there was a continuing rage, apt to surface at any time, that had endured decades after the Second World War years. Thus in the middle of his portrait of *Milton the Puritan*, published in 1977, he suddenly remembered the 'metaphysical moonshine' of the 'millenarian types straight out of the seventeenth century' to which he had been exposed when '[a] boy in Nonconformist Cornwall'. There was, he recalled, 'a club-foot tailor named Freeman, who, in the intervals of quarrelling with his wife, spouted interminable confused brabble from the Book of Revelation'. There was also 'an intermittent china-clay worker. . . who varied bouts of drinking with bouts of inspired Biblical trash'.[21] A dozen years later, Rowse was still capable of such vitriolic outbursts, a revealing passage in his *Friends and Contemporaries* in 1989 remembering with still-fresh passion (and not a little embellishment, no doubt) the joy he had felt at escaping violent, narrow-minded, claustrophobic, working-class Cornwall for the delights of Oxford:

I had enough of that. . . working-class village where I was born and brought up, on its way to becoming a slum. . . at the farm at the end, madness, the farmer cut his throat in the lunatic asylum; a few cottages along, an old widower hanged himself in the spence; next door, a sun-struck soldier drove his wife to prostitution and would beat her, the two little kids were starved to death (the woman stole my mother's only gold brooch, gift of a friend). . . around the corner a poor single woman, with two children, earned her living as a prostitute and died of syphilis. In the cottage above her, a poor little boy was murdered by a lout from the next village. A nice young fellow at the end—I went to elementary school with him—died of syphilis picked up in the town.[22]

Explaining Rowse

There were few serious attempts during Rowse's lifetime to offer a considered analysis of this difficult relationship with Cornwall. Denys Val Baker's assessment stands out as an early, albeit fleeting, insight of quality, and it was not until after Rowse's death that Valerie Jacob's affectionate and often moving memoir *Tregonissey to Trenarren: The Cornish Years of A.L. Rowse* (2001) was able to offer a sustained account of Rowse's life in Cornwall, which, though understandably lacking critical edge and indisputably loyal, was full of implicit evidence and opportunities for us to read between the lines.[23] It was no accident that Denys Val Baker and Valerie Jacob were writing from Cornish perspectives, though their work was separated in time by almost half a century, for both were able to draw from reservoirs of personal local knowledge to penetrate their subject matter and to write about it with confidence and authority—the one a writer living and working in Cornwall, the other a Cornishwoman, bard and local historian.

In recent years, other contemporary writers have also drawn upon their own funds of Cornish knowledge and understanding to try to tackle Rowse. For example, John Hurst's shrewd analysis in the collection *Cornwall Since the War* (1993) has gone some considerable way in the task of contextualizing Rowse and, amongst other things, in providing a balanced assessment of *A Cornish Childhood*. A familiar figure on the Cornish academic and literary scene, Hurst has written authoritatively on the Cornish poets Jack Clemo and Charles Causley, and in dealing with A.L. Rowse has returned to the familiar but often unsatisfactory comparisons made between the taut work of Rowse and the milder, more lyrical outpourings of that other mid-Cornwall autobiographer, Anne Treneer.[24] Brenda Hull thought merely that Treneer's happy, carefree 'attitude contrasts strongly with Dr Rowse's bitterness at his lack of opportunity'.[25]

Hurst offers a more penetrating insight, agreeing that *A Cornish Childhood* 'is, indeed, a work without illusions, and with undertones of bitterness', but insisting that Rowse had 'been able to view the childhood experiences with a degree of objectivity, distance lending proportion', and that '[t]here is also a genuine affection in the book for people, as well as for the traditional patterns of Cornish life, already changing in those early years of the [twentieth] century'. Nonetheless Rowse's childhood *was* difficult, argues Hurst, contrasting it with that portrayed in 'the more idyllic, more kindly *School House in the Wind* by Anne Treneer (1944)'. As Hurst concludes: 'Anne Treneer's background in Gorran school-house was altogether more sympathetic and supportive than Rowse's in Tregonissey, so it is scarcely surprising that the book is warmer and more relaxed'.[26]

Similarly, Alan M. Kent, in his *The Literature of Cornwall* (2000), has offered an enlightened, turn-of-the-Millennium analysis of *A Cornish Childhood*, together with a brief but illuminating over-view of Rowse's other literary work, setting Rowse firmly within the context of modern Cornish writing. Kent, himself a product of the china clay country into which Rowse was born, empathizes with Rowse's predicament, recognizing the complexities and inherent difficulties of Rowse's relationship with Cornwall. Perceptively, Kent notes that 'Rowse invests so much emotional and poetic energy in a Cornish landscape and culture which he so clearly loves and feels patriotic about'. But he also observes that '[t]he love–hate relationship which Rowse had with Cornwall could not be solved, because for much of his life he was drawn between two cultures', Cornish and English.[27]

Kent's identification of a 'love–hate relationship' with Cornwall, together with his sense that Rowse struggled to resolve the Cornwall/ England dichotomy that dogged him, provides telling insights into the life and work of Rowse. Yet these insights, fundamental as they are to understanding A.L. Rowse and Cornwall, are largely absent in Richard Ollard's otherwise impressive books: his biographical treatment *A Man of Contradictions: A Life of A.L. Rowse* and his edited volume *The Diaries of A.L. Rowse*. The biography, fittingly, begins and ends with Cornwall, and Ollard knows enough of Cornwall to agree that '[i]t is not at all English' and to explain to his readers that '[a] fierce poverty, a fierce independence, are its human characteristics'.[28] He understands the contexts of *A Cornish Childhood* and Rowse's classic history, *Tudor Cornwall* (1941),[29] and he deals sympathetically with issues of background, class and family, and with Rowse's important Cornish friendships, such as those with the antiquarian Charles Henderson and the journalist Claude Berry. There is acknowledgement of Rowse's political travails in 1930s Cornwall, and an appreciation of a Cornish dimension in his love affair with America. Similarly, the *Diaries* are peppered with Cornish references and allusions, and the dustcover notes tell us that throughout his career Rowse remained 'rooted in Cornwall',[30] although it must be said that in wielding his editorial pen Ollard has excised from the volume some of the more significant Cornish material that lies hidden in Rowse's journals.

But in neither book is Cornwall, despite its continual presence in the background, given the prominence that it deserves. Similarly, John McManners, in his obituary of Rowse in the *Proceedings of the British Academy,* although again recognizing the abiding presence of Cornwall in the background, prefers to interpret Rowse's behaviour and career in terms of a perceived series of slights and rejections—his being passed over for a studentship at Christ Church, his loss of the Wardenship battle at All Souls in 1952 to John Sparrow, and so on—a psychological explanation in which there was 'a fatal flaw in his temperament which was insidiously taking him over'.[31] But this is to underestimate the place of Cornwall in the make-up of A.L. Rowse. Far from being merely the backdrop to Rowse's life, whether in the guise of the smothering provincial society he strove to escape or as the 'little land' (as he called it) forever fixed in his heart, Cornwall was more than that: it was the ever-present continuum in his life, a principal determinant of his behaviour and of his career, and it produced a commitment which Rowse—despite alternate attempts at rejection and embrace—could never shake off. In short, understanding Rowse's passionate but paradoxical relationship with Cornwall is a key, perhaps *the* key, to fully understanding the man himself.

But if McManners, like Ollard, had underestimated the significance of Cornwall in explaining Rowse, he was in no doubt about the relationship between Rowse and the Cornish people. Elsewhere Rowse was 'an eccentric', an 'impossible figure whose insults no one took seriously', but in Cornwall (according to McManners) there was only ever uncritical embrace: '[i]n Cornwall, he was revered'.[32] Quite why the Cornish were so ill-equipped to share in the otherwise universal criticism, McManners did not explain. But in his assumption of unwavering Cornish loyalty he had unwittingly alighted on one major and contentious dimension of Rowse's relationship with his native land: what *did* local people think of him?

'Thank God for being overrun by the English'

In 1999, two years after Rowse's death, the historian Norman Davies published his massive volume *The Isles: A History.* A vast panoramic book in which Davies ranged over the whole history of 'these islands' (the 'Atlantic Archipelago' as historians are apt to call them these days), *The Isles* drew together the disparate perspectives that had emerged over the past decade or so in the 'new British historiography', the new approach to the writing of British history in which the hitherto dominant Anglocentric perspectives had been replaced by those stressing the individual but interconnected historical experiences of 'four nations' (England, Ireland, Scotland, Wales). Shot through with paradoxical insights into the complex and often contradictory relationships between the several territorial components of these islands, the book was dedicated to Davies's forebear, Richard Samson Davies, 'English by birth, Welsh by conviction, Lancastrian by choice, British by chance'.[33] This was a dedication that in its apparent contradictions not only shed light on Norman Davies's own complicated sense of 'Britishness' but anticipated and exemplified much that followed in the volume's 1,222 pages.

And yet, despite this subtlety and sophistication, in assessing the role of A.L. Rowse not only did Davies fail to recognize Rowse's early contribution to the new British historiography (see chapter 11) but he displayed a scarcely veiled ideological hostility towards him, condemning him out of hand to the dustbin of outdated, misguided and politically incorrect historians. Rowse's *Story of Britain* (1979, 1993), for example, was 'embellished with an imperial flourish' of which Davies could not approve. But more than this:[34]

> A.L. Rowse (1903–1997) somehow penetrated the inner sanctum of the British academic establishment; and, as long-time Fellow of All Souls, acquired all the superior affectations of a caste to which he didn't belong. Rowse's specialities included the history of Cornwall and Elizabethan England. Writing profusely with verve and wit, he did much to popularize the period. But he unashamedly admired his own opinions and he did little to further the cause either of Cornwall or of non-English perspectives. Rowse's somewhat patronizing approach to Cornwall presented a little land of strange names, exotic saints, and curious antiquities which should thank God for being overrun by the English.[35]

No stranger to antagonism, Rowse had throughout his long career courted dispute (most notably regarding Shakespeare's 'Dark Lady' of the sonnets, whose identity he insisted he had discovered), but there was in Norman Davies's attack a sting which Rowse, had he lived, would have felt sorely. For the accusation that Rowse had failed to advance the cause of either Cornwall or non-English perspectives transcended the usual round of academic sniping, which Rowse was able to brush off routinely as the 'third-rate' utterances of 'bloody fools', to challenge his very *raison d'être* as a Cornish writer. As Davies saw it, Rowse had failed in his duty and had neglected the tasks that lay before him—to promote the cause of Cornwall and to elucidate a non-English view of history—all the while ingratiating himself with those very individuals and institutions that were responsible for the marginalization of Cornwall and the attendant presentation of Anglocentric interpretations of British history.

The charges laid against Rowse by Davies will be examined at length in this book, and will be found wanting: Rowse, it will be argued here, was in fact an early and extremely innovative advocate of 'non-English' perspectives in the writing of British history. Moreover, according to his own lights at least, he was a committed (if inconsistent) champion of Cornwall and the Cornish. Nonetheless, there is an earnest sincerity in Davies's vehemence that impresses the reader and demands consideration ('no smoke without fire'), not least in his shrewd recognition of the many paradoxes in Rowse's life and in Rowse's complex and not always happy entwinement with Cornwall.

There is also in Davies's remarks a hint that, in contrast to McManners's perspective, the Cornish had no cause to love Rowse—the man who had so conspicuously abandoned his duty towards Cornwall. In fact, the evidence—like much else in Rowse's life—is contradictory. While Rowse did indeed sometimes receive the adulation and the accolades that McManners imagined to exist west of the Tamar, there was in Cornwall an opposite but equally extreme and similarly uncritical reaction which thought him an 'English apologist', one who had 'prostituted his own Cornish roots. . . in an undignified scramble to scale the English establishment's greasy "luvvie" pole'.[36] Such a view was uncompromisingly nationalist, echoing Davies's assessment that Rowse had let Cornwall down.

Yet, paradoxically, it was within the same nationalist community that some of Rowse's greatest supporters dwelt. *An Baner Kernewek*, the *Cornish Banner*, official organ of the Cornish Nationalist Party, a journal not likely to smile upon those who had rejected or neglected their native land, consistently supported Rowse (even publishing his articles and poetry), and expressed great sorrow and regret when Rowse died. The magazine believed Rowse to be beyond compare, its editorial in November 1997 lamenting the loss of the great man, with no hint of shortcomings or opportunities missed or duties spurned. Dr James Whetter, the editor, mused: 'One thinks of Dr Rowse's place in history. Looking from the angle of Cornwall, one can see the little land, as he would call it, has produced no such writer ever. One thinks of Quiller Couch, Borlase, Carew, there is no one to compare. . . Dr Rowse has to be Cornwall's greatest son— ever.' Moreover, Whetter continued, 'Cornwall has lost a beacon of light, the greatest intelligence. The land will be the poorer for the loss but we have his many works to ponder and savour over the years, ourselves and future generations. Through Dr Rowse, Cornwall will survive.'[37]

James Whetter was not alone in his estimation. E.V. Thompson, cele-

brated author of a string of best-selling Cornish novels, thought that
'Cornwall has lost one of its great characters and great scholars',[38] while
Donald R. Rawe, playwright, publisher and Cornish activist, wrote in a
tribute in February 1998 that Rowse's well-regarded poem 'The Old
Cemetery at St Austell' 'commands a place in Cornish literature compa-
rable to Gray's *Elegy* in English writing'.[39] Edna Milton penned her own
memorial to Rowse's passing, published in the eulogizing *Cornish Banner*:
'Looking across beautiful St Austell Bay/ Blue skies, hydrangeas, / A.L.
Rowse, Companion of Honour, / Cornwall's greatest son, / Cross adorned,
acclaimed, renowned, / Has gone from the day. . .'.[40] Likewise, Jory
Bennett, another Rowse enthusiast, resorted to verse, his personal sense
of loss expressed painfully in his 'ALR ob. October 3, 1997':

> We were there on your peninsula
> Picking strawberries
> Unknowing –
> Your life not long since departed
> The house alone without you
> An unnatural silence descended on the place
> Land and sea motionless
> Trenarren trees locked in a silent embrace
> Why did they say you were all right?
> (The enquiry was kindly meant)
> Caution, reflex or disbelief?
> Sunlight lit our lonesomeness as we departed
> Our last memory
> The first day after your death.[41]

Such outpourings are not easily dismissed, for, as James Whetter
observed, there was in fact a solid bedrock of goodwill for Rowse in many
Cornish circles, together with an appreciation of his charitable contributions to Cornish organizations and of his support for those Cornish writers
he chose to encourage. Thus, as Whetter noted, '[w]ithin Cornwall he
aided many enterprises and institutions. The Royal Institution of
Cornwall, the National Trust, his own church at St Austell. . . Old
Cornwall Societies. He was generous. . . He helped scholars and historians, myself among them.'[42] Indeed, Judith Cook, no stranger to Cornwall
or to Cornish themes, on which she had written extensively, in 1991 dedicated her biography *Daphne: A Portrait of Daphne du Maurier* to two
people: her mother and 'A.L. Rowse, guide, mentor and friend'.[43] Pat
Munn, the Bodmin historian, in her own memoir of Rowse, published in
Cornish World in 1998, caught the warm, impish spark of friendship that
existed between Rowse and his many devotees in Cornwall: '"I shall be

79 in America", he announced to me, in November 1982, just before leaving for his favourite country after Cornwall. "And what will you be in Britain?" I asked. "Irrepressible, as usual", he rejoined. He was—and the memory of him will remain—just that.'[44] Valerie Jacob, whose *A Village Portrait* (a history of Tregrehan, near St Austell) had been enthusiastically endorsed by Rowse, thought him 'generous, unmistakably engaging with an immense sense of fun, delightful. . . profoundly endearing,. . . sensitive and thought provoking', one who 'encouraged, inspired, indeed cajoled and badgered his younger writer friends to WORK'.[45]

Even with the passage of time, such fond estimations did not diminish. The hundredth anniversary of Rowse's birth in December 2003, half a dozen years since his death, prompted a further outpouring of appreciation in Cornwall. *An Baner Kernewek/Cornish Banner* ran a fresh series of commemorative articles and poems, including an excellent essay by Derek Williams, who—dwelling on Rowse's reputation as '[o]pinionated, self-assertive, confrontational, uncompromising, passionate, elitist and single-minded'—observed that '[o]ne might not expect such immodesty to endear a person to his fellow Cornish men and women, and yet A.L.'s popularity at home appears never to have been greater'.[46] As he explained, in a recent *Western Morning News* poll of the 'Top 100 Cornish People' of all time, Rowse had come fourth, behind Richard Trevithick (inventor of the steam locomotive), Humphry Davy (inventor of the miners' safety lamp), and Michael Joseph An Gof (leader of the 1497 Cornish rebellion).[47] And as part of these anniversary commemorations, James Whetter had produced his own memoir, *Dr A.L. Rowse: Poet, Historian, Lover of Cornwall*, detailing his friendship with Rowse, particularly close in the decade before Rowse's death, offering a range of telling insights and reaffirming his belief that Rowse was '[t]he greatest scholar Cornwall has ever bred'. As he put it: 'Who else has produced so many scholarly works on such a wide range of subjects. . . Academically, intellectually, the 20th century was Rowse's century.'[48]

Of course, not all Cornish opinion was so fulsome or unequivocal. Raleigh Trevelyan, writing in *An Baner Kernewek*, noted tactfully that '[w]e who admired A.L. Rowse knew that he could be difficult, even rude, certainly impatient'. On such occasions, 'we would smile to ourselves, and let the matter pass—it made no difference to our affection for him'.[49] Caroline White, one of Rowse's several Cornish publishers in his later years, 'found the quality of his conversation exhilarating', as was his 'enthralling breadth and depth of knowledge and enthusiasm', though 'he could be extraordinarily rude about people' in public, 'and I used to dislike his cantankerous newspaper articles'.[50]

Others, however, were less charitable. John Angarrack, in his *Breaking the Chains*, an overtly nationalist analysis of the Cornish situation, thought

Rowse 'mincing' and 'limp-wristed', opining that 'Rowse is always sentimental about people and events when it suits his purpose'.[51] But
Angarrack put his finger on one of the key issues that had troubled Rowse
(and observers of his progress) in his journey from working-class
Cornwall to privileged Oxford and back to Trenarren, posing the unfathomable question: 'What forces push the Rowse. . . bandwagon? Was he
"one a' we" or "one a' they"?'.[52] Rowse would not have cared to answer
the question, nor could he, for he knew that at root there was always an
inherent tension between his striving to become one of 'they', the Oxford
don, and his (not always convincing but steadfast) determination to
remain one of 'we', a 100 per cent Cornishman. John Probert, Cornwall's
Methodist historian, less controversial than Angarrack, shared similar
concerns. In a perceptive review of Ollard's biography, he recalled an
uncomfortable story in which 'Rowse, in recent years, agreed to address
a Rotary club in Cornwall and was greeted by the chairman with the words
"You're from Cambridge aren't you Dr Rowse?" Such stupidity proved
too much and Rowse turned his back on the chairman for the rest of the
evening.' But even Probert, though complaining 'that in Cornwall he has
been overrated as an historian', could conclude that '[d]espite Rowse's
veneer there was an element of warmth with him. One wonders if he had
not antagonised so many people he might have not become a much-loved
figure in Cornwall.'[53]

And yet, as the testimony of Whetter and others showed, Rowse *was* a
much-loved figure, at least among that not inconsiderable band of Cornish
enthusiasts who saw Rowse's apparent pre-eminence as a means of
asserting Cornwall in the wider world in which he moved, and who
deferred to him as *Lef a Gernow*, 'Voice of Cornwall', the bardic name that
he adopted when at last he was initiated as a bard of the Cornish Gorsedd
in 1968. Claude Berry, one-time editor of the *West Briton* newspaper and,
like Rowse before the war, a prominent Labour supporter, recorded his
pride in 'Cornwall having. . . produced a historian of the calibre of Dr
Rowse', and in the 1971 edition of his much-loved *Portrait of Cornwall* he
wrote that the barding of A.L. Rowse had given the Gorsedd a credibility
and authenticity, a completeness, that had eluded it hitherto. 'With the
addition in 1968 of Dr Rowse, who has done more as poet, scholar and
essayist to celebrate Cornwall in the past than any other living
Cornishman', wrote Berry, 'the Bardic circle now includes all who have,
one way or another, devoted their gifts and energies to maintaining clear
and bright the Cornish tradition.'[54]

Even allowing for Berry's close friendship with Rowse over many years,
his unqualified outpouring of praise and admiration seems strangely
uncritical, especially given Berry's own instinctive Cornish patriotism and
his shrewd political sense, and it stands in stark contrast to Norman

Davies's later accusations. The point is, as Angarrack had hinted, that Rowse was, like Davies's own forebear, a man of multiple and conflicting identities, a source of difficulty and pain for him on many occasions, not least in his dealings with Cornwall, but a problem too for those—Cornish and non-Cornish, now and in the past—who have sought to understand him and to sum him up. To echo Davies's own complexity, Rowse was—of course—Cornish by birth, a birthright that by turns he celebrated and berated. But he was English by conviction (though with an inner knowledge that he could never be *really* English), Celtic by choice (his explanation for his 'one skin too few', his sensitivities and temperament), and transatlantic by accident—like so many Cornish of his time, drawn by circumstances into the wider world of the international Cornish, an intimacy and embrace that led to the publication of *The Cornish in America* in 1969.[55]

There were also issues of class and class allegiance, overlaying and complicating personal identity. Rowse strove to escape his working-class roots but as a Labour candidate in Cornwall before the war he championed the workers' cause. He also insisted, comparing himself with D.H. Lawrence, that his working-class background gave him instincts and insights that eluded dons and writers whose origins were higher up the social scale, not least the Old Etonians and Wykehamists with whom he was so routinely to rub academic shoulders. Indeed, there were tensions in his academic preoccupations that intruded far into his personal identity. There was an almost uncritical embrace of all things English (at least until England 'went to the dogs' after the war) that had to be weighed against his self-confessed Celticity, together with a similar passion for all things Elizabethan which emphatically eschewed the modern world but did not quite square with his love of contemporary America and his fascination with Cornwall's nineteenth-century Great Emigration, the greatest of Cornish themes in his estimation.

As Alan M. Kent has recognized from personal experience, to try to understand the many facets of A.L. Rowse and Cornwall takes time, patience, maturity, learning and much reflection. In his poem 'In Memoriam, A.L. Rowse (1903–1997)', published in 2002, Kent observed that as a child he had played unknowingly at Black Head and by Trenarren ('as a boy I never knew you, A.L.'), but that as an earnest young man with Cornwall in his heart he had written to the great Cornishman to tackle issues of place and identity: 'My eye on Oxford', came the rebuff, Rowse insisting that when *he* was a young man his only objective was escape from Cornwall. And so, 'At twenty', Kent observed, 'you provoked only animosity. / By thirty though, those same poems I had read and read'. And then, at last, after Rowse's death: 'So many regrets; to you, so much I want now to say. / . . . punished accents, Cornishry, I now understand. / Both your anger and your hope I feel close at hand'.[56]

This entwinement of anger and hope echoed the conflicting emotions of Glynn Valley, Holy Trinity and Black Head, rehearsing once more the tensions that lay beneath the thin veneer of 'contentment' and emphasizing yet again the many paradoxes of A.L. Rowse and Cornwall. But it is Rowse himself who should have the last word here, for it is in his own utterances that we can detect the conflict internalized within him, the personal contest between the desire to become one of 'they' and the need to remain one of 'we'. Despite all the bitterness that he had felt so keenly, Rowse had developed a proprietal, almost paternal sense of 'ownership' of Cornwall and the Cornish, expressed in the bardic name that he had adopted in 1968. When in America, researching for his book on the Cornish there, he was reminded of William Saroyan, who had 'written of himself as the one Armenian writer for his people of 300,000'. As Rowse sniffed with more than a hint of ethnic superiority, '[t]here are several times that number of Cornish folk scattered round the world and I am their voice today: *Lef a Gwernow'*.[57] It was a shame, though, struggling as he was to be one of 'we', that he could not get the spelling quite right.

2

'No Wonder I Preferred Life at All Souls'

Escaping a Cornish Childhood

Today Tregonissey, rather like Holmbush, Boscoppa, and Mount Charles, has been all but absorbed into the expanding urban sprawl of St Austell. The old 'satellite' tin and clay mining villages with their hitherto individual characters are now little more than outlying suburbs of this ungainly mid-Cornwall town. One hundred years ago, however, when A.L. Rowse was born there, Tregonissey was still its own place, perched on the hillside above the town on the north-eastern side, gateway to the 'Higher Quarter' (as it was known locally), the extraordinary white-dumped, deep-pooled, lunar-landscaped china-clay country of the moors and downs beyond St Austell. A weird, benighted land, full of pitfalls (quite literally) for the unwary, its isolated cottages and austere rough-hewn villages cheek-by-jowl with giant spoil-heaps and smoking stacks, the clay country was an astonishing amalgam of the ancient and the new.

The landscape, still full of the evidence of earlier strivings for copper and tin, and of habitations and agriculture going back far beyond medieval times to the pre-Christian standing stones, was at once primitive, remote, rustic *and* the repository of the latest technology and techniques in quarrying and extraction. Its population, deeply Cornish, rooted in this landscape, seemed to 'foreigners' strange and outlandish, sometimes even in urbane St Austell where the Higher Quarter folk were thought to be a rough, uneducated lot, to be avoided if at all possible. And yet, by the early 1900s, many had already been out mining or labouring in places as far-flung as Butte, Montana, or Johannesburg in South Africa. These migratory people were the 'Cousin Jacks' and 'Cousin Jennys' who gave Cornwall its international identity and who brought to the clay country a singular outlook in which London, or even Plymouth, was of peripheral interest and marginal relevance but where news was always eagerly awaited of the latest happenings beyond the Rockies or on the Rand.

'The Higher Quarter proper'

It was into this remarkable environment that A.L. Rowse was born. Or rather, he was born on the edge of it, on the margin (a metaphor, perhaps, for his life as a whole), for Tregonissey, Janus-like, looked both ways: it was a village of clay workers, archetypal Higher Quarter folk, but topographically it kept company with neighbouring St Austell, acquiring in the process a veneer of urban 'civilization' that rubbed off from the town. In *A Cornish Childhood*, published in 1942, Rowse described the locality for his readers, explaining that the 'village was a straggle of houses along one side of the road, where for a bit it was level before mounting the hill to Lane End, then to Carclaze, then to Penwithick, with which you were in the Higher Quarter proper'. In that sense, '[g]eographically we were on the border-line; but socially. . . we belonged to the "Higher Quarter"'.[1] Yet on occasions, the Higher Quarter seemed another world, with Tregonissey discreetly removed from its wilder behaviour and kept safe within the protective orbit of St Austell.

When Rowse was not yet ten years old, for example, the clay workers, or some of them, came out on strike for better pay. The heartland of the strike was the villages on the western side of the downs above St Austell— Foxhole, Trethosa, St Stephens, Treviscoe, Nanpean, St Dennis (all later Labour strongholds)—but news of the events filtered down to Tregonissey: 'We heard exciting rumours of what was going on in the "Higher Quarter"—and we put it down to the natural roughness of the Higher Quarter people'.[2] As Rowse mused later, 'fifty years ago, or even thirty [*c.* 1910], in the Higher Quarter, it was quite possible for a stranger coming into the village to be stoned by the children of the place',[3] and as a small boy he would beg his father to tell him stories of the Higher Quarter, enjoying the *frisson* of danger and excitement that the district and its people conjured up: 'I would get father to talk about the men of the Higher Quarters [*sic*]—a name of respect, not unmingled with fear—in the old days'.[4]

Later still, in 1953, when visiting his mother, then in advanced old age in a nursing home near St Dennis, Rowse was again struck by the 'otherness' of the people from those parts. The home was run by a Mrs Tippett, who had, as he put it, 'the rough appearance of a Higher Quarters woman'. Then, returning home from the same visit, 'I went along the road to the bus—Jack Clemo's country this, and the clay-workers coming home from day-core [shift]. Here at the corner was a Jack Clemo character—a clay area tart with curled dark hair, dangling gold earrings, trousers.' Rowse imagined that 'she took a visible interest in me at the bus-stop'. Still preoccupied with the visit to his ailing mother, he felt mildly intimidated by the Higher Quarter girl and moved away from the stop: 'I walked on in a daze

3 Rowse as a boy at Tregonissey with his Vanson grandparents and Neddy the family donkey. *Courtesy Special Collections, University of Exeter Library; photo by H. Gibbs, St Austell.*

to the next one'.[5] Here, in his fiftieth year, Rowse was still experiencing that vague sense of threat, of malevolence that had been instilled in him as a child, the knowledge that, though his father was a clay worker up at Carclaze, the village in which they lived was somehow safeguarded from the worst excesses of the Higher Quarter:

> There was Tregonissey, then, half-way up the hillside to the north-east from the town of St Austell to the china-clay uplands—the 'Higher Quarter' we called them. The words 'Higher Quarter' conveyed to our minds the sense of a civilization altogether rough and raw and rude compared with ourselves—or rather of an absence of civilization as we saw it, living next to the town, three-quarters of a mile away. The men of the Higher Quarter, the china clay villages that clustered in the high bleak uplands, were known to be fierce, fearsome creatures. . . [the] best policy was to give them no cause for offence, avoid their company, give them a wide birth, especially if, as was usually the case, they were travelling the road in groups. And indeed, when my father was a lad, a very prim-itive state of hostility subsisted between one village and another. The Tregonissey lads wouldn't allow the village to be invaded by

Mount Charles men; Mount Charles men couldn't endure the [St Austell] townsmen.[6]

This was a theme to which Rowse would return time and again, fascinated as he was by the latent violence of it all and the 'intense local rivalries' between the hardened villages of the Higher Quarter:

Mount Charles, Tregonissey, Penwithick, Stenalees, Treverbyn, each had its band of wrestlers and fighters. They met in unofficial fights as well as in the regular contests at feast-time. 'Father thinks the men now are like sheep, compared with the roughs of those days'. But they had left in their hundreds to swell the mining-camps and towns of Hancock and Houghton in the Upper Peninsula of Michigan, to Grass Valley and Nevada City in California, to tough, fighting Butte, Montana, let alone South Africa and Australia. . . At home there were the local insults each parish had for the other: at Roche 'they do knuckly down 'pon one knee' (we may imagine for what purpose); while St Stephens' people 'tried to hedge in the guckoo'.[7]

Jack Clemo country

As Rowse had remarked, this was indeed Jack Clemo country: the harsh, rather alarming environment that Clemo—eventually a poet of international stature—was to evoke so vividly in prose and poem during the years of his personal misfortune. More so than Rowse, Clemo was a child of the Higher Quarter and of the grinding poverty and stunted lives that it was apt to visit upon its working-class inhabitants, and a brief consideration of his own experience sheds further light on the clay country that provided the ever-present backdrop to Rowse's early life. Born in 1916 in a tiny cottage at Goonamarris, almost on the edge of Goonvean pit in the very heart of the clay country, Clemo came on his father's side from a family of 'rough pagans' at Trethosa. His mother's family, by contrast, 'were models of Victorian piety' (his grandfather had been a Methodist local preacher) from nearby Goonvean farm. Thought at the time to be an ill-judged union, his parents' short-lived marriage was difficult in the extreme and was characterized, as Jack Clemo put it, by unremitting '[w]orking-class poverty'.[8] His father, a clay worker, had been out in the copper mines of Butte, Montana, before his marriage back in Cornwall in 1912. Then, in 1917, soon after Jack was born, he was called up into the Royal Navy and was killed when HMS *Tornado* was torpedoed on Christmas Day that year.

After the First World War, when many of the clay workings were abandoned, closed temporarily, or put on short-time, a period of intense poverty descended on the Higher Quarter. The Clemo family felt this as keenly as any other, and young Jack Clemo was often left to his own devices as his widowed mother strove to keep her household together. 'I spent many hours in the quarries and on gravel-tips', he wrote, 'getting my clothes torn and muddy as I explored tunnels, drying kilns and engine-houses while work was suspended.' Such play gave him an unparalleled intimacy with the bizarre landscape of the Higher Quarter: 'The whole expanse to the horizons north, east and west was a chaotic litter of white cones, flat tapering sandbanks, industrial buildings, craters, and head-stocks of china-stone quarries'.[9]

It fell to Rowse and Clemo together to describe this stark, strangely primeval, sometimes threatening, and certainly dangerous environment, both men resorting to poetry and prose, fiction and autobiography, to try to convey to their readers the hidden, complex nature of the china clay country and the human struggles for survival that were played out against the austere backdrop of this all-engulfing industry. For Clemo, there was 'the mud in the kiln,. . . the wired / Poles on the clay-dump'. 'Is there a flower that thrills / Like frayed rope?', he asked, 'Is there grass that cools like gravel?'[10] For Rowse, here was 'the hard-bitten country of my birth /. . . where the china-clay country begins':

> The pyramids rise pure in colour and line,
> On the other hand, the chasms torn in the earth
> Vertiginously deep and frightening.
>   . . . china-clay
> Villages with ancient rebarbative names:
> Scredda, Rescorla, Hallaze and Stenalees,
> A hog's spine of hill mounting the western sky,
> Carluddon, Carloggas and Resugga green,
> Penwithick Stents and Treverbyn vean, a tree
> Or two in a hollow by the cemetery.
> The view to the right across prehistoric moors,
> Full of crosses, quoits and standing stones,
> Circles and monoliths and dead men's bones. . .
> Of settling-pools, clay-dries and small farms,
> Tall chimneys punctuate the tilting slope
> To where at the top of the immense, frowning Rock
> Of the medieval hermit looms and threatens,
> Broken arch of chapel an eyehole at summit,
> The eye of a needle the rich may not enter.[11]

However, while Rowse was already on the road to Oxford, having done well at school and having caught the attention of the local literati (including

'Q', Sir Arthur Quiller Couch), Clemo suffered the encroaching disabilities of blindness and deafness. He found himself socially excluded from
a wider world beyond the Higher Quarter that might in other circumstances have offered help, and was fated to remain among the clay tips to
try to develop there his genius as a poet and writer. He later complained
bitterly of the '[l]ocal gentry who knew my plight well enough, and cast
sometimes a pitying glance at me when they passed in their cars as I
slouched about the Goonamarris lanes'. These were the same grandees
who, following Quiller Couch's death and the setting-up of a memorial
trust in his honour, 'at once sent funds to the [Quiller Couch] Scholarship
Fund to enable poor Cornish boys to get a University education'.[12] None
of it came Clemo's way. He felt acutely the contrast between his own ill
luck and Rowse's good fortune, writing in a letter to him in April 1948
that '[y]ou owe so much to the schools, while I've struggled through
without their help, and with a vision they would have tried to destroy'.[13]

Clemo was grateful, however, that Rowse had read and appreciated his
recently published novel *Wilding Graft*: 'I had feared that, if you did not
read the book you would be repelled by the "mystical intensity" that has
grieved some of its reviewers'.[14] Nonetheless, he turned down Rowse's
generous offer to meet him, his explanation again drawing in sharp relief
the awful contrast between his own experiences and those of Rowse: 'I'm
still an uneducated villager myself—I became deaf before I'd even learnt
to speak grammatically, and since the past ten years I've conversed only
with my mother. I've no capacity to talk beyond a few working class
clichés.'[15] By this time, needless to say, Rowse had long since dropped the
encumbrance of his Cornish dialect and accent, affecting instead the
polished tones of Oxford academe, his prose by now equally elegant and
sophisticated. However, sensing in Rowse a possibly like-minded figure
('I detest religious humbug as much as you do'),[16] Clemo ventured to
share with him the other misfortunes that had dogged his life, hoping not
so much for sympathy but for understanding and moral support. After
all, Rowse was also the gifted, sensitive off-spring of a working-class, clay-
country family, and Clemo hoped Rowse might be moved by descriptions
of his predicaments and his suffering. Of these, none was worse than the
dreadful humiliation 'back in 1941 [when]. . . some neighbours here
became very suspicious about my friendship with an evacuee girl billeted
in the village'. As Clemo explained, '[s]he was only nine, but I had to
endure a revolting psycho-analytical test by Dr Coleman of Bodmin
asylum before they were satisfied that it was an innocent friendship'.[17]

Remarkably, Rowse responded to Clemo's *crie de coeur,* the pathetic
details of Clemo's travails having struck a chord somewhere in his psyche,
and he wrote to the Royal Literary Fund recommending financial support
for Clemo's work. Rowse's intervention was successful, and soon Clemo

was writing to Rowse to explain that he had received £100 from the Fund. This was a promising start but 'I'm just scraping along on £2 a week, which doesn't give me enough comfort or security to tackle any further work that demands prolonged effort'.[18] Rowse redoubled his efforts and, encouraged by Clemo's publisher, Chatto & Windus, wrote to the Prime Minister in the hope of procuring a Civil List Pension for Clemo—the first in a series of petitions by Clemo supporters that was eventually successful. Claude Berry, editor of the *West Briton*, also encouraged support for Clemo, writing to Rowse in 1949 to add his voice to the cause and admitting that 'I'm lost in admiration of that spark of genius being blown so doggedly and desperately and successfully into a flame in that hovel among the clay dumps'.[19] A decade later and Rowse was still offering Clemo practical support, in April 1959 clubbing together with the poet Charles Causley and other Cornish literary figures to buy Jack Clemo a typewriter for his forty-third birthday.[20]

Church or Chapel?

But if Rowse felt a working-class, clay-country affinity with Clemo, looking north metaphorically, as it were, into the interior of the Higher Quarter to express common cause with a fellow Cornish writer, in other respects he was happier to gaze down from Tregonissey into St Austell proper, the town in his childhood having offered the twin 'civilizing' solaces of Church and secondary school. The Higher Quarter was solid Methodist country, the clay district dotted with the typically Cornish wayside and village chapels of the Bible Christians, Wesleyans, Primitive Methodists and other denominations which together gave Cornwall its overwhelmingly Nonconformist flavour. Rowse, however, though attending chapel from time to time and on special occasions, was not a Methodist. In a land where religious affiliation spoke volumes about an individual's ethnicity, class, culture, locality and (to a degree) political sympathies, it mattered whether one was 'Church' or 'Chapel'. Rowse's father was vaguely Methodist by background, as befitted a family of clay workers and tin miners, but his mother was fiercely Anglican—a loyalty that impressed the young Rowse, guiding him towards the Church and from the earliest days instilling in him a sense of alienation from Cornish Nonconformity, a deep-seated suspicion of all its norms, assumptions and prescriptions that he would carry through his entire life. As he reflected, 'Nonconformity was a cause very far from the heart of someone brought up a rather High Church Anglican'.[21]

His mother's Anglicanism was a result of brushes with the gentry, her parents living and working on the Carlyon family estate at Tregrehan, near St Austell, and she herself as a young woman having worked as a domestic

5 Rowse as a chorister at Holy Trinity, St Austell, during the Great War. *Courtesy Royal Institution of Cornwall.*

4 Holy Trinity Church, St Austell. *Courtesy Charles Woolf.*

6 Rowse—scowling, far right—at Carclaze Elementary School *c.* 1907, aged 4. *Courtesy Royal Institution of Cornwall.*

servant at St Michael's Mount, the fairy-tale castle of the St Aubyns, set on an island off the Cornish coast near Penzance. For her, Anglicanism was more refined, there was 'more reverence to church', as she put it, certainly when compared to the 'rough' Bethesda chapel at Carclaze that her husband, like many other Tregonissey villagers, had once attended. Something of this rubbed off on Rowse, not only a burning resentment that *he* had not been born into the gentry, but a sense that as an Anglican 'one belonged to a minority. . . a minority which considered that it was superior'.[22] He relished this aura of 'superiority', and the feeling of being apart, different from the ordinary people (the 'Noncs') that lived around him. But he reserved his greatest contempt for the social-climbing small businessmen of the locality, those who 'went to the Wesleyan chapel, that temple of the worship of money and success',[23] and even as a youngster he detected a link (of which he did not approve) between their Nonconformity and their 'unthinking' commitment to the Liberal Party.

In other respects, however, the attraction of 'Church' was aesthetic. In contrast to the stark chapels of the Higher Quarter, Holy Trinity at St Austell was a fine example of a medieval Cornish church, architecturally pleasing and tastefully decorated within, full of historical objects and incidentals to satisfy the curiosity of a young, inquiring mind. As Rowse readily admitted, his imagination was stirred by the ritual of the Church: the priest in his vestments, incense, the language of the Prayer Book (especially the 'Comfortable Words' that he found so appealing), the hymns and choral anthems sung with precision by a well-trained choir (of which he became a member). Cornwall, despite—or perhaps because of—its domination by Nonconformity, had become a home of the Anglo-Catholic movement, with 'High Church' Cornish clergy wedding their Anglo-Catholicism to an emerging Celtic Revivalism which celebrated Cornwall as the 'Land of Saints' and looked back to the ancient days of 'Celtic Christianity in Cornwall'. For the young Rowse, all this was a far-cry from the artless working-class existence just up the hill at Tregonissey. The theatre and beauty of the Anglican Church in Cornwall contrasted sharply with what he saw as the philistine austerity of Nonconformity.

As a boy Rowse had already visited Blisland church (later to become a firm favourite of John Betjeman), that 'sanctuary of Anglo-Catholicism',[24] as Rowse described it, on the edge of Bodmin Moor. The visit introduced him to the pleasures of 'church-crawling' and confirmed tastes that would auger well for his Oxford days. He was encouraged by friends with similar sensitivities, including Dorothy Common, a school-friend with whom he corresponded towards the end of, and just after, the Great War. Knowing Rowse's religious leanings, she had assured him that '[y]ou are a clever person, Rowse, no mistake about it—you'll make your mark in the world. . . I wonder what you will be eventually—Archbishop

I expect.'[25] Later, having moved house from Stenalees, near St Austell, to further afield in mid-Cornwall, she wrote to him enthusiastically from her deliciously appropriate new address, redolent as it was of all that she and Rowse admired: 'St Anthony's, St Mawgan, St Columb, Cwl. Land of Saints'.[26]

Even when, as a fervent young socialist, Rowse became an atheist—or very close to one—he never lost his affection for the Anglican Church or his appreciation of its style: 'Noncs have no taste, because lower-class'.[27] In 1935 he penned an enthusiastic review for the *Spectator* of *Twenty Years at St Hilary*, the touching memoir of Rev. Bernard Walke, the celebrated Anglo-Catholic vicar who had been persecuted by Protestant evangelicals, from both within and outwith Cornwall: 'his life at St Hilary has been a work of art—for the parson of St Hilary is a more than an eccentric, he is an artist, a mystic, a saint; and that life is one of the glories of Cornwall'.[28] In his later years, as his political ideology shifted, so Rowse's criticisms of the 'irrationality' of religion became less strident, his theological position moving in time to something like a semi-agnostic 'faint conviction' (as Betjeman described such mild faith). All the while, however, he had continued to command a reputation as being something of an Anglo-Catholic sympathizer, and was a loyal and liberal supporter of Cornish church restoration funds—such as those at Luxulyan, Charlestown and his own Holy Trinity. As John Betjeman once reminded readers in *Books and Bookmen*: 'He is High Church and not a puritan'.[29]

Hardly a book in the house

School had offered salvation of a different kind. As Rowse explained in an interview with the magazine *Vogue* in 1980, contemplating the early years of his life: 'I loved my schooldays from beginning to end—rather differently from the Old School Tie gang, so many of whom have written to say how miserable they were'. This was not just a case of Cornish country schools, with their kindly teachers and relaxed routines, being somehow friendlier, compassionate, more welcoming than the harsh Spartan regimes of the English public schools. Rather, it was far more to do with personal fulfillment, with the joy of learning and the exhilaration of self-expression. As Rowse made plain, '[f]or me, a working class boy, school was a liberation from the constriction and boredom of working class life'.[30] There was, he tells us, hardly a book in the house at Tregonissey— though his aunt had a fascinating history of the Tudors, which he often dropped in to consult on his way home—and he suffered from being 'an exceptionally sharp and sensitive lad in a very ordinary working-class home'. There was, he said, 'no one to encourage me (except at school: hence my devotion and passionate gratitude to it)'.[31] When Rowse, as a teenager, began to purchase a few books with the meagre funds that came his way, his mother was exasperated at the manner in which they cluttered up the home. 'If any more books come into this 'ouse, I'll burn 'em', she cried.[32] Oddly, his father, who in all Rowse's accounts appears a more passive, less passionate, less intelligent personality than his strong-willed mother, exhibited a sneaking admiration for his son's determination to thwart this resistance to more books. Coming home on leave from his work in the iron mines of Northamptonshire, his reserved occupation in the Great War, Rowse's father gave him the money to purchase a full set of *Nelson's Encyclopedia* from the booksellers in St Austell.

Such generosity was very much the exception rather than the rule, however, and for the most part Rowse's quest for knowledge and his creative spark went unnoticed, unremarked and unrewarded at home. At school it was a different matter, first of all at the elementary school at Carclaze, where the release from boredom at home and the excitement of drawing, reading and writing offered stimulation such as he had not known before, and, even more importantly, at the secondary school down in St Austell where the intellectual loneliness he suffered at Tregonissey was relieved by contact with teachers who recognized his talent, and in lessons and extra-mural activities that encouraged him to be himself. He discovered literature, reading widely but forming a special affection for the work of Sir Arthur Quiller Couch, the Cornish writer and Oxbridge scholar whose authentic treatment of historical themes—particularly Cornish ones—appealed strongly to the young Rowse. He also wrote his own prose and poetry for the school magazine, he took the part of Malvolio in the school's production of *Twelfth Night* (prompting his life-long enthusiasm for Shakespeare), and in such activities formed rewarding friendships with other pupils of both sexes, ameliorating his overwhelming sense of being on his own, of having to live his life in his head.

Most especially, he formed a mutually appreciative relationship with the curiously named Mary Blank, a keen young teacher of English able to enthuse her teenage charges (Dorothy Common also wrote affectionately of her) and who was, Rowse said, 'my patron saint'. She was 'golden-haired and blue-eyed', a strict Wesleyan from Camelford who—much to Rowse's distress—married a missionary and left for India. Tragically, within a year she was dead, from complications arising from childbirth. 'All I have of her', wrote Rowse in sorrow, 'is my name written in her plain forward-sloping hand in a book that she gave me, my Shakespeare; and the manuscript of a sonnet she wrote.'[33] The loss of Mary Blank, deeply disturbing as it was at the time, seems to have been the only serious reversal in what was otherwise an extremely happy and enormously rewarding time at school. It was a period which (as Jack Clemo was to note so ruefully) not only made up for the educational deficiencies of Rowse's home life

7 Sir Arthur Quiller Couch boating at Fowey. This is a photograph from Rowse's personal collection: he has scribbled on the back 'Q crossing the river'. *Courtesy Royal Institution of Cornwall and Hulton Press Ltd,* Picture Post.

but equipped him with all the necessary basics for the academic and literary career that lay ahead.

From the young Rowse's perspective, however, the positive experiences of secondary school and Church served only to emphasize the contrast with home at Tregonissey and to cause increased anxiety about what might be in store for him in the future. The solace of Church and school was not enough, and he had to look for new opportunities to fully establish his personal identity and to discover and then pursue his destiny. In the long term, that meant university. In the short term, he took advantage

of the expanding horizons opened up by the growing independence that
came with adolescence, discovering beyond St Austell a Cornwall that was
strikingly different from both the town itself and the forbidding wastes of
the Higher Quarter that he knew already. Earlier forays, well before the
Great War, courtesy of the Pentewan light railway and Sunday school
outings, had acquainted him with the coast along St Austell Bay, tantaliz-
ingly close and yet so far during the normal routine of life at Tregonissey.
Now grown older he was able to explore the locality—if not exactly at his
leisure, then certainly with a degree of freedom.

An early place of pilgrimage, accessible from Tregonissey on foot, was
Carn Grey. This was a rocky granite outcrop typical of the 'tors' that punc-
tuated the igneous backbone of Cornwall but situated deliciously—a
'splendid vantage-point', as Rowse called it—in a spot that afforded in
almost every direction breathtaking views out across Cornwall. 'Those
evenings at Carn Grey were a feast of solitary sensuousness', he wrote.
Looking in one direction, he could gaze down upon his 'beloved'
Luxulyan Valley, granite-strewn and dripping with moist undergrowth,
and out across to 'the dark woods of Tregrehan' and 'the darker woods of
Crinnis'. Other views took in Helman Tor and distant Brown Willy, away
on Bodmin Moor, along with the Civil War country of Lanhydrock,
Boconnoc and the River Fowey. These latter perspectives reminded him
of his elementary school days when he had read Sir Arthur Quiller Couch's
The Splendid Spur, set in Cornwall in that period: 'I thought of the melancholy King [Charles I] sleeping all night in his coach surrounded by his
guards in the park at Boconnoc. . . Bevil Grenville there and Hopton and
Mohun: I saw the King on his charger, as he appears in the picture,
bestriding all that peninsula, towering above the horizon'.[34] There were,
too, vistas out towards St Austell Bay, away to the Gribbin, the headland
beyond Fowey, and across to Trenarren and Black Head, the sea beckoning enticingly on those days when an almost Mediterranean clarity of
light descended on Cornwall, making granite and water sparkle and sharp-
ening colours, edges and outlines. On such days, Rowse's thoughts
returned to those early Pentewan picnics and the simple pleasures of the
beach and cliff-tops. In particular, his imagination was drawn to the
country house of Trenarren, on its headland in the Bay, for which he had
already developed a fascination, surpassing even the enchantment of Carn
Grey.

'The house of my imagination. . . the place is mine'

Eventually, in 1953, in his fiftieth year, Rowse would take possession of
Trenarren, but for the four preceding decades the house had symbolized
the unattainable in his life: situated in the same parish in which he had

been born but a world away from humdrum, working-class Tregonissey. Passing by on his expeditions to Black Head, Rowse had often peered in through the open gate to the intriguing house beyond, a window to a world beyond his grasp but a tangible expression of ambition. Trenarren was something to hold in the mind's eye and to be striven for. Once, he passed by with his parents and '[m]y poor father', with one of his occasional flashes of insight and sympathy, 'knowing about my fixation. . . looked in at the gate, and said to my mother: "I dare say he will come to live here one day; but I shan't live to see it"'.[35] In the 1920s, when he was first up at Oxford, it was Trenarren that was often uppermost in his mind when his thoughts strayed back to Cornwall: 'I want to go back and refresh myself at Carn Grey and Trenarren', he confided to his diary when the pressure of work began to tell.[36]

The passion did not dim with the passage of the years. In June 1934, while preparing the manuscript for *Sir Richard Grenville of the Revenge* (published in 1937), Rowse thought suddenly of Trenarren: 'I have broken off in the middle of writing at my book, because there came into my mind too powerfully the haunting image of how the road looks at Trenarren just where it turns in to the house, that narrow neck of land where the trees open and you come suddenly into full view of the bay'. He admitted, '[t]here is anguish in thinking of it so much: is it that I shall never live there after all?', and he remembered the episode of his father's prophetic visit to the gate: 'The pathos of that memory and how I used to talk to him about it has entered into my thought of the place. I see it so frequently, never more clearly than when I am away from home.'[37]

A few years later, at Oxford still, his sleep disturbed by the abdominal pains that racked him then (an illness that would almost cost him his life), he awoke crying, with 'the recurring thought of the headland at Trenarren, the fine smell of sea-laden turf and camomile and gorse, the scrambling lane among the blackberries to Black Head, the deep water breaking at the head, the little cove where I love to bathe'.[38] In calmer, happier moments he mused on the history of Trenarren and the 'generations of its occupants', admitting that he saw himself as one day being part of that pageant, 'since I always think of myself some day living there, that exquisite view between the two screens of trees to the sea mine, the shelving lawn from the front of the house, the hedges with the first primroses and the sound of the sea outside everything'. The Hext family, the owners of the house, were the focus of his curiosity. He knew that they had come originally from Devon, although not directly to the St Austell district but via Constantine and Madron in the West. One Arthur Hext of Constantine was baptized at Madron in 1593 and buried in St Austell in 1650. His son Samuel was described as 'of Trenarren' when buried at St Austell in 1680. But, Rowse noted in his diary, '[t]here is no crowded family of Hexts at

Trenarren now. For some years the house stood empty. . . Often in the past ten years I have been devotedly watching it, no smoke comes from the chimney, the place shut up, empty silent.' This was, he said, 'the house of my imagination, the gate I have never been inside. . . the place is mine'.[39]

But if Trenarren, the headland and the bay were Rowse's private Cornwall, so different in every respect from Tregonissey and the bleak country of the Higher Quarter, the contrast between these two (or three) Cornwalls, so closely juxtaposed, was never quite resolved. Trenarren might be the Cornwall of his heart but the 'real' Cornwall, to which he really 'belonged', lay elsewhere. Even in 1970, years after moving to Trenarren and when, ostensibly, the struggle over place was over, he returned to the contest in a broadcast on BBC Radio 4, inviting his listeners to consider the contrast between the St Austell Bay in which he now lived and the china-clay country of his birth and childhood, between the inherent rough-and-ready democracy of the Higher Quarter and the squire-like environs of Trenarren:

> Many of you will know it [the St Austell district], and how beau-tiful our bay is, the headlands and beaches, the hilly countryside all round. And then the astonishing china-clay area, with its moun-tainous peaks of white sand-burrows—like a landscape of the Moon. That is the real Cornwall to me: a little land of hard work and hard workers, of industry; the china-clay wagons creaking down through the village [Tregonissey] to the little ports, or the railway station, the shunting of trucks, the men's voices. Ours was a very free and independent-spirited place. There was no squire in this china-clay community.[40]

Here the 'real' Cornwall, the china clay country, seemed to have won the contest, and perhaps Rowse had achieved the best of both worlds, living, as he had always hoped, in the squire-like opulence of Trenarren, within sight and sound of the Cornish sea, but still professing loyalty to the workers and the hard work of the industrial Cornwall from which he sprang. This was, though, a literary papering over of the cracks, for while by 1970 Rowse had already begun his rapprochement with Cornwall (his fields of conflict were moving elsewhere, notably into realms Shake-spearean), there remained to the end an underlying antagonism which even as late as 1989 prompted him, unprovoked, to rail yet again against the Tregonissey of his childhood. 'I suppose it is the charm of the old folk ways that attracts people in *A Cornish Childhood*', he mused, 'But I could write an account of it [Tregonissey] that would give the other side of the coin. . . It would show that we do not have to go to the Congo or Central

America, the Mau Mau Reserve or Viet-Nam for horrors.'[41] Grotesquely exaggerated no doubt, Rowse's comparisons nonetheless conveyed the depths of his convictions and of his enduring bitterness. Beneath the veneer of supposed reconciliation, of the one Cornwall with the other, and of himself with Cornwall, there remained in fact a divide as significant and as painful as when, not long after the Great War, he had been the gifted St Austell schoolboy trying to find his way to Oxford.

Indeed, even when, in 1922, he had made his triumphal journey to Oxford, escaping at last the constraints of working-class Cornwall, the paradox of this relationship was already writ large. Despite the joys of embracing the glittering prizes of an Oxford education, and of a newly won privileged way of life, there remained his professed loyalty to Cornwall and his determination to maintain his links with home. He insisted that '[t]his [new life at Oxford] did not mean that I cut my emotional ties with my family and with my original environment. . . I was deeply rooted in Cornwall and in my home and was, moreover, absurdly loyal.'[42] Vacations back in Cornwall allowed him to return to all those old haunts that he had discovered and nurtured in earlier years, venturing, he recalled:

> to those beloved sequestered spots that had given me inspiration and renewal in my schooldays, Carn Grey and Luxulyan, high up in the hinterland above the bay, moorland country all granite boulders, bracken and gorse. . . . It was all so intensely Cornish, unalloyed by strangers coming into the town [St Austell] and its ugly spreading suburbs. . . There were the names the old vanished people reaching back to antiquity had given the places where they lived. Tregonissey, in its original form Tre-cunedwid, meant the hamlet of the tribal chief. . . Carclaze, the big claypit in which father worked, meant the green camp. . . Methrose. . . the cultivated land in the heath. . . the little Tudor manor-house. . . [a]nd so on to beloved Luxulyan, i.e. Loc-sulyan, the place of Saint Sulyan, with his holy well: target, terminus, paradise of all these walks.[43]

'I was an unknown, unrecognised younger brother'

But elsewhere there was little of this fond loyalty to Cornwall. Rowse thought himself another D.H. Lawrence. He once toyed with the idea of writing a book on 'Lawrence and Cornwall',[44] and even perhaps one on Lady Chatterley. Rowse shared Lawrence's working-class background and insisted that it gave him, like Lawrence, understanding and insights that eluded those 'sentimental middle-class intellectuals' for whom (the

Irish Times wrote) he held a particular Lawrence-esque 'contempt'.[45] '[My] nerves vibrated in sympathy with his', he said, comparing himself to Lawrence, 'I was an unknown, unrecognised, younger brother'.[46] Once, when still a young man, on a visit to Nottinghamshire, Rowse sought out the coal-mining village of Eastwood, Lawrence's birthplace, and in his identification with Lawrence's modest roots he saw too a striking similarity between Eastwood and his home district:

> The first thing that struck me about Eastwood—and what surprised me—was that, allowing for differences in colour and accent, it might have been a clay-village at home in Cornwall. . . . There was the same rawness and rudeness about the place—as it might be Bugle or St Dennis—the rough edged angularity, the sharpness, the hideousness. Everything recent and ugly and Philistine, the chapels in evidence: a working-class and petty-bourgeois community. Nothing of the grace of life: no taste, no culture, no relenting: nothing whatever to stay the mind on or comfort the elect soul. How he [D.H. Lawrence] must have felt about it, once he had come to know something better—just as I used to feel about St Austell and the china-clay district.[47]

For 'Eastwood', then, Rowse read 'Tregonissey'; and for both he read 'poverty'—not just in the material sense but culturally, socially, intellectually and, for him at least, in the inability to express or fulfil himself or to form relationships in the village that would give full vent to his imagination and lift his loneliness. Strangely, the complexity of this 'poverty' has not always been recognized sufficiently by observers of Rowse. John McManners in his lengthy obituary article wrote ironically that the young Rowse was 'poor but well-fed and warmly clothed'—surviving photographs show a chubby well-wrapped child—and he has complained that Rowse 'insists too much on the handicaps which added to the glory of breaking through to the world of Oxford'.[48] But as Rowse was the first to admit, in the midst of the material poverty that characterized the clay country in the post-Great War years, his family was relatively well-placed when compared to many others. In addition to his father's job in the clay pit, there was the family shop in Tregonissey (where, much against his will, the young Rowse was required to work in his spare time) that helped to supplement their income: 'We made no more money than what we lived on. We paid our way, had good, plain food and clothes, never got into debt and had no savings.'[49] During the clay workers' strike, just before the First World War, the striking families were allowed by Mrs Rowse to put purchases 'on the slate', debts to be picked up later, but despite this pressure on cash-flow '[w]e never went short ourselves. . . I never realized then how much we owed to the shop'.[50]

This was an admission Rowse was not afraid to repeat. In 1956, for example, he wrote the Foreword to *A Cornish Waif's Story*, the anonymous account of an illegitimate Cornish girl 'handed over to an organ-grinder with a hide-out in the slums of Plymouth'. It was a pathetic tale that drew (like Clemo's predicament) a sympathetic response from Rowse: 'I used to think of my early circumstances, the restricted opportunities, the lack of any understanding in a working-class home, for long with resentment. How much more reason had this Cornish girl.' Indeed, 'I thought I knew all about working-class life, the disabilities and handicaps, the disappointments and frustrations; but this book has been a revelation to me'.[51] Here, uncharacteristically, Rowse was for once pulling his punches, for while his family may have avoided the worst of the very serious conditions that afflicted the clay district in the inter-war years, they were nonetheless living in its midst. In fact, the shop that had kept the family going for so long was at last given up in 1921 because it was no longer paying its way, the spread of unemployment dampening demand and spending power in the locality.

The following year, 1922 (when Rowse first went up to Oxford), was one of the worst, perhaps *the* worst, in the twentieth century, not just in the Higher Quarter but throughout Cornwall. This was the era of Cornwall's 'great paralysis'. The pre-1914 attempts at economic diversification having come to little, despite the brief surge of energy and optimism in the years after the turn of the century, the full weight of early de-industrialization was now brought to bear upon Cornwall in those days long before the welfare state and governmental policies designed to ameliorate the worst effects of structural change in regional economies. In 1919 there had been 'talk of a total cessation of Cornish mining',[52] the price of tin having collapsed after the war. The railway strike that year and the dreadful Levant mine disaster in the October added to the general gloom that overshadowed the Cornish economy. The closure of Wheal Grenville, near Camborne, in early 1920, heralded the latest (and worst) crisis in the tin industry, while for a time during 1921 Giew (part of the St Ives Consolidated group) was the only tin mine actually at work in Cornwall, the rest abandoned or lying idle, an eerie silence descending upon the mining country and prompting a renewed burst of emigration as miners and their families left for the goldfields of Ontario or the automobile factories of Detroit.

John Rowe, later to become a distinguished Cornish historian and a close friend of Rowse, hailed from a Cornish mining family (his father had been out in Canada and Western Australia), and he recalled that '[h]arrowing tales have been told of the distress prevalent in Cornish mining districts during 1921 and 1922'.[53] Reports of near-starvation, despair and great deprivation surfaced from across Cornwall, from St Just-in-Penwith in the far west to Gunnislake on the Devon border. At Roskear, near Camborne, the kindly teacher, Mr Truran, was reduced in the Depression years to secretly handing out shoes to the poverty-stricken children in his care.[54] A choir of unemployed Cornish miners toured Britain to raise funds and to try to draw public attention to the plight of Cornwall. Abroad, Cornish communities in South Africa, Australia and America rallied to the cause of Cornwall, as they had done in the 1870s and other times of distress, redoubling their efforts in the sending back of money to help the needy at home. Camborne Police Station became an emergency distribution centre for clothing for the unemployed and their families, as the local Poor Law Guardians struggled uncomprehendingly to meet a crisis that threatened to overwhelm them. And things did not get better. Male unemployment rose to 65 per cent in Gunnislake and 40 per cent in Redruth during the difficult winter of 1935, and for the entire period 1929–38 the average unemployment of insured persons was 32.9 per cent for Redruth, 22 per cent for Camborne, 28.4 per cent for Hayle, and 15.6 per cent for Penzance.[55] These, of course, were principally the hard-rock mining districts, but there was fearful hardship in the china clay country too in the period after 1918, especially in 1921 and 1922, the years when the Rowse family shop was forced to close and when A.L. Rowse made good his attempt his 'escape' to Oxford.

'The tramping business is becoming a profession'

Seen earlier in the twentieth century as the natural successor to copper and tin, re-inventing Cornwall's extractive pre-eminence anew, china clay had indeed brought new prospects to the Cornish economy. It soaked up spare labour and spare technology as the hard-rock mines decayed—though the miners themselves thought it humiliating to have to 'go to clay'—and responded to growing international demand as more and more applications for china clay products were developed. However, export markets disappeared during the Great War, and by 1917 annual production in the china clay industry was only half of the pre-war peak of 860,000 tons achieved in the more optimistic days of 1912. Inexorably, profits turned to loss, and in 1921—the year before Rowse went up to Oxford—English China Clays, the principal producer, suffered a hefty deficit of £32,000. Although, in 1923, there were signs of an upturn, that the worst of the clay crisis was already over, events were to prove otherwise, the American slump of 1929 and the ensuing 'Great Depression' perpetuating and worsening the industry's malaise.

By the close of 1932, the industry's output had fallen by 40 per cent since 1929, the price of china clay by more than 30 per cent. A survey of

Cornwall and Devon, carried out by the University College of the South West (the embryonic University of Exeter), showed that Cornwall's economic predicament was worse than Devon's, and far worse than the United Kingdom's as a whole, pointing the finger of blame at continuing over-reliance on extractive industries, including china clay. St Austell's average unemployment for 1929–38 was 15.8 per cent, and that for Liskeard 17.4 per cent, neither as high as for the worst-affected hard-rock mining towns, but bad enough when compared to elsewhere in Cornwall and Devon, and especially so when compared to the rest of the UK. The Exeter survey noted that the 'St Austell and Liskeard areas suffered principally from the contraction of china-clay working'[56] in the inter-war period, adding that the china clay industry had been particularly susceptible to changes in international economic conditions:

> Some two-thirds of Cornwall's large output of china-clay were sent abroad and a substantial slice of this was for the American market. Not all the forces which operated to depress national export affected the export of china-clay but some were of obvious consequence, e.g. the pre-1931 over-valuation of sterling, the calamitous decline of American demand during the early thirties, the growth of economic nationalism accompanied by widespread resort to bilateralism in international trade, rigidity of domestic costs of production.[57]

Inevitably, these global, macro-economic trends affected the lives of real people, their micro impact detected all too easily in the villages of the Higher Quarter and its hinterland. By January of 1921, English China Clays had already shortened its shifts by one hour, while many of the industry's smaller concerns had put their employees on short time or had abandoned their pits altogether. The supply of china clay by now far outstripping demand, those men who were retained were given tasks such as removing overburden (the soil and stone that lay above china clay deposits) or pipe-laying, there being no sense in actually extracting clay and adding it to the industry's already seriously overstocked reserves. As R.M. Barton has observed, 'in many cases this was done only to provide the men with employment'.[58] Others were less fortunate, some of those thrown out of work finding alternative employment with St Austell Rural District Council on water, sewage and road work schemes, but many— especially the younger, single men, only recently returned from the unspeakable horrors of trench warfare—took to sleeping rough and to walking the high-hedged lanes of the district in search of odd jobs and perhaps a little sympathy. By the summer of 1922, the *Royal Cornwall Gazette* newspaper could report that there were so many on the road that 'the tramping business is becoming a profession'.[59] In the autumn, Rowse's own father was laid off for a time, one of twenty men sent home from Carclaze for lack of work.[60] For those lucky enough to remain in employ in the pits, wages fell. The price of clay was cut in July 1921 and January 1922, and again six months later, and wages were reduced accordingly. A decade later and the story was the same, the *Cornish Guardian* noting in May 1932 that the standard rate for china clay workers was to be reduced to 11d per hour.[61.]

Well-fed or not, Rowse railed against the searing injustice of it all, accompanying his father to local meetings of the Labour Party, a prelude to his later political activities. He burned with indignation against the complacency of the local middle-class Liberals who, he considered, were effectively colluding with the Tories in condoning this frightful state of affairs. But at precisely the same time, he longed to escape this all-pervading sense of poverty—poverty of the spirit as well as of the purse—and to seek fulfilment elsewhere, to achieve the higher education and socio-economic opportunity that, plainly, Cornwall was in no position to provide. When, eventually, his quest was complete, when he had made his way first of all as an undergraduate at Christ Church and then, aged only twenty-two, he had secured his Fellowship at All Souls, he looked back with a certain disbelief at what he had achieved and at the extraordinary contrast between the privileged yet stimulating environment of Oxford and the stifling, unrelieved mediocrity of Tregonnisey. As he put it: 'No wonder I preferred life at All Souls'.[62]

'The high road that leads across the Tamar into England'

In the business of escape there had been no half-measures. Rowse never tired of emphasizing his version of Samuel Johnson's adage—'Dr Johnson said that the finest road a Scot ever sees is the high road that leads from Edinburgh into England: much the same could be said of the Cornish and the high road that leads across the Tamar into England'[63.]—and in preparing himself for this great journey he had already set about abandoning working-class, Cornish ways. Church and school had pointed to the path ahead, Anglican liturgy and Shakespearean plays revealing new dimensions to the English language, and he worked hard to eradicate his Cornish accent and to expunge Cornish words from his vocabulary. He recorded with feeling 'the struggle to get away from speaking Cornish dialect and to speak good English. . . for was it not the key which unlocked the door to all that lay beyond—Oxford, the world of letters, the community of all who speak the King's English, from which I should otherwise have been infallibly barred'.[64]

There were, however, more practical keys that also had to be acquired

8 C.V. Thomas, one-time Chairman of the Higher Education Committee of Cornwall County Council. Although Thomas was a key figure in securing Rowse's passage to Oxford, his status as a leading Nonconformist ensured Rowse's hostility.
Reproduced from Cornwall Education Week Handbook, *Truro, 1927.*

9 A.L. Rowse, the recently elected Fellow of All Souls, Oxford, in 1927.
Reproduced from Cornwall Education Week Handbook, *Truro, 1927.*

if the door to Oxford was to be unlocked, and the most important of these was funding, the means to get to university and to pay his way once there. In those bleak years after the Great War, the number of 'County Scholarships' in Cornwall for aspiring students had been cut to just one. The examination, held in Truro, lasted four or five days. Rowse grew in confidence as he went from one test to the next, and his final essay was a triumphal analysis of the literary work of Sir Arthur Quiller Couch. He concluded: 'What Thomas Hardy is to Wessex, Q. is to Cornwall'.[65] Rowse was prescient in his choice of Q as a theme, for it was Quiller Couch who championed Rowse's application for the scholarship, speaking up for him in the County Education Committee and disregarding the spoiling note passed to him as he spoke: 'Do you know that this boy is a socialist?'[66] Rowse clinched the scholarship, with Q persuading some of the grandees on the County Council—C.V. Thomas, G.T. Petherick, F.R. Pascoe—to put their hands into their own pockets to top it up a little. Rowse recorded his indebtedness to them but it was to Q that he owed the greatest gratitude. Already Rowse's hero, Q, the distinguished literary figure who in prose and poem had brought alive the Cornish landscape, had now emerged as Rowse's personal supporter, his champion no less. Although they had not yet met, this put in place a friendship that would endure until Q's death in 1944, in which Rowse would always defer to Quiller Couch as mentor and superior scholar, an unfailing source of wisdom and advice. He was, Rowse told St Austell Old Cornwall Society in a lecture in January 1937, the 'most eminent of living Cornishmen'.[67] And as he observed years later: 'The Cornish have not been much of a literary folk. . . But for those of us who do write, he is the head of us all.'[68]

Fleetingly grateful to C.V. Thomas and the others, Rowse would later return to his scornful estimation of such men, as on one occasion when travelling by train to St Ives and espying at Carbis Bay 'the Philistine sea-side villas of Camborne mining magnates: I thought of C.V. Thomas, smug Wesleyan hypocrite, with his pomposity and his penchant for the girls of the sixth form whom he took in a special Bible class'[69] ('all very harmless of course',[70] he added later). But for Q there was none of this sneering contempt, for, although active within the Liberal Party in Cornwall, Quiller Couch was altogether a higher being, Rowse thought, beyond the criticism that he enjoyed levelling at the 'Noncs'. After all, Q, though a Liberal, was not a Nonconformist but an Anglican, and this, Rowse imagined, accounted for his shy good grace and gentlemanly manners. This was in contrast to most Cornish folk—'[t]hey are a *mean* people, the Cornish, because organised Nonconformity is organised meanness'[71]—but Q was spared the worst of these Cornish traits, Rowse thought, not only because of his Anglicanism but because in reality he was only half-Cornish:

Q. was half-Cornish, half-English. Though to the world he appeared as a Cornishman, wholly identified with Cornwall, for which he spoke, I have often thought that the English side was uppermost in him. He had none of the characteristics of a Celtic temperament. It is odd that most of those of Cornish stock who have made their names as writers are only half-Cornish. Matthew Arnold. . . [s]o too the Brontes—Branwells of Penzance on their mother's side. Keats had Cornish blood and name. . . William Golding and Charles Causley, half and half, like Q.[72]

According to Rowse, it was this 'English side to Q. [that] gave him equanimity, his control and balance'.[73] Although Cornish on both sides of his family, '100 per cent native'[74] as he never tired of reminding those who would listen, Rowse aspired to Q's 'Englishness', discerning within it the qualities and style of the Oxbridge don, some of which Quiller Couch had acquired (Rowse admitted) from his upper-middle-class background and public-school education, but most of which reflected natural inheritance. Equally, though aided by favourable circumstances, Q had made his way from Cornwall to the glittering prizes of Oxford and Cambridge (he was Professor of English at the latter and a Fellow at the former), establishing a shining example that Rowse was determined to emulate. Q, then, was Rowse's role model, and Rowse was committed to following in his footsteps, the more so now that Q had so explicitly, so publicly, lent support to his quest.

Fortified by Quiller Couch's support, and the county scholarship, Rowse looked elsewhere for further funding to secure a place at Oxford. He had failed to get a scholarship at Exeter College, thought historically to be the 'natural choice' for Cornishmen going up to Oxford; his unsuccessful interview there 'was the first time that I had ever crossed the Tamar into England'.[76] But with the encouragement of Quiller Couch himself, whose advice he had sought bravely, Rowse redoubled his efforts for a place at Christ Church—and was successful. To this was added a further grant, from the Drapers' Company, and at last Rowse had just enough to go to Oxford. This time of preparation had been an anxious one, however, precipitating the 'grumbling' appendix and abdominal troubles that would pain him for years, the agony and the worry associated with the periodic attacks an unsettling portent of what lay ahead. For the moment, however, there was room only for elation. As he wrote: 'More fortunate than Jude, I was going to Oxford. Those lights have held my eyes ever since.'[76]

3

'You're No Rowse'

The Mount—Mabel—Montana

O n 11 October 1922, A.L. Rowse arrived at Christ Church forsaking Tregonissey and Cornwall in that darkest of years. He left behind the spiritual and material poverty that—he believed fervently—had dogged his life thus far, and against which he had fought determinedly. In the process he escaped the constricting, uncomprehending embrace (as he saw it) of his family: especially that of his mother, Annie, and, to a degree, of his father, Richard (Dick). But as Philip Larkin (for a time Visiting Fellow at All Souls, and a correspondent of Rowse[1]) reminds us, the ability of our parents to continue to influence us, even if unwittingly or against our will, is powerful, insidious, reaching into the new, ostensibly independent life that has been established beyond the bosom of the family.[2] If this is true for humankind as a whole, as Larkin avers, then it was especially so for Rowse—and in a very important sense his attempt to escape his Cornish childhood had only just begun in 1922. His singular relationships with his mother and his father and the extraordinary facts of his family history ensured that his parents, and his memory of them, would continue to exercise a great deal of influence over him long after he had left home. Although, in one respect, there is in Rowse's experience a universal timelessness, part of the tragedy of human existence, there is also a specifically Cornish dimension: played out against a backdrop distinctly Cornish and determined by the forces at work in Cornwall's history.

Rowse's recollections, published and unpublished, of his family are complex and sometimes contradictory. If there is a hero, then it is his elder sister, Hilda ('Hoola', as he called her as an infant) who provided the motherly love and attention that was otherwise absent and who was a constant source of reassurance and guidance.[3] Eventually, she married and went to live in North America, but she retained a special place in Rowse's affections and even in later life he sought her opinions and listened to her judgements. His brother, George, by contrast, was temperamentally unlike Rowse in almost every respect, demonstratively masculine and (in Rowse's estimation) lacking in creativity and sensitivity, and of only average intelligence. In 1944 Rowse recorded in his journal 'my early fear and hatred of my brother'.[4] But George went to Western Australia for a time, and for Rowse it was now essentially a question of out of sight, out of mind.

As Rowse no doubt observed with ironic satisfaction, his family circumstances in several respects echoed those of D.H. Lawrence, not only the working-class, mining-village background, but also the relative socioeconomic positions of his mother and father. His father, Richard Rowse, sprang from a large, rough brood of uneducated miners. His mother, uneducated too but intelligent and quick-witted, had, like Lawrence's mother, married a little beneath herself, settling for second-best. Her own family was a little higher up the social scale and with affectations that set

10 Annie Vanson—Rowse's mother—before marriage: head-strong and sexually attractive.
Courtesy Royal Institution of Cornwall.

11 Rowse's father in Johannesburg, South Africa, *c.* 1883–1885 aged 18–20. On the back, Rowse scribbled: 'Richard "Dick" Rowse, poor fellow, in Jo'burg'.
Courtesy Royal Institution of Cornwall.

them apart from the normal run of Higher Quarter Nonconformists. Indeed, Annie Rowse, a proud woman, never forgot that she was that little bit better than most: not only becoming a member of the Anglican Church but also joining the Tory 'Primrose League'. Her parents had been the lodge-keepers of Tregrehan, near St Austell, the country house of the Carlyon family which had made its money from Wheal Eliza, Wheal Buckler and the other copper and tin mines of the locality. This gave her an entrée of sorts into the world of the gentry. At any rate, it smoothed the way for a position in service on St Michael's Mount, the island-castle of the St Aubyn family. From there she returned to St Austell, again as domestic servant, working for the local GP, entering 'the middle-class comfort and friendliness of the doctor's, where she was treated almost as one of the family'. This was a time when '[l]ife was cheerful and kindly' for Annie Vanson (as she still was), the Doctor's wife being 'easy-going, generous', with much 'merry-making among the girls in the kitchen'.[5]

However, as was expected of a young woman, Annie took a husband, Richard Rowse, who had been working as a groom at the doctor's at St Austell. A family followed—first Hilda, then George, and finally (Alfred) Leslie Rowse (known invariably by his second name). Although Rowse was always to complain that his mother was hard-bitten and unable to show him affection, he recognized that he had inherited many of her traits—stubbornness, obstinacy, intolerance. She was, he wrote in later life, 'a beautiful bitch, hard as nails, bitter, heart turned to stone, tongue like a wasp, so absorbed a female egoist she burned up everyone within her reach. . . I recognise the same tendencies in myself, responsible for alienating friends.'[6] But when he observed her hard, unrewarding lot as housewife and keeper of the family shop at Tregonissey, he wondered with a degree of sympathy 'if she felt that life was an anti-climax after that all too short a time at St Michael's Mount' and the sojourn at the doctor's.[7] He shared some of her affectations—not least the espousal of High Church Anglicanism—and had a regard for her intelligence, even if her unwillingness to learn infuriated him. His sympathy (if not love) for her extended to his recording in his journals her endearing, amusing or apposite Cornish dialect sayings. Once, for example, she had heard Big Ben on the wireless and thought that its strike was irregular: ''e edn striking nice—all craazified'. On another occasion, she was thumbing through a book of self-portraits: 'There's some ugly ole faaces in this book—awful ugly. Tedn nice.' And then there was her terse assessment of the St Aubyn family: 'Proper old duffers, they be. Is, gid along, woudn' very sharp. After all the maidens down there.'[8]

'After all the maidens down there'

The latter comment, a throwaway line, hinted at something profound: something that Rowse would not grasp fully until he was well into his twenties but of which he had an inkling when still a teenager. Mabel, 'his aunt', lived with Grandmother Vanson, and Rowse had assumed, naturally, that she was his own mother's younger sister, his grandmother's other daughter. However, something was not quite right: 'I wasn't more than fourteen or so when a sharp intuition with Grandmother Vanson told me that Mabel was not *her* child. A silence suggested to me whose.'[9] The truth, as Rowse revealed awkwardly and obliquely in *A Cornish Childhood* (but in a manner that nonetheless shocked the reading public) was that his mother had become pregnant by a member of the St Aubyn family during her time in service at St Michael's Mount, and that Mabel was his half-sister, not his aunt. In *A Cornish Childhood*, Rowse wrote coyly (as well he might, for his mother was still very much alive) that '[i]n the background was that experience of the Mount, most romantic in its associations and memories of all places in Cornish history'.[10] That history was long and illustrious, but:

> Not much of all this, it may be supposed, entered the head of a very young, very lovely housemaid, with those wonderful dark eyes and perfect features, the exquisite line of mouth and nose, the small ears under wavy black hair, drawn straight back. A *bonne bouche*, a discerning eye would decide. Age: twenty. The reaction on her part, in terms of how many bedrooms (so much larger than Tregrehan), so many stairs and tunnels and passages in the rock; here you had to go downstairs to bed; you were for ever losing your way in such a large place. Here, too, the sacrosanct, mysterious routine of the gentry. . . the figure of the young Captain, invalided home from the East. Only a few years ago, with strange emotion, I saw his memorial, dead a year or two after that brief time.[11]

Evidently, seasoned bibliophiles were well-equipped to read between the lines in those pre-Chatterley trial days, able to divine the essentials of the matter from the beating-around-the-bush obscurity of the language. Returning to the tale in 1979, a quarter of a century since his mother's death, Rowse was no less abstruse but there was now a further admission: of the deep, lasting effect of his discovery upon his own life. There were, he said, 'stories that related to my family; one that came peculiarly close connected one side to the most romantic place in Cornwall'. He did not mention the Mount by name, because there was no need now to spell it out. However, '[h]ere was cause for trauma that lasted all my life; as with

T.E. Lawrence it fortified my distaste for the consequences of hetero-sexual relations, the vulnerability of women, and cut me off further from conventional family life'.[12] Here were themes that had already become characteristically Rowsian and here was his own explanation for it all. We are given here a window into his view of women (that bordered on misogyny), into his sexual ambivalence (and his sympathy for homosex-uality), into his professed dislike of children, and into his abhorrence of marriage and the family unit as a whole. In Rowse's reckoning, it was all his mother's fault.

His journals give a more private view of the Mount story. In November 1929, for example, he noted in his diary that several occurrences in recent days had combined to make him downcast: 'Last night, an upsetting episode when [Sir Charles] Oman [Chichele Professor of History at Oxford] asked me to look up the St Aubyns in Burke's *Peerage,* to see when they first occupied St Michael's Mount'. As his eyes scanned the entry, 'I came upon the name of "the Captain". "Francis Michael" I found his name: Captain in the Rifle Brigade, had fought in the Burmese War. His birthday, 3 November 1859; after being invalided home he died unmar-ried in March 1895.'[13] He went on:

> So he was thirty-five when he died: I shall be able to tell Mabel, who likes to have every scrap about him, and mother will tell her nothing. Once she had a photo of the Captain, which she carried everywhere with her: a handsome young fellow, no doubt felt towards him like a lover rather than a daughter. And then, careless and lackadaisical as she is, she lost it: that's like her, and I daresay like him.[14]

Musing further, Rowse imagined the Captain as a 'Peckwater hunting type' of the sort that he, as a socialist, disapproved: 'Yet the whole story, and the effect it has had on my mind, make it impossible not to think of him as a romantic figure. To have died so young, for one thing: in the prime of life. And what was it he died of?' Rowse itched to know more, and thought to ask the Captain's 'brother before the old peer dies; there's more chance of knowing from him than of getting her [Rowse's mother] to open her lips'. Understandably, his mother wanted the Captain to be thought of as 'a bad man', an unscrupulous philanderer who had taken advantage of her, a young innocent: ' "He was fast; still he had to pay for it, didn'a!" ' was all she said: the last with a kind of resentment that seemed genuine, though what it meant I am not sure even now' (in fact, the St Aubyns had made provision for Mabel's upbringing). Rowse guessed that it was his mother's experience on the Mount 'that accounts for the iron in her character. . . [i]t is clear that she has never forgiven herself', and he pondered the effects of it all on his own life: 'What a life to have lived around me, all through the years of childhood, the years of security. No wonder there was no feeling of love, even though there was security and we were all well cared for: but when I think of it, my childhood was empty of love.' In a gloss added to the diary entry when, years later, his thoughts turned again to the Mount episode, Rowse admitted that '[t]he discovery of the story was a great blow and made for an almighty complex'. As he observed, it had in his younger days conspired with other pressures and anxieties in life to make him ill but it had also made him self-reliant: 'Not good for duodenal ulcer. I inherited the iron.'[15]

As a boy, Rowse had envied the Carlyon family of Tregrehan, the house where his Vanson grandparents had worked. It was an envy that grew with the years, broadening outwards from the local gentry of relatively modest means to encompass the grandest of aristocracy in their great piles across England. He envied their estates and country seats, their status, and what he considered their easy wealth, security and leisured way of life, the access to the finer things, to quality, style, success, to the connections that secured without question or effort their place in 'the Establishment'. As a socialist, of course, he abhorred privilege, the growing rich at the expense of others, the obscenity of inherited wealth, the inequality that it necessarily implied and perpetuated. But he also aspired to the aristocratic lifestyle, and in the same breath that he defended working-class interests against the rapacious avarice of the gentry, as he saw it, so he longed to be like them and to have access to all the good things in their lives that he coveted so desperately and was sure that he would make better use of. It was infuriating, then, to acknowledge that his half-sister, the lackadaisical Mabel, was herself 'half-aristocratic', that his mother's connection with the gentry—and the Cornish gentry at that, and at St Michael's Mount of all places—had been illegitimate.

In an interview in the *Evening Standard* in April 1977 he remembered vividly the frustrations he had felt about the tantalizing proximity, yet absolute impenetrability, of the gentry and their lives: 'D.H. Lawrence and I were both rendered irritable, angry and resentful at being born in circumstances inappropriate to an aesthete. . . our people were servants in country houses and I knew fools were being born there instead of me'.[16] Two years later he added that: 'All my mother's people had been brought up on the estate at Tregrehan, that William-and-Mary house with the portico and the sunken Italian garden. . . Why wasn't *I* born there?' As he put it: 'I should have been better suited to it than the nitwits that were, or many of the other asses who didn't appreciate the historic houses and possessions they had inherited'.[17] When, in September 1967, Rowse, now a Cornish celebrity, was invited to lunch with Eva Robartes at Lanhydrock—who continued to live on the estate, near Bodmin, after it had been handed over to the National Trust—he recorded that '[a]ctually I don't care much for the *stimmung* of the Robartes family, Liberal, Gladstonian, Parliamentarian and therefore Low Church'. This was not at all how the gentry should be: 'If I belonged to an historic family I should naturally like its tradition to have been Cavalier-Tory, Royalist, Laudian and High Church'.[18]

'It has left a great scar'

However, as Rowse had acknowledged, the effect of the Mount discovery upon him went much further than the enhancement of his already covetous love–hate relationship with the gentry. As we shall see in Chapter 4, amongst the more profound consequences of this revelation were the effects that it was to have upon his attitudes to women and to matters sexual. For Rowse, the 'trauma', as he described it, of the Mount discovery was kept alive by the continuing difficulty of his relationship with his mother: a battle of wills, interlaced with moments of remorse and regret—certainly on his part, and occasionally on hers—that lasted until her death in 1953. In 1925 his parents had moved into a council house in Robartes Place, St Austell, where his mother continued to live after his father's death in 1934, and which served as Rowse's home when he was down from Oxford. The contrast between this overtly working-class environment and the surroundings to which he had become accustomed at Christ Church and, latterly, All Souls was enormous, a gulf that made him increasingly uncomfortable and resentful. In 1940, however, he purchased his own home, a delightful villa, 'Polmear Mine', on the outskirts of St Austell, literally and metaphorically on the road to Trenarren. His widowed mother moved into her son's new home, but despite its superior appointment, secluded, well-stocked garden and superb views, she missed the noisy informality and intimacy of the council estate. As Rowse recorded: 'ungratefully, she never did like it: it was away from the fatuities she liked to view from the front room of the council house'.[19]

Encroaching old age and infirmity further soured the relationship between mother and son, though pangs of guilt and a repressed sympathy, even love, continued to affect Rowse. An insight is provided in an entry in Rowse's diary in September 1951. About to leave Cornwall for the new term at Oxford, Rowse observed his mother in low spirits and seemingly in decline, wondering if this would be the last goodbye. When he asked her briskly 'what's wrong?', she replied: 'I dunnow. I'm feeling all down-'earted some'ow.' The pathetic words touched Rowse:

> Heart-breaking, but it's too late. This phrase pierced all my defences, my deliberate hardening—for I could not break down,

or allow her to. Underneath she knows that there is the same nature of a good son that I have been to her all these years. But no sense of her responsibility in ruining it. . . All sorts of thoughts thronged in my mind as I saw her sitting up in her old calico night-dress—the body that gave me birth, the chief justification for the existence she has ruined, the pity that assailed me because she had only death to look forward to, done, no one to console her loneliness.

He continued:

Touched by the hopelessness of the situation and that this might be the last time I should see my mother, I said [in response], 'I dare say you are'. Then relenting, 'Mabel is coming to look after you while Beryl [the housekeeper] has her holiday'. 'Yes, I know', she said submissively. It all adds up to another stroke of Fate, which I regard as my personal enemy. Yet, confronted by the human situation, against my conviction of what is best for me, for her, for all of us, I could not but soften, be wounded. For is it possible that underneath I am the less tough, as I have been much the more damaged by it all—the unspoken facts of the family life?

At length he had to take his leave of her. 'I went away pierced to the heart by that phrase, "I'm all down-'earted some'ow"', he wrote: 'Illiterate, she has the gift of striking out a phrase that knocks one out. All my gift of phrase comes from this determinedly illiterate woman—she will *not* learn, ever. So I went back to say goodbye.'[20] In fact, his mother struggled on for another two years, testing Rowse to the limit as he tried to moderate the increasingly bitter confrontations between his mother and the housekeeper, while pursuing a punishing programme of work. Eventually, over Christmas 1952, on the doctor's advice, she was put into Barncoose, the grim hospital—a former workhouse—under the shadow of Carn Brea in the midst of the Camborne–Redruth mining country, where so many Cornish folk went to die. As Rowse put it, 'neither Beryl nor I could bear the smell or the filth'[21] of his mother's continuing presence at Polmear Mine, and something had to be done. Rowse paid for his sister, Hilda, to come home from British Columbia, and he had hoped that she would stay for a time. But it was a disastrous visit, his mother shocking Hilda with the stories of all the men she had had in her life: 'they were barely on speaking terms before very long. . . The old bitch was too much for her, as she is for everyone.'[22] And yet, once again, Rowse took pity, removing his mother from the dread workhouse atmosphere of Barncoose and arranging for her to go to a pleasant nursing home near St Dennis, in the china clay country above St Austell, run by one Mrs Tippett.

12 'Polmear Mine which I owned and where I lived 1940–1953', explains Rowse in his inscription on the back of the photograph. *Courtesy Royal Institution of Cornwall.*

13 Rowse's mother, in old age, gazes from the window at Polmear Mine. On the back of the photograph, Rowse wrote: 'My Mother at Polmear Mine 1940–1953, the atmosphere of which, my home, she ruined. Psychotic, not exactly "mental" as my brother said. They [his brother's immediate family] kept well away, and left me to it— thought "I liked it". I liked me poor little *place*, my *own* home. A.L.R.'. *Courtesy Royal Institution of Cornwall.*

Over Easter 1953, Rowse visited his mother at the nursing home: 'I asked her about Barncoose: she didn't like it there, she liked it here, Mrs Tippett was wonderful'. This was the final act, Rowse recognized, 'no going back now, this was the last home, this strange house her last home. She understood and accepted: no complaining any more. . . And now, this sunny Easter afternoon, perfect acceptance.' When it was time to say goodbye, 'I bent down and she kissed me. I had not kissed her for years, after all the trouble she gave rise to—her lips trembled, that beautifully shaped mouth losing its lines, and she began to cry a little, not much.' And then, '[a]s I went out, I heard her say to her "company" (Mrs T) "That was my son. He is my baby. Is he like me?"—eagerly'. This was too much for Rowse. As he made to leave, he found that he could not speak to the nurse: 'she saw that I had broken down'. Gratefully, he accepted a cup of tea and sat for a while in the garden to gain his composure. Later, after he had travelled homewards, 'I got off the bus at the corner [and] I could face the world no longer. . . Nobody in the fields, I found myself shaken with sobs—like when father died: it had all been too much. . . No mystery now: it is all over: childhood, youth, mankind all over, and I a man in middle age—and I suppose now, a marked man, a famous man—shaken to the core.'[23]

This sense of finality, of the last chapter in a painful episode, was given still greater weight when, in August 1953, Rowse moved out of Polmear Mine and at last into Trenarren, the house that he had coveted for so long which had now become available for rent: 'This evening [31 August] for the first time here at Trenarren I saw a magpie on the lawn. "One for a death", I said. . . and my mind turned to my mother in that house on the roadside at Foxhole.' Shortly afterwards, Mrs Tippett rang him to say that his mother might pass away at any time, and that she was asking for him. Rowse made his way to the nursing home, to find his brother George there already. It was a cool meeting: 'the inanity of the conduct of his life, its poor spirit and commonplace failure. . . they would not even take her [mother] off my hands for a week, to give Beryl a holiday'.[24] Almost a month later, and his mother was still hanging on, 'making the maximum nuisance of herself in death as all through life.' Together, at the nursing home, Rowse and his mother recited the Lord's Prayer. She feared, she said, 'the coals of fire' that would be her lot for all the wicked things she had done in her life but Rowse reassured her that 'all sins are forgiven'.[25] Three days later, on Monday 28 September 1953, Rowse recorded in his diary: 'Yesterday at 4.20 in the morning, the 17th Sunday after Trinity, my mother died'.[26]

Of all those who wrote to him offering condolences, none was more valued by Rowse than his old school-friend Noreen Sweet. As he rightly observed, Noreen knew more about his mother and his family circumstances than virtually anyone else, for Noreen and he had been confidantes since their teenage years. He responded to her kindness in a letter of cathartic quality that stands as an eloquent summary of all the conflicting emotions that he felt then:

> That was so kind of you to write to me so sweetly. I was very much touched since you are one of the very few people to know the whole sad background. . . My mother became gentle and sweet at the end—alas, all too late; for all of her life she had been fierce and hard and unkind—well, you know what a trouble and what a trial all her life, and the deep scar she made on my life. . . Of course, she had inexhaustible courage, fortitude, dignity—she was indomitable. But it all went on too long. In spite of everything, I was devoted to her all my life, and was (I think) a good son to her. But those last years were too, too much, and the sad thing is that I ceased to love her—she had exhausted all that. There remained only a long drawn-out misery, sometimes more than one could bear. It has left a great scar.[27]

A quarter of a century later, Rowse reflected on the great sense of release—tinged though it was with pain—that he had felt at the death of his mother, an emotion heightened by the acquisition of his beloved Trenarren: 'When she died, I was at length free. At that moment, Trenarren at last fell vacant, the place of my dreams ever since I was a schoolboy.'[28] The reality was, however, that these twin events had by no means created the emotional break that he had craved so desperately. Indeed, remembrances of his family history continued to trouble him, remembrances that were so intimately connected to the history of Cornwall that it was impossible to avoid them, or to put them to the back of his mind, for as long as he was preoccupied with that history.

'Dear Dick Rowse'

In the late 1950s Rowse began to consider the possibility of writing the history of the Cornish in America (see Chapter 8), of examining perhaps the most important strand of Cornwall's nineteenth-century 'Great Emigration'. He envisaged a project that would look back to the embryonic days of the first Cornish contacts with America in Elizabethan times but would concentrate on the heyday of the North American mining frontier, spilling over into the early years of the twentieth century when the Cornish emigrants—the Cousin Jacks and Jennys—were still important in that land. But this focus on the Great Emigration and on America rekindled thoughts of his own family history. His father and uncles had been out mining in South Africa for a time. Two uncles, including the adored 'Cheelie', had died out there, while many other Tregonissey folk had been in South Africa or had gone to the United States and Canada. Rowse's own sister, Hilda, had emigrated to British Columbia, and his brother, George, had spent some time in Western Australia. Emigration—to America, South Africa, Australia—was as much in the blood of the Rowses as it was in that of any other Cornish family of that period.

Inevitably, as Rowse began to turn his attention to the subject of Cornish emigration, so thoughts of his father, long since dead, and others of that emigrant generation, began to fill his mind. In many ways, Rowse's father, 'dear Dick Rowse'[29] as he had once been moved to call him, had existed in the shadow of his wife, lacking her passion and her dominating manner. Quite why Annie Vanson had married Richard Rowse was not clear, though years later, for once alluding to the Mount experience, she admitted to his face: 'I married 'ee to cover up me shaame'.[30] The kindly doctor at St Austell, it seems, had done a little match-making, introducing the headstrong Annie Vanson to his steady, reliable groom, Dick Rowse. Though never really a meeting of minds, the marriage appeared to work well enough, although the young A.L. Rowse—with temperamental characteristics not unlike his mother's and sensitivities that distanced him from the plain, practical disposition of his father (and his brother George)— seemed very unlike Richard Rowse and that side of the family.

For Richard Rowse was one of a 'family of sons' whose father, Alfred Rowse, had died young of 'miner's complaint' (phthisis): they were 'all of them miners,. . . a rough crowd, a hard-drinking, hard-fighting, swearing, dancing, singing lot. . . not at all respectable'. Born in 1864, Richard Rowse was one of the younger sons, put upon and bullied by the older boys, and in consequence he 'shut himself up in reserve and silence, said nothing because he was afraid of them, became a slave and a drudge for them about the house'.[31] He was, said Rowse, 'a man of simple texture, upright, hard-working, honourable, of a distinctly Puritan cast of character. . . uneducated, unintrospective, unsubtle. . . [with] no means of self-expression. . . silent, reserved, discontented, a less satisfactory man, and less successful than he might have been'.[32] But despite his Puritan disposition, and his habit in earlier years of attending the Bible Christian chapel, he 'was not in the least religious. He was of a rather cynical humour. . . a sardonic character. . . and would say in his cynical, sensible way: "It's always the Bible-thumpers who are the greatest hypocrites".'[33] In this prejudice he had something in common with his younger son, but there was little else that drew them together, nothing much in the way of shared interests or mutual sympathy.

Indeed, as Rowse grew older and approached his teenage years, so he grew further away from his father, the latter paying little attention to his son's burgeoning curiosity and desire for knowledge, seemingly always preoccupied with this or that practical task, forever making things with his hands, an activity 'which he loved and for which I had an evident distaste'. There was also his constant irritability, which made Rowse afraid of him. But there was a gentler, more kindly side to his character, exhibited occasionally in spontaneous acts of generosity and, notably, in his decision to keep his son on at school and then to support his quest to get to university. Years later, looking back with regret, Rowse recognized this, but at the time there seemed only friction and disharmony. When, in the Great War, his father went away to the iron mines of the south Midlands—in Oxfordshire and Northamptonshire—Rowse felt an overwhelming sense of relief: 'For me, the most important consequence of the War was that it took my father away from home. That I regarded as a great blessing.'[34] Then, in November 1918, when there was news of the Armistice and the capitulation of Germany, and the church bells rang out in St Austell and an impromptu furry dance wound its way joyfully along Fore Street, Rowse felt only gloom and foreboding: 'father would be home again from the iron-mines'.[35]

In fact, as Rowse later acknowledged, the return from war service was not as bad as he had anticipated, and as well as supporting the plan to get to Oxford, his father began to take some interest in his son's growing political awareness, accompanying him to local Labour Party meetings and the like.[36] But it was not yet a meeting of minds, nor was it likely to become one, though Rowse tried to be a good son after he had established himself at university, providing for his father in his later years and ensuring that his retirement was at least comfortable. When, in March 1934, his father died suddenly and unexpectedly, Rowse, in London, was assailed by mixed emotions. Receiving a letter from George saying that their father was very ill, Rowse immediately telephoned the hospital but it was already too late. He left straight away for Cornwall:

> All the way home in the train I was in the same state: not so much stunned, as frozen. In my sleeper I tried to go on reading my book on the archaeology of Cornwall. I had been reading about the megalithic chamber-graves of Cornwall, the pots containing human ashes, the cult of the dead, this weekend in Oxford while father was dying. I ought to have known something was wrong. . . All that weekend I was in a dazed condition, not knowing what to do with myself, though there was as usual plenty to do: I put it down to being fagged. . . On the homeward journey, I could not read, nor could I sleep.[37]

To this self-reproach, the awful feeling that he had ignored the portents and his own intuition, was added a strange sense of emotional detachment from what was happening. At St Austell station, 'George had come to meet me in a downpour of rain. We met in silence and then carried on a conversation about the arrangements for the funeral. Not even the sight of mother in misery, standing at the stove, broken and crying, moved me much. Nor all that morning.' There was further self-reproach, for being away when his father was so ill: 'what agony he must have gone through in that last week to die; and I could not be near to help him. . . I wished I had been there every moment. . . the nurse told me that all through the last day he was asking for his young son—I can't believe it'.[38] Rowse went to see his father's body in the chapel-of-rest in Truro—'[i]t wrung my heart to see him, like a little child, a wax doll in his small coffin'—and then he sought solitude and solace in the city's cathedral: 'It was not until I reached the little chapel at the back, in a remote corner, with the picture of Christ blessing Cornish Industry, that I was overcome by grief, finding words for what I felt'. It was only then that he felt able to reflect upon his father's life, 'the hardness of it, the unending labour. . . He had worked at china clay all his days; at the end nothing but pain, and this was absolutely the end.' He was glad that he had been to the chapel to see his father for that very last time: 'but, alas, that image of him lying there is how I always see him now. For it was thus that his life summed itself up and came to a close.'[39]

These last lines, penned in 1937 as he reflected on those events of three years before, seemed to draw a line under his father's life, to offer the final word in that uneasy, unfulfilled relationship between father and son, to resolve the matter, allowing Rowse and others to move on. In fact, of course, Rowse returned in detail to his father in *A Cornish Childhood*, published in 1942, rehearsing for all to read the shortcomings of his father's family background and the nature of their own difficult relationship. These were unpalatable insights that for some readers appeared unnecessarily candid, as if Rowse was deliberately recording for posterity the limits of his relationship with his father. Indeed, he may well have been, for whatever the sense of finality that he had experienced in March 1937, the reality was that the memory of his father would never be far below the surface of his consciousness. It lurked there, and in the 1960s, as he conducted research for *The Cornish in America*, it surged to the fore as Rowse contemplated yet again the details and uncertainties that pained him. For, far more serious even than the tale of St Michael's Mount and his 'half-aristocratic' half-sister, Mabel, was the thought, the *possibility* that Richard Rowse might not be his real father: a suspicion hinted at, perhaps, in *A Cornish Childhood*. 'I have never supposed since my childhood that I was wanted', he wrote, 'later I regarded my appearance as a regrettable accident—and such, I have subsequently gathered, was the case.'[40]

14 Annie Rowse (standing) and Hetty May (née Coombe). Rowse imagined that Hetty's husband, Fred May, was his real father. He scribbled enigmatically on the back of the photograph 'My Mother and Mrs May—who wonders?'. *Courtesy Royal Institution of Cornwall.*

15 Evidence that eluded Rowse: a photograph of F.W. May's van, confirming that his business was in West End, St Austell. It is not clear whether the butcher behind is May himself or one of his employees. *Courtesy Valerie Jacob.*

''E i'dn your father'

The seeds of doubt about his paternity had been sown in Rowse's mind at an early age, but in a confused manner that was not easy for an immature mind to grasp, and it was not until he had reached adulthood that it all began to make sense and that the full import of what he had half-heard, misunderstood and been rebuked for as a boy dawned upon him. In May 1928, for example, he observed that:

> An odd memory comes back to me after some fifteen years: the strong rancid smell of the saddler's shop at the bottom of East Hill [St Austell], to which father would send me with bridle, or belt, or whip for repair. Old Samuel [Clemo]—had a way of quizzing little boys, grey eyes wide-open in glassy stare behind pince-nez, shifting to and fro. 'You can't ride a horse', he would tease, 'What d'you want a bridle for?' 'D'your father give you the whip? That's what little boys ought to have!' I was rather daunted by the old fellow, brought up by the women as I was—I found the male atmosphere, as in the barber's shop too, a bit frightening. Then, ''e i'dn your father'. I took this seriously, reported it at home, after which I was not sent again.[41]

Nearly forty years on, in October 1965, Rowse remembered the story slightly differently. The saddler at the bottom of East Hill was now Kellow (not Clemo), and young Rowse had been sent on an errand to fetch 'Uncle's medicine'—his uncle's hair-dye. But the outcome was identical: '"Who's your father?" When I said Richard Rowse, "Oh no: he id'n your father" I was very vexed and told what he said when I got home'.[42] But there was more. In 1931, as a political candidate canvassing during the general election campaign, Rowse was door-knocking in Polgooth, a former mining village near St Austell: 'an elderly man gave me a scrutinising look. . . and said, "You're no Rowse"'. Campaigning in Truro brought similar results: 'only now do I know the meaning of the greeting from the riff-raff of Truro women-folk, "Bring out your love-child"'.[43] At the time Rowse thought that they had meant Mabel, his half-sister, but now, on reflection, the full horror became apparent—or at least he thought it did.

The year 1965 also saw the publication of *A Cornishman at Oxford*, the second of Rowse's autobiographical volumes. In it he referred obliquely to the paternity issue, mirroring the tentative treatment afforded the Mount episode in *A Cornish Childhood*. In the opening pages of the book he acknowledged that, with hindsight, he had now a better understanding of the difficulties his father had faced in life, and was glad that he had given him 'care and protection' in his last years—'more than he got from those more indubitably his own'.[44] Equally opaque was his intimation that, as he had prepared the material for the book's Prologue, 'I came across something that upset me strangely. It was just the marriage-certificate of my mother and father all those years ago, 21 February 1893, at Charlestown church. There it was, all in order.'[45] Much later in the book there was a further clue, an insight into the 'nasty experience' of Christmas 1925, when the general merriment occasioned by his successful elevation to a Fellowship at All Souls that year was marred by a spiteful, jealous letter from abroad. 'A horrible letter arrived from the M.s in Montana: as an ironical Christmas greeting it must have been meant. Written by the youngest daughter, to my mother, it was obviously inspired by her mother and contained just the sort of charge which rends families and makes people miserable.'[46]

There had been considerable fuss in the press about his success at All Souls, and Rowse imagined that news of his good fortune must have made its way to America (Cornish newspapers were still routinely crossing the Atlantic in those days) and fallen into the hands of a 'family with whom we had been on such close—too close—terms in old days in the village, now emigrated to Montana'. The mother had found it all too much to take, Rowse guessed, prompting her daughter to write the unpleasant note: 'I read the letter to my mother', recorded Rowse, 'then tore it up and burnt it, so that no evidence of it should remain'. But the damage had been done: 'it added renewed strain and dubiety to my own make-up, increased the sense of insecurity, provided another trauma and was followed by another attack of ulcer. . . is it any wonder that I have no relish for family life?'.[47]

Fred May and Annie Rowse

The 'M.s' to whom Rowse referred were the Mays, originally from Polgooth (perhaps the unpleasant old man who had scrutinized him there was a relation, Rowse thought). The disgruntled mother was one Hetty May (née Coombe), the 'too close' relationship alluded to no doubt in the damaging letter from America being that between her husband, Fred May, and Annie Rowse. For the story—true or false—that was common knowledge in Tregonissey, and so unfairly imparted to the young Rowse by the sly saddler of East Hill, was that Fred May had got Annie Rowse pregnant, eventually slipping across to America to avoid the gaze of gossip-mongers who guessed at the paternity of the little boy in the village. Annie, in the meantime, so the story went, had passed off the newborn babe as her husband's son, the offspring of Richard Rowse; the infant in question, of course, was Alfred Leslie Rowse.[48]

Rowse never did find out for sure whether the story was true or not. Even in the 1990s he was still agonizing over the matter, returning to the circumstantial and sometimes conflicting evidence to see if there was anything he had missed. It was certainly a plausible story, and one that was characteristic of Cornwall's Great Emigration. Amongst the great many motives for emigration was the desire of individuals—usually young men—to escape the consequences of what they had done at home, with girlfriends, wives and other men's wives left, quite literally, holding the baby back in Cornwall. As Rowse observed, Fred May's passage to America had been a typically Cornish one, travelling first to New York, the eastern landfall, then across to Chicago in Illinois and on to Butte, Montana—'a Cornish objective',[49] as Rowse termed it—before settling at Helena in that locality. There had been Cornish folk at Last Chance Gulch, where Helena grew up, since the 1860s when gold was discovered there. The *West Briton* newspaper noted in December 1865 that Cornish miners from across America and from Cornwall itself had been amongst the first on the goldfields.[50] The best days of Montana gold seemed to be over by the 1870s but silver-lead discoveries perpetuated Butte and its environs as a mining district long enough for the copper-laded 'richest hill in the world'[51] to be discovered. Thereafter, Butte became a magnet for Cornish emigrants, and although never as overwhelmingly 'Cornish' in composition or culture as Grass Valley in California or Moonta in South Australia, it took its place in the iconography of Cornish mining alongside destinations such as Virginia City, Kalgoorlie and Johannesburg. This was the country where:

> He can take the eight penny strike
> And bend it in his hand –
> The strongest little Cousin Jack
> That ever struck the land.[52]

The Cornish struggled with the Irish for control of the miners' trade union, as they did elsewhere on the mining frontier of the Far West of America, and they formed Cornish carol choirs and brass bands as they had done at home and across the globe. Alongside the ubiquitous Cornish pasties, there were wrestling matches and drilling matches, the former conducted according to time-honoured Cornish rules with contestants wearing the unmistakable Cornish jackets, the latter a Labor Day or Fourth of July spectacle as 'champion' double-jack teams competed to strike straight, deep holes into the hardest granite.[53] With this strong repertoire of Cornish connections, Butte, Montana, inevitably featured on Rowse's itinerary as he toured America in the 1960s, garnering material for his forthcoming book on the Cornish over there. When, eventually, it

was published in 1969, he devoted a dozen of its pages to the Cornish at
Butte. There were still many hundreds of Cornish surnames in the district,
he noted, from Angelly, Angwin and Carkeek through to Uren, Varcoe
and Warne, together with any number of patronymics that in the context
were likely to be Cornish, such as Richards and Hicks. But, he added,
there were still others of Cornish descent not yet accounted for: 'none of
this exhausts the number of Cornish: the Polgooth family of May, for
instance, is represented by daughters whose married names are Roddy
and Bielman'.[54] Although he did not say so, these were amongst the
Cornish-Americans that Rowse imagined to be his half-sisters.

In fact, Rowse had visited his supposed half-sisters in 1964, arriving in
Helena, Montana, in October of that year: 'I have attained this strange
objective after the years. Shall I find out from it what Fred May really was?
I have no doubt that he was my mother's lover'—but was he his natural
father? In an astonishing stroke of luck, he mentioned to the elderly cleaner
in his hotel room that he was looking for the May family, and, coincidently,
it turned out that she had known Phyllis, one of the May sisters. Phyllis's
brother-in-law lived locally and was contacted by telephone: 'He put me
onto Beryl, the youngest, born over here, called Mrs Bielen [*sic*], who knew
all about me; said that I was her mother's [i.e. Hetty's] hero (she couldn't
bear me as a child)'. Hetty, the mother, had died two years before at the
age of 93, but Nora, another of the sisters, was also living locally: 'She was
overjoyed—after fifty years. . . She told me that Alec, Mildred—who
wrote my mother the venomous letter—and Phyllis all live at Seattle.'[55]
These, then, were the putative half-sisters, the Cornish-American siblings
that bound Rowse tightly to the Cornish emigrant world of the mining
camps of the American West, confirming the personal intimacy and sense
of 'belonging' that was at least in part behind his drive to tell the story of
The Cornish in America.

And yet, no sooner had he made contact than the issue was suddenly
resolved, or apparently so, Rowse noting in his diary on 19 October that
'[t]he important question is answered, the question I came all this way to
have answered. No son of Fred May, but of Dick Rowse. Rather disappointing in a way—Fred May was a so much more interesting character,
if a less good man.' Nora, it seems, had convinced him of this: she 'thinks
there is no family resemblance'. Persuaded, apparently, by the authority
of Fred May's eldest daughter, Rowse regretted the 'false trail' he had laid
down in *A Cornishman at Oxford*, though he was still insistent that '[o]f
course Fred and Annie were lovers; but also Dick played with Hetty, when
he took the groceries over late on Saturday evenings. . . Over here Fred
was free with the women, bore no good name.' He went to visit the graves
of Fred and Hetty: 'It was very moving to see them and to know their story
so closely intermingled with ours in the village'. Later in the day he was

driven over the mountain to Butte itself: 'Touching at last to be in Butte, Mecca of so many thousands of poor Cornish miners. Apparently, Fred May first went there. . . In those days it was wild and raw, plenty of fighting, drinking and twenty-four brothels—a miners' community.'[56.]

Noreen Sweet lends a hand

Back in Cornwall, however, Rowse was not so sure about it all, and the doubts resurfaced. When his mother lay dying in the nursing home in 1953, he had asked her cryptically for the truth: 'I. . . asked her if she had anything to whisper to me. "No, I haven't got anything to whisper", she said. I wasn't going to press her any more; if she has got a secret, she can keep it to the last.'[57] Now he wished he had known more; had more hard facts to go on. Searching for further leads, he turned to his friend Noreen Sweet, writing to her in April 1965:

> Can you get yr [*sic*] mother to tell you all she knows about *Fred May* of Polgooth (who married Hetty Coombe)—was a butcher at West End, St Austell, left for America 1909. I have a very special reason for wanting to know—you can probably guess or may know already. Since you know everything about me, you may as well know that he was my father. Some old people in Polgooth may have known—though keep it to yourself at present. I went to see his grave in Helena, Montana—though I never had a word from him in life. Isn't it all a strange story?[58]

Loyal and dutiful as ever, Noreen set about the task Rowse had given her, replying a month later from her home in Boxford, near Colchester, with all the details she could muster. It was not much but there was an interesting pen-picture of Fred May's father:

> I went back to Polgooth and could talk with my mother. The result is most disappointing. She must be the only survivor in Polgooth of that generation, her mind still alert and memory attentive. More than that, she was at work in Fore Street, St Austell—head dress-maker at Broad's—up to her marriage in October 1904, when she came to Polgooth. Yet she cannot recall a *Fred* May nor has she any recollection of a butcher's shop in the West End, apart from the one *we* remember as Hoare's, which at the time of your birth she insists was Nancollas.
>
> How strange all this. I remember years ago your wondering, but I never took it seriously and thought you didn't.
>
> Not much love lost between the Mays and the Sweets. This Fred

May was presumably one of the numerous progeny of the thrice-married 'old maister' as he was known when I was a child, whom I remember vaguely as a patriarchal figure twice as large as life, lording it over one and all at Chapel anniversaries, tea-treats and choir meetings. On the whole an aggressive difficult brood.

I think you will find one daughter is still alive—nee *Lily* May, now Stocker, in the St Austell area I believe. Curiously, I heard at Easter that some descendant in America had been at Polgooth trying to discover more of the family history.[59]

It is not clear whether Rowse was able to follow up this lead, or to build on any of the information in Noreen Sweet's letter. But there was something that chimed with his own belief, the brief character sketch of Fred May's father impressing him especially. It is also possible that his sister Hilda had told him more. It transpired that she and her husband Edwin had travelled down to Montana from British Columbia back in the 1920s and had visited Fred May: 'he told Hilda that Annie was the only woman he had ever loved'. On a separate occasion, Edwin (a cabinet-maker) had found Annie's love-letters in a locked draw and had destroyed them, along with the secrets they contained. Whatever the case, Rowse now thought that he had at last sorted out the true facts of the matter. In his journal in October 1965 he recorded solemnly that:

> A great blow befel [*sic*] me this year, which has taken a great deal of adjusting to. It is strange—like so much in my life—that I should have had to wait until my 61st year before I learned the true fact of my paternity, and that—as I have for many years suspected—I am really Fred May's son, not dear Dick Rowse's, who fed me, clothed me and brought me up.[60]

In a sort of stream of consciousness—an attempt to get the matter off his chest, to pour everything out on paper—Rowse rushed on, as though he needed to record it all while the memory was clear, lest it should again become confused or forgotten:

> There was only one man in her life she [mother] ever loved—she told me that, though she did not add that that was Fred. I know that she was the one woman he really loved—wanted her to leave everything and join him in New York. (She did tell me that. Her only comment: 'Did 'ee think I should be such a fool'). . . She was fool enough to let him give her a baby. But I can blame neither of them for that: they were swept away by the passion, they were both highly sexed. . . I suppose I was always spoiled and protected by

Mother—her love-child, though it was never admitted. There were people in the village who suspected it. . . In the family it was not admitted, though Hilda knew.[61]

Hetty, Fred's wife, also knew the facts, thought Rowse, and so disliked him intensely when he was young: '*She* evidently knew whose child I was'. Fred May had at first gone to America on his own, only later, in the Cornish way, making arrangements for his wife and family to join him. In the interim, he had sent home remittances to support them (as did many an emigrant Cousin Jack in those days), and Rowse noted the irony of the fact that while Hetty waited for the next money draught from Montana, she was allowed credit by Annie Rowse in the family shop. Before Fred had gone to America, Rowse imagined, he must have paid visits to the shop when Richard Rowse was up at the clay pit at Carclaze. Feeling the slight suffered by his cuckolded father, he repeated his earlier view 'that later on, when Fred had absconded to America, Dick used to give Hetty a turn when he took groceries over on Saturday nights after dark'.[62]

'Obstinate and prejudiced in the old Cornish way'

Always concerned about whose traits, temperaments and physical char-acteristics he had inherited, Rowse had readily identified and admitted his mother's influence, the Vanson side, in him. He had always seemed so little of a Rowse, however, '[b]ut now I know where the other side comes from: the magnetic way of looking at people, according to Hilda, living life dangerously, the disdain for my own family—*his* characteristics according to her'. Moreover, 'his daughters out West—my half-sisters!—told me that he was indomitable, fearless, his courage was such that no set-back daunted him', a strength of character that Rowse now liked to think that he too had developed, and was 'obstinate and prejudiced in the old Cornish way'. He recalled that '[w]hen I at last got to Montana last October, Nora didn't believe that I was Fred's son', persuading him that he had been wrong all along. However, '[w]hen I got to Seattle, Mildred's husband recognized my family looks, and Phyllis was sure that I was'. As he put it: 'what chance had I, with *her* for a mother and *him* for a father?'.[63]

Convincing himself that the case was finally proven, the whole matter self-evident, Rowse struggled now to conjure up his own memories of Fred May:

> My earliest memory of him is that time in the slaughter-house at Tregonissey, after a killing, he took me up in his arms and shut me inside the slit carcase of a pig. I remember reacting violently, aged three, kicking him in the stomach and using *all* the swear-words I

had heard him use. . . He let me down; I took refuge with Dick
[Rowse]. A symbolic gesture. They exchanged smiles.[64]

The idea of some kind of tacit understanding, even alliance, between
Fred May and Richard Rowse appealed to A.L. Rowse as he pondered
the question of his paternity, relieving a painfully difficult situation of
some of its angst and sting, somehow making things all right. It was probably wishful thinking but it was important to Rowse as he constructed a
sense of who he was and where he came from. In the end, he convinced
himself, the combination of genes that created him had been fortuitous in
any case, for it had given him the unique blend of talents that he had been
able to deploy so effectively in life.

But as Rowse had already admitted to himself, there was actually something rather attractive about the idea of being Fred May's son. After all it
would bind him all the more tightly to the 'greater Cornwall' that he
believed existed across the Atlantic, giving a strong American dimension
to his sense of personal and Cornish identity. Just as his strange relationship with the Cornish gentry, through his half-sister Mabel, was tantalizing
and intriguing, introducing a romantic aristocratic element into the heart
of his family story, so there was a *frisson* of excitement in being *almost*
Cornish-American. For all their extraordinary trauma and anxiety, these
singular personal encounters with the Cornish gentry and the Cornish in
America had conspired to affect the way Rowse thought of himself as a
Cornishman, adding St Michael's Mount and the mining camps of
Montana very firmly to the repertoire of Cornish places that he liked to
think of as 'his'.

4

'She Made Me Detest the Very Nature of Women'

A Mother's Legacy?

From the days of his earliest childhood, A.L. Rowse was alert to the imagery of Cornish folklore and to the legends that had attached themselves to the antiquities of the Cornish countryside. 'Historians are apt to be specially interested in the folklore, people and stories, of their native parish or county', he wrote, and '[a] local historian is bound to much interested in folklore'.[1]

Cheek-by-jowl with the modernity of an industry that tended to sweep all before it, there was in the china clay country of his birth, despite those encroaching quarries and tips, a wealth of ancient monuments to delight the folklorist and the antiquarian. First and foremost, in Rowse's estimation, was Roche Rock. This igneous intrusion near Roche village seemed to erupt abruptly from the surrounding landscape, an extraordinary landmark visible for miles across neighbouring Goss Moor. As Rowse explained, the 'outcrop of granite rocks is sufficiently dramatic; but on top is a hermitage for an anchorite, with his now roofless chapel on top of that'. Built around 1400, according to Rowse, this building once housed 'an unknown hermit. . . a confessor—a kind of psycho-therapist to all who came for spiritual advice; they in turn would have kept him supplied with food and drink on his draughty perch'.[2] That was the story for public consumption, rehearsed in guide-books and popular histories. But Roche Rock had an earthier relevance in the living folk-practices of the Higher Quarter people, Rowse thought, one in which he expressed an at least equal interest: 'what a centre of fertility rites the place was, half the population in the old days conceived there—wasn't the hole in the rock a fertility symbol?'.[3]

At a time when many historians, especially the more fastidious empiricists amongst them, were only too glad to leave such folk-practices safely in the hands of the anthropologists, Rowse was keen to consider sexual matters alongside other facets of human social behaviour. His own family experiences had taught him that behind the ordered, straight-laced façade of Victorian restraint and respectability—'Nonconformist humbug',[4] as Rowse would have it—there was often a complex web of sexual indiscretion and deceit. In *Tudor Cornwall*, published in 1941, he was concerned to peer into the 'inner lives' of sixteenth-century Cornish people, revealing forced marriages, bastardy, fornication, and the like: 'The passions no doubt were simpler, stronger, more immediate with such people than now, held in check by no reason, their only control the fears, the superstition of their religion'.[5] Later, in *The Elizabethan Renaissance: The Life of a Society* (1971), Rowse devoted an entire chapter to 'Sex', though complaining that such extensive treatment was still too cursory: 'One cannot do justice here to the sex-life of the Elizabethans: it would need, and merit, a whole volume—one of far greater significance than most works of historical research'.[6]

He went some way towards providing that volume himself with his *The Case Books of Simon Forman: Sex and Society in Shakespeare's Age* (1974). Based in part on Forman's autobiography, transcribed a century before—'Victorian prudery prevented its publication'—the manuscript was presented now to the reading public in the spirit of a historian's specialist contribution to the work of 'psychologists, anthropologists and, possibly, medical men'.[7] Rowse's own preoccupation with Shakespeare's life and work included discussion of the playwright's sexual orientation and proclivities, and revealed among other things—to Rowse's satisfaction at least—the identity of the Dark Lady of the Sonnets. She (Emilia Lanier) was a 'rampant feminist', while the unwitting Shakespeare (said to have suffered at her hands) was, in Rowse's estimation, aggressively heterosexual: 'Shakespeare is the bawdiest of Elizabethan dramatists, with the natural bawdy of the highly sexed normal heterosexual, possibly the sexiest writer in the language—to anyone who knows the full possibilities of innuendo in contemporary usage'. Rowse certainly did, enjoying the 'rude fun' of it all.[8]

As Rowse intimated in *A Cornish Childhood*, his interest in matters sexual—so evident in later writing—was manifest at an early age. He recalled reading *John Halifax, Gentleman* at elementary school in Carclaze: 'I remember [it] for quite the wrong reason—for the extreme sexual excitement I derived from it, from the passage where the wife announces to her husband that she is going to have a baby'. As he observed so disarmingly, '[i]t only shows how impossible it is to keep sex out. Nobody on earth would have imagined that this would have been the effect of the chastest of Victorian novels on a small boy of ten.'[9] He was also fascinated by one of his Tregonissey neighbours, Jack: a ne'er do well who nonetheless 'had a wonderful way with animals, as with women', and kept a string of 'fancy-women' down in the town in addition to his long-suffering wife in the village, and who intrigued the young Rowse by showing him 'a wooden phallus, carved and painted, that he had made'.[10] And then there was the experience of his own brother, George, in the Army of Occupation in Germany after 1918, upon which he mused in *A Cornish Childhood*: 'The usual things happened, the landlady where he was billeted taking the opportunity of her husband's absence. . . My brother quite enjoyed himself'.[11]

Nature versus nurture?

However, despite this early and enduring interest in heterosexual relations, Rowse's attitudes towards sex were made complex and to a degree unfathomable—to him as well as to observers—by a growing disgust for the physical characteristics and bodily functions of women *and* by his burgeoning interest in, and sympathy for, homosexuality. During his early days at university Rowse eschewed all interest in sex, disturbed no doubt by the contest unravelling in his head.[12] For Rowse it was the classic 'nature versus nurture' debate: was one born with such predispositions or were they the result of an individual's life experience? He resolved the question in his own mind by insisting that, while it was the traumatic impact of his own mother's infidelities and personality that had put him off women for life, humankind (himself included) was in fact naturally sexually ambivalent. Thus one individual was as likely to be attracted to a member of one's own sex as to someone from the opposite. But, he added, this latent homosexuality was generally repressed—not least by legal sanction—in favour of heterosexual activity because of the basic need of society, throughout history, to reproduce itself.[13]

As we saw in Chapter 3, Rowse's 'distaste for the *consequences* of heterosexual relations'—the messy agony of childbirth, the objectionable presence of children, the stifling constraints of family life—was attributed by him to the influence of his mother: to the abiding knowledge of her promiscuity, the traumatic details of his family history (including doubts about his own paternity), and her 'hard-as-nails' personality that did not begin to provide the young Rowse with the love he craved.[14] This latter deficiency was exacerbated with the passage of the years as mother and son lived a strained life of close-quarters estrangement. As Rowse confessed with more than a tinge of regret in a letter penned in November 1953, shortly after his mother's death, to his old school-friend and trusted confidante Noreen Sweet: 'I think she made me detest the very nature of women'. It was, he wrote, 'a great pity but these things, though irrevocable, are not rational'.[15.] A dozen years later, and Rowse was still writing to Noreen on the same subject, torturing himself as he wrestled with the memory of his mother. The irony that Noreen was herself a woman seemed not to occur to him: 'You know more of the inside of my early life than almost anyone living. You know what a bitch my mother was— enough to put one off women for the rest of one's days.' The fact that he recognized himself in his mother only served to make things worse: 'And, of course, I am very much like her and share nearly all her defects of character and temperament'.[16]

Sometimes, indeed, the very thought of women overwhelmed him with revulsion and repugnance. One extraordinary passage provides a sharp insight into this emotion, hidden not in the depths of his journals, where it might be kept safely to himself, but rather published for all to see in his autobiographical volume *A Man of the Thirties*. Here he recalled how once, in the 1920s, he had been returning to Cornwall on a particularly busy train: 'Homeward bound in the train I was put off by *l'odor di femina* in the crowded summer compartment. . . a smell exudes from their twisted hair and their bodies, under their arms and from their bodices: sweat, rigor vitae, lactesence, the torrid essences, the languescence of women'. Pausing for a moment to reflect on this, he added: 'Women should always wear perfume'.[17] Likewise, the mere thought of Mary Blank, the gentle, pure, pretty teacher whom he had adored at school, suddenly in the anguished throes of the childbirth that killed her in the oppressive heat of India, was deeply alarming. Sometimes, it was merely the routine everyday incidentals of life that disgusted him, a growing hostility towards the 'idiot people' in general aimed specifically at females: in a street in Falmouth in June 1934, for example, '[h]ere the Fools come, gabbing about their ailments, especially the women'.[18]

But if it was his mother who was responsible for this aversion to women, then it was Bruce McFarlane, the Oxford historian and close friend of Rowse, who first suggested to him that the uncertainty he felt on matters sexual might be the result of natural inclination: an innate homosexuality rather than merely the outcome of his unfortunate family experiences. McFarlane was, it seems, a practising homosexual in the physical sense, but Rowse was not, at least as far as we can tell. He was deeply alarmed by homosexual advances when a young man at Oxford, and was at pains to explain—in the not entirely tasteful language of his age—that '[o]f course, sodomy and homosexuality are not interchangeable terms: neither one need imply the other'. The latter, he thought, was capable of ranging from 'the physical to the platonic and ideal, with its. . . expression in literature and the arts'.[19]

Nonetheless, McFarlane's intervention had brought clarity to his thoughts, and in pondering his own orientation Rowse recognized and gave voice to what he considered the 'feminine' side of his own make-up and that of other like-minded aesthetes: the ability to appreciate art, beauty, music, literature, and the wonders of nature, in contrast to the brutish 'masculinity' of the sports-field or the mechanic's workshop. He was also sure that the angst experienced by many young scholars at Oxford in his day was the result of repressed homosexuality, and he argued strongly for both the liberal toleration of homosexuality in society as a whole *and* a more enlightened understanding that would accept this orientation as natural rather than perverse. At times, Rowse seemed to argue that bi-sexuality was really the natural state of humankind, a reflection of the intellectual position he had arrived at in consideration of his own situation. In his *Homosexuals in History* (1977) he made plain his view that, hitherto, heterosexuality had been celebrated and homosexuality repressed because of the human race's fundamental drive to perpetuate itself in the face of pestilence, disease and famine. Now, however, with modern medicine and food aplenty (at least in the West), the survival imperative was not nearly so dominant, and this ought, he thought, to be reflected in the changing sexual mores of society, with both orientations—heterosexual and homosexual—being regarded as equally valid.

'In a world from which women were eliminated what an appeal he would have for men'

In later years—just as he exaggerated outrageously the irascible, contrary elements of his personality as part of his 'Rowse act', providing for his public what they expected to hear, see and read—so Rowse affected overtly camp characteristics for his audiences: the saucy wink, innuendo and *double entendre*, the wandering hand. This was, however, to trivialize a serious side to his being, to deliberately obscure through frivolous superficiality the depth of his feeling about this intensely personal subject. An earlier, more telling, more authentic insight is provided in the private recollection in his journals of a cliff-top walk—probably in the company of his old school-friend Len Tippett—in south-east Cornwall in the warm autumnal glow of mid-September sunshine in 1930:

> Tregantle Fort, coming up to it with strong western sun in our eyes. Two young soldiers, in their vests, coats off, sit jauntily on a gate. One fair and lithe. . . white arms and muscles; the other, less interested, dark, also enjoying the hour, sea-wind and sun. The younger interested in the impression he makes on the passers-by, dances up and down the gate, face radiant with *joi de vivre*. We pass. 'In a world from which women were eliminated what an appeal he would have for men'.[20]

Indeed, there were men who did have such an appeal for Rowse. There was, for example, Norman Scarfe, the young man who as a schoolboy had first met him when submitting an essay in a competition that Rowse had sponsored. Rowse had by then purchased 'Polmear Mine', his villa on the outskirts of St Austell, a kind of proto-Trenarren with mature gardens overlooking St Austell Bay, and there he first entertained Norman Scarfe to lunch. A few years later, in June 1944 when Norman was in the first wave of the amphibious assault on D-Day, Rowse in his anxiety thought again of their first meeting and 'that fascinating lunch. . . that beautiful Sunday in Spring, the rhododendrons and camellias out, the hot sun on the lawn. . . you as a schoolboy wanted to know me, went in for an essay prize I was asked to set, took the trouble to go round and see the Cornish churches in order that you might win and so get in touch with me'. He went on, re-living the exhilaration of the moment, 'we are meant for each other and are happiest in each other'.[21] But in a gloss penned thirty years later, in 1974, he added a more sober perspective: 'It could not last on this level. And it did not.'[22]

In fact, the intensity of their friendship endured for some years. In the early 1950s it ameliorated the growing despair Rowse felt in consequence of the animosity that had developed between his mother, who had come to live with him at Polmear Mine, and his housekeeper, Beryl Cloke. Here, for example, is his diary entry for 21 December 1952, penned at Oxford on the eve of his return to Cornwall for the Christmas break: 'tomorrow I have to go down there to the disquiet and unhappiness of my own house—it cannot be called a home—with those two miserable women in it creating an intolerable atmosphere. Thank God, Norman comes down next Saturday to keep me company.'[23] Rowse and Scarfe also went abroad together, and Rowse encouraged him to go up to Oxford. But Scarfe only got a Fourth, much to Rowse's horror, and although he managed to acquire a lectureship in history at Leicester under the wing of Rowse's old friend and fellow Cornishman Jack Simmons, at length Scarfe abandoned his formal academic career to go to live in Suffolk—again to Rowse's horror, and to the abiding damage of their relationship.

Before Norman Scarfe, there had been Adam von Trott, whom Rowse had met in Germany in 1928. They were in touch for the next half a dozen years, writing and meeting when they could, the rising star of Hitler in the end getting in the way of their relationship and bringing it to a tragically abrupt halt. Although von Trott was a German patriot—wishing to restore Germany's pre-Versailles boundaries, and denying that anti-Semitism existed in his country—he was opposed to National Socialism and was implicated in the plot to assassinate Hitler, forfeiting his own life in the recriminations and executions that followed. In the intensity of his friend-ship with Adam von Trott, Rowse had felt all the ambiguities and ambivalence that assailed him when his thoughts turned to matters sexual:

'the relationship was so complex. . . Adam was dominantly heterosexual, as I was not; on the other hand the thought of physical relations was strongly repressed in me, conceivably more so than with him'.[24] He added, echoing again the theme he thought so important, 'love and sex were not synonymous',[25] implying once more the salience for him of the 'platonic and ideal' homosexuality that was more a meeting of minds than of bodies, an intense emotional companionship based upon a like-minded enthusiasm for the arts and culture.

The *Economist* magazine, reviewing in August 1979 the newly published *A Man of the Thirties*, recognized the significance of the von Trott episode and wondered whether it was not the key to understanding Rowse the man, asking rhetorically: 'Is his "intensely pure" love affair with Adam von Trott, first, fondly and frankly told here, the explanation of it all?'.[26] The answer, of course, must be 'no' (and in fact Rowse had already devoted a chapter to von Trott in his earlier *A Cornishman Abroad*). But the periodical had put its finger on at least part of the story: the importance for Rowse, in the absence of a satisfactory relationship with his mother (and therefore, in his estimation, with other women), of his relationships with men.

Although never as intense as the friendships with Norman Scarfe and Adam von Trott, Rowse's relationships with Bruce McFarlane and other Oxford colleagues—notably Richard Pares and Geoffrey Hudson (the latter half-Cornish)—were often particularly close and contributed enormously to shaping and enriching his life. However, amongst those male friends who influenced, guided and helped form his tastes and enthusiasms, none was more significant than Charles Henderson, a fellow Cornishman who shared (perhaps even created) Rowse's interest in Cornish history and was responsible for unlocking for Rowse the hitherto remote, inaccessible, far-flung parts of Cornwall that had been beyond his reach (Henderson owned a car), including the muniment rooms of the great houses from which Rowse would have previously been excluded automatically. Henderson's role in enthusing the young Rowse, which ranged from help in the enormously difficult task of reading and transcribing early historical documents to the seemingly effortless dating of fonts and benches in Cornish churches, is addressed in Chapter 11. But it is important to note here the Cornish connection, not only the significance of Henderson's infectious enthusiasm for Cornish history but also the qualities of intimacy, exclusivity and mutual identification lent by their common 'Cornishness'. This was an ethnic dimension to their relationship that they had felt strongly when they first met at Oxford and which they carried over when at home in Cornwall, an agreeable and extremely satisfying sense of superiority, of 'belonging' in Cornwall, of being able to claim the 'hereditary right to Cornwall' that both men felt to be so important.

16 Charles Henderson the Cornish enthusiast—about to be barded at the first Cornish Gorsedd at Boscawn-Un in 1928. *Courtesy Royal Institution of Cornwall.*

18 Noreen Sweet: 'early school friend and to the end' as Rowse scribbled on the reverse. *Courtesy Special Collections, University of Exeter Library.*

17 Charles Henderson (hatted) with his bride Isobel Munro and a friend, Umberto Zanotti-Bianco, during the newly-weds' honeymoon in Italy in 1933. Rowse's inscription on the back of the photograph reads: 'Charles Henderson with death in his face'. *Courtesy Special Collections, University of Exeter Library.*

'So much hereditary right to Cornwall'

Henderson's pride in being Cornish was considerable. And although his research was focused principally on the local and the antiquarian, preoccupied with facts and details, he would occasionally lift his eyes to grander themes, proffering generalizations that lent Cornwall an importance in the history of these islands that far outweighed its relatively small size and remote situation. Thus, in his essay on St Ives, we learn of the special role of Cornwall in the propagation of the Christian religion in the centuries following the departure of the Legions. 'In Cornwall and the Celtic lands the missionaries planted Christianity',[27] he wrote, emphasizing Cornwall's position within the Celtic world and postulating a Celtic Christianity that had carried the Word throughout the Isles. Similarly, in his *A History of the Parish of Constantine in Cornwall*, there was his firm insistence that '[t]o study the history of a parish such as Constantine is to understand in large measure, the history of Britain'.[28] He was, moreover, adamant that the qualities that made Cornwall unique, a land apart, were shared in equal measure by all its constituent districts. As Rowse recalled, Henderson 'always used to insist. . . that we should never underestimate the Cornishry of East Cornwall', even though 'some of us may think of West Cornwall as a kind of *Bretagne bretonnante*, a fastness of Celtic purity'.[29]

Despite this fierce attachment to Cornwall in all its manifestations, Charles Henderson was—as Rowse often liked to remind him—only one quarter Cornish. Yet, as Rowse was forced to admit, Henderson's ancestry had opened the door to a network of 'county' family connections that he, for all his much-vaunted 100 per cent Cornish descent, could only dream of. As Rowse and Isobel Henderson (Charles's widow) observed in their introduction to Henderson's *Essays in Cornish History* (one of the few examples, incidentally, of collaborative writing by Rowse):

> Charles Henderson's only quarrel with Cornwall was that it had given him no more than a quarter of his blood. His father, Major J.S. Henderson, is half Scotch and half of the Irish family of Newenham: his mother is a Carus-Wilson from Westmoreland. Both, however, were born and bred in Cornwall, and a portion of Cornish ancestry came to him through his mother's mother, one of the Willyams of Carnanton who entered the Duchy in the sixteenth century by the gift of an Arundell manor. He was glad to claim so much hereditary right to Cornwall, and it happened against his wish that he neither began nor ended his life there, but was born in Jamaica and died in Rome.[30]

Thus it was, Rowse observed, that '[h]e had the advantage—though only one-quarter Cornish, as I used to tease him—of being connected, through his mother, with a number of the county families, and so most doors, not all (one rather mean exception was Tregothnan of the Boscawens), were open to him'.[31] As Rowse elaborated, explaining the extent of this connection, Henderson's mother on her 'Cornish side. . . was related to the Williams clan, famous gardeners, who had made such a fortune out of the Industrial Revolution, then married into the county families and acquired half a dozen of its finest estates'.[32] Here there is a hint of Rowse's self-confessed envy and his love–hate relationship with the gentry, sharpened, as we have seen in earlier chapters, by his knowledge of Tregrehan—where his Vanson grandparents worked—and his mother's experiences at St Michael's Mount. Yet in his friendship with Henderson, Rowse had at last gained that entrée to the world he craved: not merely the research opportunities amongst the dusty documents behind closed doors but to the drawing rooms and dining rooms of the great houses, to the lifestyle that intrigued and attracted him. His first-ever country-house weekend was with Charles Henderson at Penmount—'a draughty spot off the road to Newquay looking down on our little cathedral city'[33]—and thereafter Henderson took his working-class friend under his wing, introducing him to the country houses of Cornwall and to the people who lived there, like Killagorden, tucked away in its hidden valley, home of the Toms family and 'crammed with old family china'.[34]

Rowse had already learned the delights of tramping the Cornish countryside, with his jaunts to Luxulyan and Carn Grey and the forays to Trenarren and Pentewan, and in Charles Henderson he found a like-minded enthusiast. In 1901 Henderson's parents had returned to Britain, living first at Okehampton in Devon before moving across the border to Falmouth and then Hayle, with the young Charles staying whenever he could with his grandfather at Penmount, the house into which he would himself move in 1923. From these strategic places, Henderson was able to explore much of West Cornwall, developing an intimate knowledge of parishes such as Constantine, Mabe and St Just-in-Roseland, while the later acquisition of a family car allowed him to lift his sights to Cornwall as a whole, leading to his much-vaunted familiarity with every church, farm and lane from the Scillies to the Tamar.

Nihil Cornubiense alienum a me puto

Henderson liked to claim '*nihil Cornubiense alienum a me puto*'[35] ('nothing Cornish is alien to me'), a catch-cry that Rowse himself took up in later life. In his growing authority as a Cornish specialist Henderson received the blessing of Henry Jenner, patriarch of the Cornish-Celtic Revivalist movement and (from 1928) Grand Bard of the Cornish Gorsedd, together with the academic endorsement of the University College of the South West at Exeter, which in 1924 appointed him its peripatetic extra-mural Cornish Studies lecturer in Cornwall. But Henderson did not have the field entirely to himself. A.K. Hamilton Jenkin, the mining historian and folklorist, was, according to Rowse, a rival and critic of Henderson. He was, Rowse said, 'a mean man' who suffered the twin disabilities of being 'a middle-class Quaker' and 'married not very happily'. And '[t]hey did not like each other. . . Jenkin was nothing like such a nice man as Charles'.[36]

However, Charles Henderson had the happy knack of appealing to all types of people across the bounds of class, religion or political allegiance: a 'common touch' that found him as welcome and as much at ease when speaking in remote village halls as he might be when dining in the great houses of the gentry. There was also something endearing in his manner, a self-effacing quality that allowed others to readily accept his authority in matters Cornish. Fondly, Rowse told the story, in several places and several versions, of their experience together 'in a small country church' in Cornwall when 'a clergyman came up to him and said: "We are not sure of the date of this font: Mr Henderson has not yet seen it"—but, whether out of shyness or malice, he did not reveal himself'.[37] In another story, Henderson was talking to an unknown companion in a train: the 'stranger remarked on the ineptness of the name New College [at Oxford] for so old a foundation: he answered that Newquay was existing in 1480 or before: and the stranger, who proved to be Sir Richard Edgcumbe, rejoined: "Then you are Mr Henderson"'.[38]

Rowse was happy to defer to Henderson's superior credentials: content to be led as together they explored Cornwall. Much of the territory was entirely new to Rowse though already familiar to Henderson, and he claimed that there was never any sense of rivalry between them. They settled upon a convenient division of labour—Henderson was a medievalist, while Rowse embraced the Tudor period—and if there was a latent competition between the two it did not show. But if a sense of shared Cornishness underpinned this working arrangement, lending that intimacy and exclusivity in which both delighted, then there was in the personalities of the two men something complementary, a quality that drew them together and gave their relationship a vitality and depth that went far beyond their synergetic interest in Cornwall. Ironically, Rowse and Henderson had first met, not in Cornwall, but at Oxford in early 1928. Rowse had already encountered Geoffrey Grigson—the son of an East Cornwall clergyman—whom he did not like. 'I was more taken with another Cornish associate whom I met this term', Rowse recalled later, 'Charles Henderson, who was to become one of my dearest friends'. Rowse recounted the amusing circumstances of their meeting: 'I was surprised when this red-faced giant of 6 feet 7 inches, dining in Hall one Sunday night turned out to be he. I thought I had caught sight of him as a pale-faced attendant one day at a seminar. . . That turned out to be Hamilton Jenkin. . . and Charles and Jenkin were mutually exclusive.'[39]

Thereafter, the two 'became inseparable'. In Cornwall, there were the expeditions together—'I can see us now', Rowse wrote in 1979, 'on the top of Trencrom in view of both seas, Bristol and English Channels, the wind in our hair, faces plunged into "splits", homemade blackberry jelly, Cornish cream streaking the corners of our mouths'.[40] When, later, Henderson went back to Oxford as a history tutor at Corpus Christi, '[d]ear Charles was like a large faithful dog, who came around every afternoon to All Souls'. In the end, Rowse, for all his affection for Henderson, became 'impatient'—there were so many other things to attend to—and 'told him that there wasn't anybody I wanted to see every afternoon of my life'.[41] Nonetheless, their friendship blossomed, and although Rowse was by now involved with Adam von Trott, there was in the Henderson–Rowse relationship more than a hint of the intimacy that Rowse reserved for the closest of his male friends. Charles was, he said, along with Bruce McFarlane, one of a brace 'of the closest and dearest friends of my Oxford life'.[42] He was 'the kindest of men, totally without malice'; he was 'pink and boyish'[43] and could be very entertaining and amusing—as in the story, remembered by Rowse but told by Henderson against himself, regarding the occasion when he had been invited to give a talk in a village hall in Cornwall. The chairman had droned on for more than an hour in his introductory remarks, and when, finally, Charles Henderson was asked for his address, he promptly announced that it was 'Penmount, Truro', and explained that he had to leave now to catch his train![44]

'To know him is to love him'

For his part, Charles Henderson was as predisposed as Rowse to intimate male bonding. Indeed, perhaps more so than his friend, he was attracted to the male physique. As he once remarked in conversation with Rowse: 'It's extraordinary what a difference not having to wear clothes makes. These young men come here [Oxford] looking perfectly ordinary, nothing out of the common. They take their clothes off, and they look like young gods.'[45] In the years before he met Rowse, Henderson had been closely involved with one Fred Maxse, an Oxford undergraduate who had been having difficulty with his studies and whom Henderson had readily agreed to help. Years later, Rowse wrote, with perhaps a hint of retrospective jealousy: 'Charles became extremely fond of this backward boy'.[46] Certainly, Henderson in his diary in September 1925 had recorded that Maxse was 'first my pupil and then my true intimate friend'.[47] They had already spent more than two months together in Italy and it was agreed with Maxse's father, Sir Ivor, that young Fred should go down to Cornwall for a couple of terms to be tutored by Henderson before returning to Oxford to take his finals.

In early October, Henderson left for Cornwall, with the prospect of Fred Maxse joining him later: 'If Fred and I had been saying goodbye for ever we should have been quite broken hearted. . . after a last glimpse of that clear bright face, I felt a great blank in my life. I couldn't get him out of my mind for the rest of the journey.' As Henderson mused: 'We have been together for nearly 10 weeks and have never been separated. We have always (except at Bondo [in Italy]) shared the same room and I can there-fore claim to know Fred better than anybody. To know him is to love him.'[48] Lady Maxse wrote to Henderson, thanking him for the attention that he had lavished on her son—'a window has opened in his soul'[49]— and Fred lovingly followed his mentor up and down Cornwall as he gave his lectures. Thus on Tuesday 13 October Henderson lectured on 'Aspects of the History of Liskeard' in the town of that name, the two of them spending the night in Webb's Hotel where 'we had a dismal cold supper and longed for Italy'.[50] When, at Christmas, it was time for Maxse to return home for the festivities it was '[a] dismal day for me in every respect. Cold damp and foggy and Fred's final departure',[51] only the prospect of the two of them going to Rome at Easter keeping Henderson's spirits up.

A few years later, Henderson formed a similar attachment with Sandy Rendell, another Oxford undergraduate whom he had taken under his wing. Rowse thought Henderson 'humbly in love' with Rendell, noting that '[w]hen Sandy was taking his Schools, Charles would get up at 6.a.m to lay a fire for him to work by before breakfast!'.[52] Alas, Sandy did not reciprocate. According to Rowse, it was this case of unrequited love that threw Henderson into the alternative, female arms of (Mary) Isobel Munro, whom he shortly married. It was a 'dynastic marriage', as Rowse disparagingly described it, for Isobel was the daughter of the Rector of Lincoln College, Oxford: 'Charles. . . at the height of his love for Sandy was desperately miserable and finding that Sandy was not in love with him, and later, off the rebound, married Isobel'.[53] Rowse, again more than a little jealous, thought Henderson's behaviour rather unnecessary and over-reactive: 'Not that Charles meant to go to bed with him—"I'd rather shoot myself", he said: it was all platonic, rather un-adult'.[54]

Writing in his journal, Rowse recorded the distress the episode caused for all concerned. There was, for example, an agonizing journey from Oxford down to Cornwall with Charles Henderson and his sister Chrys (Christobel). To Charles's preoccupation and Rowse's unsympathetic response was added the fact that Rowse was suffering acutely from his latest spell of duodenal trouble and, worse, that Chrys appeared to have a crush on *him!* 'On that journey down that summer, we were a miserable party', Rowse wrote later, 'Charles inwardly moaning over Sandy, Chrys over me, me over my guts gradually killing me.'[55] Charles and Rowse were to leave together for the Isles of Scilly the next day, but despite Henderson's insistence to the contrary, Rowse was determined not to stay overnight at Penmount, where he might fall prey to Chrys. There was a 'conflict of wills as we drew near the parting of the roads in Lanivet' in mid-Cornwall, one route continuing on to Truro, the other turning south for St Austell. Rowse wrote: 'He [Henderson] was determined that we should drive straight to Penmount, to give Chrys a chance of getting at me—she had a downcast expression (at Polmear later she said she would "like to"—I'd have been trapped). I was determined to go home to squalid 24 Robartes Place [his parents' house]—next day Charles and I were bound for the Scillies.'[56]

For Rowse, the thought that Henderson might be match-making was adding insult to injury. For Charles to be distracted by Sandy was bad enough but for him to try to foist Chrys on him was worse, a kind of betrayal. And yet, all this was relatively trivial compared to what was to happen next. As Henderson prepared for his forthcoming marriage to Isobel Munro, 'he tried himself out with one of the girls from the Drawing School he was attending—"poor little Cecilia was the butterfly broken on the wheel", with the aid of a French letter'. Remembering, perhaps, his mother's experience on the Mount, Rowse did not approve of this further example of the upper classes taking liberties with the lower, observing that: 'She was lower class; I did not much appreciate her being taken advantage of for Charles's apprenticeship for marriage. However, like Spender, he found that he "could", and graduated to marrying Isobel Munro.'[57] Rowse also found the episode inherently distasteful—he had 'had her on the floor of his room in college'—but most especially he was jealous of the idea of Henderson marrying Isobel: 'Of course, I was jealous at his marrying, I resented losing him'. Rowse imagined that Henderson could not possibly enjoy heterosexual activity, and with self-congratulatory triumph he recorded in his diary that neither did Isobel: 'Funnily enough, she didn't much care for sex either: it always made her feel sick, she told me'.[58] But in the end it did not matter whether Henderson and his new bride would be sexually active. 'Alas',[59] Rowse wrote later on the invitation card that he had received for their wedding, not so much because the match itself pained him but of its consequences—for Charles Henderson was to die suddenly on honeymoon.

'His death brought him back to me'

Charles and Isobel Henderson were married in June 1933 and set out on their honeymoon tour of southern Italy two months later. Charles had been complaining of chest pains for some time and at Monte Sant' Angelo of the Gargano he suffered a severe heart-attack while visiting the shrine of St Michael—the Anglican patron of Cornwall, as Rowse and Isobel were to note later. He died in Rome eleven days later, on 24 September, and was buried there in the Protestant cemetery, near that other 'great Cornishman, Edward John Trelawny'.[60.] For Rowse, this was a devastating event, one that at a stroke deprived him of one of his closest friends and robbed Cornwall of its most esteemed scholar. 'Sunday afternoon in Oxford, the trees as heavy and full as so many summers before, also heavy in the air bells ringing', wrote Rowse in July 1934, still miserable almost a year after the event, 'And from time to time I say to myself, Charles are you really dead? Can it be that you are dead?'[61] And yet death had had the effect of releasing Henderson from Isobel's embrace and restoring him to Rowse. Rowse could now claim Henderson's mantle in the study of things Cornish and preserve the memory of Henderson as he was: drawing a veil over his new interests and the portents of a different life ahead, and rooting him forever in Cornwall. Moreover, there was now no possibility of competition between the two men, the potential for rivalry between Rowse and Henderson that may have lain in the future no longer an issue. In fact, if anything, Henderson's death allowed Rowse to assert a quiet superiority with the passage of the years (see Chapter 11), to observe that Henderson had been an antiquarian rather than a trained historian, that really he had been incapable of writing good prose, that his wider knowledge of history and literature was limited.

Publicly, Rowse supported Isobel in her loss, collaborating with her in the edited collection of Henderson's essays and helping her in other ways too, but in private he was less forgiving:

> I always blamed Isobel for running him off his feet. In a way his death brought him back to me. But how different things would have been if he had lived. I should have tapered off so close a friendship when he was married—which I resented. Then too I partly succeeded to his place in Cornwall; but only partly for politics came between and alienated me bitterly. He would have gone on to a conventional family life, perhaps become President of Corpus. I should have gone on as before, increasingly without him. Death brought him back to me, and I remained ever faithful to his memory.[62]

He wrote, for example, a poem in Henderson's memory, publishing it privately as a card-covered pamphlet, *Extempore Memorial*, a very public expression of his devotion and his loss:

How should my life have become so bound,
So mixed with his that by his death,
I now see never that ridge of land,
The familiar road, the stone-pines on the edge
    leaning to the wind, their driven shapes
    fantastically flanking the forsaken house [Penmount];
Nor ever see the curve of hills
Encircling the lighted city [Truro]
    through nocturnal mists, June night of stars,
    or by the January moon;
Nor ever walk in the funereal woods,
    the waters in my ears falling,
    letting fall their drops upon my mind,
    and in my heart:
Nor know all these in the flesh, or in the mind's eye,
    but they are his, being made so by his death?[63]

Rowse also dedicated *Tudor Cornwall* to Charles Henderson, 'First of Cornish Scholars',[64] part of his attempt to keep his memory 'green',[65] and in spare moments across the years Rowse's thoughts would drift back to those carefree days spent in Henderson's company:

> In the Tube I suddenly think of Charles, and see him and me sitting in the afternoon sun of late July by the shallow inlet, like a lake, of Porthellick on St Mary's in the Scillies—where Sir Cloudsley Shovel's body came ashore. Two great rocks stand out to sea on either side, through which narrow channel the tide rushes in and out. At high tide the shallow basin is full to overflowing, the water coming right up to the rim of grass, where we sat in the sun after bathing. . . Christ, how brief it all was![66]

The funeral of Isobel Henderson in April 1967, which Rowse attended, was another occasion on which to remember Charles. The early, untimely deaths of both Bruce McFarlane and Richard Pares, his Oxford colleagues, had affected Rowse deeply. But before either of them there had been the loss of Charles Henderson: '1933 was the year of Charley's death: the death that upset me most and over which I grieved longest'. Isobel herself had been ill with TB after Charles's death, having to have a lung removed, and as a chain smoker courted the throat cancer that finally killed her. 'Another life, younger than mine, rounded up and ended', Rowse sighed, though there was in the continuing survival of Chrys Henderson, also at the funeral, something ironic that irritated him and reminded him of the repugnance he felt towards women. There was

'Chrys, froosy and dowdy as ever', with her 'unappetising legs. . . such a clumsy, *gauche* cow'.[67]

'Women who have fallen for me'

If the irony of Charles's early death and Chrys's survival caused Rowse a grim, inward smile, then there was also the irony of what he termed 'nostalgia': the deep-seated emotion of tender, unconditional affection that a mother, lover, or life-long friend might feel for another. Despite his professed aversion to women, he reflected that—insofar as anyone felt this 'nostalgia' for him—it was almost always members of the female sex. Writing in his diary in August 1936, nearly three years—as he observed—after Charles's death, he explained:

> Some of the subjects of [my]. . . nostalgia now surprise me, though I reflect how little I have been the subject of such nostalgia for others. For my mother—but only since I grew up and became a man, moreover a sick man, as a child hardly at all, not much love there, and that has left a deep mark on my mind. I suppose that that has meant no response to the women who have fallen for me. . . When I have been the subject, it has *always* been on the part of women: Noreen [Sweet] certainly, Chris [*sic*] Henderson, now Betty [Stucley]. . . Very little from the menfolk.[68]

Here again was the underlying influence of his mother. But there was also the intriguing suggestion that, despite his self-confessed sexual preferences, it was always women and rarely men who found him attractive. He insisted, as he had done before and would do so again, that he felt no desire for women. But there is certainly evidence to the contrary, as Rowse would on occasions concede: ranging from his earliest sexual stirrings to the several long-term intimate friendships that he retained with women throughout most of his life. There were also some surprises that cast at least partial doubt on his own self-image as the fastidious misogynist who, despite homosexual sympathies, eschewed physical contact and sought instead the cultured delights of high-minded, platonic love. There is, for example, an extraordinary diary entry in April 1933, a time when he was in the capital delivering a series of lectures at the London School of Economics. He observed that 'Guildford Street. . . was a regular beat for poor tarts. One had to run the gauntlet as one made for Russell Square down Kingsway for my (dreary) lectures at the L.S.E.' On one occasion, he recorded, '[o]ne of these young ladies hailed me close with: "Have a fuck. It'll do you good"'. 'Would it, though', Rowse pondered, adding with youthful bravado 'I usually steered clear'. Half a century later, reviewing and correcting his diaries to ensure their suitability for his posterity, he struck out the daring (truthful?) 'usually', replacing it with an emphatic 'always'.[69]

Should this evidence appear unreliable, there are other pointers elsewhere. In December 1952, for instance, Rowse was a guest—along with Sir Robert Menzies, the Australian Prime Minister—at a dinner at Clivedon, and found himself sitting next to Joan Hammond, the celebrated Australian opera singer. He was captivated. Here was '[a] woman to write home about, with the luscious, glittering, sexy look of an Italian prima donna, black mane of hair, incriminating smile, pretty mole on her cheek'.[70] Closer to home, in Cornwall, he was impressed by the sexually attractive Jean, the wife of Derek Tangye—author of the *Minack* series of books. On one occasion, exploring West Cornwall with his friend David Treffry, Rowse arranged to visit the Tangyes. He did not much take to Derek Tangye, disliking his 'glum, middle class Cornish look'. Nor did he care for his work: 'hasn't much talent for description (too journalistic)— *she* is the real spirit of the place: dark, pretty, loving, and with the shrewd look in her eye by no means evident'.[71] Later, the Tangyes returned the compliment, visiting Rowse at Trenarren. 'Do I really like the Tangyes?' he asked his diary: 'They certainly make up to me prodigiously. But he doesn't know me. He is a completely masculine type, with male physical clumsiness. . . Jean is far more attractively female, firm little apple-breasts like a girl, I felt as she leaned seductively to me.'[72]

There was something mischievously exotic in Jean Tangye that made her attractive to Rowse, and there was the same quality in yet greater quantities in Marthe Bibesco, the exiled Romanian princess whom he had first met in the late 1950s at Sir Robert Abdy's house at Newton Ferrers, in East Cornwall. Marthe Bibesco had known the Russian Court before the Revolution and was friendly with the Hohenzollerns of Imperial Germany. In the Second World War, as Romania was overrun by the fascists, she had escaped to South Africa, but her only daughter, Ghika, was captured by the Nazis and, on liberation, incarcerated by the Communist regime. Taken together, Ghika was in captivity for all of a dozen years. Meanwhile, Marthe had made her way to Cornwall, seeking a retreat far from the metropolitan seats of Europe, and settled at Tullimarr, the Regency house (mentioned in Kilvert's famous diary) at Perran-ar-worthal, between Truro and Falmouth. Rowse admired her for her courage and strength of character, as well as for her aristocratic credentials: 'She had been one of the richest, as well as most beautiful, women in Europe. . . she never once complained of what she had lost, or what they had all suffered'. Her magnanimity impressed him, as did her 'zest for life, she was a *great* woman, besides being a great lady'. When she had to make a living by turning her hand to writing, she confided to Rowse, comparing her new life with the grand old days, that 'I like this better'. Rowse was bowled over: 'I thought it wonderful of her'. Moreover, '[i]t was an honour for Cornwall that she should have chosen it', though 'the small-minded Cornish gentry in their crevices did not appreciate their acquisition—too ignorant of Europe (they had all been Appeasers), let alone of European literature'.[73]

'We became playmates', Rowse explained, 'with all Cornwall to explore, with me—her "Professor"—as guide.' Indeed, '[s]he became very patriotic about Cornwall; I promised that when Cornwall was happily cut off at the Tamar from insanely tax-ridden England, she should become *Madame la President de la Republique Cornouaillaise*'. She gave Rowse lunch at Tullimarr—'a feast of fresh lobster from Falmouth, and on top of that, out of Cornish patriotism, a proper Cornish pasty'—and in their adventures across Cornwall they ranged as far as Landulph on the Tamar and, searching for antiquities, to the remote corners of the Higher Quarter, above St Austell, 'with me as chauffeur, the Princess anxious not to go too fast along Cornish roads and lanes'. At Landulph, Rowse showed Marthe Bibesco the tomb of Theodore Palaeologus, a descendent of the Greek Emperors of Constantinople, 'my obedient pupil taking down the inscription which I dictated to her'. In the Higher Quarter, they ventured to Roche Rock—that 'exciting upthrust of rocks high up on the moor'—with its ancient fertility rites. 'In one of the recumbent rocks at Roche', Rowse wrote, 'like an Irish bawn, there was a suggestive deep hole, filled with water, into which one cast a copper and made one's wish—such was the folklore. I had often enacted the ritual, and had been televised doing it; the Princess was game, and followed suit.'[74]

A quarter of a century and more since his explorations with Charles Henderson, here was another enthusiastic companion delighting in the hidden haunts of Cornwall: a woman this time though still of aristocratic hue, but with the role of master and pupil emphatically reversed: 'All in all, she was the most remarkable woman I have ever known'.[75] But did he love her, or she him?:

> I have now the obscure and humble feeling that I may have failed her. Could it be expressed in the one word—love? The thought then never occurred to me—I should have thought it presumptuous on my part. There was the difference in age, every sort of difference—and yet, in spite of that, a deeper kinship of spirit than I realized. I regarded her with admiration, deference, a fascination that was partly historic and partly personal. But I did not love her; it never occurred to me that possibly she might have loved me.[76]

The disclaimer was vintage Rowse, a retreat to the comfort zone that enabled him to keep women at arm's length, while remaining true to his own self-image and retaining his much-prized independence. He had dealt similarly with Betty Stucley, with whom he had stayed at Speke's Mill, in North Devon, when he was undertaking field-work research for his book *Sir Richard Grenville of the Revenge,* published in 1937. She claimed descent from the Grenvilles and introduced Rowse to Grenville country, the marcher lands of the North Cornwall/North Devon borders. The two ventured as far as Hartland as Rowse absorbed the topographical milieu that underpinned the book he was writing. By all accounts, it was an idyllic time, tramping 'across country full of the scents of honeysuckle in the hedges, meadowsweet in the ditches, saxifrage and comfrey' to destinations such as Bideford and Woolfardisworthy (which, Rowse noted, Betty pronounced 'Woolsery'). He enjoyed this '[f]ooling my life away in Devonshire lanes', but as he added later, delightful as Betty's company was, he was not going to allow himself to be ensnared by her: 'I wasn't and I was not going to, marrying Betty would have been a fatal mistake'.[77]

'I love you. . . with the utmost chastity'

More significant was the relationship with C.V. (Veronica) Wedgwood, first Rowse's gifted student at Oxford, and later editorial assistant at *Time and Time* and Jonathan Cape, as well as author of a number of distinguished books on seventeenth-century Europe, including several on the Civil War. Intellectually, Veronica Wedgwood was very much to Rowse's taste, and together they visited the Civil War sites of Cornwall, including the Boconnoc estate—'dripping with memories of the Civil War, of Braddock Down and Charles I sleeping in his coach by the hedge, the house itself asleep at the end of long drives in from the tangle of roads between the Fowey and Looe rivers'.[78] As well as warming to his Cornish enthusiasms (always a good tactic), she was also a stunning beauty: full of a gentle, aristocratic grace that appealed to Rowse. When he was in London they saw a good deal of one another, relishing each other's company as they dined out or went to the theatre. In later life, Rowse was insistent that there was never any question of their being married—a point of view endorsed by mutual friends who agreed that it would have been an impossible match—although he conceded that there was a point in their younger days when they had come close to engagement: driven by the match-making skills of Veronica's mother, Lady Wedgwood.[79]

Rowse also claimed that Veronica was the more ardent of the two in the relationship, an assertion borne out in the flirtatious and occasionally adoring tone of her correspondence. Letters spanning the period from the early 1930s to late 1960s were routinely addressed to 'My dearest Trelawny' (an allusion to that other great Cornish patriot, Bishop Jonathan Trelawny of 1688) and 'My darling Trelawny'. When he had been ill with his duodenal ulcer she wrote in the tenderest terms: 'My love, dear Tre, look after yourself carefully won't you? Don't overdo yourself and get really well. Bless you.'[80] She was always eager to meet up—'I do frightfully want to see you my dear. . . Please, when can we meet?'—and each letter was concluded with an affectionate signing-off. 'Yours, ever so soft, sentimental, and feminine' was one farewell; another, more playfully, was 'Love & xxx' with a postscript to explain that the latter was '[a] sign they put on beer barrels. It has nothing to do with amorous salutation.'[81.] She was content, too, to sign herself as 'Your devoted disciple', in January 1957 insisting that still 'I regard myself as a small conscientious drummer boy marching along behind the Great Drum Major, hopeful and aspiring'.[82] When Rowse, in a generous review of one of her books, had described her as 'master' of her subject, she replied provocatively in a letter: 'How wise of you to let me emerge "as a master"—though emerging as a mistress would have other charms'. Likewise, writing to assure Rowse that he was a 'Great Man' and 'what a darling', she re-affirmed that 'I love you very much'—though adding with a rueful irony that aptly reflected the truth of the situation—'with the utmost chastity'.[83]

The relationship had not developed into the passionate affair that Veronica Wedgwood desired and Rowse resisted, though the friendship endured. It was ruptured eventually by the award in 1969 of the Order of Merit to Wedgwood—an honour that Rowse thought should rightly be his—and by her disagreement, in the same year, with Rowse over the identity of the Dark Lady. Of the former, she wrote to Rowse that 'it is excessive but it's certainly nice'; of the latter, she told him that 'I have read your book on the Sonnets and re-read what you say in your Shakespeare, and I'm terribly sorry to disagree with you'.[84] Veronica Wedgwood was no longer pupil but master, something that Rowse could not stomach. As he put it perfunctorily: 'This ended my friendship with her'.[85] Even so, he did contribute a chapter to her *Festschrift*, published in 1986 and co-edited by Richard Ollard, later to be Rowse's biographer.[86]

The real nature—and the significance—of their relationship, perhaps, was to be found not in the repressed sexuality of Wedgwood's letters, nor in Rowse's inability to respond to their seductive content, but rather in the intellectual stimulation that the two scholars had given one another, not least in their formative years when they had been finding their ways as writers and establishing their areas of interest and expertise. As will be argued in Chapter 11, Veronica Wedgwood's insistence on flying in the face of the received wisdom of the time by viewing the Civil War in terms of 'three separate countries, England, Scotland and Ireland, and two civilisations of a wholly different type, the Normanised Anglo-Saxon and the Celtic',[87] had informed Rowse's early contribution to the 'new British history', while his similar insistence on the distinctive place of Cornwall and the Cornish in these matters likewise impressed her. We see, for example, in her *Seventeenth-Century English Literature* (1950) her insightful—and, for its time, wholly atypical—appreciation of the plight of the Celtic languages at the hands of increasingly dominant English, her sympathetic analysis taking care to include consideration of Cornish: 'The Celtic tongues, Gaelic and Welsh, were fast becoming the marks of barbarism; Cornish was dying on the lips of all but the fisher folk'.[88]

'Nobody to correct her cheap style'

However, this mutual influence could not last. Wedgwood's growing stature and authority disturbed, and at length overturned, the comfortable master–pupil relationship that Rowse had cultivated. In those instances where such relationships did endure, it was where Rowse remained assured of his scholarly superiority, and there was no better example of this than his friendship with Daphne du Maurier, the writer of romantic fiction who had made Cornwall her home. Initially, Rowse envied du Maurier her leisured lifestyle and the apparent ease with which her work found publishers: 'Yes', he admitted, 'I was jealous. . . there was so much money, so little struggle'.[89] He also regretted the way in which her novel *Jamaica Inn* had led to the vulgar popularization of the moorland hostelry of that name. In September 1954 he visited the public house with his friend David Treffry: 'For the first time I set foot in Jamaica Inn', he wrote, 'beginning of dear Daphne's appalling world-wide celebrity'.[90] Similarly, he thought *Rebecca* a 'lower level' version of *Jane Eyre*, and as for 'Max de Winter for name of a Cornishman or family, pure Hollywood! It should have been Carminow, or Godolphin or Penhallow. The sinister Mrs Danvers?—one wouldn't have kept her on as a housekeeper for a fortnight'[91] Likewise, *Vanishing Cornwall* was the work of 'an inveterate romancer', an outsider whose view of Cornwall would contrast inevitably with the more 'authentic' perspective of the insider—himself.[92]

By 1967, however, when *Vanishing Cornwall* was published, Rowse's reputation had—in his estimation at least—surpassed du Maurier's, as had, perhaps, his bank balance. This allowed envy to be replaced by a patronizing tolerance, Rowse smiling at her ineptitudes and accepting her absurdities. Daphne, for her part, sensed a mellowing, sending Rowse a belated copy of her book *The Loving Spirit* and inscribing it: 'A.L. from his student, with love'. By 1977, when she sent him a copy of her autobiographical *Growing Pains*, he had become 'A.L., my Professor and dear friend', for in the preceding decade Rowse had undergone his 'conversion' (as he called it), now viewing Daphne du Maurier as a capable and gifted writer, or at least being prepared to describe her as such in public. 'When I re-read *Rebecca* now I see it as the triumph it is, perfect *in its own terms*', he wrote, while even the success of Jamaica Inn with the passing tourist trade had become a good thing: 'luck again: it must help to keep that exciting melodrama fresh and green'. *My Cousin Rachel* 'has always been a favourite of mine', he insisted, and *The House on the Strand*, a novel set in Cornwall both past and present, was 'original and ingenious'.[93]

Rowse and du Maurier became correspondents, she carefully pursuing the pupil–master relationship, though having little success in persuading him of her 'Bacon theory', confiding to her friend Oriel Malet that he 'says he will poison me if I suggest in *Winding Stair* that Bacon had anything to do with the Shakespeare plays'.[94] 'Utter rubbish of course',[95] was Rowse's response to her theory, penned in irritated manner in the margins of one of her letters to him, but generally their correspondence was affectionate. Rowse should be awarded 'a K.B.E. in my opinion', she opined, for 'I think of you often, and all you have done for literature and for Cornwall'.[96] Invariably, she signed off playfully as 'Madame Non-Non!', which he rather liked, ending her letters more often than not with an endearing salutation: 'love to you, if you can bear it'.[97]

But Rowse had already by this time—the 1980s—decided that he could not bear it, or at least that earlier thoughts of a more intimate relationship with Daphne du Maurier should be firmly discounted. The late 1960s, however, had been a different story, the years of Rowse's 'conversion', and in 1967, two years after the death of Daphne's husband, Tommy 'Boy' Browning, he had made a rare but all-important visit to her home at Menabilly. Daphne had recently celebrated her sixtieth birthday (Rowse was by now in his sixty-fourth year), and *Vanishing Cornwall* had just appeared in the bookshops. Rowse confided in his diary that he had still 'no high opinion' of her work, including *Vanishing Cornwall*, 'which I can't much like, and envy its sales'. But she had suffered, he thought, from 'so unintellectual a life, not really educated', and regretted that she had had 'nobody to correct her cheap style' of writing.[98] And yet he discerned promise, a quality that placed Daphne du Maurier above the normal run of romantic novelists. Indeed, Rowse wondered whether it was not too late to take her under his wing, to point her in the right direction, but also, in growing together as master and pupil, that they might make some sort of personal alliance—she across St Austell Bay at Menabilly, not a million miles from Trenarren.

Arriving at Menabilly, Rowse found that Daphne had lost none of her sexual allure, 'her figure lithe and youthful as ever'. There was an immediate mutual attraction, he sensed, and he wondered whether he should make a pass at her. There she was, 'coiled up on her sofa like a young girl: her eyes giving themselves to me completely. . . Upstairs, as we went around the bedrooms I thought "How would it be? Nobody in the house".' A moment's reflection deterred him, however: 'it would have been a mistake; no passions aroused'. And yet, as they toured the house, he reflected on the unrelieved masculinity of 'Boy' Browning. Entering 'the General's room', which she had not had the heart to touch since his death—'a boy's room, totally unsophisticated: full of caps and cups and racquets and odds and ends of sports tackle—like the bedroom of a school prefect or captain of boats at a university'—Rowse wondered whether she might have made a more profitable marriage to someone of greater sensitivity, someone with a more subtle, feminine side. The General dead, there was now the possibility of starting afresh: 'How would it be if she married some one more sophisticated, more complex, less of a boy and less of a man?', he thought, '[s]he might get a new lease of inspiration'. But again, it seemed impossible: 'she is solitary; and so am I, too old to turn open a new leaf and make new adjustment now. It would certainly make the headlines, though!' Daphne, too, had agreed 'that her essential life was solitary', and although, Rowse imagined, 'she must have enjoyed being fucked by the handsome soldier', she and her late husband had lived, she had intimated, increasingly separate lives, reinforcing her solitary nature and (again like Rowse) encouraging her own sexual ambivalence: 'Neglected, he went off the rails at the end, drink and drugs and a lower-class girl at Fowey. He must have been breaking up.'[99]

When it was time to go, the two of them having spent the afternoon deep in a nostalgic 'heart-to-heart' that ranged from the old days of Sir Arthur Quiller Couch to the prospects of life after death, Rowse prepared to say his farewell: 'I took leave to kiss her, which she took in good part—though I got the impression that she didn't want to be touched'.[100] Here, then, was the final evidence he needed. Thereafter, they would develop their mutual admiration society—increasingly important to Daphne after her unhappy move from Menabilly to nearby Kilmarth—but there was to be no thought of something more.

It is difficult to gauge how serious Rowse had been in his testing the water with Daphne du Maurier. But there was in his musings the sense of a man, advancing into old age, suddenly aware of his loneliness, willing at last, perhaps, to rid himself of the shackles of his mother's memory and his family's past, and able now to grasp the full extent of his sexual ambivalence. He understood now how his inability to identify with overtly masculine expressions of maleness had led him to question the boundaries of gender, drawing him into intense same-sex relationships with those exhibiting oppositional feminine characteristics but also, paradoxically, attracting him to those women who were themselves overtly feminine. The move to Trenarren, shortly before his mother's death in 1953, he had tried to see as a watershed in his life, the first part of a 'coming home', while his determined attempt in the mid-1960s to settle once and for all the question of his paternity cleared at least some of the clutter from his personal baggage. The overture to Daphne du Maurier, if that is what it was, in September 1967 came then at a significant moment: a point of reassessment in which he contemplated the years of old age and, eventually, retirement that stretched ahead of him. Daphne might have been an obvious choice—already living close by, recently widowed, enthused by Cornwall and by now an extremely successful author, though not distinguished enough to rival her potential suitor or to disturb their master–pupil relationship. Yet, as Rowse himself admitted, it was never a realistic proposition, and as retirement from All Souls loomed at the end of 1973, his thoughts turned again to his old school-friend, the constant, patient Noreen Sweet.

'A remarkable woman, with very remarkable gifts'

At secondary school in St Austell, years before, Noreen and Rowse had been close friends, and they had developed a mutual enthusiasm for Labour Party politics. Noreen had also worked as a party activist in support of Rowse during the 1930s when he was a parliamentary candidate in Cornwall. In the general election of 1935, when Rowse had performed well, coming within 3,000 votes of the victorious Conservatives in Penryn and Falmouth, Noreen had written to Rowse enthusing about the experience: 'Yes, they were great days. . . I can't tell you how heartening it was to be working for something one really cares about'.[101] Concerned that his mother might not have fully appreciated the scale of her son's achievement, she had also written to her, admitting that '[w]e couldn't help feeling sorry that Leslie didn't come out on top' but also explaining that 'there is much to be pleased about' and that 'I have a feeling that the next election is half won already!'.[102] Rowse, in turn, wrote to Noreen, thanking her for her support, a certain non-committal awkwardness evident in his letter as he searched for the right words to express his affection and admiration for her but without suggesting that there was more on offer in their relationship than he was able to give:

> I can't tell you how grateful I am for the magnificent help you were during the Election. I can only say how much it was appreciated, and what pleasure it gave me to have you beside me. One thing more I shd [*sic*] say, for I may not have so good an opportunity for some time—it is evident that you have grown into a remarkable woman, with very remarkable gifts of your own. You know that they are all proud of you—I have told you that before—the Labour men and women of Penryn-Falmouth; but I am particularly so—perhaps you knew that, though I have not before had an opportunity for saying so.[103]

Noreen was too shrewd to imagine that it was worth her while to wait for Rowse, preoccupied as he was with so much else, and in 1938 she married Christopher Vivian. Rowse was assailed with mixed emotions at the wedding, wondering amongst other things whether in earlier years he had unfairly given her false hopes, and whether indeed he had done the right thing: 'I felt a tug at the heart. It should have been I that was marrying her.'[104] Yet their relationship remained close, evidenced, for example, in their correspondence in the 1950s and 1960s on subjects as intimate and delicate as Rowse's mother and his paternity, and as time went on he began to think of her as his 'Miriam'—returning to his self-confessed affinity with D.H. Lawrence to compare his life with that of Paul Morel, the principal character of Lawrence's semi-autobiographical *Sons and Lovers*. It was a comparison that he did not keep to himself, letting it slip obliquely in a collection of essays, *The English Past*, in 1951, including a hidden allusion to one 'N' (Noreen) in the place of 'M' (Miriam). Impossible for the casual observer to divine, the reference was obvious enough to Noreen herself. She wrote:

> It was only on Sunday that your new book came into my hands. I had returned from a few exhilarating days in town to find it here. What a deflated N. I was by bedtime! I had spent the evening accompanying you to Max Gate and Hardy, to Haworth and the Brontes and finally to Eastwood and to Lawrence. Already I had been disapproving of the frequent asides, extraneous and artisti- cally a mistake, when suddenly I found myself involved. Yes—woman or no in the far-off days, now I was startled into protest! How could you, I thought, draw the parallel, suggest indeed that there was anything resembling the Lawrence–Miriam story in our undemonstrative and intermittent association. I went to bed without finishing the piece. . . really deeply hurt that I, at least, would recognise the reference, and indeed those who know us both.[105]

Rowse was mortified, replying tactfully that '[i]t was so nice to hear from you—if only to get a wigging', though admitting that 'I was so dejected the morning I got your letter. Alas, what *could* I have said? I hadn't got a copy of the book in the house, and I couldn't remember anything v. naughty. Then Claude [Berry] sent me a copy.' Reading his text again, he agreed to alter it in subsequent editions (he was true to his word) but he insisted that 'I am very sad if you felt hurt. . . it was not unkindly meant. For I have the greatest admiration for Miriam—and always thought of you as Miriam.'[106] Claude Berry, observing the exchanges, hoped that 'you have declared peace with Noreen and that a treaty will soon be ratified',[107] and indeed it was a tribute to the strength of the relationship between Rowse and Noreen Sweet that the incident did not lead in the end to a Wedgwood-like rupture. Quite the opposite; Noreen proved an enormous help to Rowse in the subsequent decade and more, as he struggled with family problems, and when Christopher Vivian, Noreen's husband, died suddenly in 1968, Rowse was one of those friends who rallied round. He wrote to her, agreeing that 'no ill in life is equal to this one', though 'I expect you to be a stoic', reassuring her that 'of course, you were right to marry Christopher: he was so much nicer a character than I', and reaffirming his view that 'I have never thought of marrying, was always determined not to—I always regarded it as, for me, a trap'. Moreover, 'I have had a wonderful life, for which I am insufficiently grateful. But I'd never have *shared* it with anyone, of either sex: they would have found me intolerable.' And yet, despite the characteristic disclaimers, there was something else: 'I hope you will give me a good mark for being happy that you and Christopher were happy—for inwardly I cd [*sic*] not but have a little twinge of envy'.[108]

When, in early 1969, Norman Pounds—an academic friend who had worked on the economic geography of medieval Cornwall—wrote from America to tell Rowse that Noreen was not coping well with widowhood (a recent letter from her 'was positively suicidal'),[109] Rowse again lent a hand. Invitations to visit Cornwall became more frequent, and much of their old intimacy was restored, Rowse hoping that 'we may see more of each other'. February 1975, for example, had Noreen '[d]elighted to hear from you—I had been tempted to telephone for news. . . I can't reach Cornwall much before Easter',[110] and although Rowse had earlier cautioned against the thought of moving back home after all those years— '[y]ou mustn't think of retiring to Cornwall, alas, you wd [*sic*] find it too remote & unrewarding'[111]—he began to change his tune. By the summer of 1975 Rowse was scouring the local newspapers for details of houses for sale. He had noticed, he wrote to Noreen, 'enormously expensive grand flats' at Heligan, the old Tremayne family house, now sold-off and refurbished, over-looking St Austell Bay, though he suspected that cost made them a 'no go'. However, he had also seen an attractive house advertised at Duporth, hardly any distance from Trenarren: 'Don't forget that spot—we should all be near'.[112] But it was not to be, though Noreen lived until 1993, for Rowse had left it all far too late. In any case, as in *Sons and Lovers*, Noreen Sweet and A.L. Rowse, like the Miriam and Paul Morel of D.H. Lawrence's imagination, had years before realized—and tacitly agreed—that the shadow of his mother was just too strong, and that for better or worse Rowse would have to make his way through life alone.

5

'A Deep Anxiety to Do His Best for Cornwall'

Confronting the Politics of Paralysis

'When I was a boy in the village at Tregonissey some of the villagers hadn't enough to eat, while the Edwardian upper classes stuffed themselves with all the good things going. That needed putting right.'[1] This was how Rowse, writing in 1979, explained his early conversion to Labour Party politics. As we have seen in earlier chapters, in the years before the Great War and, more especially, in its aftermath, there was real suffering in Cornwall as the local economy struggled to respond to overwhelming structural change. Even the dynamism of the china clay industry succumbed to disastrous slumps in international demand during the conflict and on into the 1920s and 1930s. Attempts at economic diversification had been only partially successful, and the apparent success of china clay earlier in the century had merely disguised the deleterious consequences of continued reliance on a monolithic, extractive single industry.

Hard times had confronted Rowse personally, and although they had not prevented him from going to Oxford, they had provided an unfortunate backdrop—with the family shop being given up as no longer profitable, and Rowse's father laid off from the pit at Carclaze in the autumn of 1922, Rowse's first term at university. This was a contrast that Rowse found hard to bear and, relieved as he was to have escaped the working-class constraints of Tregonissey, he worried about his family left behind. He was also incensed by the wider injustice of it all: 'the working class should have had a better deal'.[2] Home for the summer vacation in 1923, for example, he was depressed 'by the fact that father has only one pair of boots that doesn't take water. All the others are no good when the winter comes on, and he can't afford to wear his best boots. I have just had a pair soled, and he has to wear those. I ought to give them to him for good, but that and a rather worse pair are all I have.'[3] But the problem was more than a question of leaky footwear, as he recorded in his diary:

> This is the sort of thing that appears likely to increase during the next two or three years—as if I hadn't enough of that already in my life! Lack of money has handicapped us all from our earliest years. And one can see how it affects all families around one. But it is a new experience to feel that we are approaching rock-bottom. Mother and father, after more than twenty years in the shop at Tregonissey, retired with a fortune of £100. That was two years ago; they now have £40. Everything depends on my life.[4]

Embracing Labour

The responsibility weighed heavily on Rowse's shoulders, and there was great frustration that, as in other areas of his life, the conditions that he had struggled so hard to escape were still able to exert an enduring influence, albeit at a distance. There was a whiff of despair. In December that year, however, something extraordinary happened—for the very first time, a Labour government was formed, under Ramsay MacDonald. Here at last was evidence, it appeared to Rowse, that something might be done: that there was now an opportunity in the political process to materially affect the lives of working people, to generate policies for the common good rather than to bolster the interests of 'the businessmen and the profiteers' who had run Britain since the decline of the Liberal ascendancy.[5] However, any euphoria was short-lived. In the ensuing nine months, Labour devoted its energies to demonstrating that it was fit to govern, laying aside the temptation to introduce a raft of socially and economically innovative legislation. Despite this cautious approach, the minority government was out-manoeuvred by its opponents in the Commons. MacDonald requested a dissolution, and in the subsequent general election Labour prospects were damaged by the leaking of the so-called 'Zinovieff letter', a forged note, allegedly from the international Comintern, calling on British Communists to rise up and overthrow the government. Although the Labour vote went up in the election, so did the Conservative (with the Liberal share declining sharply), ushering in a period of Tory rule under Stanley Baldwin.[6]

The effect on Rowse was two-fold. In the short term, the maddening experience of Labour coming to power, only to be ejected, re-doubled his commitment to the party, fostering his determination to pursue social justice and the creation of greater opportunities for those from working-class backgrounds who were (like him) prepared to work hard and to seize the chances that came their way. In the longer term, as we shall see, he was increasingly frustrated by Labour's continuing inability to make

19 A.L. Rowse performing his civic duty as a Parliamentary candidate for the Labour Party in the Penryn and Falmouth Constituency. *Courtesy Special Collections, University of Exeter Library; photo by E.J. Russell.*

20 Rowse's election flyer, 1935. *Courtesy Special Collections, University of Exeter Library.*

21 Claude Berry, life-long friend of A.L. Rowse, editor of *Cornish Labour News* and later the *West Briton*. *Courtesy Royal Institution of Cornwall; photo by G. Sandy, Truro.*

sustained headway. This was true in the UK as a whole where, despite its replacement of the Liberals as the principal alternative to the Tories, it fell victim to its own internal dissension and ineptitudes, and in Cornwall in particular where—in marked contrast to most other areas of Britain—the old Liberal–Nonconformist nexus remained robust in the face of the Labour challenge.[7] Rowse was to dedicate the next decade and a half to the cause, two-thirds of it as parliamentary candidate in the Penryn and Falmouth constituency, only to reflect years later that 'I deeply repent every moment I spent as a Labour candidate, when a young man, propaganding to make things better'.[8] Although Rowse was active in the Labour Club at Oxford, it was Cornwall that was the battlefield, and the ultimate 'rejection' that he was to experience at the hands of the Cornish electorate re-doubled and re-asserted his aversion to much that characterized contemporary Cornwall.

Brought up in the democratic atmosphere of the Higher Quarter where no-one said 'sir' to anyone, and with memories of the heroic stand of the clay-work strikers of 1913 still fresh in mind, the young Rowse had begun to take an interest in Labour politics before going up to Oxford, persuading his father (hitherto, a Liberal voter) to accompany him to local party meetings. Yet behind this enthusiasm there were already misgivings, a sense that the working people would never be able to grasp the opportunities that lay before them or wake up to the situations that they should confront: 'I was a Labour man, inevitably and—with my temperament—keenly, aggressively, loyally, though not without some scepticism'.[9] Thus, in January 1922, after a Labour Party meeting in Carclaze:

> I come away from a mtg. such as that held tonight in deep despair. There wasn't a soul except Joe Harris, the chairman, [C.A.] Millman the organizer *and myself*, who understood a thing about the Labour programme, the cause of the present state of affairs, or the necessity for the altering of our social system. I watched the face of each man that came into the room; and upon each one was an expression of sheer, stupid ignorance. Perhaps there was one man who had a faint glimmering of intelligence and whose face was less blindly stupid than the rest—and he said that he was not converted to the Labour Party! Oh God! How can these people grumble about the present state? They won't make one move themselves and there is such work to be done—such leeway to be made up![10]

It was a pattern that replicated itself time and again, and on occasions the speakers were no better than their audiences: 'Tonight to a Labour meeting at Mevagissey, as last night at Carthew. . . A motley crowd of fishermen had assembled along the arms of the quay, with speaker at the strategic point of contact. And what use he made of it! What a speech he gave us!—pure, tub-thumping mob-oratory.' Worse still, 'he was completely out of touch with his audience. . . When it came to questions he was worse than helpless'.[11] Similarly, a meeting at Tregonissey Lane End, '[a] tame but homely affair', attracted a lacklustre audience where the workers' dogs seemed more intelligent than their owners, and where the key-note speech was all but intelligible: 'What's wrong with these Labour speakers?. . . I notice an inability to say things simply with all these half-educated Labour speakers.'[12]

At Oxford, the atmosphere was more congenial, the debate more refined, and Rowse responded positively and with some relief to the intellectual climate in which he found himself. He was attracted, like many of his contemporaries, to the Marxian explanation of history to which he was now exposed. Much later, even after he had abandoned his Labour allegiances, he could still claim that 'to be a good historian in our own time one needs to have been something of a Marxist'.[13] He was also drawn into the world of G.D.H. Cole, founder of the University Labour Club at Oxford. Rowse was one of those undergraduates who used to meet at Cole's house at Holywell, and who—enraged and emboldened by the General Strike of 1926—formed the 'Cole group' at the university. Amongst its number was more than a sprinkling of able young men who later went on to make names for themselves in British public life and letters—Hugh Gaitskill, Evan Durbin, Michael Stewart, W.H. Auden, and (surprisingly) John Betjeman—and together with Cole, R.H. Tawney and A.L. Lindsay (the Master of Balliol) they provided what Elizabeth Durbin has called 'an oasis of socialist discussion and teaching'[14] at Oxford. The 'Cole group' and the Labour Club also provided contact between these socialist intellectuals and senior Labour politicians. It was in this environment that Rowse first met Ernest Bevin, whom he much admired with his bluff, no-nonsense working-class approach. It was here too that he had first espied Ramsay MacDonald, with whom he fancied he had some Celtic affinity: 'the Highland laird in him. . . [a] Celt, he was a man of distinguished sensibilities'.[15]

Politics and the Younger Generation

Later, Rowse was to question—and, at length, disown—what he saw increasingly as Cole's unrealistic, unhelpfully theoretical contributions to debate. 'Of one thing I am certain', Rowse wrote in 1979, 'not one of the Left intellectuals could republish what they wrote in the thirties without revealing what idiotic judgments they made.'[16] Rowse was drawn instead to the work of John Maynard Keynes at the London School of Economics,

seeing in it practical relevance for policy-making by future Labour governments. Thus in *Mr Keynes and The Labour Movement*, published in 1936
and dedicated 'To Herbert Morrison, In High Hope of the Future', Rowse
insisted 'that there is little or no divergence between what is implied by
Labour policy and by Mr Keynes'.[17] Before that, however, in 1931, Rowse
had published his *Politics and the Younger Generation*, a volume dedicated
to G.D.H. Cole and betraying all the influence of his Oxford group. There
was much on the 'intellectual bankruptcy' of modern Conservatism, the
'defeatism' of contemporary Liberalism, and a conviction that genera-
tional issues were on Labour's side: 'One finds again and again, in country
villages in Cornwall it may be, or in provincial towns, or in an academic
society like Oxford, that the strength of Liberalism is in the older generation, and that the young men are mainly Labour'.[18] In a work given
principally to theoretical generalizations, he allowed himself some Cornish
examples, showing how a socialist administration might deal, for instance,
with the problem of absentee landlordism:

> As for the absentee landlord, his incidence varies. One may be
> influenced by the consideration that five out of the six estates
> around my home-town [St Austell] in Cornwall have absentee
> landlords. Their ownership is no longer justified; the only justifi-
> cation for the existence of a landlord, if any at all, is that he should
> continue to look after his land. Those of them who continue to exist
> in the future will have to be as much workers as anyone else. As an
> immediate measure, county councils and other local authorities
> should exercise strong powers to break up such an estate into small
> holdings and to administer them.[19]

There was more, Rowse's preferred socialist solutions revealing a hint
of a nascent Cornish nationalism and a resistance to tourism and the
newcomers who came in its wake:

> There are plenty of men who have long wanted an outlet on the
> land. Instead of which, one sees the most cultivable soil being given
> up to jerry-building and ribbon development; or country houses
> and their domains being turned into clubs and hotels and golf-
> courses for the bourgeois and the *nouveaux riches*. Again, it often
> brings money into a vicinity, as in Cornwall it does. But the money
> so spent is a dead loss to the country at large; and, for oneself, one
> would prefer the old Cornish type, hard-working and close to the
> soil, independent and eternally productive, to the new population
> of lodging-house keepers and hotel waiters.[20]

If all this was designed to ring bells of appreciation back home in Cornwall, it was misconceived. Hard-working Cornish types were alarmed by what they read elsewhere in the book, not least by Rowse's reflections on religion. Although, as Methodists, many would have approved of his call for the disestablishment of the Church of England, and perhaps even of his suggestion that churches, as 'heritage' artefacts, should be found new roles in the community, few would have subscribed to his view that in a rationalist socialist society religion would survive only in 'providing purpose for the defeatist, hope for the spiritually helpless, consolation for the sick and the neglected, a message of certainty for the dying'.[21] To some, this seemed perilously close to atheism, to which was added an equally dangerous advocacy of free love and an attack on the institution of marriage and thus the family. Rowse believed that there were several areas of individual interest, including sex, 'which are not by their nature susceptible of external regulation' and that 'I am in favour of freedom precisely where conservative minds want regulation'. Moreover, '[n]or need the bondage of the marriage tie be held necessary for the procreation of children', he wrote, '[i]n the future we shall have a greater broad-mindedness on this and other issues; the birth and care of children will be more important than the pretences of an outworn morality'.[22]

In the safe environs of the 'Cole group' such ideas might be advanced, disputed and adopted or rejected in the spirit of intellectual exchange and the quest for 'truth'. Elsewhere, they were contentious and controversial; the *Catholic Times* condemned the book as the 'Godless politics of the "New Age"'.[23] And in Cornwall such views were dynamite. The *Western Morning News* newspaper ran half-a-dozen lengthy articles composed of what Rowse later admitted were the most damaging extracts from *Politics and the Younger Generation*, a deliberate attempt to discredit the aspiring Labour politician.[24] For by this time, Rowse had already been adopted as prospective parliamentary candidate for Penryn and Falmouth, joining the political fray in the period of turmoil leading up to the formation of the National Government in 1931. Only recently, in August 1929, the *West Briton* had reported approvingly of his likely adoption—adding that 'Mr Rowse's rapid rise to fame has brought real distinction to Cornwall'— while the *Cornish Guardian* had agreed that he was a 'brilliant young Cornish scholar', who at 'twenty-seven years of age is regarded by members of the Labour Club at Oxford University of which he is an ex-chairman as one of the pivots around which the Club revolves', adding that 'he has an attractive though not fluent style of speech, and gives the impression of possessing a well-stocked brain'.[25] In fact, despite these accolades, Rowse's adoption had been by no means a foregone conclusion. Sir John Maynard, 'an Anglo-Indian of some distinction',[26] was the preferred candidate of both Transport House and the local party officials, but at the

selection meeting Rowse won the solid support of the clay country delegates, picking up enough other votes to carry the day. '[W]e don't wish
for a better candidate than yourself',[27] wrote Bill Stone of St Austell.

Rowse as Labour candidate

Thereafter, Rowse had begun the usual round of activities expected of a
diligent candidate, such as taking up the cases where individuals sought
pensions, compensation or redress: 'Penryn. Mrs Jenkin, husband injured
1907, died 1914, stonemason therefore insurable' and 'a Carn Brea
villager, age 57, whose husband had died in 1914: a tin-miner, an insurable occupation. To intercede for her.'[28] He had also begun his assault on
the Liberal Party, for although in Cornwall the Liberals had won all five
seats in the 1929 general election, elsewhere in Britain they had continued
to stumble towards what seemed like certain annihilation. After the
débâcle of the 1924 general election the Liberals made only a limited
come-back in some areas of rural England and far-flung parts of Scotland
and Wales, with Labour surging ahead as it consolidated earlier successes
and made striking advances elsewhere. Winning 288 seats in the House
of Commons (as opposed to the Conservatives' 260 and the Liberals'
derisory 59), Labour was once more in power, with MacDonald as Prime
Minister: a minority government again but this time one able to claim the
moral mandate of the people.

This was the era which Christopher Cook has dubbed the 'Age of
Alignment', the period in which British politics was transformed into an
essentially two-party, Labour versus Conservative, contest. Cook has
argued that between the general elections of 1922 and October 1924 the
party system had changed irrevocably—the fatal point of Liberal downfall was reached in 1924, and by 1929 the Liberals had slipped back too
far to be an effective force, their role by now usurped by Labour.[29]
Moreover, after 1918 Nonconformists in Britain had become markedly
less politicized, with church attendances falling and bonds with the
Liberals disintegrating. As Stephen Koss has put it, by 1935 'Radical
Nonconformity, once a force to be reckoned with in national life, was not
dormant but dead',[30] replaced by the secular socialism of Labour.

But, as Koss also observed, the Liberals in this period were able to retain
'considerable loyalty among Nonconformists of particular persuasions in
isolated areas'.[31] Cornwall was one such place. Nonconformity held up
well here as it declined elsewhere, with the Liberals remaining as the cred-
ible radical alternatives to the Tories despite the advance of Labour in
other parts. In the 1920s, argues Garry Tregidga, Liberalism in Cornwall
'was still sustained by the forces that had motivated the party before the
war: a deep reverence for the cause of Gladstone, the moral fervour of

religious nonconformity and a belief that the Liberals were still a potential party of government'.[32] The Liberal triumph in Cornwall in 1929
confirmed all this, but was in marked contrast to the party's fortunes elsewhere. Even into the 1930s, as the Liberals descended into utter confusion
on the British political stage, there was still in Cornwall, as Tregidga put
it, a 'more conducive environment'[33] for the successful advocacy of
Liberalism—if only there had been coherent leadership at Westminster
capable of capitalizing upon it.

Indeed, if this period was for Britain as a whole the 'Age of Alignment',
then for Cornwall it was characterized by the 'Politics of Paralysis'.
Cornish politics mirrored the inertia apparent elsewhere in the Cornish
economy and society, and—notwithstanding encouraging socialist interventions at St Ives and Camborne in the 1918 general election—failed
conspicuously to embrace the cause of Labour. The relative strength of
Cornish Nonconformity helped to explain this situation. But it was also
the case that rapid de-industrialization had retarded the development of
trade unionism and a wider Labour movement in Cornwall. The apparent
shift towards a more militant unionism in the 1860s and 1870s amongst
copper and tin miners—mirroring a similar militancy in the South Wales
coalfields—had been cut short by a succession of crises in the Cornish
mining industry. As a result, the industrial base that might have nurtured
a successful Labour movement shrank rapidly, the would-be leaders of
men emigrating to Australia, America and South Africa where they helped
forge the great miners' unions of the New World.[34]

It was this situation that confronted the young Rowse as he began to
prepare the ground in Penryn and Falmouth. His assault on the Liberals
was firmly under way by the New Year of 1930. Rowse recognized that
if Labour was now to make headway in Cornwall then it had to smash the
Liberal–Nonconformist nexus. 'I have for some time been waiting for an
authoritative pronouncement from Cornish Liberalism as to what line it
is going to take', he wrote provocatively that January, 'now that it is evident
that the Liberal party can never command a majority in the country again.'
Out-voted by Labour and riven with leadership disputes, the Liberals had
had their day, Rowse argued, and the illusion of unity and strength in
Cornwall had to be laid bare for what it was. '[W]hen I came home to
Cornwall I was astonished to find what little inkling Cornish Liberals had
of the situation', he wrote, 'as people well know if they don't yet know it
in Cornwall, the rift in the higher direction of Liberalism is from top to
bottom. . . and it is irreconcilable.' Elsewhere in Britain, he pointed out,
Labour had already eclipsed the Liberals and was now in government for
the second time: 'the Labour party is the natural party of the working
people. . . as a Cornishman, I should be sorry if I thought Cornwall was
going to be left behind'.[35]

'Practically a non-believer, if not an atheist'

When the Liberals returned fire, it was not to refute Rowse's claims but to respond in the name of outraged Nonconformity, carefully avoiding his unpalatable political analysis by exposing instead his alleged 'atheism' and his commitment to 'advanced socialism'. One 'W.J.F', for example, wrote to the local press from Camborne, condemning Rowse's 'devilish'[36] religious views, while the choice excerpts from *Politics and the Younger Generation* in the *Western Morning News* had done their own damage. As Rowse acknowledged, 'bright remarks from a young progressive about religion and sex were made use of by opponents'.[37] Supporters rallied to his defence, of course. A correspondent signing himself 'Working Man' wrote to the *Cornish Guardian* in October 1931 declaring that '[i]t is surely passing strange that he should be called an atheist when he has thrown in his lot with a political party that in their doctrines are nearest to the religious doctrines of Christ'.[38] A Labour Party meeting in Falmouth in the same month complained of attempts 'daily to try to influence the Nonconformist electors of the division to believe that he was practically a non-believer, if not an atheist'.[39] The damage had been done, however, and in attempting to break the Liberal–Nonconformist nexus, Rowse had allowed himself to be portrayed as attacking Nonconformity itself: an interpretation encouraged by the badly timed and injudicious remarks in his already infamous book, intended though it was for intellectual Oxbridge colleagues rather than the ordinary working folk of Cornwall.

Indeed, many radical Nonconformists in Cornwall, who in other circumstances might have considered abandoning the Liberals for Labour, felt compromised. The Rev. T.W. Slater, for example, a Methodist minister from 'up-country' working in Cornwall, had warmed to Rowse and his new book. *Politics and the Younger Generation*, he wrote, 'brings him still further into the limelight and shows him to be a man of parts, a keen student of economics, philosophy, history and politics, with an exceptional gift for expressing himself by pen'. But the gratuitous attacks on religion were unworthy, Slater thought, and 'I am sorry that Mr Rowse should go out of his way to speak about "parts of the country (obviously meaning Cornwall) formerly afflicted by Methodist revivalism"'. Moreover, 'Christianity was stated to be a myth',[40] a view, according to Slater, that was ill-judged and unnecessary. Far from smashing the Liberal–Nonconformist nexus, Rowse had merely confirmed its enduring strength in Cornwall, at best betraying his anti-Nonconformist prejudices, at worst acquiring an unenviable reputation as an atheist.

Meanwhile, the political climate in Britain had already changed unrecognizably. The second Labour government faired little better than the first, the confident predictions of Rowse and others undone as events on the international stage pushed the United Kingdom towards an ever more parlous socio-economic position. Confidence in the British financial system appeared to be faltering and, as unemployment rose, cut-backs were effected to try to keep the economy stable. MacDonald, under pressure from the Conservative and Liberals, proposed yet further cuts in government expenditure, including a reduction in unemployment benefit, to which his Labour Cabinet was naturally resistant. As MacDonald admitted, 'the proposals as a whole represented the negation of everything the Labour party stood for, and yet. . . [I] was absolutely satisfied that it was necessary, in the national interest, to implement them if the country was to be secured'.[41] The logic of this situation, as both MacDonald and his opponents within the Labour Party realized, was the end of the Labour government and its replacement by a coalition in pursuit of the 'national interest'—something that had become inevitable by late August 1931 when the National Government was set up under MacDonald. Despite support in the country for the new government, things continued to get worse, a deflationary Budget exacerbating the underlying problems, and departure from the Gold Standard combining with the mutiny of the Royal Navy at Invergordon to create an air of jittery uncertainty. To bolster the government's mandate, MacDonald called a general election. The majority of Labour MPs, inevitably, had refused to join the National Government, and in the ensuing election a great many were simply swept away, leaving in the new parliament a rump of just 52 members. The Conservative-National coalition and their 'Samuel' Liberal allies won a thumping 554 seats.

For Rowse, the 1931 election was a baptism of fire. Still reeling from the personal attacks in Cornwall and dismayed by MacDonald's manoeuvrings at Westminster—which Rowse labelled 'taking action completely contrary to the interests of the working class'[42]—he had entered the campaign on the defensive. Electioneering was exhausting, an uphill battle that almost sapped his will to go on. Retreating on one occasion to the familiar solace of Clark's Restaurant, in Truro, he confided in his diary:

> I have the room to myself. . . I have slunk in here for a moment's peace in the political faction fight. The backlash of the atheism rumour has hit me, wearing me down. Just here from a meeting in Victoria Square, where Joe Bennetts (my Labour Agent) noticed that I was done up and sent me away. I came here for the sake of old memories, and am absolutely alone.[43]

By contrast, his Conservative-National opponent, Maurice Petherick—an old-fashioned Tory—was quietly confident, offering continuity, stability and reassurance to an anxious electorate and expecting to be returned as its MP. His election leaflet appealed: ' To One and All. I am not a wobbler. I am a Cornishman who has been amongst you for many years and I know the needs of the Division.'[44] In the event, Rowse did surprisingly well, given the unpromising circumstances, trailing third with a respectable 10,098 votes. The Liberals were the runners-up with 14,006, and Petherick won the Penryn and Falmouth seat, as he always thought he would, with 16,388. A. Browning Lyne, editor of the *Cornish Guardian* (and a Liberal supporter), conceded that Rowse had indeed done rather well: 'I was surprised that Mr Rowse polled so many [votes] though I did not expect the Labour vote would slip back in Cornwall to the extent that it did elsewhere in the country'.[45] Reflecting on this, however, all Rowse could remember was the anguish of it all:

> The catastrophe of 1931 was upon the Labour Movement, and I was caught unawares as a candidate for Penryn and Falmouth, in the hopeless circumstances of our leaders, MacDonald and Snowden [Chancellor of the Exchequer in the second Labour government], having gone over to the enemy. We were in utter confusion—how the Tories, the City, the upper classes must have chortled—Liberals too, for they ganged up with all the rest, leaving the Labour Party naked and defenceless.[46]

In retrospect, Rowse felt that he had been 'trapped' in 1931.[47] He had performed well, despite the 'atheism' charge locally and the crisis at national level, and there was now a real opportunity to build upon his modest success: to begin in earnest the task of persuading Liberal voters— especially the working classes—that their future lay with Labour. He was grateful for the continuing support of grass-roots Labour activists in the constituency, especially in his own china clay country, and felt a strong moral obligation to go on. He was also aware that, notwithstanding the apparent strength of Liberal Nonconformity, there was now a record of Labour activity in Cornwall upon which he had to build, and in the Higher Quarter itself there was the particular legacy of the 1913 clay workers' strike. Although the eastern villages in the district (Bugle, Roche, Penwithick, Carclaze) had remained mainly Liberal, the more westerly settlements, where support for the strike had been strongest (St Stephens, Treviscoe, Nanpean), were now Labour strongholds and an important resource for Rowse as he tried to consolidate his local power base. Sam Jacobs, revered leader of the 1913 strike, whom Rowse admired as 'a spiritual father... guide, counsellor and friend... a voice speaking for the poor and downtrodden',[48] had died in June 1931, but there were others to carry on his work in the clay country and its hinterland. Their simple devotion touched Rowse, their loyal, unfailing attendance at party meetings and events a source of sentimental pride:

there is the personal side—the pleasure of seeing and recognising one's friends' faces among the audience. . . A meeting at St Blazey without Mr and Mrs Cooksley or Mr Mason. . . wouldn't be a meeting for me. . . The same is true of Mr Clyma, and his son and daughter, my old school-mates at Sticker; of Mr Chapman and his fellow workers at Roche; Mr and Mrs Yelland and Mrs Samuel Jacobs at Trethosa (how much I miss my old friend Sam Jacobs there, what a great man he was); Miss Meagor [*sic*], who is one of the ablest and most active of our young recruits; and Mr Stoneman and Mr Best at St Dennis. . . Wherever there is a little group of Labour workers in a village, there are my friends.[49]

'The young Cornish David of the Labour Party'

If the warm, affectionate tone of this piece seemed strangely at odds with earlier, exasperated descriptions of Labour meetings in Cornish villages, then the change in tenor reflected not so much the mellowing of a maturing Rowse but rather the sophistication of a new political strategy. For while Rowse was to continue with his insistence that Liberalism had had its day, he was careful now not to antagonize Nonconformist opinion, instead courting Methodist ministers and going out of his way to embrace Nonconformist concerns such as temperance and the abolition of tithes. At a Labour meeting at Tregonissey Lane End he declared that he 'was utterly opposed to tithes and considered the Church of England should raise funds for their churches in the same way the Nonconformists raised funds for their chapels'.[50] He had become, indeed, a 'Political Wesley',[51] as he described himself, preaching the message in the Cornish country-side just as the Wesleys had done almost two hundred years before: 'what nicer thing can there be than to be home in Cornwall, on a June evening in open-air, out in the country lanes all smelling of honeysuckle, or up in the china-clay district with the fresh breeze blowing across the downs'.[52] The Rev. T.W. Slater was among those won over by the seductive rhet-oric, responding in kind with a wealth of biblical allusions to extol the virtues of the newly re-invented Rowse—'the young Cornish David of the Labour Party', the 'youth from the sheep-folds' who would 'confront the Philistine giants, and with his staff in his hand and his sling and five smooth stones, turn the tide of battle and win a well-fought fight for his side'.[53]

This new appeal to Nonconformist opinion, as well as learning from the mistakes of the 1931 campaign, was part of a drive towards the construction of a more overtly Cornish agenda, an attempt to popularize Labour's image and to engage with local issues, to create a 'Cornish socialism'—as it was known by its advocates—that would be relevant to the working people of Cornwall.[54] In 1932, as part of this new strategy, *Cornish Labour News* was launched, edited by Claude Berry: a close friend of Rowse, a Labour Party member, and a journalist of some distinction with considerable experience in Cornwall and London. He had worked on-and-off for the *Cornish Guardian* in Bodmin where he had crossed swords with A. Browning Lyne. 'Lyne had tired of my Socialist propaganda', he wrote to Rowse in November 1929.[55] Berry moved to London to work on Fleet Street but was forced back to Cornwall by ill health, taking up again as assistant editor under Lyne but confiding to Rowse that '[s]trictly between ourselves, however, I'm not happily settled'.[56] By 1931 things were no better: 'You see, Leslie', he wrote to Rowse, '[after] a long period of dissatisfaction and sometimes disgust. . . [I am] not prepared to go on indefinitely with "the Guardian". . . It is an atmosphere of miserable hostilities, open and veiled, of a sycophancy that is nauseous, of incompetence parading as a controlling force, of responsibilities shirked.' Moreover, he confessed: 'My heart and soul were in building up the Labour movement here. . . I love Cornwall'.[57] Eventually, and not without further trials, Berry found his niche in the *West Briton* in Truro, spending 34 years with the newspaper, 18 as its editor. But in 1932 he was delighted to accept the editorship of *Cornish Labour News*—a vehicle at last for his unrestrained expression of Labour opinion and commitment to Cornwall. Rowse had been the guiding hand in his appointment.

Both Rowse and Berry recognized the need to project Labour as the natural successor to the Liberals in the perpetuation of the Cornish radical tradition. As well as embracing Nonconformist themes they sought to usurp long-cherished Liberal policies, such as commitment to free trade. Using *Cornish Labour News* as his platform, Rowse argued that the National Government had introduced tariffs to the detriment of Cornwall to support 'up-country' industries:

> Tariffs. . . may be all right for the motor car industry or glove making, but we don't make gloves or hosiery or motor-cars in Cornwall. That is what concerns us. What earthly use can tariffs be to the china-clay trade?. . . it is time that Cornish industry was considered as well as Morris' Motor Cars. What I have said about china applies also to tin mining, slate quarrying and Cornish agriculture which doesn't want to be strangled with a wheat quota but needs cheap feeding stuff for cattle.[58]

In articles such as 'Cornishmen in Revolt', which evoked the spirit of Trelawny and of the 1497 rebellions, and 'A Cornish Working-Class Leader', which was about the Chartist William Lovett, Rowse and Berry cultivated their 'Cornish socialism'.[59] The opening by Ernest Bevin of the

Transport and General Workers Union's 'Foxhole New Hall' in September 1933 provided the occasion for a passionately pro-Cornish editorial from Berry's pen. 'It has long been the belief of Socialists in Cornwall that the latent radicalism of the Cornish people will one day be kindled into a fiery cross that will lead to the transformation of social conditions in the Duchy', he wrote, arguing that many of Britain's greatest social, political and technological advances had had their roots in Cornwall. 'Methodism owes much to the enthusiastic devotion of Wesley's Cornish followers', he enthused, 'Liberalism had in Cornwall one of its sheet-anchors; the development of the mineral resources of the world was made possible by those Cornishmen who, generation after generation, have taken their skills to every land.' And what the world 'owes to the inventive genius of Richard Trevithick none can tell'. As in the past, so in the future Cornwall was well-placed to lead the way—'[n]o place offers a better hope than Cornwall', Berry wrote—and the china clay district, with the proud memory of the 1913 strike and now the honour of Bevin's visit, was in the vanguard: 'And to Foxhole has come the privilege of being one of the pioneer villages in the struggle to win working-class emancipation'.[60]

Similarly, when George Lansbury, Labour leader in the Commons between 1931 and 1935, paid a 'Cornish Visit' to Camborne and St Austell in the autumn of 1933, *Cornish Labour News* readers were urged to 'give "G.L." a real Cornish Welcome'. It was important, the newspaper stressed, to 'show the veteran leader of the workers that there are still twenty thousand Cornishmen who must know the reason why poverty still stalks the county, when the lavish gifts of God are destroyed to provide profits for the few'.[61]

'Cornish socialism'

This appeal to Cornish patriotism had also struck a chord with Celtic Revivalists in Cornwall. Although Rowse had hitherto kept the Revival at arms length, criticizing efforts to revive the Cornish language as a waste of time and a deflection from the real issues facing Cornwall, he and Berry were now—as part of the new strategy—more amenable to the movement, welcoming its proponents under the unifying banner of 'Cornish socialism'. Most notable of these was E.G. Retallack Hooper, 'Talek' as he was better known in Revivalist circles, who later became both Grand Bard of the Cornish Gorsedd and chairman of Mebyon Kernow, the Cornish nationalist organization founded in 1951. Reviewing in *Cornish Labour News* a booklet by another Cornish Bard, A.K. Hamilton Jenkin, which called for the nationalization of Cornish mining, Retallack Hooper took the opportunity to articulate his own vision of 'Cornish socialism':

Cornish socialism must be definitely Cornish—by which I mean that we work for the new economic system to be applied in Cornwall in a Cornish way. Our industries—notably mining and china-clay, fishing and farming—demand treatment that cannot be dictated by ready-made up-country methods. . . That we have a Celtic history, language and mentality is not to be despised but rather to be worked for. It is humanity itself that must come first and good causes must be built on *economic* freedom of the people themselves. . . so many of our best Cornishmen being deprived of a right to live by a system which piles up armaments on one hand and preaches to Bible societies on the other. Omseveagh why gone-sugy Kernow! [Arise—workers of Cornwall!].[62]

Retallack Hooper was also active in the proto-nationalist Tyr ha Tavas (Land and Language), formed in 1933 with its 'primary aim to serve Cornwall and the Cornish People'. Tyr ha Tavas was an organization committed to 'the unity of persons of Cornish birth or descent who value their Cornish heritage, and who desire to maintain the outlook, individualism, culture and idealism characteristic of their race', and who would show 'what Cornishmen have done and what they can still do to help the World'.[63] As Tregidga has argued, Retallack Hooper formed an important bridge between *Cornish Labour News* and Tyr ha Tavas.[64] In playing the Cornish card, Rowse had proclaimed his own intense attachment to 'every lane and field and village of home', flirting with Tyr ha Tavas as it strove to develop its political influence by lobbying MPs and parliamentary candidates, and emphasizing that 'all I want to be is a spokesman for the Cornish people'. If the movement was serious in its pursuit of 'Cornwall for the Cornish',[65] he said, then it should support him for his was the only chance of achieving a Cornish Prime Minister.

There is little doubt that Rowse's 'Cornish socialism' strategy did much to raise consciousness and to win the confidence of local voters—the first edition of *Cornish Labour News* was said to have achieved a circulation figure of some 3,000—and he approached the general election of 1935 more strongly prepared than in 1931.[66] However, Rowse by no means had things his own way, and even in his clay country heartland there were voices vehemently opposed to his. At Carpalla, near Foxhole, for example, there was Percy Harris, a dyed-in-the-wool Liberal Nonconformist activist: 'an inflated frog in a small pond', as Rowse described him.[67] Harris saw through Rowse's attempts to woo Cornish Nonconformity. '[I]t is pathetic to see Mr Rowse appealing for the support of the Free Churches for his Socialistic proposals', sneered Harris in the local press, especially when the saintly Liberal candidate adopted for the Penryn and Falmouth constituency—Sir Ronald Wilberforce Allen—'was a Methodist before a politician, having been reared in a Methodist manse. . . [and] for many years now has been preaching and speaking almost every Sunday. . . and opened bazaars in every quarter of Methodism'. In contrast to Rowse's cynical agenda, Harris argued, Wilberforce Allen's 'motives are pure, and his life-long association with the Methodist Church. . . is not for the benefit of party politics, but in the interests of the Kingdom of God'. Taunting Rowse, Harris declared that 'Mr Rowse knows he cannot win in a three-cornered fight, and he has even confessed it to a friend of mine. It is easy to discern the symptoms of defeat.'[68] A fortnight later, Percy Harris was again gracing the pages of the *Cornish Guardian*, pouring scorn on the thought that Rowse might be genuinely concerned for the diminishing influence of Nonconformity in British life, in a sly aside again raising the spectre of Rowse's 'atheism': 'It is a great pity that Mr Rowse does not accept the Christian faith, but he need not shed crocodile tears over its waning influence'.[69]

Such attacks hit their mark, unsettling a community for whom religious conviction was still important. The atmosphere of the time was remembered vividly years later by Ken Phillipps in his autobiography *Catching Cornwall in Flight*. In 1935 Phillipps was still at infant school at Roche, in the heart of the Higher Quarter, and a 'few days before the election a Mr Salter from big school came across, urging Miss Richards [the teacher] to vote Labour'. As Phillipps recalled:

> The class was set to silent reading; but no way. . . was I going to carry on silent reading with this lot going on. I recall that Miss Richards was pale and tight-lipped as she repeated: 'I stick to my guns, I stick to my guns, I will have nothing to do with that Mr Leslie Rowse. I have it on good authority that that young man is an atheist.'[70]

'When I look into my heart, what do I see? A Fascist'

If there were voices hostile to Rowse in his Higher Quarter backyard, there was opposition of a different sort elsewhere in his constituency. As we have seen, Rowse's strength lay within the china clay district but there were other areas of the far-flung electoral division that also held pockets of Labour support. For example, there was the tight-knit community of railway workers at Highertown, Truro, the granite quarrymen of the Penryn district, and, most importantly, the dock workers in Falmouth. Rowse had to work hard to win the confidence of this latter group, with whom he had little in common and about which he knew less, and Jack Donovan, the dockers' trade union leader, was equivocal in his support

for Rowse. Rowse described Donovan as a 'tall dark craggy type, prog-
nathous jaw and big teeth', and admitted that 'I could sense that I wasn't
his choice'. He felt, however, that as time went on 'Jack rather warmed to
me',[71] though it was never to be a meeting of minds and after the 1935
election they clashed over strategy. Earlier, Rowse felt that Donovan had
been less than helpful, notably in Falmouth itself when he was canvassing
there. In June 1934, homeward bound and waiting for his train at Penmere
Platform on the branch railway to Truro, he scribbled impressions in his
diary of the 'open-air meeting on the Moor at Falmouth' that he had just
held. It was, he wrote, '[a] miserable affair; nobody there at the beginning,
no organisation, no backbone, the people good for nothing'. In fact it was
Gala Day in Falmouth, the 'big yachts racing' and everyone crowded at
the waterfront: 'My chairman, the Trade Union secretary (Jack Donovan)
had rushed back from the harbour, bronzed and healthy, never having
given a thought to the meeting or seen to it that anybody came. Fancy
allowing it to clash with a gala in the harbour!'[72]

In a mood that reflected the angst of Labour meetings more than a
decade before, Rowse forgot the cheery picture of rural idylls painted only
recently in *Cornish Labour News*:

> I began to speak in a tornado of noise, heavy buses creaking into
> the Moor from Redruth, from Constantine, Penryn, and out again.
> Private cars and motor bikes contributed their quota; then a wire-
> less shop with a particularly loud speaker blared forth music into
> the square. (Was this deliberate, against a Labour meeting?). No
> making myself heard: I spoke about Modern Progress.
>
> Here at Penmere there is at least a little peace. I look down into
> the valley. . . to the working-class houses of Swanvale, each with
> its wireless mast. Is this the sort of life I want to make for these
> people? Their spoon-fed complacency, their cult of pleasure—and
> what pleasures! This is the world that those I detest have created.
> Would not the innate inertia, the passivity, the swinishness of the
> masses win in the end of any ground one might make?[73]

In the darkest of moments, when he felt like this, Rowse despaired of
himself: 'When I look into my heart, what do I see? A Fascist. Only when
I look into my mind do I see that I am a Socialist.'[74] But the battle went
on, the election year of 1935 witnessing the redoubling of his attacks on
the Liberals. He continued his efforts to prise Nonconformist voters away
from the Liberal Party, asking publicly: 'have my Nonconformist friends
ever considered the real reason for the decline of their influence. . . It is
directly due to the fact that their older generation have gone on attaching
themselves politically to the Liberal Party.'[75]

In the *Western Morning News* he returned to his favourite theme, the demise of the Liberal Party, demanding that its adherents be honest about their impending doom: 'why not be candid with our Cornish people and say so?'.[76] In the *Falmouth Packet* he likewise called on '[d]ear old Isaac Foot' (the darling of Cornish Liberalism, personifying as he did the tenacity of the Liberal-Nonconformist nexus in this period) and 'dear old Wilberforce Allen' (his Liberal opponent in the constituency) to acknowledge their imminent defeat: they 'knew perfectly well that the days of the Liberals were up'.[77] But there was to be no such acknowledgement. One angry correspondent in the *West Briton* in June 1935 expressed incredulity that Rowse should ask 'Liberals to forsake principles, profound beliefs, and liberty to join a Party that nearly ruined this country when they were in power—a Party that puts its particular class first and the country and Empire last'. Here there were intimations of deep religious and ideological hostility: 'If Cornish people are true to their traditions, and deep-rooted beliefs, then Mr A.L. Rowse will not represent them at Westminster. Cornwall has fought for religious freedom—and won.' And so the debate went on, the discouraging evidence elsewhere in Britain and Rowse's own political analysis cutting little ice with those who were adamant that: '[t]he Liberals of Cornwall have in the past elected, and can elect in the future, Liberals to Parliament. . . to secure the liberty which our fathers sacrificed so much to gain'.[78]

By June 1935 MacDonald had retired as Prime Minister, and had been succeeded by Baldwin. To the continuing woes of the Depression years had been added growing difficulties on the international stage. There was the attack on Manchuria by Japan—which Britain had been shown powerless to prevent—and the restless expansionist spirit in Hitler's Germany, together with the Italian invasion of Abyssinia (an affront to the beleaguered League of Nations) and the stalling of disarmament negotiations. Despite the general mood of uneasiness, the National Government had held up well, and when the general election was called there was little likelihood of its being defeated. Labour, now under the leadership of Clement Attlee, sought to take advantage of pro-League of Nations feeling, and in the election Labour gained a slightly higher proportion of the popular vote than it had in 1929, its previous best performance. The Conservatives, however, managed to hold on to enough of the Liberal votes they had gained in 1931, securing a comfortable 432 seats compared to Labour's 154 and the Liberals' tiny 20.

'We have had a magnificent fight in Penryn and Falmouth'

In Cornwall, the election resulted in the return of one 'Lloyd George Liberal', one 'National Liberal', and three Conservatives. Liberalism had survived in Cornwall, as its adherents had said it would, albeit in battered form, but the real victors were the Conservatives.

For Rowse, the 1935 general election was a bitter-sweet experience. He had the satisfaction of forcing his Liberal opponent into third place, cutting into the Liberal–Nonconformist vote in the way that he had hoped, but the Tory vote had held up—as it had done across Britain—and Petherick was returned again as the Conservative MP for Penryn and Falmouth. Nonetheless, Rowse had come within 3,000 votes of the winning candidate, his 13,105 votes outdone by Petherick's 16,136 but convincingly ahead of Wilberforce Allen's disappointing 11,527. Reporting the results, the *West Briton* observed on 18 November that '[a] striking feature was the accession of strength of A.L. Rowse', echoing Rowse's view that '[t]o have been placed second and to have added three thousand votes for Labour in this division is something to be proud of'.[79] Later, as the political dust settled, the *West Briton* further noted that 'Mr A.L. Rowse has been congratulating the Labour party in Truro on the remarkable advance in its voting strength at the last election. That is quite right and proper. So is his prophecy that at the next election the Labour Party will win the seat.' But as the editorial added with prescient insight, 'much water will flow up and down the Fal in the next four or five years'.[80]

In many respects, the 1935 election represented the high point of Rowse's political career. As well as knocking the Liberals into last place and substantially increasing the Labour vote, his campaign team had proved loyal and effective. Noreen Sweet, his admirer, had worked tirelessly in his support. F.L. (Fred) Harris, the son of a railway signalman from Tywardreath, had gone on from Fowey Grammar School to Wadham, Oxford, a county scholarship boy like Rowse, and had come back to Cornwall to pursue a life-long career in adult education, being appointed resident tutor in Cornwall in 1935 by the University College at Exeter. A firm believer in community action, Fred was glad to lend a hand in the campaign, and remained a fund of sage advice for Rowse over many years. Then there was Ethel Magor, from Foxhole, who was, according to Rowse, 'a good sort: a mass of dark auburn hair, buxom figure, a winning smile. A most loyal spirit and a generous helper, she made it to Oxford, if only to Ruskin.'[81] As Rowse put it, reflecting on these willing friends who believed in him and shared an idealistic view of Cornwall's future: 'We were a team; we pulled together, no quarrels; I have never forgotten any of them'.[82] Of the result itself, Rowse told the *Cornish Guardian* that 'it has delighted me',[83] while in the December 1935 issue of *Cornish Labour News* he explained all to his committed party workers: 'Well, we have had a magnificent fight in Penryn and Falmouth and I hope you are not disappointed with the result. For I certainly am not: I am delighted as if I had got in.'[84]

Reviewing press reactions to the result, Rowse detected a common theme: 'Why should they regard the Penryn–Falmouth result as so significant? I think that it must be because they realise it points to a Labour victory at the next election.'[85] He had heard already, he said, from many Liberal supporters who wished they had voted Labour, and as for those working-class Tory voters who had allowed Petherick to get in:

> Poor, deluded things—they did not know any better. They were led to think that their interest and well-being is the same as the interest of the wealthy, the industrialists, the landowners, the owners of slum property, whose slums they inhabit. But they will not always be deluded. One day they will come to see things as they really are. It is the business of Labour to open their eyes, to convert their own working people; especially as it is clear that a fair proportion of the middle-classes, the shopkeepers, teachers, bank-clerks, professional workers, are coming over to our side.[86]

In Truro, added Rowse, there were some 3,000 working-class Tory voters. If they had all voted for him, he would now be their MP. If they could be won round in the years ahead, 'there will be no doubt about our majority in 1939'.[87]

Towards a Lib–Lab pact

In focusing on the presumed forthcoming general election in 1939, then, Rowse's strategy was two-fold. Firstly, having successfully eroded the Liberal vote, he now needed to turn his attention to the Tories—to try to undermine the hitherto solid Conservative vote through a determined appeal to working-class Tories. Secondly, the Liberal vote had to be dealt with further and, Rowse calculated, this was to be achieved not through the attempted final annihilation of Liberal support in Cornwall but rather through a local Lib–Lab pact—an alliance that would build an effective radical coalition against the Tories in Cornwall and which might be a model for joint action elsewhere in Britain. He had toyed with the idea before the election, and in November 1935, in the election's aftermath, he had complained to the *West Briton* about 'Liberal and Labour people cancelling each other out, splitting the progressive vote and letting the Tory in—in what used to be a progressive constituency—on a minority vote'. There were important lessons to be learned here, he thought, and 'this may not happen next time; Liberals and Labour may be fighting shoulder to shoulder in Penryn–Falmouth and in the country at large'.[88]

Turning his sights on the Conservatives and the National Government, Rowse told a Labour meeting at Mevagissey in May 1936 'that Mr

Baldwin is not a great leader',[89] and at Nanpean he explained that 'the Tories were determined to place the burden of balancing the Budget upon the unemployed' and that Cornish workers were being discriminated against: 'They had delayed for years to introduce a proper unemployment insurance scheme for farm-workers and fishermen. The fact was they had no intention of producing one.'[90] Increasingly, however, Rowse's political energies were directed towards the prospect of Labour–Liberal co-operation. Although Wilberforce Allen, the Liberal candidate defeated in 1935, had warned that 'it would suit the Labour Party's book to eliminate the Liberals', insisting that any 'attempt to force the electorate to chose between two Parties, and only two, is bound to fail',[91] Rowse's strategy seems genuinely to have been to combine the radical vote in the face of Tory resilience rather than a device to subsume the weakening Liberals.

The *Cornish Times*, however, was cautious about the proposal. Speaking from Isaac Foot country—the newspaper was published at Liskeard, close to the old Foot family home at St Cleer—it reminded its readers that '[i]t is an open secret, of course, that the Labour Party is desperately anxious to secure the return to the House of Commons of Mr A.L. Rowse, the brilliant young Cornish scholar. . . and it is perfectly obvious that Labour's only real chance of getting a Cornish MP for some years is in that constituency [Penryn and Falmouth]'. Labour's plan, then, was for 'an arrangement with the Liberals in North and/or S.E. Cornwall in return for a straight fight with the National Government in Penryn–Falmouth', a proposal that, as the newspaper admitted, had attractions for at least some Liberals. Mr John Foot, indeed, had advocated '[s]omething of the sort' recently, while 'Sir Francis Acland [MP for North Cornwall], speaking at Gunnislake, suggested that the two parties might come to an "understanding"'.[92] Nonetheless, the Penryn and Falmouth Liberals had made their views plain on the death of Wilberforce Allen in 1936 by immediately announcing their intention of selecting his successor: thus 'letting the cat amongst the pigeons with a vengeance!'.[93] Rowse continued to insist, however, that such an 'understanding' was necessary if public confidence in the political process was to be rebuilt, and was delighted when in November 1938 none other than Isaac Foot himself—the personification of Cornish Liberalism in this period— appeared to endorse his view.

On the wider stage, Rowse's proposal had also won considerable attention. The *Manchester Guardian* noted that Rowse had advocated a Lib–Lab pact throughout Britain to reduce the Conservative Party to the 'position of permanent minority which is its proper and rightful place in the political life of the country'.[94] In the *News Chronicle*, moreover, Rowse had written several articles explaining his scheme and calling for 'a better understanding between the Liberal and Labour Parties'.[95] Closer to home, however, as the *Cornish Times* had detected, opinion was split, and suspicion of Rowse's motives was not confined to his Liberal opponents. Jack Donovan, for example, was still wary of Rowse and no doubt expressed the views of the Falmouth trade unionists as a whole when he declared opposition to the pact idea in *Cornish Labour News*.[96] Rowse's principal opponents, though, were a group of intractable Liberals within Penryn–Falmouth who, whatever was said by the likes of Sir Francis Acland or Isaac Foot, were determined that Rowse should not be handed the seat at the next general election. This hostility to Rowse was deep-seated and personal, and he knew it. In particular, '[s]o far as my own constituency is concerned, I am well aware that there is one leading Liberal who would do anything to prevent me being returned. He would rather see Penryn–Falmouth handed over to the Tories and all the chances of an understanding in Cornwall blown sky-high'.[97]

This leading Liberal was, as Rowse wrote in his diary in 1939, one 'Crabbe [*sic*] at St Austell [*sic*, actually Mevagissey]', a 'humbug of a Nonconformist Liberal who attacked me politically',[98] and Rowse found especially wearing the contest between the two men that had developed in the Cornish press in the late 1930s. H.H. Crabb, President of Penryn and Falmouth Liberal Association, a local businessman in the building trade, had accused Rowse of anticipating the 'next slump', an indicator, he thought, of Labour's defeatist and negative thinking on such subjects. This provoked a weary response from Rowse in the *Cornish Guardian* in March 1938 in which he made it clear that 'nobody but a fool would accuse me of wanting one. Everybody here in Cornwall knows perfectly well that I quite a deplore a slump as much as anyone.'[99] Distracted by illness once again, Rowse went abroad for a short break, and on his return found to his annoyance that Crabb's interventions had continued. He tried to be light-hearted in his response:

> I do not know what has gone wrong with poor Mr Crabb—or rich
> Mr Crabb, as the case may be. But here I am, returned from a stay
> abroad where I hoped to get better, to find him still crabbing away
> in my absence. I am sure he'll be sorry to learn that I haven't come
> back any better, though in a mood of unusual good humour, and,
> I had hoped, at peace with all the world. What I should really like,
> however, would be to be able to eat a good, rich Cornish crab. But,
> alas, my miserable digestion will never allow me.[100]

Beneath the humour, however, there was anger and frustration: 'to take him seriously, I don't very much mind Mr Crabb crabbing me; I am so used to it. There are so many people who do it, that it seems rather a pity that he couldn't have thought of some better subject. . . something a little more original.' And as for the suggestion that Crabb had gleaned Rowse's economic views from the *Political Quarterly*, '[d]oes anybody see Mr Crabb taking off to bed with him such high-brow literature. . . ? Not on your life!'[101] The exchanges became increasingly acrimonious, and Crabb, though a Liberal, was a supporter of Neville Chamberlain—Baldwin's successor as Prime Minister—in his attempts to seek an accommodation with Hitler and to avoid war. Rowse, by now a convert to the anti-Appeasement cause, was seen by Crabb and others in Cornwall as unnecessarily alarmist and, in a speech reported in the *West Briton*, was condemned by Crabb as 'anti-British'. Indeed, demanded Crabb, '[w]hat right has Mr Rowse to chide the people of Cornwall with disloyalty because of their attempt to foster friendship with Germany'.[102]

'The Tories. . . have Europe exactly where Mussolini and Hitler want it'

In the exchanges between Rowse and Crabb we see all the ingredients of Rowse's impending disillusion at the end of the decade: Liberal Nonconformist intransigence (as he saw it) preventing political progress in Cornwall; small-minded personal attacks on him by opponents (sometimes within his own party); the debilitating effects of illness; and, increasingly, a blindness—not least amongst the electorate in Cornwall—to the looming threat of Hitler's Germany. The press, or parts of it, had echoed the responses to what was seen as Rowse's tiresome carping about the Germans. Suggestions that an insufficiently prepared Britain would risk military defeat by Germany were considered 'defeatist'. In an explicit attack on Rowse—together with Richard Acland, the Liberal MP for Barnstaple in North Devon, and John Foot, now a Liberal candidate in Cornwall—the *Western Morning News* criticized 'the doctrine of force. . . advocated with particular earnestness by. . . three young men [who] to judge by their political activities. . . are alike in having time on their hands'. These youngsters were not inclined to put their money where their mouths were, the newspaper thought, 'while drawing dismal pictures of the ruin they believe to be pending over England and vigorously denouncing Government inactivity none shows the least willingness to render any form of national service'. Indeed, 'Mr Foot and Mr Rowse are. . . anxious about Czecho-Slovakia, whose maintenance, it seems, is "an essential part of our security". And there apparently the matters are to rest so far as they individually are concerned.'[103]

This was personal criticism calculated to inflame Rowse. The suggestion of indolence, even moral cowardice, hurt at a time when he had striven to overcome physical illness so as to fulfil his obligations as a political candidate. But more than this, the attack was characteristic of what he saw as, at best, a blinkered inability to perceive the real implications of Hitler's ambitions and, at worst, an open sympathy for or collaboration with the Nazi regime. 'Down here in Cornwall. . . the Chamberlainite Lord Lieutenant actually had Ribbentrop down to tout him round the country houses',[104] Rowse asserted later, and when a German pocket-battleship visited Falmouth harbour he was appalled when Joseph Hunkin, the Low-Church Bishop of Truro (a former Nonconformist), went aboard to say prayers: 'what was it *for* but to sink British sailors'.[105] For his part, Rowse continued to be what the *Cornish Guardian* called 'outspoken' about the German threat. On one occasion, for example, he told an open-air meeting at Bugle that '[i]f you have bullies to deal with it is no use running away from them, if you do you will only be worse off in the long run'. As he put it, '[y]ou have the Tories giving way all along the line and they will have Europe exactly where Mussolini and Hitler want it'.[106] By March 1939 Rowse could insist that his warnings had all come true. The Prime Minister and the Tories had been thoroughly 'duped' by Hitler and his allies: 'We could not afford to let Franco win; and yet they did it. We could not afford to let Mussolini have Abyssinia, yet they did it; or let Hitler have Czechoslovakia, yet they did it'.[107]

It was especially irksome that Maurice Petherick, the Tory MP for Penryn and Falmouth who had on two occasions defeated Rowse, was an uncritical supporter of Appeasement. In early 1938, the two men clashed in a debate in St Austell. The *West Briton* observed that Petherick 'hoped General Franco would win' in the Civil War in Spain. He also thought, it was reported, that '[t]he only way to stop Hitler's immense and growing power would have been to go to war', something to be avoided at all costs, while anyway 'surely we had no right to dictate to another country [Germany] what form of government it should have'. Rowse was astounded. There could be no avoiding a crisis with Hitler, and as for Spain, there was the spectacle of 'a gallant people. . . trying to emancipate themselves from a reactionary Church and absentee landlordism, and because they were trying to do that, they were being bombed into submission'.[108] It came as no surprise at all to Rowse when war finally did come on 3 September 1939:

> sitting on the beach at Pendower, nothing but a towel on after my bathe, an hour after the declaration of war—the second in my life-time—against Germany. . . [a] good omen that this is the day of Cromwell's victories? Naseby, Dunbar, Worcester. Nothing of that inspiration in the dreary spiritless speech of Neville Chamberlain, which we gathered to hear in the Nare Head Hotel.[109]

The outbreak of war meant that what would have been an impending general election was put on hold indefinitely, thus robbing Rowse of the opportunity of winning Penryn and Falmouth, at least in the short term. For all the difficulties locally, morale had remained high among his party workers, and it seemed no time at all since November 1937 when, after the euphoric Bournemouth conference of that year, the *Cornish Labour News* had announced confidently that it was now 'straight forward to a Labour Government'.[110] John Legonna, one of Rowse's devotees, half-Cornish and half-Welsh, and later an adherent of both Plaid Cymru (the Welsh nationalists) and Mebyon Kernow, had campaigned for him in the late 1930s: 'Another "push" and he [Rowse] ought to be in sight of winning!', he wrote excitedly. In 1938 he had spent the summer on the Labour Party Clarion Youth Campaign, in and around St Austell, camping with the other young activists at Charlestown until an unseasonal storm swept their tents away. The Labour organizers found them alternative accommodation in St Austell Town Hall. As Legonna later recalled; '"[d]rying out" meant, understandably, a lot of running about in birthday clothes and the hilarities of fitting into nondescript borrowed clothes. . . giving way to love-making',[111] an exhilarating if not entirely responsible or productive way of supporting Labour's cause in the constituency. Rowse had gone along with it all, publicly encouraging the air of optimism and good fun despite the growing threat that he had foreseen, and despite his bouts of illness, private doubts and personal frustrations. But the outbreak of war changed everything. Although he was to reflect soon enough that it had actually saved him from a life of politics that might have killed him, in the short term there was only anger and disillusion.

Forty years later, Rowse still recalled vividly 'the misery of that decade, what I had to put up with in the way of ill-feeling, personal insults, whispers about my family—when I was largely right about Baldwin, Chamberlain and those old men ruining the country'.[112] For the moment, however, he remained active, throwing such weight as he had behind Churchill's leadership. As early as November 1939 Rowse was urging the creation of a federated 'United States of Europe' as a war aim, and in 1940 he was calling for an alliance of the British Empire, America and the Soviet Union to defeat Germany and ensure a lasting peace thereafter, advocating for the future a federal German state in which the influence of Prussian militarism would be diminished.[113] But in Cornwall he had already lost heart. Claude Berry had resigned from *Cornish Labour News* after the 1935 election, and thereafter Rowse had contributed only infrequently, the newspaper losing its distinctly Cornish flavour as the 'Cornish socialism' strategy gave way to advocacy of the Lib–Lab pact. The final edition of *Cornish Labour News* came out in June 1939, the paper succumbing like much else to the impact of war. It was another indication if any were needed that the heady days of the mid-1930s were well and truly at an end.

Inwardly, Rowse had already recognized that his enthusiasm was waning, appealing to his own sense of duty for the strength to go on. In early 1936, for example, he had told himself firmly that 'however much one may be discouraged by the incompetence of the right side, disillusioned by continual defeats, lack of any sense of power, one must go forward with the cause (and people) one believes to be right'.[114] Publicly, he had professed delight at his impressive performance in the 1935 election but privately, as he admitted later, he had long nurtured his disappointment at the result and the 'rejection' implicit within it. He had come out smiling, but '[i]t was easy enough to smile. Little did anybody there know what was in my heart.'[115]

Now that the war that he had foreseen was upon them, he had little inclination to go on as a candidate. Instead, he blamed those who had refused to take heed of what he had said for bringing catastrophe upon themselves. 'As a political candidate with a responsibility to the people in my own part of the country, the county of Cornwall', he wrote, 'I warned them again and again of the fateful indolence and irresponsibility of the man who was Prime Minister of Great Britain. They preferred not to listen; they are paying for it now.'[116] Or, as he told a Labour meeting in St Austell in July 1942, the electorate in the 1930s had kept out of power those very politicians (himself included) who might have done something about it all: 'If the people suffer through putting second-raters in power they have only themselves to blame'.[117] Or, as reported in the *Cornish Guardian* in the same month: 'That is what I mean by the idiot people— the people who voted for Baldwin and Chamberlain'.[118] Privately, he was even more scathing, condemnatory even, returning to gloss an earlier diary entry, that of June 1934 when he had addressed the Labour meeting on Falmouth Gala Day:

> What an innocent I was—and yet not so innocent. I knew what was happening in Germany. . . I was a fool to waste my time trying to open the eyes of the Idiot People—Modern Progress—but I was not so innocent. All the while I was building up my ulcerated resentment: when the time came, *they should pay for it, not I.* And, my God, later on, one afternoon in 1940, they did!; after the Fall of France, I watched from the high road by St Just [-in-Roseland] the bombing of ships in the same harbour [Falmouth] by a German plane. They made excellent targets, and we had no defences.[119]

'You are the voice of Cornwall, and you must speak for her'

Speculation about Rowse's political future was now rife in the Cornish press. The *Cornish Times* asked 'how does Mr Rowse hope to find a seat in the House of Commons'[120] and the *Western Morning News* wondered whether he would 'persist in his Labour candidature'.[121] Rowse himself had already told close friends, such as Claude Berry, that he was about to call it a day. The precipitating factor was the replacement of Herbert Morrison, for whom Rowse had the greatest respect, by Arthur Greenwood as Labour Party Treasurer. Rowse put pen to paper on 9 June 1943, writing to J.H. Bennetts, Secretary of the Penryn and Falmouth Divisional Labour Party, to tender his resignation: 'At the moment of saying goodbye', he confessed, 'I cannot but think of the many times we have stood together in the Market-place at St Austell, or on the Moor at Falmouth, or on the open hillsides in the china clay district, doing our best to open the eyes of our own people to their own welfare'.[122] But his patience was wearing thin, he said, while illness had taken its toll, and the unkindness of enemies in Cornwall had discouraged him:

> We were not always very successful—they [the working class] are very slow on the up-take—and I am not naturally patient, though I have plenty of affection for the genuine and simple of heart. During all the years in which I have been a candidate. . . I have had a constant struggle with illness. In London in 1938 over those two very serious operations I nearly died; it took nearly a year before I got back my strength. And this last winter I had a recurrence of the old duodenal trouble, which made me realise that I cannot ever afford to take risks with my health or put any undue strain upon it.
>
> Our Labour people at home, and you in especial, have been wonderfully understanding and forbearing with me. . . [n]ot so everybody in Cornwall; but that is merely what one would expect. Along with a good deal of kindness of heart, there is a very unpleasant strain among some Cornish people. And I do not wish to come into contact with it any more.[123]

Looking to the future, Rowse emphasized his intention of abandoning politics for good, a course of action that would, he noted, leave 'me free to say exactly what I think about Cornwall and Cornish people.' 'So far as Penryn and Falmouth is concerned', he went on, 'I think you ought to have a younger and stronger candidate—if possible, one with local connections and with a deep anxiety to do his best for Cornwall such as I once had.'[124] The *West Briton's* commentary on all this, no doubt penned by Claude Berry, was to acknowledge that '[o]bservers of Mr Rowse's career are not surprised by this break. It was bound to come. While his ardour for social reforms and his sympathy with the underdog remain undeniable', the editorial insisted, 'he has never had enough tolerance for human frailties and incapacities to ride easily with a party which has many sets.' But the break was all to the good, the paper thought, for while Rowse had been 'steadily piling up votes' and 'might have won it in time', those 'admirers of his real work, which is literature, will have no regrets. . . The politician in this instance is probably less important than the poet and historian.'[125]

Tactful, balanced and placatory, this assessment might have taken the sting out of Rowse's resignation and dampened any backlash. But Rowse had also written an open letter in the *Manchester Guardian*. 'I despair of the Labour Party', he announced, 'such a talent for snatching defeat out of the jaws of victory. There was never a party with such an infallible nose for the second-rate, and such a distrust and dislike of the first rate.'[126.] He had also written to George Shepherd, National Agent for the Labour Party at Transport House, who did not take kindly to Rowse's tone. 'As a very plain man I am somewhat mystified by the different reasons which appear to have determined your retirement', he complained: in his note to Shepherd, Rowse had emphasized the undue length of time he had been a candidate, in the *Manchester Guardian* he had stressed the Morrison affair, in his letter to Bennetts he had concentrated on health issues. Shepherd also accused Rowse of being out of touch with the party, criticizing his 'lack of contact with the Movement'. Rowse's suggestion that Michael Foot—later to be Leader of the Labour Party—might be an appropriate successor in Penryn and Falmouth was met with derision, and '[f]inally, I like not your term "Party hacks". This is a slander on the many men and women who have devoted their life service to the Labour Movement.' Taking particular aim at Rowse, he added: 'It may be that many of them lack polish and educational attainments, but they are entitled to admiration rather than scorn for their loyalty and their ability to play with the team'.[127]

It was Claude Berry who provided the solace and understanding that Rowse needed at this moment, writing to him privately as the news broke in the press. 'I've known for some time, of course, that the break was coming', he admitted, 'and I had the insight to tell Win [Berry's wife, also a Labour activist] it has probably come when I heard the B.B.C. report of the Morrison-Greenwood voting.' It was still a shock, however: 'All the same, it's a bit sad and heartbreaking. . . Being Cornish, now that the end has come, I'm full, of course, of memories of the earlier years. . . and a bit sick that we shan't speak together again at all those places I got to know so well.' But that was to be sentimental: 'that's pure sloppy Cornishry.

You've done the proper thing, and I'm absolutely convinced of its sound-ness. There's still greater work ahead for you, and we shall be terribly proud of you.' There was also a piece of advice: 'I'd like to find you mellowing with the years—but never, please, as mellow as dear old "Q" [Quiller Couch]: only that wouldn't be you'.[128] They kept in touch, and in the months ahead Berry continued to offer support, encouraging Rowse to pursue his Cornish interests in other directions, in literature and history, and assuring him that '[t]hese few b's whom you loathe, and who dislike and fear you, are the very ones who would rejoice if you abdicate'. Indeed, Berry went further, insisting in March 1945 that 'you must be, you are, the voice of Cornwall; and you must speak for her'.[129] In 1945 this was not an accolade that Rowse was inclined to accept—though in later years, as we shall see, it became his catch-cry.

6

'Haunted by Cornwall'

A Case of Mutual Rejection?

'I saw them as nuisances, cluttering up the path with their corpses.'[1] This was how, half a century later, A.L. Rowse looked back with undiminished contempt for those Liberal Nonconformists who had stood in his way in Cornwall in the fateful 1930s. For all the apparent attempts to woo Nonconformists to Labour's cause, or even to construct a Lib–Lab pact, he had never lost (he admitted) hostility to those who had perpetuated the Liberal–Nonconformist nexus in Cornwall at a time of rapid political change elsewhere: 'In contemporary conditions, one was either a Tory or a Labour man—anything else was irrelevant. Why go on with a Liberal Party, dead since 1924?'[2] As he explained, '[t]he prime task for Labour was to bring home the futility of going on being Liberal'. But it was not to be; 'backward Cornwall, smothered as it was in Nonconformist Liberal humbug' became 'a fossilised survival', Cornish Liberalism 'the political expression of Nonconformity', the 'little chapels out in the china-clay district virtually Liberal recruiting stations in my time'.[3]

And yet, as Rowse only rarely bothered to acknowledge, his strategies had been in large measure successful, for although the Lib–Lab pact did not happen, he had been able to win over the Nonconformist vote as well as converting working-class Tories. So successful had he been in this, indeed, that in the UK-wide swing to Labour in the post-war election of 1945, the Labour Party at last won Penryn and Falmouth, returning Evelyn King as Cornwall's first Labour MP. This, in turn, laid the foundation for Harold Hayman's lengthy period as Labour MP in the reconstituted Falmouth and Camborne constituency in the 1950s and 1960s, and, it might even be argued, for Labour's revival there in 1997—which Rowse lived just long enough to see. For Rowse, however, there was to be no sharing in these victories, no pride in having prepared the ground work, no pleasure or relief that Labour had at last a foot-hold in Cornwall.

22 The Longstone at Mount Charles, St Austell—near Rowse's house, Polmear Mine—the site of the 1948 Gorsedd and the subject of one of Rowse's short stories. *Courtesy Charles Woolf.*

'Stopping all contact with Cornwall'

To begin with, he was by now heartily glad that he had abandoned politics, allowing him to pursue his academic and literary interests uninterrupted and to re-build his precarious health. In any case he was now firmly disillusioned with Labour. Although he remained a card-carrying Labour member until 1956—when he resigned from the party over its attitude to Suez[4]—he was already drifting to the political Right and increasingly critical of the Labour movement. But more than this, Rowse had made a conscious decision to turn his back on Cornwall, to retreat from public life, to affect an air of almost hermit-like reclusivity, to cultivate an anonymity that eschewed all contact locally. As he put it in June 1943: 'So far as I am concerned, stopping all contact with Cornwall will enable me to concentrate on writing, which is infinitely more pleasure and is far more worthwhile'.[5]

Naturally, there were moments of regret, chinks in the armour of his self-imposed isolation that appeared from time to time, especially when erstwhile political supporters expressed bewilderment at their sudden abandonment:

> When I threw it all over, I had my bad moments the first few years—all that work, and energy, and time wasted! Once when I happened to be down on the quay at Mevagissey, where I had often spoken on summer evenings during vacations when I might have been enjoying myself abroad, one of the fishermen looked up from his boat and said, 'You don't come down to see us much now'. It went to my heart. Some of those fellows around my home did not forget me; I felt sad at deserting them.[6]

This was an emotion that returned from time to time. It was expressed especially well in his poem 'The Parting', which reflected the Mevagissey incident, a telling and surprisingly candid insight in which Rowse owned up to what had become—and would continue to be—one of his stock behavioural devices: the deployment of pride to mask an inner hurt:

> Tonight as I sit by my fire, solitary in Oxford,
> I hear the cry of my people three hundred miles away,
> Saying—'Do not turn away from us wholly,
> Do not desert us utterly'.
> I see the faces in the flames turned to me,
> Pathetic, beseeching, I recall the fisherman
> Painting his boat in harbour, down by the quay,
> Looking up and saying, gently, reproachfully,

'You don't come down to see us much nowadays'.
And I turned away, feeling I had deserted them,
Tears in my throat so that I could not speak
Until I found words of pride
To hide the sensitive place and said
'There is a limit to what one can stand, you know',
And was surprised to see
He understood perfectly and complained
No more, but turned to his work,
Accepting the fact.[7]

Later in the poem Rowse revealed 'a hurt irreparable / In the inmost recesses of consciousness / The wound opening inwards / The spirit too proud to admit an injury'. But in the background there was also 'the enemy that hates /. . . / Rejection with contempt, defeat with scorn'.[8] This was a fixation which pervaded a yet more self-revelatory poem, 'Home Coming to Cornwall: December 1942', in which he laid bare the desolation he felt after what he saw as the endless trials of the 1930s. Here we encounter Rowse returning home on the old Southern Railway line that ran through Launceston and around the northern edge of Bodmin Moor, skirting the Atlantic coast as it made for Wadebridge, the Camel estuary and Padstow. We see him responding to the dramatic landscape illuminated by the moonlight, a ripple of excitement stirring him as he crosses the Tamar:

It is night and we are entering Cornwall strangely:
The sense of excitement wakens me, to see
Launceston perched on a shoulder like Liege,
The young moon white above moving clouds.
The train halts in the valley where the monks prayed,
Under the castle-keep the Normans ruled
And Edward the Black Prince visited. We stop
At every wayside halt, a signal-box,
An open waiting shed, a shrub or two,
A friendly voice out in the night, a lamp—
Egloskerry, Tresmeer and Otterham—
And out upon the shaven moonlit moor.

The train continues where 'The seawind blows from the Atlantic coast' and 'In that strange wavering light upon the downs / That look towards Rowtor where King Arthur hunted / The red deer, and met at last with Modred'. But before these patriotic stirrings could command his full attention, Rowse remembers the other, darker side of his Cornwall:

> In the moment of breathing in my native land
> I remember to hate: the thousand indignities,
> The little humiliations, the small insults
> From small people, the hidden enmities,
> The slights that hurt the sensibilities. . .
> The biting word that freezes sympathy,
> The instinctive expectation of a blow
> To pride or self-respect or decency. . .
> The meanness of the moneyed middle-class,
> The slow passivity of the workers that know
> Not their own interest or their enemies. . .

He ends with a keen remembrance of 'The million fond stupidities that make / A modern electorate', and declares:

> Alone with myself I could beat my head against
> The walls for rage and impotent defeat.
> Quick! Shut the window. Pull down the blind
> Over the lovely landscape. Shut out the sight![9.]

'I have come back to my old vomit'

So in poetry, so in prose: returning home to Cornwall in July 1945, this time by the more familiar Great Western route, over the border bridge at Saltash and on via Liskeard, Rowse penned in his diary lines of gloom and despair as the train reached Bodmin Road station. 'I have come back to my old vomit', he wrote, 'As the train goes further into Cornwall, draws nearer every moment to home, I find my face set. The Cornish mood settles on my spirits that have been cheerful all day: suspicion, moroseness, dislike steal upon me almost unawares.'

'I was not expecting it', he added:

> I looked out upon the jewelled waters of the Hamoaze [the neck of the river Tamar at Saltash, the border between Cornwall and Devon] with love and pride. Then, as I draw near the scene of defeat and so many humiliations—I dislike even the sound of their voices, soft, homely, comforting, that are native to me. I am fearful of anyone speaking to me. I don't want to be recognised or to have to speak to anyone.[10]

Earlier, Rowse had tried to explain his attitude to Noreen Sweet, his old school-friend and confidante, insisting that he was absolutely serious when he said that he 'will not reply to any letters coming from Cwll [*sic*,

Cornwall] (except from old friends), on the grounds that they are likely to be (a) asking for something, or (b) offensive, and in either case illiterate'. Moreover, he was thinking of making his books unavailable in Cornwall, of 'getting my publishers to put a ban on the sale of my books in Cornwall. So that anybody who wanted to get one wd [*sic*] have to make the journey to Devonshire for the purpose.' Indeed:

> People in Cornwall have made rather a mistake in offending me. For more and more I feel myself in a position to get my own back. And you know me well enough to know that I shall not fail to do so. When once I turn my back on them, I not only turn my back but slam the door in their face. I rather think I shall carry on a feud with Cwll till my dying days.[11]

This was not just idle talk. In early 1944—only six months after Rowse's resignation as a political candidate—the St Austell Youth Club had, in its innocence, written to him to invite him to deliver a lecture at one of its meetings. He had replied according to his convictions: '[it] should be generally known that I have a general principle against speaking in Cornwall, though I may occasionally break [*sic*] an exception'. And he explained that 'I am sorry for you—since it is not the fault of you young men. I should have quite liked to have come and spoken to you. But as things are I only do that kind of thing outside Cornwall nowadays.'[12] The *Western Morning News,* in the past no particular friend of Rowse, caught wind of the story, reprinting his comments for all to see and adding its own editorial perspective: 'while as a historian he glories in the Cornish past, he has no time (as the saying goes) for the Cornish present'. In fact, the newspaper noted, Rowse had now determined that it was a 'waste of time' in 'speaking to people in Cornwall who failed to take their opportunity in the past ten years' to support him electorally. There was for Cornwall deep sorrow in this decision, the paper thought, for 'Mr Rowse wasn't a carpet-bagger. He was a "native son" and had good reason to think that at some future time of asking he might succeed. . . No doubt Cornwall will survive this deprivation. But an open animosity in a distinguished Cornishman is a thousand pities.'[13.]

The *Western Morning News* was not alone in its opinions, and there was genuine dismay in Cornwall at the attitude that Rowse had struck. Self-styled 'SICK of Mr ROWSE' wrote to the press from Marazion, for example, noting that 'Mr A.L. Rowse has decided that in every respect Cornwall is not worthy of his services or even his notice and that he has resolved never again to speak publicly in the county'. Had it not occurred to Rowse that the feeling might be mutual, the correspondent thought: 'Is it not about time this young man realized that the dislike is not only on one side and that the great majority of people in Cornwall have no desire that he should speak to them?'.[14] Rowse was not to be moved, however, and a year later he was still adhering strictly to his principle. As he noted in his diary:

> This morning at Oxford a letter came from a Nonconformist minister at Newquay [the sympathetic Slater?, one wonders]: would I give a lecture, preferably on my theme of 'The English Spirit' [the title of his recently published book] or 'Churchill and English History'? After expenses met the proceeds would be devoted to church purposes. I should be advancing the interests of the Christian religion. . . [a]fter years in which a political candidate and a public figure but because I was a *Labour* Party candidate, no such invitations from those miserable local Wesleyans were forthcoming—do they think I would now? It was on the tip of my pen to reply in those words; instead I merely regretted that I couldn't accept his "novel, if kind, offer"'.[15]

In a later gloss, appended to this entry, Rowse observed that the success of *The English Spirit*—especially in America, where Lord Halifax had presented a copy to President Roosevelt—had prompted an all-too-late response in Cornwall: 'This new found popularity had its reverberations in obtuse Cornwall', he wrote, 'though having ceased to be a political candidate, I was determined that they should see me no more as a public figure, nor hear me—they had their chance throughout the Thirties'. Again he had considered the possibility of withdrawing his books in Cornwall, 'stipulating with my publishers that my books should not be sold in Cornwall—but then, that would have been my loss'.[16]

'A person at war with himself'

However, it was not *The English Spirit* that was to be remembered in Cornwall as the quintessential Rowse but rather *A Cornish Childhood*, published a couple of years before in June 1942—almost exactly twelve months before his resignation as a political candidate.[17] Conceived during his illnesses, as Rowse explained much later to his bibliographer, Sydney Cauveren, *A Cornish Childhood* had started life as a social history of a Cornish village, Tregonissey, but had soon adopted an autobiographical tone. This was a cathartic process, no doubt, as Rowse mapped out the book in his head as he lay desperately ill in hospital: 'I lay there remembering all the things that gave me pleasure and thinking about bathing on the Cornish beaches because I was having a very high temperature and all that'. And, '[w]hen I began to get stronger and to recover, I found that the book was all there in my head. Just write it out, easily.'[18]

Subtitled *Autobiography of a Cornishman*, the book covered the period of Rowse's life up to age nineteen and his departure for Oxford. It has been almost continuously in print since its initial publication, acquiring the aura of a classic: a work of literary nostalgia, to be considered alongside books such as Laurie Lee's *Cider with Rosie* or Flora Thompson's *Lark Rise to Candleford*, volumes that record and bring to life a Britain long-since vanished. By the time Sphere Books brought out their cheap Cardinal paperback edition in 1975, aimed at the popular mass market, *A Cornish Childhood* had exactly that reputation, the back-cover blurb explaining that '[i]t evokes memorably and with great charm life in the little village where he was brought up, the village whose customs, characters, and stories had remained unchanged since early Victorian times. . . a moving self-portrait, and a portrait of a generation'.[19]

In Cornwall, and indeed in much of Britain, *A Cornish Childhood* had had a very different reception when it first appeared. In a society gripped by war, the book seemed inappropriately self-indulgent, and although it was dedicated 'To my mother and the memory of my father', with both parents thanked in the Preface for their contributions to the book and to his life, Rowse's frank, pithy descriptions of working-class family life, his oblique but nonetheless shocking revelations about his mother, vague hints about his father, and his shameless parade of diverse prejudices, combined to offend and outrage many readers. Variously interpreted as an attack on the family, an attack on religion, and an attack on moral values generally, full of self-praise and self-promotion, *A Cornish Childhood* was condemned by more than a few. Warren Hamilton Lewis, who read the book in 1947, thought it 'well written' but found it 'intolerable' and thought it should have been subtitled 'Self Portrait of a Shit'[20]—an assessment that probably mirrored the private thoughts of a great many others.

Many 'up-country' readers must have found their personal constructions of Cornwall—and their experiences there as holiday-makers —offended by the gritty realism of Rowse's text. For the austere picture of clay-country life painted by Rowse—or, indeed, his near contemporary, Jack Clemo—contrasted starkly with popular Home Counties imaginings of the 'Delectable Duchy' and the 'Cornish Riviera'. These visualized an exotic, semi-tropical, quasi-Mediterranean land of mystery and romance, a paradise no less, a construction that had been marketed vigorously by the Great Western Railway in the interests of mass tourism. In 1928, in the midst of the economic crisis that had blighted Cornwall and had motivated Rowse as Labour candidate, the Great Western's tireless publicity machine had published S.P.B. Mais's classic guide *The Cornish Riviera*, a genuinely charming volume that did much to capture the English imagination: 'Everybody has dreamt of a land where the sun always shines but never proves harmful, where it is always warm but never enervating, where we may bathe in winter and take active exercise in summer. We had to have a name for this Elysium, so we called it the Cornish Riviera.'[21] There was more:

> You may go there with the idea that you are in for a normal English holiday, and find yourself in an atmosphere of warlocks and pixies, miracle-working saints and woe-working witches. . . You may go there intent only on tennis, and find yourself at the end of a fort-night a devotee of holy wells and Celtic crosses.[22]

For all the nostalgia that *A Cornish Childhood* might later evoke, Rowse's Cornwall was no Elysium, and no doubt many up-country readers were confused, annoyed, or even disturbed by the intervention of his social realism into their imagined scenes of mystery and romance. At the very least, working-class life at Tregonissey seemed only incidentally connected to the Cornwall of S.P.B. Mais and the Great Western Railway. Not only had Rowse unashamedly, even indecently, abandoned his native heath, but in so doing he had painted a pen-picture that was wilfully subversive, criticizing home and family as well as undermining those reas-suring, fondly held imaginings of tourist Cornwall, offending deeply those who had warmed to the seductive purple prose of Mais and the Great Western.

The press reviews came thick and fast, from outside Cornwall and also from within. The *Cambridge Review*, always an important indicator of informed and educated opinion, considered the context in which Rowse had conceived *A Cornish Childhood*: 'Here is the Cornwall of his child-hood', explained the *Review*, trying to evoke the socio-economic paralysis of Cornish society and culture, 'a queerly melancholy society, crumbling away under the impact of competition' from abroad. The book was 'frank but not endearing', thought the reviewer, and was 'marred by a lack of humour and an air of uncritical [self] admiration'. There was also, the reviewer continued, 'a series of indiscriminate and liverish outbursts against all sorts of conditions of men', so that the intellectual components of the book were 'a mere jumble of prejudices thrown off with a brilliant literary technique, a minimum of reflection, and less logic'. Within this confusion, '[t]he working classes are castigated. . . [t]he middle classes are mean, selfish and small-minded. The intellectual Left are mere deluded idealists.'[23] *Time and Tide*, another important test of cultured opinion, was less condemnatory, finding within the volume 'colour, warmth and affec-tion'—even for 'the little shop he served and loathed'—but warned readers that they would be 'alternately attracted and repelled' by the book's contents.[24] The *Observer*, meanwhile, suggested that the book revealed Rowse at 'three levels: the Cornish historian, the self-analytic, and the man of developed opinions and prejudices'. The first two suffered at the hands of the third, the newspaper thought, and urged that, having got so much off his chest after so difficult a time, Rowse should now take stock and start again: it hoped, it said, that 'in this book, Mr Rowse is shedding his dead self, and that he will soon [achieve] a greater objectivity and a greater magnanimity'.[25]

Intriguingly, one of the most thoughtful and incisive commentaries on *A Cornish Childhood* was that broadcast in 1943 on the *Listener's Bookshelf* programme of the Palestine Broadcasting Service (an arm, of course, of the British Mandate's administration in that territory). It admitted that 'the book is important because it is fiercely honest, and gives a picture of a section of society that has been very little written about, working class life and education in a remote Cornish village'. But there was also 'a dangerous error in his [Rowse's] opinion of the people', the programme explained, for '[l]ike all intelligent working class intellectuals he rejects the romantic glamour that is sometimes thrown over the harsh facts of working class life'. This in itself was acceptable: 'But he is not content with this. He despises the working class.' Searching for explanations for this unsettling and deep-seated animosity, the programme observed that '[t]he savagery of the attack is caused no doubt by the deep wounds his sensitive nature received in the lonely struggle to success': the inner loneliness of his family life, a home without books, the battle to get to Oxford. But the outcome was, alas, a 'reactionary' state of mind, a condition that was at the very least a 'disturbing symptom in a prospective labour [*sic*] candidate'. Rowse was, the programme concluded, 'a person at war with himself'.[26]

'There are dark places in the Celtic mind'

Such was the view from the Holy Land. An alternative perspective was glimpsed in *Life and Letters Today* in a review by 'Bryher'—a *nom de plume* suggestive of the Scillies, and therefore a Cornish sympathy—which put its finger on the book's inherently paradoxical nature: 'It is a long time since I have read a book that is at once so delightful and so irritating as Mr Rowse's autobiography'.[27] *The Times,* again with a qualified sympathy, recognized the same paradox but put it down to the complex characteristics of the Cornish race, of 'the inborn contradiction, which tends to be in Cornish people, of harshness and gentleness, caution and impulsiveness, gaiety and brooding melancholy, assurance and diffidence'.[28] This was a perspective that attempted to offer a specifically Cornish explanation for both book and author, to account for the society that was being described and to penetrate the Cornish psyche of Rowse himself. This was also the approach adopted by Elizabeth Bowen, who in the *Tatler* drew

upon her credentials as an Anglo-Irish novelist to present Rowse as mercu-
rially Celtic, a writer imbued with all the faults and the brilliance of the
Celtic temperament. 'I admire him', she said, 'for being so bitter against
the members of the more fortunate classes. . . Yes, the spirit that runs
through *A Cornish Childhood* is, decidedly, a haughty one.' But this was
down to Rowse's Celtic blood: 'this is an affair of heredity. Mr Rowse
appears to be almost purely Cornish on both sides. . . To be Cornish is
to be Celtic, and all Celts seem to exhibit a sort of aristocratic intransigence. They have natures that quickly and thunderously cloud over, and
they are touchy in a way that the Anglo-Saxon finds incalculable.'[29]

Rowse was grateful for this review. The notion of the Celts as inherently 'aristocratic' appealed especially, and was one he was to use
frequently in the years ahead. After all, Elizabeth Bowen was herself indisputably aristocratic—and, indeed, a Celt—and therefore should know.
Moreover, her husband, Alan Cameron, was half-Cornish (a Lanyon on
his mother's side), so she had had plenty of opportunity to observe the
Cornish character at close quarters, and to appreciate its subtlety and
nuances. Rowse was similarly grateful to Rosalie Glynn Grylls (Lady
Mander, as she had become on marriage), who contributed her own
review to the *Cornish Guardian* after his book had received a mauling in
that paper from the pen of its editor, A. Browning Lyne. She had tired,
she said, of the 'reviewers' attitude' to Rowse that had become commonplace in commentaries on *A Cornish Childhood*. What was missing, she
explained, was an appreciation of Rowse as Cornishman, and as a
Cornishwoman herself she was in a position to furnish this: 'What matters
and what will last is its Cornishness', its 'Cornubiality', for '[w]e are
Cornish, One and All', and the book would stand as a fitting memorial to
that condition. The bitterness, frustrations, anger and disappointments
that Rowse had vented were not merely, she thought, the results of the
limitations of working-class family life or the rebuffs he had encountered,
but reflected the deep complexity of his Celtic inheritance. Here there
were, she said:

> moods. . . which probably only a Cornishman would understand:
> those sides of our character which led an observer once to say. . .
> 'There are dark places in the Celtic mind where wild beasts lurk'.
> They come, not from family maladjustments or later misunder-
> standings, but from the fundamental maladjustments of the Celtic
> people: lost children of the Mediterranean who find themselves in
> foreign climes—the outlines of their character made more angular
> in the north, blurred in the Island of the West, and at once
> 'rigourised' (to coin the word) by the native scene and mellowed
> by the prevailing air in Cornwall.[30]

There was an unbridled romanticism in this that was typical of the style cultivated by Rosalie Glynn Grylls—no wonder she became a devotee of the Pre-Raphaelites, author of the highly regarded *Portrait of Rosetti*—an other-worldly whimsy which seemed to say much about her own uncritical embrace of nineteenth-century English stereotypes of 'the Celts' and actually very little about Rowse and life at Tregonissey. No matter; she had tapped into an important *genre*. 'The thing about the Cornish', she wrote in the *Cornish Review*, 'is that they are not nice: exciting and attractive but not nice. . . The essence of Celtic truth is that it is faithful to mood, fickle to fact.'[31] Although at odds with Rowse's social realism, she thus appealed to an explanatory Celticity that he found persuasive and was himself to adopt. Certainly, Rowse warmed to her, forgiving her her Liberal Party affiliations (her husband was a Liberal MP, and she had once been a candidate herself), and approving of her Oxford connections. Like Mary Coate and Veronica Wedgwood, Grylls had been at Lady Margaret Hall. Indeed, Rowse went out of his way to maintain a life-long, consciously Cornish friendship with Grylls. Years later, when in New York, he contrived to meet up with her for lunch with Alan Curnow, the New Zealand poet of Cornish descent, and later still, in September 1988, as she lay dying, he wrote to Katherine Munro (Charles Henderson's sister-in-law) to reflect on Rosalie's recent visit to Cornwall: 'It was wonderful that she had such a good time down here just before this, seeing the places she had known years ago, old Grylls and Glynn places'. Alas, 'I now rather fear for the worst—no reason going on as an invalid. Give her my love if she recovers consciousness.'[32]

As a writer of note, Rosalie Glynn Grylls in her stout advocacy of *A Cornish Childhood* may have won Rowse some converts. Charles Causley, just emerging as a Cornish poet of consequence, wrote approvingly from his native Launceston that the book 'stands up and batters its environment'.[33] In the *Royal Cornwall Gazette*, moreover, one 'Onlooker', from St Austell, mounted a spirited 'defence', as he called it, of 'Mr A.L. Rowse, the writer and historian (and politician) who I think one may safely remark has rocked the literary world, to say the least, by his frank and honest autobiography'. Like Elizabeth Bowen and Rosalie Glynn Grylls, 'Onlooker' felt that a proper appreciation of the elusive Cornish character was crucial in any estimation of the book, and that most reviewers had failed to attempt this. 'It is a book I shall read again', he wrote, 'and one which every true Cornishman will understand. It is probably because nearly all the reviewers are not Cornish that their reception has been such as it is.' Indeed, '[t]o understand the "outpourings" of such a distinguished Cornish writer as Mr Rowse I feel it is definitely not the job of a "foreigner"'.[34]

Down in Penzance, W.H. Rowe felt much the same but offered a more cautious assessment, recognizing that many in Cornwall had been offended by *A Cornish Childhood*. 'There must be many Cornishmen', he wrote, 'who grieve that one of them who has shown such admirable grit in his initial struggles should now be so embittered in his reflection on his fellow country-men.' And yet, Rowe went on,'there is a bitter foundation for much of what he pronounces', one that should be considered, acknowledged and understood when weighing up the book. Besides, he added, Rowse had fallen victim to the nostalgia that stalked all Cornish folk who had left their native heath, a familiar malaise that afflicted alike the emigrant to the distant lands of the New World and those who merely sojourned up-country, a condition whereby the fond imaginings of home nurtured in the exile's breast could never be matched by the mundane reality encountered on the return. 'All Cornishmen love their country', he said. 'It is in their blood. They cannot help it—But this love fails to extend to their brethren Cornishmen when they return home, and Mr Rowse cannot conceal his disappointment.'[35]

'Mr Rowse's terrible drawback'

Written with a telling insight that reflected Cornwall's all-pervading experience of exile and return, Rowe's analysis added a further dimension to those apologies and defences of *A Cornish Childhood* that had appealed variously to Celtic temperament, Cornish blood, and the unfathomable spirit of Cornwall. More convincing, perhaps, than the more fanciful expressions of Cornishness, it still did not cut much ice with many detractors in Cornwall. One S. Church, from Pengrugla, near Pentewan, for example, was exasperated that Rowse 'with all his learning, has learnt little from life', and regretted 'the egotism and almost contempt for common people in *A Cornish Childhood*'.[36] The *Western Sunday Independent*, in its review of the book, offered the by now all-too-familiar criticisms. There was 'a number of disagreeable features', the review alleged, including 'an excessive carping at some aspects of Cornish life', a deficiency that 'hideously disfigures' the book: 'Mr Rowse's terrible drawback is a complete lack of tolerance: his admiration of the aristocracy must be balanced by a contempt of the middle class, and latterly of the "idiot people"'.[37] The *Cornish Guardian*, as Rosalie Glynn Grylls had noted with disquiet, had emerged as a particular critic of *A Cornish Childhood*, with A. Browning Lyne—Liberal Nonconformist in sympathy and hostile to Labour—writing a lengthy review article in which he ranged across further notices of the book, from the equivocal to the downright antipathetic, that had appeared in other publications, Cornish and metropolitan, politically Right as well as Left.

Browning Lyne explained to his readers that Rowse 'examines his origins, his family, the village of Tregonissey in which he was born, and the social milieu of the people; but he examines them as mercilessly as he portrays his own complex character and the characters of others'. This was a serious flaw, and '[m]y own regrets are so pronounced that I could almost wish the book had never been written'. He feared, he said, that it 'will give offence to many', adding that 'I was very sorry Mr Rowse had indulged in so much contemptuous criticism and displayed so much intolerance of those with whom his dazzling career had brought him into association'.[38] This was not just the view from mid-Cornwall, Rowse's stamping ground and the *Cornish Guardian*'s patch, but reflected a universal anxiety. In the *New Statesman,* he noted, Raymond Mortimer had attacked Rowse's 'savage contempt' for working people, while Howard Spring in the *Daily Mail* detected that a 'queer note of intolerance, arrogance and self-satisfaction runs through the book', though he admitted that it was highly readable and could be recommended 'with all my heart'. The *Western Independent,* meanwhile, had identified passages that would 'give intense pain to many people', adding with wry insight: 'He has his cudgel always ready. When he sees the head of a Nonconformist or a "bourgeois" he hits it—and hard.'[39]

For Rowse, the all-too-familiar repetitiousness of such reviews was depressing, and when Joseph Hunkin, Bishop of Truro, added his voice of disapproval, he was outraged, fulminating against 'one Hunkin, a former Nonconformist, who unforgivably attacked *A Cornish Childhood.* . . I never spoke to the man again: his loss—I did not want to know him'.[40] Hunkin's reaction further confirmed Rowse in his Anglo-Catholic sympathies. Though he remained an agnostic—if not an atheist, as his critics alleged—his quizzical aside in *A Cornish Childhood* suggesting that he was a 'High Church unbeliever' puzzled the Rev. L.V. Jolly of St Eval, who wrote to the papers to say so, sparking another round of shrill correspondence in the press concerning Rowse's supposed religious beliefs and affiliations.[41] The *Western Morning News* noted the 'lively controversy', and observed that '[a]s a Parliamentary candidate in Cornwall, Mr Rowse, in the controversial days of piping peace, sought to unite the old Liberals with the new Socialists'. This was less than a year before Rowse's resignation as a political candidate, with speculation rife that he was about to 'throw in the towel', and the *Western Morning News* could not resist a further needling remark: 'If he persists in his Labour candidature it will be interesting to see, in a constituency famed for its devotion to religious subjects and where "the vast majority went to chapel", the fate of one who says he "loathes Protestantism"'.[42]

There can be little doubt that the furore that greeted *A Cornish Childhood* genuinely took Rowse aback. The public response added to the unbearable climate of late 1942 and early 1943, reinforcing the sense of rejection by Cornwall and the Cornish, and further persuading him to abandon his parliamentary aspirations and to turn his back on Cornwall. When, eventually, he did resign and copies of his resignation letter found their ways into the press, journalists and editors recalled *A Cornish Childhood*. As well as remarking ironically that a retreat from Cornwall would benefit Rowse's health—'[i]t is much to be hoped that congenial literary work in congenial academic surroundings will restore it'—the *Western Sunday Independent* compared the tone and content of the resignation letter with that of Rowse's autobiography. 'This is an echo of the most deeply resented passages in Mr Rowse's fine book "A Cornish Childhood". It suggests an obsession.'[43] Likewise, when Rowse, true to his word, began to turn down offers to speak to local groups, the *Western Morning News* thought this unfortunate attitude reminiscent of the 'lamentable chapters'[44] of the now infamous book. Not surprisingly, it had been Claude Berry—a close friend of Rowse and a Labour activist—who had anticipated the political fall-out and negative publicity that *A Cornish Childhood* might generate. In a characteristically subtle review in the *West Briton* written shortly after the book's publication in June 1942, Berry noted both strengths and weaknesses in the new work, as well as the potential for damaging criticism:

> The book at once takes its place among our Cornish classics as naturally and inevitably as Mr Rowse has been taking first place since he toddled up the hill from Tregonissey into Carclaze School before he was four. . . [but] there are hard things and even harsh things that gentle spirits will come upon to their hurt and vulgar spirits no doubt (with an eye to future damaging in political combat) to their delight.
>
> It is fitting perhaps that this notice of 'A Cornish Childhood' should be written by one who came from a working-class family, poorer even than Mr Rowse's, and who, although altogether less complex, brilliant and distinguished, has shared something of this life of which he writes without subscribing to all his judgements upon it.[45]

'Dogged by ill-health and made cynical by celibacy'

It would be unfair to interpret Berry's comments as a disclaimer but there was an element of discomfort, even foreboding, in his remarks: a sense that Rowse had once again landed himself in hot water. As the above indicates, Berry was largely right in his assessment, though the predictable reaction of the Liberal Nonconformists was ameliorated—to Rowse's enduring delight—by the Celtic-Romantic imaginations of Elizabeth

Bowen and Rosalie Glynn Grylls. Their support, however, notwith-standing the affinity of their views with aspects of Cornish-Celtic Revivalism in this period, did not imply the wider support of the Revivalist movement in Cornwall. Despite the engagement of E.G. Retallack Hooper and other Revivalists with *Cornish Labour News*, together with Rowse's own contacts with Tyr ha Tavas, the movement as a whole continued to eye Rowse with some suspicion and even enmity, especially as he had criticized efforts to revive the Cornish language.

Certainly, this was the position of Edwin Chirgwin, a Cornish bard (with the bardic name Map Melyn) and one-time secretary of the Gorsedd (1944–60), a self-taught Cornish language specialist who composed verse in Cornish. As Brian Murdoch has noted in his *Cornish Literature*, Chirgwin 'has been singled out, quite properly, as a poet of considerable stature',[46] and there is little doubt that he should be accounted an indi-vidual of some significance in the literary and cultural history of twentieth-century Cornwall. Chirgwin was headmaster of St Cleer School, near Liskeard, from 1925 until his retirement in 1956, with the exception of a brief interregnum in 1941–42 when he was in Gibraltar as a government censor, and he was a member of the parish church in St Cleer—in whose churchyard he lies buried.[47] He had taught his pupils the Lord's Prayer and Creed in Cornish, a measure of his commitment to the language and to his belief that the Cornish Revival should not be the preserve of the few but ought to touch the lives of everyone in Cornwall. He was, like Rowse, a man of strong views with a keen sense of history. As an Anglican, moreover, he had common ground with Rowse, and was far removed from the stereotypical Liberal Nonconformity that Rowse so despised.

However, despite these apparent similarities, Chirgwin and Rowse were very different characters. Chirgwin's strong sense of social responsibility was offended by Rowse's reckless treatment of family secrets and his care-less expression of wounding prejudices. Shortly after the appearance of *A Cornish Childhood*, Chirgwin, recently returned to Cornwall, settled down to craft an important essay: one which remains unpublished and yet stands as a valuable critique of Rowse's work. It was written from the perspec-tive of a self-confessed Cornish patriot anxious to preserve the best in Cornish life but also to reconcile Cornwall to the demands of modernity. Paradoxically, like Rowse, Chirgwin was well aware of shortcomings in the Cornish mind-set, but for him Rowse was part of the problem: a product of the negative features of Cornish society rather than the anti-dote he had claimed to be. As Chirgwin explained, 'Mr Rowse is the most gifted of living Oxford Cornishmen, and being a Cornishman he is a man of intense likes and dislikes'. This was partly a question of racial inheri-tance, for '[a]s a rule Cornishmen know nothing of compromise or

half-measures. Whatever they like they are enthusiastic about, and whatever they dislike they detest very thoroughly and either ignore it or attack
it.' But it was not merely a function of genetic predisposition, for in Rowse
Chirgwin saw a hang-over, a relic of the pre-1914 era, of the religious and
political intolerance that he imagined to have characterized early twentieth-century Cornwall:

> Being individualists par excellence they [the Cornish] have a
> marked tendency to intolerance and bigotry, and down to the
> outbreak of the war of 1914 this intolerance pervaded the whole
> religious and political life of the County. Their innate Fascism was
> disguised by enthusiasm for the principles of the Liberal Party, and
> their innate Paganism was disguised by a love of ritualistic
> Christianity (as we know it) by one section of the community, and
> by a detestation of all ritual by another and larger section.

Although Chirgwin regretted the 'unadulterated indifference' that he
detected in contemporary Cornwall, a result of the pendulum having
swung too far the other way after the Great War, and though he worried
about a new generation 'that has lost all sense of values', he nonetheless
welcomed the decline of intolerance and bigotry that had become apparent
after 1918. As he put it: 'With the marked decline of organised religion,
the fading out of the Liberal Party as a national force, the passing-away
of the pre-1914 generation, and the break down of hard and fast lines
between other political parties, much if not all this intolerance has
vanished'. And yet Rowse, who claimed to represent the new, was,
Chirgwin thought, actually an anachronistic survival, one whose prejudices reflected the hates of old Cornwall: 'throughout his work he betrays
himself as a typical Cornishman whose feet are in the pre-1914 years'.
Moreover, though typically Cornish, Rowse 'was not a patriotic
Cornishman', for not only had he opposed the revival of the Cornish
language but in his constant appeal to pre-1914 sentiment he was in
danger of opening old wounds, of resurrecting dead animosities, of
perpetuating divisions at a time when the Cornish should be working
together. As for *A Cornish Childhood*, '[o]nly a Cornishman could have
written [it]. . . and only a Cornishman can attempt to review it because
the whole atmosphere of the book is essentially Cornish'. Generously,
Chirgwin admitted that, '[h]aving an overdose of original sin in my make-
up I have enjoyed the book, but I closed it with mixed feelings nonetheless,
a feeling of bewilderment being not the least of them'. Indeed:

> Had I not known the author was a comparatively young man I
> should have been deceived into thinking that this book was the last

word of a disillusioned old man dogged by continued ill-health and made cynical by celibacy. I am convinced that it contains much which in the years ahead the author will regret having written.

The worst of this was that 'Mr Rowse has deliberately and unashamedly exposed all the family secrets of which he is almost the sole custodian. He turns family skeletons into marionettes for public entertainment', an unforgivable betrayal when '[b]lood should be thicker than water', and when there are those 'who still believe that certain phases of family life are sacred and confidential'. As Chirgwin observed, '[n]o one has ever charged Mr Rowse with any attempt to seek popularity', and in *A Cornish Childhood* Rowse had set 'his hand against every man, and consequently, every man's hand against his'. But for all the fuss and bother that the book had caused, the enduring reaction in Cornwall would be plain enough: 'Most of his Cornish readers will close the book with the apt quotation, "Ephraim is joined unto idols, let him alone!"'. This attitude is also very Cornish and will not be resented by the author.'[48]

'Tormented again this evening about Cornwall'

But Edwin Chirgwin was wrong; utterly so. The unending stream of reviews, some equivocal, mostly hostile, had arrived in tandem with the final crisis of Rowse's political career, reinforcing his overwhelming sense of rejection—most painfully, at the hands of the Cornish—his own very public repudiation of Cornwall matched by responses from the likes of Chirgwin who were happy to see him go. The mid-1940s were the nadir of Rowse's personal relationship with Cornwall, and however successful his literary and academic career might be elsewhere, this perceived rejection left a dark hole in his life. In his diary, he recorded his 'official' position, the one for public consumption but also the one that he tried to convince himself was true: 'Cornwall: The Summing Up—after the years as a political candidate I find that the less I have to do with Cornwall and Cornish people the happier I am'.[49] But it was not quite true. At Oxford, he was acutely aware that colleagues and acquaintances were almost all English—and certainly not Cornish—providing entrée to a stimulating environment in which he moved happily enough but to which, ultimately, he did not 'belong'. His position at Oxford, in other words, was a facade that—so long as it was maintained—protected him from the awful reality of his Cornish inheritance. The moment his guard was down, however, the moment his circle of friends was preoccupied elsewhere, his attention for a second not held by the glittering Oxford lights, then his thoughts drifted back to Cornwall. He remembered that he was Cornish, that Cornwall was the source of the angst that welled in his heart:

Alone in a restaurant in London, haunted by Cornwall—the obsession that awaits me around the corner when I am away from my friends, nearly all of *them* English, associated with Oxford. They have given me happiness, with them I am gay, cheerful and contented. They exorcise for me those bitter memories, the endless disappointments, the nausea: the impertinences from people one wouldn't wish to know; the familiarities from people one would rather forget; the treacheries and worse, the letting down by friends; the misunderstandings with the stupid, and even with the well-intentioned the inability to get to the point, the gift for saying the wrong thing. The futility of my own family and relations, a liability to carry on top of everything else.[50]

Such thoughts were likely to assail him at any time, and to be triggered by the slightest thing. This produced a response akin to panic, an anxiety that would compel him to rehearse yet again all those incidents that he would rather have forgotten. In November 1948, for example, he chanced across a report in a local newspaper explaining that the Cornish Gorsedd would hold its next annual bardic ceremony at the Longstone, near St Austell. Not only was the Longstone field next door to his house, Polmear Mine, but as Patron of St Austell Old Cornwall Society it would fall to him to welcome the assembled Bards. The prospect was too awful to contemplate:

Tormented again this evening about Cornwall. Almost everything about or from Cwll [*sic*] is capable of torturing me. Tonight it was a paragraph in the *West Briton* to say that the Gorseth had accepted the invitation of the St Austell Old Cornwall Society to hold their Gorseth on Sep 3 next year at the Longstone next to my house— the Longstone of my story. Like anything of that sort it clutched at my mind and set the old familiar hammers working. What should I do? I am still nominally Patron of the St A. O.C.S. and should be there to receive them. But it is unthinkable that I should be there, that I should allow myself to be seen by them.

If it was term time at Oxford, then he could gracefully bow out, his apologies to the Old Cornwall Society expressing his regrets but noting the pressing business of student essays, lectures to prepare, college administration, and so on. But unfortunately, it would not yet be the end of the summer vacation, as people well knew:

I am always at home in early September. These idiotic festivities will be in the field next to my house. The house itself will be pointed out, will be an attraction to the gaping sight-seers. Some of them may come in—people who know me may try to call, expect to see me, in my absence come and talk to the old woman [his mother], interview her, get [her]—all too easy—to make a fool of herself for the newspapers.

And so it all came flooding back again, Rowse railing as ever in his diary against 'the stuck-up pretentious. . . Nonconformist middle-class. . . people made of asbestos like Wilson Harris or Percy Harris, people with no human face. . . the people who have made the dominant Cornish mentality'. Here, in his diary, was a furious stream of consciousness that dwelt upon the 'endless small insults and detractions, the indignities offered, the refusal of any ordinary civil recognition'. There was the time, he noted, when he had not been invited to the unveiling of the War Memorial, though his Tory opponent had, and the occasion when he was left off the guest list for the opening of the new school, and the fact that not once during his candidature had he been asked to address the local Chamber of Commerce. In 1948 it still rankled: 'it was the kind of thing I was expected to swallow from these people again and again in Cornwall'. That was then: 'Now no-one knows why I never appear there; why I never accept their invitations, or allow myself to be seen or heard if possible'.[51]

In the end, of course, Rowse relented, and the fierce insistence that he had maintained through the 1940s, that he would for ever turn his back on Cornwall and would never again speak or appear in public there, began to crumble. Back in 1942, before his resignation but when he had first threatened to abandon Cornwall, the *Western Sunday Independent* had taken him at his word, though doubting his long-term resolve. Rowse might indeed try to 'cut away from the place and never see it again', the paper thought, but 'he loves every field and lane and hedgerow in Cornwall', a bond so deep that the desire to escape 'is not likely to become strong enough to conquer him. His nostalgia of Cornwall is more powerful'.[52] The newspaper was right, as it turned out, for time was beginning to heal the wounds of his political candidature and *A Cornish Childhood*. But it was not until a decade later that A.L. Rowse was again routinely appearing in front of Cornish audiences. Even then he did so with misgivings, irritation and a heavy heart. In June 1953, for example, he had a speaking engagement at St Ives. But only 'half a dozen rows had gathered to hear the leading Cornish celebrity', he complained, 'I reflected on Glasgow a fortnight before with 400 to hear what I had to say—I hadn't expected any other: I know Cornwall too well'.[53]

7

'Not Being English, Alas—
But Hopelessly Cornish'

Embracing Churchill's England

In April 1945, with the Second World War not yet won, Arthur Bryant—biographer of Charles II and Samuel Pepys, and author of a string of patriotic English histories—wrote admiringly of A.L. Rowse and his unswerving devotion to his country's cause. '[I]n an age when every left-wing publicist and almost every intellectual decried patriotism', Bryant declaimed, 'Mr Rowse, who is both',

> Stood for his country's honour fast
> And nailed her colours to the mast.[1]

The country to which Rowse had accorded such unqualified loyalty was not Cornwall, on which he had so recently turned his back and whose rebuffs he had felt so keenly, but England. While Cornwall had sneered about his religious beliefs (or lack of them), his family secrets, his warnings about the Germans, churlishly rejecting his solutions for a better future and casting aside his carefully crafted autobiography, so England had at the eleventh hour thrown off the Appeasing coterie that had almost ruined her. Instead, England had embraced now the visionary leadership of Winston Churchill: at first standing alone against Germany, as Elizabeth had against the Armada, and then—in the time-honoured tradition of English foreign policy, and in the manner advocated by Rowse—marshalling the grand alliance that would secure the victory. This, at least, was Rowse's view, and in giving up on Cornwall—and, to all intents and purposes, on the Labour movement—his attentions and affections were now directed firmly elsewhere. Now he looked to the newly re-awakened England, roused at last from the somnolent 1930s and alive again to her historic role: that of fashioning under Churchill's inspiring guidance a mighty coalition of the English-speaking peoples to lay low the enemies of civilization.

23 Rowse the anglophile scholar ponders the latest news as he begins to fear for England's future. *Courtesy Special Collections, University of Exeter Library and Douglas Glass.*

24 Rowse in characteristic pose, putting right the ill-informed and correcting the errors of their ways. *Courtesy Special Collections, University of Exeter Library and Douglas Menzies.*

Arthur Bryant, champion of England's greatness, saw the transformation that had occurred in Rowse, recognizing the passing of the old persona—the 'passionate Cornish scholar and poet'—and the emergence of the committed Anglophile, devoted to Churchill and determined to see the destruction of Nazism, the Axis powers, and all their works. It was a remarkable metamorphosis, Bryant observed, for 'Mr Rowse is—or was—a man of the Left, even at times of the extreme Left'. And yet the shift was not after all so surprising, he thought, for while it was inevitable that Rowse's working-class background would at first point him to the Labour camp, so his instinctive understanding of England's destiny would lead him eventually and inexorably into the company of those who celebrated her history and championed her interests. As Bryant explained:

> The son and heir of a long line of Cornish miners who fought his way through harrowing anxiety and constant struggle to Oxford, sensitive to every slight—real or imagined—as a born artist must be, a warm-hearted and hot-blooded observer of the national scene around him, he gravitated mentally into the political ranks of the intellectual Left.

But Rowse was never happy or at home with the intellectual Left, thought Bryant, and although Rowse might share genuinely in its condemnation of the social and economic policies that had brought misery to millions of working—and unemployed—people in the 1920s and 1930s, he was uncomfortable at the way in which the Left railed against all the traditional institutions of Englishness. In Bryant's words, Rowse:

> found himself aligned with men whose fundamental attitude was instinctively repugnant to his nature; a poet, an historian, a meticulous scholar, an instinctive aristocrat and a passionate patriot, he took his place among the long-haired, ill-disciplined intellectuals who, ignorant alike of the past and the character of their country, sincerely set out to discredit and denigrate, not merely the reigning economic beliefs and practices (in which they were only too right) but every virtue, institution and achievement that had made her great and glorious.

It was an analysis with which Rowse must surely have agreed. Those excruciatingly difficult last years as a political candidate alongside colleagues with whom he increasingly disagreed, and from whom he felt alienated, were still fresh in memory—as Bryant knew:

> They blackguarded the Fighting Services, cried out against courage

and discipline, and tried to break up the Empire. And Mr Rowse, because he hated the blinkered men of business who failed to give his country the imaginative leadership for lack of which she was dying, found himself forced to march with such critics while growing daily more repelled by their ignorance and their suicidal rootlessness.

It took the outbreak of war, however, to convince Rowse that this was so. The precipitating factor in his personal realignment was the emergence of Churchill as war-leader, a crowning moment that at a stroke—or so it seemed to Rowse—rescued the country from its plight and restored something of the old glory that he had grown to love during his research into Elizabethan England:

> From this dilemma Mr Rowse. . . was rescued in the terrible spring of 1940 by the collapse of the England of the money-changers and phrase-makers and the dramatic emergence of an older England under the leadership of Mr Winston Churchill. For this reason, I believe, Mr Rowse owes a gratitude to Mr Churchill.[2]

'An Elizabethan in our own time'

Bryant was right about Rowse's sense of indebtedness to Churchill. Rowse was later to write an extended history of the Churchill family, and in 1943 he had dedicated his short book *The Spirit of English History* 'To the Right Honourable Winston S. Churchill: Historian, Statesman, Saviour of His Country'.[3] The volume that had prompted Bryant's passionate and illuminating review, however, was Rowse's *The English Spirit*, published in 1944 and again in 1945: a vigorous collection of essays that, as people began at last to see the first beckoning glimmers of victory, caught the mood of the moment.[4] As C.V. Wedgwood put it in *Time and Tide*: 'In and out above the darkened horizon of war-time historical writing, now blazing heavenwards in a shower of sparks, now crackling with furious energy, shoots the spirit of A.L. Rowse'.[5] There were similar accolades in the *Daily Telegraph*, the *News Chronicle*, the *Tatler* and elsewhere, with the book receiving a rapturous reception across the Atlantic and even raising a murmur in Cornwall, the site of his only too recent rejections and humiliations.[6] This was the kind of flattery to which Rowse responded, confirming for him the rightness of his decision to abandon his commitment to Cornwall and to set out his historical and literary wares on a grander stage where they would be welcomed by people equipped to appreciate their quality.

The book itself ranged across a variety of historical and literary themes, but was bound together by the common thread of Englishness. The opening chapter was devoted—inevitably—to 'Mr Churchill and English History'. This was a hagiographic celebration that saw Churchill as both the encapsulation of English history—descendent of Marlborough and craftsman in his own time of a Grand Alliance—and chronicler in his own right of England's story. 'I wonder', Rowse thought, 'how many people, when they see that so familiar, so endearing, bulky figure on the films or railway platforms returning from one of his innumerable journeys, think how much of English history is embodied in it?' Too few, he suspected, but: 'I always think of it: it moves me to think of these patterns in our wonderful long history as a nation. It is evident that Mr Churchill himself is conscious of it; but then he is a historian. . . dominated from his boyhood with the desire to play his part in the nation's history.'[7] Churchill's six-volumed *The World Crisis* was in Rowse's estimation perhaps the finest of books on the Great War, but Churchill had also engaged—Rowse reminded his readers—in a wide variety of other historical writing. There was Churchill's own commentary on his illustrious ancestor, the Duke of Marlborough, and innumerable pieces on disparate themes, many of them drawn from personal knowledge or experience: 'Nobody in our time can have had such an infallible nose for history on the wing: guerrilla warfare in Cuba (this while on leave from the army at home), expeditions on the North-West Frontier (sharp fighting but good sportsmanship), Omdurman, the Boer War'.[8] Especially, Churchill had caught all the ancient splendour of the battle of Omdurman, Rowse thought, recording for all time a spectacle never to be seen again, the sixty thousand Dervishes rushing forward under the Mahdi's banner to engage Kitchener's gatling-guns. Then there was Churchill's gripping account of his own escape from a prisoner-of-war camp in Pretoria, providing a pen-picture 'as thrilling as anything that R.L. Stevenson ever wrote'.[9]

But it was as war-leader that Churchill had reached his apogee, Rowse insisted, securing for ever his central position in English history. In this achievement Churchill had displayed all the qualities of an earlier age, in the process rekindling England's pride and self-respect: 'In himself the Prime Minister exemplifies the grander and more robust standards of an age which was certain of itself, which had an infinite soaring confidence—when statesmen were not afraid to be poets, historians, philosophers, theologians, voyagers on uncharted seas of discovery'.[10] This was, of course, an allusion to the age of Elizabeth, Rowse's own chosen field of research in which he was fast emerging as a leading scholar. His *Tudor Cornwall* had appeared in 1941 and even more ambitious projects were already on the stocks. Speaking with this authority, he was certain that 'Mr Churchill is made in an Elizabethan mould. But then he is a man to whom English history has been both inspiration and the call of duty.'[11]

Elsewhere, Rowse maintained this eulogistic estimation of Churchill's life and work. In the London *Evening Standard* in November 1944, on the eve of the great man's seventieth birthday, he contributed an article on Churchill as hero, returning once again to the theme of his being '[a]n Elizabethan in our own time'.[12] Likewise, the *Sunday Dispatch* commissioned from Rowse 'Five Years of Churchill', a glittering article to sit alongside its 'Moment of Victory' leader in its edition for 6 May 1945.[13] With the war against Germany won, there was already a general election on the horizon, and the political implications of Rowse's unswerving and high-profile support for Churchill—a Tory—were now obvious, as the press was quick to spot. In *Vogue*, on the eve of the election in July 1945, Rowse confessed that '[i]f I were in Mr Churchill's constituency, I should certainly vote for him'. But lest this be seen as an uncritical embrace of the Conservative Party, or the final repudiation of his Labour links, he was quick to add that 'if I were in Mr Bevin's [constituency] I should vote for him'. Ernest Bevin's bluff, no-nonsense, common-sense brand of social democracy still exercised an appeal for Rowse. The bottom line, he explained, was that 'wild horses wouldn't drag me to vote for some useless old Labour hacks; equally, nothing would induce me to vote for some hoary old Tory reactionaries'.[14]

But in any case, Rowse's devotion to Churchill was not, nor could it be, party-political. As he observed years later, '[h]undreds of people knew him politically. . . my acquaintance with him was something different—over history':[15] their mutual interests in the sagas of the Churchill family and of the English-speaking peoples but also Churchill's own towering role within the story of England. 'To me as an historian', Rowse explained, 'my contacts with Churchill were contacts with history, direct and live',[16] with a man whose own ancestry was steeped in history, who relished, understood and wrote history, and who had himself made history on the grand scale. Moreover, in Rowse's estimation, Churchill was far, far more than a mere politician. Like Rowse, he had also suffered at the grubby hands of petty political operators, but had risen above it all to fulfil his greater destiny: 'Churchill was not like a politician—as a matter of fact, he was not a good politician, but he graduated—in his sixties and seventies!—into a statesman'.[17] It was this graduation that had rescued England in the nick of time and had restored her confidence and grandeur, creating amongst other things the conditions that had allowed the unqualified expression of Rowse's own unbridled admiration and enthusiasm for England and all things English.

'A deep love for English things'

In all this there was, of course, the thorny question of Rowse's Cornishness, something that he had always defined as oppositional to the

Englishness that he now embraced so passionately. One could not be both Cornish and English, he had insisted time and again, for the categories were mutually exclusive. Indeed, as recently as 1942, in *A Cornish Childhood*, he had complained that '[p]eople do not realize that to be Cornish is a very different thing from being English'. The Cornish were a Celtic race, he said, with very different temperaments from their English neighbours, and he admitted that at Oxford 'I find life in the English environment one long struggle with one's temperament: so many things you must not do or say, or perhaps even think, such sedateness, such sobriety and self-control, the comfortable and instinctive adherence to correctness and convention'. And yet, he did not hold this against the English; in fact, he rather approved of it. 'The old dears', he wrote affectionately, 'how much I admire them for it—but how very unlike them I am!'[18] There was, in this expression of affection and approval, and in the regretful admission of his own 'difference', the mechanism that Rowse was to deploy to resolve his personal tension between Cornishness and Englishness. He could never really be English, he thought, but he could admire—or even acquire?—the superior qualities of the English people. His status as an 'outsider' in their midst gave him an objectivity in his estimation of their worth that no doubt eluded the English themselves.

In marshalling his material for *The English Spirit*, Rowse explained, he had been struck anew by his enduring love for England and Englishness. This was something that he had scarcely been aware of or able to articulate fully before the heightened danger of war. 'In bringing these essays together', he wrote, 'I am surprised to find how consistent and strong is the theme that runs through them: something more than pride in, a deep love for, English things.' There was the countryside and the towns, 'with their memories of the people who inhabited them and of things that took place there—all so much alive for me', and the places associated with names so central to the English tradition: 'Thomas More and Elizabeth, George Herbert and Hampden and Clarendon, Swift and Horace Walpole, William and Dorothy Wordsworth; the Tower and Hampton Court, Rycote and Great Tew, Trinity Great Court and the High, Wilton, the Close at Salisbury'. It was, no doubt, he said, the grave threat that had lain over all this that had awoken his latent love (and that of others) of English things and 'their being very precious to us'. It was this great peril, perhaps, that had allowed the English to give voice to hitherto private thoughts: '[i]n the usual English way, perhaps, we were shamefaced and shy at saying what they meant for us'.[19] Here Rowse was remarkably close to uncritical, unconscious self-identification as English but in the next breath there was a disclaimer, asserting an oppositional Cornishness that explained why he could articulate so readily sentiments which the English hesitated to own. 'Not being English, alas—except by conviction—but hopelessly Cornish, I am not ashamed but proud to say it for them.'[20]

Indeed, Rowse continued, '[i]t is important. . . both for us and for the world that the English should understand themselves and that the outside world should know what kind of people they are to whom they owe (as a Cornishman I say it) so much'.[21] To the casual observer, '[i]t may seem presumptuous on the part of a Cornishman to write about the English spirit, to attempt to define the indefinable', but there were certain advantages in this: 'there are things a Cornishman can say, and even see, which an Englishman perhaps could not'. The English, he insisted, were very unselfconscious, not knowing what they were really like—'a charming trait'—and (equally charming) caring even less. Insofar as they had a view of themselves, it was as a 'dull, plodding, humdrum, hard-working sort of people' but in fact they were the opposite: 'far from being hardworking, they are lazy, constitutionally indolent. They are always being caught lagging behind, unprepared—again and again in their history it has been the same.' But when roused, confronted, in a corner, up against it, they were magnificent: 'they more than make up for it by their resourcefulness, their inventiveness, their ability to extemporise, their self-reliance'. Thus, he said, the English were among 'the most brilliant of modern nations', adding that '[a] Cornishman, who is sufficiently of them to appreciate them and yet is different enough to see them with a certain objectivity, may say that'.[22] Englishmen were too reserved to say it themselves: '[p]erhaps a Cornishman—one of the numerous minorities happily included within the creative amalgam that is Britain—may be allowed to answer for them'.[23]

Elsewhere, he continued in similar vein. In an article in the *Daily Despatch* in November 1945, for instance, he explained that '[a]s one who sees the English people a little from the outside, as a Cornishman, I am filled with admiration for them'.[24] Earlier, in October 1942, he had written for the *Listener* about Germany's barbarous treatment of its now subject peoples—Poles, Serbs, Czechs, Russians, Norwegians, Dutch, Belgians, French. He expressed horror and outrage at German excesses and atrocities, and contrasting this appalling behaviour with the 'tolerant and liberal' outlook of the British Empire, not least England's gracious historical accommodation of Cornwall: 'Cornishmen, one of the racial minorities within it [the Empire], may bear witness to the essential kindliness and tolerance, perhaps too great tolerance, of the English people'.[25] It was wartime, of course, and anything less than this would have seemed inappropriate, unhelpful, even subversive, but there was in Rowse's uncritical gratitude for England's treatment of Cornwall a fawning sycophancy that would have grated with the likes of Tyr ha Tavas and which echoed the age-old dilemma faced by Cornish people who owed their livelihood to the patronage of the English state.

As far back as the fourteenth century, the Oxford scholar John Trevisa had sought to defend his Cornishness while at the same time embracing Englishness, attempting to resolve a medieval tension surprisingly like Rowse's twentieth-century conundrum. Cognisant that Cornwall was one of the chief constituent territories of Britain, Trevisa was nonetheless nervous about contemporary assertions that Cornwall was not actually part of England. As Mark Stoyle has observed, 'Trevisa protested too much',[26] his anxieties telling us much about the ambivalence of a medieval Cornishman conscious of his separate identity but owing his scholarly *raison d'être* to the English ecclesiastical and literary establishment. Similarly, in the early seventeenth century, Richard Carew, author of the *Survey of Cornwall*, celebrated Cornwall and Cornishness but was careful to apologise for the Cornish 'commotions' (the Tudor rebellions), projecting himself as a thoroughly modern Renaissance Englishman, in the process deriding the Cornish language—which he did not understand—and stressing instead the 'Excellency of the English Tongue'.[27] As Mark Stoyle has also observed, 'Rowse was the intellectual and spiritual heir of Carew'[28] in so many ways, distancing himself from the allegedly parochial norms and values of what he considered 'traditional' Cornish society—not least Liberal Nonconformity—and embracing instead the mores of the English Establishment. It was a familiar pattern.

In Rowse's case, however, as we have seen, the background to this shifting allegiance was traumatic in the extreme. His absolute rejection by Cornwall (as he saw it) had coincided with the dramatic rise of Churchill and the assertion—as Rowse and Bryant both thought—of an older England, reminiscent of the unbounded confidence of the Elizabethan age. And yet, as we have also observed, there was no question of a simple replacement of one identity by another, an abandonment of Cornishness in favour of Englishness. In a twentieth-century version of a much older device, Rowse had sought to reconcile his Cornishness to the demands of Englishness, an echo of Trevisa and Carew (and many others) but with a context specific to the exigencies of the Second World War. But the matter was more complex still, for despite the apparent clarity of Rowse's position—that the Cornish were not English, and never could be—the reality was that the boundary between Cornishness and Englishness remained fluid and muddled, inconsistent and uncertain, even for Rowse himself. Allusions to 'our nation' and 'us' and 'we' when discussing the nature of Englishness were a tell-tale sign that Rowse too, like many of his countrymen, had difficulty in negotiating the precise boundaries of Cornishness, of resolving the 'in England but not of England' dichotomy of Cornwall's existence.

Indeed, making the situation all the more puzzling, Rowse argued that

'[f]or patriotism to be true patriotism, it must attach itself to a really significant entity, a nation or state that has achieved some greatness, that
possesses a tradition and a record that means something to civilisation'.
Thus England was a legitimate object of true patriotism, not least his own.
But what of Cornwall? This was more problematic, for:

> we get to a border-line with the smaller indeterminate nationalities
> which are really agglomerations of tribes with very little conscious
> corporate existence. I appreciate the point well as a Cornishman:
> devoted [*sic*] as I am to Cornwall and its history, is there such a
> thing as Cornish patriotism? It comes, I think, under the heading
> of what we call 'local patriotism': not a bad thing—a good thing
> rather, provided it is kept in proper perspective.[29]

In the context of the war years, Rowse's attempt at resolving the
tensions and defining the boundaries between Cornishness and
Englishness may have been convincing, or at least convenient, but there
was little rigour in his distinction between 'true' and 'local' patriotism,
while the question of whether the Cornish should therefore be considered
English went unanswered—despite his protestations elsewhere.

This puzzling contradiction, by no means unique to Rowse, was the
abiding essence of 'old Peggy's conundrum', as it has been dubbed. This
is a reference to A.K. Hamilton Jenkin's fascinating insight into the
complexity of identity formation in nineteenth-century Cornwall, a tale
that is for us a useful tool in attempting to divine the elusive and sometimes confusing characteristics of modern Cornishness.[30] In his *The
Cornish Miner*, first published in 1927, he told the illuminating story of
Peggy Combellack, a 'school dame' typical of the sort who offered a rudi-
mentary education to young children in Cornwall in the days before the
Education Act of 1870. Venturing into the realms of geography, old Peggy
asked for a definition of Cornwall's status: 'Hes Coornwall a nashion, hes
e a Hiland, or hes a ferren country?'. The brightest pupil answered that
Cornwall was none of these—not a nation, nor an island, and certainly not
a foreign country. 'What hes a then?', inquired Peggy. 'Why, he's kidged
to a furren country from the top hand', replied the pupil, to the great
approval of the other children as well as Peggy herself. The 'furren
country' to which Cornwall was 'kidged' ('joined', from the Cornish
language) so tenuously ('from the top hand') was, of course, England, a
paradox that exemplified the contradictions and uncertainties of Cornish
identity.[31] Cornwall, in the estimation of Peggy and her pupils, was not a
nation in its own right and yet it was also not part of England. In the days
of Cornwall's nineteenth-century industrial pre-eminence, this separate
identity, though lacking clarity, could be asserted with confidence. But by

the time Rowse, with his working-class background, began his entrée into the English Establishment, the glory days of Cornish industry were already over, Cornishness no longer assertive and the uncertainties and irresolution inherent in Peggy's conundrum now correspondingly of greater consequence—not least for Rowse himself.

'Loyalist Westcountrymen'

Indeed, having with at least some conviction and perhaps plausibility created a niche role for his Cornishness in the advocacy and celebration of things English, Rowse was on occasions tempted to go yet one step further—to subordinate Cornwall to the notion of a wider 'West Country'. This was an amorphous and ill-defined territory that somehow faded into middle England somewhere beyond the Stour and the Bristol Avon, and in which an Anglo-Saxon Wessex shaded imperceptibly into Celtic Cornwall, the whole exhibiting some kind of unity in its diversity. At such times, Rowse became a 'West Countryman', the ultimate blurring of the boundary between Cornishness and Englishness, especially when he looked east across the Tamar border to make common cause with like-minded friends and colleagues who shared his tastes and sympathies. Shaking off all the frustrations of being Cornish, and all the negative emotions he associated with Cornwall, Rowse was on such occasions glad to embrace England's West.

Winston Churchill had been born at Bleinheim, in Oxfordshire, on the extremity of Hardy's Wessex, but his real claims to West Country roots stretched back to medieval Dorset: to 'the country on either side of the main road from Dorchester to Sherborne',[32] whence hailed the earliest Churchills. 'The Churchills are by origin a West Country family',[33] explained Rowse in the Preface to his *The Early Churchills*, published in 1956 and dedicated 'to Arthur Bryant, in friendship and love of the past'.[34] There were branches of the Churchill clan throughout Dorset, Somerset and East Devon. On his mother's side, Winston Churchill was also American, and here Rowse detected another West Country connection, for the West Country was 'that part of England which is closest—not only geographically—to America and which, along with East Anglia, made the most marked contribution to the historic foundation of the American people'. In the recent war against Germany, he added, the role had become somewhat reversed. Under Churchill's direction, the West Country had played host 'in the heroic months of 1944' to thousands of United States servicemen: 'The old West Country became in those unforgettable days, happily and naturally, an American colony'.[35] Churchill was thus tied inextricably to the West Country, and Rowse liked to think of himself and Churchill as West Countrymen together, sharing common bonds and outlook. '[I]t is not inappropriate', he observed, 'for a Westcountryman to write the story of this family whose origins lie across my road from Cornwall to Oxford.'[36]

The Later Churchills, bringing the story up to Sir Winston's own time, was published two years later, in 1958, and combined volumes were to follow, including an abridged *The Churchills: The Story of A Family* that appeared in 1966.[37] In this latter edition Rowse admitted the twin motivations for the study: the West Country associations of the Churchill family and his particular admiration for Sir Winston. 'I was first drawn to the subject by their West Country origin', Rowse observed, 'but this was confirmed by the inspiration afforded in our own time by the career of the family's greatest son.'[38] A cursory glance at the volume quickly reveals the extent to which it is peppered with 'West Country' references and allusions. We find, for example, that Sir Jonathan Trelawny, seventeenth-century subject of the Cornish patriotic ballad, was one of a group of 'loyalist West Countrymen'.[39] Later Trelawny, Sir Joseph Tredenham and Mr Boscawen, all Cornishmen, are described as inhabitants of 'West Country houses', while the Foxes are a 'West Country family'.[40] Sidney Godolphin, from near Helston in West Cornwall, Lord High Treasurer under Queen Anne, had been long, we are told, a close friend of John Churchill, Duke of Marlborough. Rowse was anxious to effect a territorial and cultural affinity between the two and stressed that '[t]hey had a similar West Country background. . . Godolphin and Churchill were both West Country Royalists by origin'.[41]

This yearning for a West Country affinity, prompted as it was by a desire to claim common cause with Churchill, and given additional impetus by Rowse's estrangement from Cornwall, found literary expression beyond the confines of the *Churchill* books. As early as 1945 Rowse had published his *West Country Stories* (in fact, almost all the chapters were Cornish), including a fictional essay on 'All Soul's Night'. Among the *dramatis personae* in this story was a Rowse-like Oxford don who took an 'almost fatherly interest' in the 'long file of young men coming up to the University from the West Country. . . Anybody of West Country connections had a claim upon his attention, if not upon his affections.'[42] Similarly, Rowse's edited collection *The West in English History*, published in 1949, with memory of Churchill's victory still bright, was explicitly West Country in tone. Consisting of the texts of some eighteen radio broadcasts from the BBC West Region (based in Bristol), the book was—as its Foreword noted—a collaboration between 'a West Saxon producer from Gloucestershire (Gilbert Phelps)' and 'a Celtic historian from Cornwall (A.L. Rowse)'. It contained contributions from a range of authors who in their work showed the West Country to be a place whose 'unity is a product of its diversity', even if, as the Foreword admitted, no one was quite sure of the geographical extent of this supposed 'region'.[43]

A fine essay by F.L. Harris, Rowse's old friend and ally, on 'The Industrial Revolution in Cornwall' provided a specifically Cornish angle but the rest of the collection was decidedly West Country in flavour. Some of the pieces were place-specific, like John Summerson's piece on Bath or C.M. Macinnes's on 'Bristol and the Slave Trade', while others were all-encompassing—such as John Betjeman's sketch of 'Victorian Provincial Life' or Jack Simmons's 'The Civil War in the West'. The one exception was Rowse's own 'Tudor Cornwall', echoing the title of his major book published earlier in the decade, but even here the straightforwardly Cornish perspectives of 1941 had given way to a West Country gloss. It was now Cornwall and Devon together, rather than Cornwall alone, that had been forced by Tudor intrusion from their erstwhile isolation into the mainstream of national life, and likewise the rebellions of 1497 and 1549 were now best described as events of collective West Country historical significance. Then there were the 'West Country families that took to the sea',[44] Cornwall and Devon men together, 'Raleighs, Grenvilles, Killigrews, Carews, Tremaynes', and in the capital itself 'the brilliant court of Queen Elizabeth had a strong West Country contingent'.[45] These were themes echoed in Rowse's later book, *The Elizabethans and America*, published in 1959 (with its very Plymothian dedication to 'Nancy Astor, this tribute for Plymouth and Virginia'), Rowse explaining to his readers that '[t]his book cannot but have a West Country bias. For a notable consequence of the emergence of America was to bring the West Country very much to the fore, in the front-line of oceanic discovery and of the war with Spain.'[46]

'Our own Westcountry Wessex'

For Rowse, the high point of this love affair with the West Country—and, by proxy, Churchill?—had been in 1953, on the eve of the Coronation of Elizabeth II, when he was asked to write a Coronation preview for the *Western Morning News*. He chose as his theme the role of the West Country in the creation of the English system of government, emphasizing an ancient and historic link that went back to the house of Wessex, to the days of Alfred and Athelstan. But there was no room, it appeared, for Cornwall, the Cornish or the Celts, in this assessment. Instead, there was only a proud insistence that all West Country folk should honour the West Country origins of the Constitution. 'It all springs from our own Westcountry Wessex, the kernel of the Anglo-Saxon kingship', he announced with authority, 'Wessex became the foundation of the English monarchy'.[47] Dogmatic and exuberant, Rowse's claims had overlooked the separate experience of Cornwall, its historical relationship with

Wessex, it own constitutional peculiarities, reducing it to a mute and decidedly minor component of the 'Westcountry Wessex' whose signifi- cance was to be remembered on this special occasion.

As it happened, Rowse, in the guise of a *Western Morning News* reporter, was able to attend the Coronation in Westminster Abbey. He felt, however, that he should have been invited on other grounds, as an impor- tant public figure, perhaps, or as a leading historian and man of letters, and that it was somehow degrading to sneak in as a mere 'press-man' (as he put it): 'As usual, in my life, I had to make the grade myself: I was going to have an inside view in the Abbey, but as a press-man'. But, having such a lowly view of jobbing journalists, Rowse had not realized that members of the press might be required to dress up for the occasion, and he arrived wearing only a lounge suit: 'It had not occurred to me that even the press- men would be wearing full evening dress, and that is what we in the transept were supposed to be wearing. . . When I got inside I realised that I was the only person there who was under-dressed.' Somehow he managed to suppress his embarrassment and anger but the experience had shaken him, taking him down a peg or two and reminding him that, for all the Anglocentric pretensions that he had affected, he was not a member of the English Establishment. He remembered his Cornish working-class roots, and even his Labour affiliations: 'At one moment I found myself thinking in *Daily Worker* terms: perhaps, after all, the only one in that large congregation to do'. Here was 'a demonstration of the upper classes in force. What was I doing there? Alone, as always, with no-one to talk to. . . looking on but not belonging.' A mute and decidedly minor component of this collection of grandees, he was pleased after all that he had come in the wrong outfit: 'I was glad I had come in my best dark suit and not rigged myself up like the rest'.[48]

But there were other emotions, too, and Rowse was lost in admiration for the young, beautiful Queen, so assured despite her tender years and so full of regal dignity, the whole occasion redolent of continuity in a thou- sand years of English history: 'the most magnificent spectacle in the world, but the spectacle had meaning. . . Elizabeth's coronation, and the Conqueror's, and George IV's and Victoria's'.[49] Indeed, had not the new Queen pledged her life to the service of the Empire and Commonwealth? Was not Churchill back in power as Prime Minister, the post-war Labour government having been undermined (in Rowse's view) by the 'constant weakening of the economic position. . . by the death of their real leader Bevin and by the squabbles and divisions endemic in the party'?[50] In short, was this not the birth of a new Elizabethan Age, could one not hope that the resilience and determination shown by England under Churchill's war-leadership might be perpetuated afresh? Rowse wished that it might be so, but he was not sure. Although he approved grudgingly of much of the social progress achieved by Attlee's government, he feared that the fortunes of the Labour Party in power had smacked too much of the 1930s, while the independence of India already spoke volumes about the shift in England's power and prestige on the world stage.

'A new Elizabethan age?'

Nonetheless, Rowse cheerfully pressed forward with a book that caught the spirit of the moment, *An Elizabethan Garland*, published in 1954.[51] It was part of an upsurge in popular enthusiasm for the idea of a new Elizabethan Age, a feeling that the new Queen—energetic and vivacious— was already adding new colour to a country made drab by rationing and austerity. One of the crack expresses from King's Cross to Edinburgh, for example, had become *The Elizabethan*, while even as Rowse put pen to paper, Elizabeth and her dashing naval husband were in the midst of a brilliantly successful royal tour of Australia. *An Elizabethan Garland* looked back with pride to the days of Elizabeth I—the most glittering in English history in Rowse's estimation—but it also took stock of the present, introducing a comparative aspect that weighed the periods, one against the other. His essays on 'The Coronation of Elizabeth I' and 'Coronations in English History' were straightforward enough: stressing continuity in the English experience, and inviting the reader to make his or her own comparison between recent events and those of long ago. However, the final chapter, 'A New Elizabethan Age?', struck a more complex note. Here was a tougher assessment that struggled to disentangle the romance and emotional appeal that the idea of a new Elizabethan period might have for a war-weary people. Seductively attractive as this vision was, did it go beyond what—given current economic, political and cultural conditions—the England of the 1950s and beyond might reason- ably be expected to achieve?

Rowse understood the will and strength of popular opinion, and sympa- thized with it, though he considered it superficial and not thought through adequately:

> With the accession of a young Queen, at just the same age as that of the first Elizabeth when she came to the throne; at her side, at the head of our affairs, a man [Churchill] who is already in his life- time an historic figure; the wars, we hope, over: what more natural thing than that the people should wonder whether another age may not be opening to us like that which has proved itself unforgettable in the memory of the English peoples? The thought has been presented to many people's minds. It occurred to me at a different moment and with, I hope, more substance—since those adventi-

tious circumstances are but appearances on the surface of society—
at the end of the war.[52]

In other words, it was not merely the coronation of a new Queen, whose
name happened to be Elizabeth, that might rebuild England anew,
refreshing though her accession had been, but rather the ability to sustain
into the period of peace the indomitable spirit that had been cultivated
during the war. There had been no doubt about England then: 'The war
was another heroic age—in the whole history of the English people their
finest hour. Even more so than that of the Elizabethan struggle with
Spain.'[53] This was not to underestimate the Spanish threat, dangerous to
England as it had been, but the Spain of Philip II was after all a civilized
country, integral to the European tradition, whereas Hitler's Germany was
something altogether more alien and sinister. Compared to the
Elizabethan confrontation with Spain,

> [e]ven more depended on the struggle against Nazi Germany. It
> was the hardest struggle we have ever been through, the nearest
> thing in our history. Our very survival depended on it: if we had
> been defeated we should have been destroyed; the Germans would
> have made no mistake about us. Europe would have been subju-
> gated—and remade in the Nazi model. What that model was we
> can see from its consequences, in Belsen and Auschwitz, the mass-
> murders of millions of human beings.[54]

Strong words indeed, and Rowse meant every one of them. He felt,
however, that the English were not yet fully aware of the enormity of what
they had faced, or what they had achieved—'[i]t is difficult for people to
grasp the significance of an experience like that at the moment of passing
through it: they lack imagination'. He himself was well aware of it,
however, and: 'I wondered then if we could not keep going in our lives
something of the inspiration of those years and dedicate ourselves to
achieving something worthy of the men who gave everything that the
nation might live'.[55] This, then, was Rowse's aspiration for the future, his
hope for England's destiny. But it was a tall order: 'The question is: can
there be a New Elizabethan Age for us?'.[56] From the evidence of the war,
and Churchill's leadership—to which he devoted a short chapter in *An
Elizabethan Garland*—the answer was 'yes', but elsewhere the portents
were not so favourable. To Labour's disarray and the first signs of retreat
from Empire, was added continuing economic difficulty. This was in
marked contrast to the first Elizabeth's reign, he argued, when there was
a period of sustained growth and an expansion of wealth, a time when the
great palaces and country houses, together with 'most of the English

villages from Cornwall to Northumberland', were rebuilt. The Reformation had 'toughened and braced up the country; it greatly stimulated its wealth and energies', and the Renaissance had led to an in-pouring of 'all the accumulated knowledge and experience of Greece and Rome, France, Italy and Spain', prompting an era of great scientific, artistic and literary flowering, not least the incomparable writings of Shakespeare with which Rowse was increasingly absorbed.[57]

In contrast, he thought, in 1950s England there were few indicators of such spirit and excitement. The whole 'intellectual temper and tone of the age' was 'definitely adverse', he complained, 'with far too much criticism of every kind' in every field of endeavour: in literature, art and music, but especially the 'carping, denigrating criticism in politics—particularly from the Left intellectuals—of the country's past, its whole record, its institutions, the British Empire, our rule in India, whatever comes to hand'.[58] To this was added 'far too much self-consciousness, too great a self-awareness, too much sophistication',[59] all of which was bad for the 'intuitive' processes of real creative activity. There was also a sense that social reform, even if it had not yet gone too far, had thrown out too many babes with the bathwater, and had yet to deliver what its adherents had hoped for, 'caught as we are in the discomforts of the transition to a new social order, experiencing so far the positive losses of the old rather than the promised delights of the new'.[60] Too great an emphasis on equality had in any case a deadening effect on art and enterprise, he added, especially when it was enforced, as in Soviet Russia with its 'castrated social conformism'. Indeed, '[h]ow could anyone derive any inspiration from anything without standards, without sense of quality, without pride of ancestry or hope of posterity?'.[61]

The Victorians, by contrast, were in spirit far closer to the Age of Elizabeth I, with their energy, confidence and vision, and their very tangible achievements at home and across the globe. And yet, despite this unpromising litany, all was by no means lost for contemporary England, Rowse thought, and there was still time to rekindle and perpetuate the wartime ethos. In particular, the arts and sciences were still far more productive than in most other countries, 'because the degeneration attendant upon mass-civilisation has gone less far here than elsewhere', and '[t]hat leads me to a more hopeful reflection: the wind of inspiration blows where it lists; human genius is unquenchable; civilisation itself is a tough plant—it springs up anywhere, like stinging nettles among the ruins'. It was, he said, like 'willow-herb flowering inextinguishably on the bombed-sites of London'.[62] It was in this metaphor, so apt for the image of an England rising phoenix-like from the ashes of the Blitz, that Rowse placed his hopes for the future, willing England to meet his expectations and daring her not to let him down.

But, privately, Rowse was already pessimistic about the future. As ever, he generalized from personal experiences, his triumphant sense of being proved 'right' about the Germans and Appeasement, of standing together with Churchill, already fading as he struggled with the difficulties of post-war life. Churchill himself was now well past his prime, suddenly appearing the elderly man that he was, though he and Rowse consulted each other on their books, Rowse on the *Churchills* saga, Churchill on his *History of the English-Speaking Peoples*. Churchill had suffered a stroke in June 1953, a fact which was kept secret from the public at the time. His Prime Ministerial load was lightened thereafter but he did not resign from the Premiership until April 1955. When Rowse dined with him in July 1958, he 'was shocked to see how much he had aged. . . unsteady on his feet. . . It was sad to see him: still the centre of attention, the embers of a great fire, all the force gone.' Rowse sat next to him during the meal: 'I made a few attempts to talk, single sentences, so as not to burden him' but, as Rowse admitted to himself, Churchill was 'a bore when he didn't want to speak'.[63] The Churchill of his imagination and of his earlier acquaintance was failing fast; it was unquestionably the end of an era. Rowse felt this keenly, pondering its consequences, and in a curious case of putting the record straight retrospectively, he produced in 1961 his *All Souls and Appeasement*, so that when Churchill was no longer able to remind public opinion that Rowse had *not* been one of the prominent Appeasers of inter-war All Souls, here was an enduring testimony to ensure that no one would be in any doubt.[64]

'You are lucky not to be a Professor'

To the slow demise of Churchill was added Rowse's growing disaffection with Oxford, and with All Souls in particular. Much earlier in his career, in 1926, he had failed to win the History Lectureship at Christ Church, his original college (before All Souls), even though he had been invited to apply for it and was given to understand that he was in with an extremely good chance. Although Rowse later admitted that Christ Church had probably done him a favour in turning him down, allowing him to continue as a free spirit rather than being tied down too rigidly to a tight programme of teaching, this was nonetheless the first of a series of 'rejections' that he was to hold against Oxford. Worse was to come in 1950, and worse still, in 1952, a double rejection that led Rowse to reassess the shape of his academic future in the years ahead.

The Chichele Professorship at Oxford had become vacant in 1950, and with the encouragement of G.M. Trevelyan, the eminent historian whom he emulated and admired, Rowse had applied for it. Trevelyan sent supportive words from Cambridge—'I certainly hope you will obtain the

Chair, and I shall be very glad to be a referee'[65]—but Rowse was pipped at the post by Ernest Jacob, who had once been his tutor. Trevelyan was surprised by Rowse's defeat and offered his commiserations, adding 'Jacob is a good man'.[66] Sir John Neale, the distinguished Tudor historian at University College London, with whom Rowse was also close, was equally surprised and sought to offer an explanation: 'I hope you won't feel too disappointed. They have evidently gone by seniority and felt that Jacob must have a chair.'[67] Moreover, '[y]ou know, you are lucky not to be a Professor, if being one involves (as it usually does) an interminable round of committees on top of teaching. . . [c]ount your blessings!'.[68]

Rowse seized on Neale's perspective, and did count his blessings, repeating time and again how glad he was not to have acquired a professorial chair. But the further rejection, of 1952, cut deeper and was less easy to explain away. By a process of 'buggin's turn', Rowse had become Sub-Warden of All Souls, normally a lightly-loaded and routine affair, but when the Warden fell ill, Rowse found himself taking on almost all of his onerous duties. In 1951 the Warden died and Rowse, still Sub-Warden, presided over the election for the successor. Urged by friends to stand himself, Rowse refused to do so, only to find that the newly elected Warden was also made unfit for office by illness. Encouraged once again to put his name forward, Rowse relented and did so, but in the ensuing contest he was defeated by John Sparrow. Rowse felt betrayed by his colleagues, and although in later years he would try to make light of it all—'it was an almighty deliverance. I did not want to spend my life on committees deciding who should cook, or cook up, what'[69]—at the time he was hurt deeply by what he called the 'Stop Rowse!'[70] campaign. For months he brooded on it, his diary recording periods of self-reflection and outbursts of anger and dented pride. In Easter 1954, for example, he ranted:

> So the jealous and the hostile, stupid, unsympathetic family, unde-
> pendable or false friends, active enemies or the merely
> uncooperative—they can just now Fuck off! Cornwall, Oxford, All
> Souls—they have all done their best to hold me back. Now, well-
> off, independent, celebrated, fulfilled in my work, with my pleasant
> rooms in college for home, Trenarren to retreat to, the best houses
> in England open to me—they can all go to hell![71]

To all this was added what Rowse took to be the failing of England itself. For despite the cautious optimism of *An Elizabethan Garland*, England had soon proved unable to perpetuate the heroic spirit of the war years, thus confirming Rowse's worst fears. Without a leader of the stature of Churchill, she proved unable to assert her position on the world stage or to tackle problems at home. From this perspective, Rowse was glad not to have presided over All Souls in the 1950s and 1960s, in his estimation a time of accelerated national decline. As he reflected years later: 'I was lucky to miss out on the country's downward plunge after Suez, the age of Harold Wilson and Dick Crossman. . . of rioting students occupying university premises, holding up lectures and examinations'.[72] As early as December 1952, before the collective lift in spirits occasioned by the Coronation, Rowse had expressed his misgivings about the future. He was worried by the growing confrontation between the West and the Soviet bloc, and deeply troubled by domestic problems at home. 'These days I am sick with apprehension at the way things are going in the world', he confided to his diary. Here he was 'in a muddle of proofs, parcels, letters to answer, Christmas cards, books arriving for me to review' but finding himself 'paralysed, as not infrequently these days, these mornings after reading the papers. What is to come of us?'[73]

'What do the idiot working classes think they are up to?'

Increasingly, he felt that the working classes, emancipated by the war and at last accorded their dues through the welfare state, were in the process of 'wrecking what is their own show'.[74] The coal industry, now in the hands of 'the people', had taken on more workers, and so productivity had fallen, while the response of the railways to the gross inefficiencies of national-ization was merely to put up fares again: 'What do the idiot working classes think they are up to? They *think* nothing of course.'[75] This was to be the common theme for all the years ahead. In 1962, for example, Rowse wrote that there was now little prospect of 'Britain achieving any recovery under the burden of the welfare state'. The very word 'England' disappeared gradually from his contemporary vocabulary. Having lost all lustre and romantic appeal, it was now replaced by the more prosaic 'Britain' that (in his view) described more accurately the drabness of modern society. 'We live in perpetual crisis', he complained, 'the country isn't paying its way: the working people aren't playing the game. Their status has improved, but they aren't giving an honest day's work in return.'[76] In 1968, in his diary, there was more of the same: 'gnawed constantly by worry about Britain. . . I wonder if anybody takes the decline of Britain, her ruin, as badly to heart as I do?'[77]

By the 1970s, Rowse had drifted further to the political right, having long since resigned from the Labour Party. His reactionary outbursts in the press were enjoyed enormously by both adherents and detractors, the former admiring him for saying what they thought privately but could not possibly put in print, the latter laughing at his preposterous posturing. In the *Sunday Telegraph Magazine* in August 1977, for example, Rowse asked: 'why is the working class, especially the trade unionists, so daft as to be wrecking its own show?'. Although writing in a Conservative-aligned journal, he wanted to 'make it clear that I write as an old-time Labour man, not as any kind of reactionary'. He admitted that in the 1930s the working people had had a raw deal—some with not enough to eat and many suffering the consequences of appalling insanitary conditions. But now the workers were 300 per cent, or even 400 per cent, better off, he said— and yet they were all shirkers. The grammar schools had been ruined by the comprehensive system, at university 'all they want to do is sociology— which means shouting your mouth off about society', and 'now the chickens are coming home to roost'.[78] Britain was on the edge of bank-ruptcy:

> That is what is happening to this contemptible society blue-printed by the lily-livered liberal illusionists ever since 1945. Nobody likes it, and we can all see that it is breaking apart. Would you like to know what the last words of the great man Ernest Bevin were on the matter? No illusions with him; he knew ordinary people and what they were like, through and through. His last words were: 'The buggers won't work'.[79]

Just as Rowse had turned his back on Cornwall all those years before, so he had now given up on England. It was, however, a complex process. For all the railing against the manifold shortcomings of contemporary Britain, as he saw them, his fondness for the historical England of his imagination—principally, but not exclusively, Elizabethan—remained undiminished. It was expressed in his continued outpouring of books and articles on historical themes, and most especially—as he turned, imper-ceptibly at first, from history back towards his first love, literature—in his devotion to Shakespeare. *William Shakespeare: A Biography* appeared in 1963, the first of more than a dozen major Shakespearian titles that were produced over the next thirty years or so, culminating in his *My View of Shakespeare*, published in 1996, the year before his death.[80] But even here there was 'rejection' and controversy to confirm all his worst suspicions about modern Britain and contemporary society. His 'discovery' of the identity of the Dark Lady of Shakespeare's Sonnets—Emelia Lanier, he insisted—was greeted not by the adulation he expected but rather by the scepticism of the Shakespearean academic establishment. Even C.V Wedgwood doubted him—it ruined their relationship, as we have seen— and those who might have been persuaded by his arguments were put off by a dogmatic style that would admit no uncertainties in the evidence and no alternative interpretations. George Steiner in the *New Yorker* in March 1974 spoke for many when he remarked: 'Dr Rowse obsessively overbids his hand. The more the pity, as his suit is strong.'[81] Rowse, of course, was furious.

'I don't like the modern English'

Retreating ever further into the nostalgia in his head for the 'real England', the England of Shakespeare and Elizabeth, Rowse churned out volumes such as his *Eminent Elizabethans* and *In Shakespeare's Land*. The former, published in 1983, was a modest collection of biographical essays. It included a fond portrait of Bess of Hardwick, one of Rowse's favourite characters from the Elizabethan period. She was 'the most remarkable woman in Elizabethan England. . . a constructive, creative woman on the grand scale',[82] and Rowse wrote with an intimate affection as if he had known her, as though he had been her personal confidant, in his extraordinary imagination living more happily in the sixteenth century than in the demotic twentieth. Subtitled *A Journey Through the Landscape of Elizabethan England*, *In Shakespeare's Land*, was published in 1986 when Rowse was in his eighty-third year. It was an excuse for collaboration with John Hedgecoe, the distinguished photographer, in a profusely illustrated volume that in its contents wandered through southern England, carefully avoiding all traces of urban modernity and allowing Rowse to indulge his passion for places such as Compton Wynyates, the Tudor 'perfection' near Stratford, or Baddesley Clinton, another fine Warwickshire manor house.[83] There were other volumes, too, such as *The Tower of London in the History of the Nation* (1972) and *Oxford in the History of the Nation* (1975), together with his *Heritage of Britain* (1977) and *The Story of Britain* (1979), all abundantly illustrated flights of historical nostalgia, if not actually fancy.[84]

But the reality was that Rowse had already abandoned England. Psychologically and ideologically, he was turning away from the country that had failed to live up to his aspirations and expectations. Physically too, until he became too old to travel, he spent more and more time in the United States of America. His identification with America was at first glance puzzling, for surely the country was all that was now anathema to him—modern, democratic, its culture truly popular. But no, Rowse saw a different America, one whose roots were in his own Elizabethan age, a country that had taken over England's role in the world and had assumed the mantle of the English-speaking peoples when England had forfeited it, forging ahead in every direction at the moment of England's failure. Churchill's mother had also been American, of course, and in America Rowse saw reflections of the Churchillian spirit that had momentarily restored England but continued to inspire the United States, exemplified in figures such as Admiral Nimitz (whom Rowse befriended), hero of the

Pacific war against Japan. America was a great nation, one in which one could take confidence and have pride. And the fact that Americans loved Rowse's books on the Churchills and Shakespeare, reviewing them rapturously in their newspapers and buying them in their thousands, evidenced unreserved embrace rather than the familiar rejections of home.[85]

Rowse had first visited America in 1951, on the eve of the Warden crisis at All Souls, and his warm reception there and his favourable impressions suggested new and more fruitful fields of endeavour: at once he took to 'the native goodness of the American people, their extraordinary kindness, their sheer lovability'.[86] Even in *An Elizabethan Garland*, when he still held out hope for England, there was a sense that England's greatness, if it could be perpetuated, would now only ever be complementary to that of the United States and the other newly emergent English-speaking powers—Australia, Canada, New Zealand—'the fact that this country is the old, fertile hearth of all the English-speaking peoples will become of increasing importance as the younger nations, its progeny, become more important in the world'.[87] There was also the sense that the Americans, like the Cornish, were sufficiently close to the English—but also enough apart—to observe them objectively: 'sufficiently close to know, and enough outside of us to see'.[88]

But that sentiment was voiced in *The English Spirit* in 1944, before the long disappointment with England had set in. By the time that Rowse had come to know America first-hand, he was already developing an alternative perspective. As Englishness lost its allure, so Rowse's identification with it diminished, and in the shifting sands of personal identity there was—notwithstanding the continuing value of a 'West Country' that linked Churchill and Rowse, Cornwall and America—a return to a more assured Cornishness. As he travelled further in America—to Michigan, Wisconsin, California, Montana—so Rowse became more profoundly aware of what he knew already: that the Cornish, in his own time and in the generations before, had made a contribution to the development of the American frontier vastly out of proportion to their numbers, especially in mining.

Here was something to be proud of, to be built upon, and in aligning himself with America, Cornishness was suddenly an asset to be deployed: 'Ambivalence is the line', he wrote in his diary in 1960, 'Cornwall *is* halfway between England and America. I shall secure myself on the side of America, whatever happens in England'.[89] By January 1967 there was no longer any ambivalence, no doubt at all. Sitting, symbolically, in Los Angeles airport, he wrote up his diary. The English were now 'fucking idiots', slackers who lived off the welfare state to which he paid exorbitant taxes: 'I have no sentimental feeling about giving up England. After all, I am a Cornishman; and I don't like the modern English—the soft, easy-going, flaccid, slack, lazy, eleemosynary English, disgrace to their history.'[90] After all the years of estrangement, Rowse was on his way 'home' to Cornwall. But it had been already a long journey, made necessarily via the mining camps of the United States of America.

8

'The Biggest and Most Significant of Cornish Themes'

America and the Great Emigration

When A.L. Rowse first visited America, in 1951, it marked a great turning in his life. He was astonished by what he found there, and, on the eve of his 'rejections' by Oxford and his growing disappointment with England, he experienced a rejuvenating sense of excitement, a rush of adrenalin, as he contemplated what might be achieved in this young, bright, vast country bursting with energy and enthusiasm. Even he could not quite believe it. 'For in most ways I was the last man to appreciate America', he wrote, 'no longer young, set in my ways, liking old countries, cities, cathedrals, churches, houses.' But it was true: '[a]nd it made my fortune'.[1]

Defeated by John Sparrow in the Wardenship election in All Souls in 1952, Rowse wisely sought a rapprochement, and when the Huntington Library in Pasadena, southern California, offered him regular visits as a Research Fellow, the new Warden was pleased to lend his support: 'John made no objection to the ambivalent course I followed: a winter of research and writing in California, spring and autumn at All Souls, summer at home in Cornwall'. Pasadena was the ideal environment: 'The Huntington Library had everything to recommend it. Founded to study the English Renaissance, it had the advantage of both History and English Literature together on the open bookshelves. Just what I wanted.'[2] Although lonely at first ('the old friendly life in College was over; all that was past'),[3] he soon developed a new circle of colleagues and acquaintances: 'Here was a New World to learn, a happy group of new friends, none of the bitter memories of the old. Solitude, concentration on work, I was happy there.'[4] Rowse had settled now for a half-time Fellowship at All Souls, readily agreed to by Sparrow, allowing him the freedom to take full advantage of the opportunities of America. And take full advantage he did, travelling extensively and making contacts with a wide range of universities, colleges

25 En route to New York on board *RMS Queen Elizabeth*. *Courtesy Special Collections, University of Exeter Library.*

26 Having fun in America: Rowse demonstrates the Cornish furry dance in Portland, Oregon. *Courtesy Special Collections, University of Exeter Library.*

27 Having fun in America: Rowse at the Huntington Library Christmas party, 1966. *Courtesy Special Collections, University of Exeter Library.*

and libraries. In the years ahead, further Visiting Professorships, all with generous terms, appeared, and before long Rowse had visited almost every State in the Union—more, as he liked to boast, than had most Americans.

Here, at last, Rowse was able to give full vent to his aspirations and desires, doing exactly what he wanted, when he wanted, and with the resources to make it all happen. He recognized the irony of the situation, as he recorded in his diary in September 1965: 'Because I hate modern society, the welfare state, pop culture and mob-civilization I am going to the home of it all, the pattern modern state'. But, as he was quick to add, he had no responsibility or obligations in the United States, other than to do what he was paid for, and America was overwhelmingly 'an alternative to this deplorable country [England]'. Moreover, 'the Americans seem to want me more than the English do, treat me better, far more generously, with more good will'. And he grew genuinely to love America and the Americans—the sincere hospitality of the people, their friendliness, the open landscapes and wide skies of a vast continent: 'I like the people better over there. More good will, more generous. One can breathe.'[5] He was no sycophant, however, and was prepared, on occasions, to take the Americans to task, on one notable occasion in Philadelphia in 1956 conducting a vigorous argument with a young lawyer on the reasons for America's supposed unpopularity abroad. The Americans, Rowse thought, had an uncritical, almost blind assumption that their way was inherently right and that—for the benefit of the world as a whole—it should be spread across the globe:

> Theirs is a middle-class society. . . the standards are conformist and Puritan, respectability above all else, doing the right thing, being like everybody else. Liberal progressivism imposed on others, who know better, as political wisdom; democratic illusions assumed as truth; everything seen in terms of ethics, moralizing, cant, humbug—ugh, intolerable! For a moment, in arguing with that tough young Philadelphia lawyer, I sympathized with George III: this, I felt, was what the makers of the American Revolution were like.[6]

And yet, Rowse also sympathized with the lawyer, recognizing in him the unswerving determination that gave America the zeal and self-confidence to stand by its principles (even when they were mistaken) and to take the battle to the enemy when other nations might falter or shrink away: 'It is men like the young Philadelphia lawyer who. . . carry on the world's work; and, when conflict comes, they will fight it'.[7] There was a Churchillian spark here that Rowse admired (alas, the embers were already dimmed in England), so that his allegiances became ever more instinctively American. Rowse was increasingly ready to take the side of the United States in any debate or dispute. Moreover, he felt that most English commentators did not really understand or appreciate America. 'Their view is a superficial one', he thought, 'of a country that is really a vast continent: how it holds together in freedom, with free institutions (no Siberia) is the political miracle of our time.' Indeed, he insisted, '[t]hose [English] people who are mean about the United States—usually, though not wholly, on the Left—do not know what they are talking about'.[8] In any case, 'I recognised with the end of the Second World War in 1945, and the loss of Empire, that it was the end of England's great days. Henceforth the leadership of the English-speaking peoples would necessarily pass to the other side of the Atlantic.'[9]

'I am not some old English humbug'

If Rowse enthused about America, then the Americans certainly reciprocated. Alongside the welcome afforded by academic institutions, Rowse's books—especially those on the Churchills and, later, William Shakespeare—sold handsomely. When *The Churchills: The Story of a Family* appeared in 1966, for example, there were rave reviews across America—in the Boston *Morning Globe*, the El Paso *Times*, the Charleston *News and Courier*, and many more, including the prestigious *Wall Street Journal*.[10] As Rowse was happy to admit, it was America that had made him well-off—generous fellowships; fees for lectures, newspaper articles and television appearances; royalties from book sales—and in pursuit of this financial security he was prepared to endure arduous long-distance travel, successions of nights in unfamiliar hotel rooms, the strain of being the constant centre of attention at functions, with the need to make sparkling small-talk with people he did not know. He was grateful for it all, and in one of his 'Poems of America', simply entitled 'Riches', he could muse that:

> The riches of my later life offset
> Many frustrations and resentments earlier;
> Long illness, straightened circumstance,
> Hardly a day outside the parish bounds,
> Walking the road wherever I went,
> Proud, humiliated, but yet unbent,
> No scope, nor variety, rooted in depth
> And narrow intensity. Now I am content
> Within a hotel bedroom in a foreign land,
> My familiar possessions on either hand,
> The old clothes-brush known since childhood,

My faithful slippers accompanying me
Into unfamiliar, unknown territory,
Mettatuxet, Winnepesaukee, Narragansett Bay,
Where the solar geese in V-formation
Fly into the sunset and south for Louisiana.[11]

To financial success was added the recognition and popularity that Rowse felt he had been denied at home. Again, he was grateful, and for all the hard work that it entailed, he enjoyed basking in the American lime-light. As he explained pointedly in the *Sunday Times*, he was now 'a shameless success' in the United States, starring on the *Dick Cavett Show* and the *Johnny Carson Show*, two enormously popular and influential chat programmes, appearances on which were the hallmark of celebrity in America. He took tea with Jackie Onasis, he said, and he corresponded with the likes of Caspar Weinberger and Richard Nixon (in letters to the latter predicting the demise of the Soviet Union at the hands of various internal nationalisms). Television audiences loved his forthright style and his Oxford affectations, especially his 'plummy' accent and old-fashioned manners, for viewers so delightfully redolent of the 'old country', or at least of American estimations of what it might be like. The American edition of *House and Garden*—subtitled 'Creative Living: How the English Do It'—even carried an article by Rowse on the pleasures of book collecting.[12]

But, significantly, Rowse resisted the sobriquet 'English' in the United States, insisting from the first that he was a Cornishman, and—returning to his original stance—that to be Cornish was to be *not* English. 'I am enor-mously popular with the Americans because I tell them the truth', he told the *Sunday Times*, 'I am not some old English humbug'.[13] And yet, he also realized that, despite this evident popularity, by eschewing Englishness he had probably disappointed many of his American fans, some of whom thought him the epitome of the English Oxbridge don. 'I threw away something of my assets by insisting on my Cornishry, discounting anything English',[14] he admitted in his diary in October 1974, reflecting on his sojourns in the States. Helpfully, the *New York Times* tried to eluci-date his position for bemused Americans who, surprised to find that Rowse was after all 'not English', probably had not even heard of the Cornish. 'Above all', the newspaper explained, 'he would like to convince readers that the Cornish are Celts who have little in common with the Anglo-Saxon English.' This was partly because, the report said, Rowse did not care much for post-war England. But more than this, it reflected Rowse's burgeoning interest in the Cornish in the United States itself, where they had made a significant though usually un-sung contribution to the country's history. 'What is the most neglected minority group in

America?', the paper asked, 'Why, the Cornish, of course.'[15]

Rowse, then, having developed a passion for America, had decided that it was his solemn mission to draw the attention of Americans—and of the Cornish themselves—to the role played by Cornish men and women in the foundation and subsequent development of this great country. He began, according to his academic instincts and training, by tracing Cornish involvement in the early colonization of America, beginning with Virginia and then ranging out across New England, a study that was in many respects a natural extension of his existing work on the expansion of Elizabethan England. Some of this research found a home in his *The Elizabethans and America*, published in 1959, and more was to inform the early chapters of his much larger volume, *The Cornish in America*, which appeared a decade later, published on both sides of the Atlantic.[16]

Cousin Jacks

For all its panoramic qualities, both temporal and geographical, however, the bulk of this latter book was focused on the Cornish contribution to the expansion of the American mining frontier in the nineteenth and early twentieth centuries. Here Rowse detected, not the mean-spirited Nonconformist humbugs that he had despised in his youth and the years of his political candidacy, but a race of hardy, adventurous, heroic people—the Cousin Jacks—who had taken their unrivalled mining skills and technical expertise to the very edge of the known world, and had prospered there. Here, at last, were Cornish people whom Rowse could believe in and be proud of, and here too a story as romantic and as grand in conception and scope as any other in the annals of America.

At its most extreme, Rowse's enthusiasm for his new-found subject saw contemporary America, rather than Cornwall itself, as now the real home of Cornishness and Cornish ingenuity, in much the same way that he had imagined the baton of the English-speaking peoples passing from England across the Atlantic. For Cornwall, he thought, this Great Emigration—to America, and to other far-flung destinations across the globe—had been the last gasp of Cornish genius, all else thereafter disappointment and narrow-mindedness, such as he had experienced when a schoolboy and as a young man. But in America, by contrast, the spirit lived on, evidenced in the continuing self-confidence and success of those Cornish-Americans who remembered the old homes of their forebears—sometimes just a generation or two back—and yet were integral in every way to the country that Rowse now so admired. 'The bulk of the Cornish were in America anyway',[17] insisted Rowse, musing on the scale and volume of the emigration and insinuating that those who had remained in Cornwall were but a pale reflection, a sad rump: 'there may well be seven or eight times the number of people of Cornish name and descent there [in America] than there are in Cornwall'.[18]

And on top of this was the tantalizing and rather exciting possibility, perhaps even probability (see Chapter 3), that Rowse's real father might have been Fred May, from Polgooth, a Cousin Jack frontiersman who had settled in Montana in the early years of the twentieth century, thus affording Rowse his own personal connection with an American West that he now claimed as part of his Cornish inheritance: 'I am a Cousin Jack', he wrote, '[t]he rhythm I keep between Cornwall and California—where I mine away in the basement of the Huntington Library for much of my material—is very much the rhythm of the miners, my forebears'.[19] And there was much in California to remind him of Cornwall, to reinforce that sense of symbiotic connection which made him feel at home: even the familiar flora, the 'freshly-leaved crinum with its Annunciation-lily flowers' and 'the deep sea-blue of agapanthus—both serving as a link between Cornwall and California'. Further afield, in the foothills of the Sierra Nevada, were yet more intimate links, 'among the people and the memories', the enduring influence in that region of the emigrant Cornish miners whom Rowse claimed as his kith and kin.[20]

Rowse's legal father, Richard Rowse, had also been overseas for a time as part of this great movement of Cornish people and know-how, not to the United States but to South Africa, another of the enduring destinations of Cousin Jack, and to that extent Rowse had himself been born into the emigration tradition. But his early impressions contrasted strongly with the views he would develop when once he had come to know emigrant destinations first-hand, his experiences as a youngster in Cornwall exposing him to the painful, pathetic dimensions of this extraordinary phenomenon. By the time of his birth in 1903, Johannesburg had already acquired its reputation as 'but a suburb of Cornwall',[21] and, against the background of de-industrialization and dereliction at home, remittances from the Rand were eagerly awaited in mining communities from St Just to Gunnislake, a means of keeping the social fabric together in an otherwise fragmented society and economy. In 1896 the *West Briton* had 'reckoned that every week a sum of money probably from £1,000 to £1,300 is received in Redruth alone, and a like sum at Camborne',[22] and a decade later the *Cornish Post* could still insist that '[w]hen the button is pressed in Africa, the bell rings in Cornwall. . . a change of thought and action in South Africa affects the little western county which has contributed so much of the labour and enterprise to. . . the land of gold and diamonds'.[23] To this dependency culture was added the human tragedy that so often marked the Cornish experience in South Africa, not only the separation of husbands and wives, sons and mothers (to which the Cornish were already long-since inured), together with the all-too-frequent fatal accidents in the notoriously deep and dangerous Transvaal mines, but also the frightening effect of miner's phthisis on the human frame. As A.K. Hamilton Jenkin wrote in 1927, '[t]he name "South Africa" is deep cut in the heart of mining in Cornwall, not so much engraved with an instrument of steel as jagged and ghastly with the malignant quartz that hid the gold and filled the lungs of Cornish pioneers'.[24]

The death of Cheelie

It was against this background that the young Rowse had grown up in Tregonissey, and for him then it cast a melancholy shadow as well as conjuring a certain mystery and romance, a mix of emotions that he captured in *A Cornish Childhood,* and which coloured his view of the Great Emigration until modified years later by his exposure to America. Returned miners, old before their time, were familiar figures in Rowse's early years, men home from South Africa to await an early but lingering, rasping death. 'As a boy I knew several of those men', he wrote, 'and glimpsed, from the outside, something of their lives. They were regular features in the social landscape of Cornwall whom one took for granted, gaunt-visaged men, yellow-faced and with that far-away look in their eyes, while they gasped out their breath.' His own Uncle Tom had 'spent his life abroad in the mines on the Rand, dying there early of phthisis and drink, and is buried in Johannesburg'. There was, Rowse said, writing in 1942, 'something very pathetic and deeply moving in that close connection between our Cornish villages and South Africa', and in the story of 'Cheelie'—another of Rowse's uncles, the youngest of the brothers (the 'cheeld')—there was a poignancy that touched the Rowse family at its heart but also spoke for many others in Cornwall.[25]

Tom had called for Cheelie to join him in South Africa, and for three weeks before his departure he had stayed with Richard and Annie Rowse, brother and sister-in-law, the latter getting his things ready and putting his clothes in order. During those three weeks Cheelie had tinkered incessantly with an old clock that hung above the kitchen table, but which no longer worked:

> One morning about eight o'clock, some months after he had gone away, while mother and father were sitting at breakfast, the clock suddenly struck 'one' out loud. 'That's funny', said my father, 'there must be a mouse in'n'. He got up and looked; there was no mouse there. Three weeks later they got the news that Cheelie had been killed on that day, at about that time. They ever after took it as a 'token', a signal of his death: there are many such stories in Cornish families. When the poor boy was brought up to surface

dying—he was almost cut in two by the crashed skip—he said these last words: 'I've no father nor mother to grieve for me, so it's all right'. I have always taken those words of an unknown Cornish lad as equal to any of the famous last words uttered by the great. He was a brave spirit, Cheelie, and has left a fragrant and beautiful memory in my family and among all who knew him.[26]

As Rowse observed in *A Cornish Childhood*, '[i]t is only now that the strange episode which linked us to South Africa is over that I can realize the full tragedy of their lives, the price they paid'. But there was no point in being sentimental about it, he thought, for there were good times as well as bad, humour alongside the tragedy: 'if it meant aching hearts at home, many separations and much grief, there was also much fun, the enjoyment of camaraderie, the sticking together of the Cornish folk, Cousin Jacks, out there'. There were Cornish Associations to welcome newcomers, to ensure their welfare, '[a]nd at home people knew what was happening in South Africa often rather better than was happening "up the country"'. Newspapers and books were sent home regularly: one of the first papers that Rowse read was the *Cape Times*, and one of the few books in the Rowse household was a collection of views—of Table Mountain, Durban, Johannesburg. There were letters going to and fro, and 'photographs sent back: groups of Cornish miners with their native boys'. Life-long friendships were forged out there—'at Maritzburg or Kimberley you met Camborne or Redruth folk whom you would never have got to know in a lifetime in Cornwall'—and sometimes individuals settled in South Africa for good, sending home for their families to join them.[27]

'Like tales from Bret Harte or films from the Wild West'

But if it was South Africa that predominated in the mind's eye of the young Rowse, then he was also aware of an American connection, of another emigration strand that had taken Cornish folk—including members of his own family—to the mining districts of the United States. Again, there was sadness, a sense of loss, as in 'the pathetic episode told by a cousin in Father's family I met only once'. The cousin had gone out to the copper country of the Great Lakes, and when 'she arrived at the house of our old aunt in Michigan—Father's only sister—she stood outside the window looking into the lamp-lit room'. Suddenly, 'the old woman saw who it was, the tears streamed down her face, overjoyed to see somebody from home after all those years'.[28] Such bitter-sweet tales appealed to the young Rowse, sensitive and imaginative as he was, and as a teenager he had collected similar stories from Tregonissey folk, remarking years later that many of them echoed D.H. Lawrence's fictional short-story—'most authentic of Cornish themes'[29]—in which a Cornish miner returned home a stranger, unrecognised even by his own wife, after many long years in America. One such yarn Rowse had collected from his own mother, a story he regarded as quintessentially Cornish, typifying the tragedy that emigration was apt to visit on Cornish families:

> Mrs Hore must have been a termagant, led her husband a miserable life, and brought him no children. He left her and went to America, but for years sent her a decent living. She saved on it, a good bit of money. Then he stopped sending for several years, and she lost touch with him. One day, somebody returning from America told her where he was, keeping a pub with another woman, by whom he had a family of young children. Mrs Hore drew out her money, sold her things, and went out to him. She went straight to his address, knocked at the door, which, as luck would have it, was opened by him: 'So I've got 'ee now', she said. The husband died of fright on the spot.[30]

As Rowse observed, in a short story one might think this far-fetched. but 'it was in fact authentic',[31] and after all mother had insisted that it was true. But if it seemed too trite, a little beyond belief, there was tangible evidence of such lives all about in Tregonissey to which Rowse could point—like the sad existence of Annie Courtney, his mother's aunt. Her husband had been out in South Africa for years. 'Then one of her daughters followed him, the other two married and went to America; her only boy followed in the bad years of unemployment after the [Great] War.' Annie was left behind. 'She lived on there alone', wrote Rowse, 'fat, dark as a Zulu, proud-spirited, a small property-owner, too—pathetic in the end.' Eventually, her children in America sent for her: 'she went out, and died shortly after'. It was, thought Rowse, '[i]n its way an epitome of a Cornish family's history, very many of them. No one is left in this country: all of them gone abroad, not to return, the home broken up.'[32] The ruins of abandoned copper mines about St Austell seemed to tell a similar tale, yet further evidence of the dereliction and depopulation that had overtaken Cornwall: 'I hung around Wheal Eliza, the last of the mines to be worked, right up to the late 1880s, thinking of the hum of machinery and men, their voices and footsteps where all was silent and desolate now, they and their sons scattered to America, South Africa, Australia.'[33]

Sadness and loss were the prevailing themes, then, as the young Rowse contemplated the impact of emigration upon Cornwall—although he was quick to try to imagine what life must have been like for those on the new mining frontiers, to wonder at the tantalizing prospect of a strange existence so far removed from Tregonissey. In a radio broadcast in October 1940, for example, he had told listening schoolchildren that '[y]ou could not help getting the feeling of adventure if you were brought up as a child in Cornwall'.[34] As he explained:

> In my father's early days, thousands of Cornish miners had emigrated overseas to open up the gold mines of South Africa, Australia, the silver and copper mines of Montana. Pretty rough days those were in the mining camps of Johannesburg and Butte City, and many were the tales that came home to us of the happenings there—more like tales from Bret Harte or films of the Wild West than our own sedate and necessarily sober life—since we were schoolboys at home in Cornwall.[35]

In his *The Use of History*, published in 1946, Rowse had also noted the emigration of Cornish folk 'to work the mines in South Africa, Montana, Michigan, Australia', but it was not until a later edition of the book—composed after his own introduction to America—that he felt able to elaborate. 'In later years', he wrote, 'it has been a poignant experience to follow these Cornish folk overseas to their old mining settlements.' He had visited, he said, 'such places as the Upper Peninsula of Michigan, very characteristic and delightful Mineral Point in Wisconsin, Grass Valley in California and ghost-towns like Jerome in Arizona.'[36] In 1960, he recorded in his journal, he had discovered the Cornish Arms Hotel in New York: 'This is the hotel that so many thousands of Cornish folk used on their way in as immigrants, and hundreds on their way out.' Ironically, he found that the Cornish had been supplanted there by another ethnic group: 'the whole place has gone Italian; they have kept the name, but there is nothing Cornish left, and they even have no knowledge of what it means or refers to.'[37]

Elsewhere the Cornish memory was bright, however, and Rowse was moved by what he discovered on the Upper Peninsula of Michigan, the 'Lakes' copper mining country to which the Cornish (his own aunt amongst them) had emigrated in droves for more than half a century from the 1840s. Here was a Cornish strength of character that impressed him, a stoicism in the face of adversity (including the cruellest of winters, alongside the usual vicissitudes of the mining frontier) that reflected a determination to succeed, a characteristic Cornish stubbornness (as Rowse saw it) that gave them the edge over competing ethnic groups in America. Here there was evidence of a 'Cornish obstinacy' and a 'never give in' attitude, a 'tenacity and getting through situations where others would give up'.[38] At the Pine Grove cemetery at Eagle Harbor, on the Peninsula, there were tangible reminders of these qualities, and of the attendant tragedy of Cornish lives blighted and cut short. There was the grave of 'Thomas R. Job, 1870, aged 24; wife 22: "Weep not for me my wife so dear"', the inscription read. Then there was 'Peter Opie, son of James Opie and Jane Roberts, 1869–85, aged 16. Bessie, their daughter, aged 3'. As he wandered amongst these tombstones, Rowse encountered the graves of '[a]ny number of small children at two and three, and young people in their twenties—those ferocious winters and insanitary conditions, poor folk with their hard-bitten lives'. He recognized the tell-tale Cornish surnames—Rosewarne, Martin, Cocking, Rule, Paull, Sampson, Nicholls, Williams, Barrett, Kellow, Bawden, Richards, Angove, Saunders, Collins, Uren—'[an]d then there was a tough old girl who lived through the whole period, from beginning to its end, dying at a hundred when I was a growing boy: Harriet Uren, 1808–1909'.[39]

And then there were the inevitable mining accidents: 'Sacred to the memory of William Roberts who came to his death while performing his daily labor in the Amalgamated Mine, May 18, 1869, aged 28 years', recorded one memorial stone. Another was to Thomas and John Berryman, both killed in the Central Mine on 29 April 1872. Rowse read the inscription, noting it in his diary: 'They fought the fight'. But among the loss there was a redeeming humour that was also characteristically Cornish, Rowse thought, evidence of people making the best of things and living their lives to the full. 'People in U.P. [Upper Peninsula] have a strong impression of doggedness and vivacity of character', he wrote, '[s]tories of them are legion'. Of these irreverent yet insightful Cousin Jack yarns, with their disarming candour, one gave him particular pleasure, good enough to be saved for posterity in his diary, no doubt raising a chuckle whenever he returned to the entry. According to this story, a Cornish miner was standing on the pavement on Saturday night with a Bible tucked under his arm, when he was met by a colleague. 'Where be 'e goin'?', asked the fellow. 'To Liza's, the town prostitute', came the honest reply. 'But why the Bible?', was the puzzled response. 'If she be so good as they say she be, I might stop over Sunday.'

In such stories Rowse detected an authentic Cornishness, a window into the Cornish experience in those parts, and while in America he also read Newton G. Thomas's 'American-Cornish novel'[40] (as Rowse described it) *The Long Winter Ends*, published in 1941, a semi-autobiographical testament by a Cornish miner who had emigrated from Stoke Climsland to the Upper Peninsula. The book's fictional hero, Jim Holman, had likewise abandoned Cornwall for the Lakes, and in Michigan he demonstrated all the tenacity and adaptability characteristic of the Cornish, grasping to the full the opportunities that had come his way, in the process becoming archetypically American and yet retaining an abiding sense of his own Cornishry. 'The flavour of Cornwall will last in the Peninsula a long w'ile hafter the Cornishman be extinc',[41] considered the fictional Holman, echoing the belief of his creator. Rowse acknowledged that this was so, and thought *The Long Winter Ends* a 'blameless novel', finding it '[a]uthentic enough'.[42] It was an insight, he thought, into the processes of adaptation and, eventually, assimilation that confronted the Cornish in the unforgiving environment of the Upper Peninsula: 'sticking out into Lake Superior', as he told readers of the *Listener*, 'just like little Cornwall into the Atlantic'.[43]

But Michigan was only part of the story, and there were other areas of Cornish concentration to visit, to explore, to get to know:

> the Blue Mounds county of Wisconsin, the mountains of Colorado, the deserts of Utah and Arizona (where my cousin was killed in a mine accident); the wild life of Butte, Montana, which we used to hear about in the village. Best of all is beautiful Grass Valley, a Cornish settlement in the foothills of the Sierra, up above Sacramento in California. A few years ago I was given a fine picnic in the grounds of the famous Empire State [*sic*] goldmine: I've never had a better pasty, made by a third-generation Cornish-woman, nor have I tasted better saffron cake (if you don't like saffron, you are not a proper Cornishman).[44]

'No one has written about the Cornish'

All this Rowse wrote up in *The Cornish in America*, published in 1969, a book of considerable length (some 450 pages) that was the summation of his all his wanderings across the continent in search of the Cousin Jacks, a journey of eclectic research that had ranged from the files of newspapers back in Cornwall to any number of State, county, local and family history collections and publications in America itself.[45] It remained a poignant story, and sometimes a tragic one, such as he had known as a child. But now there was also heroism, triumph and achievement, a success story that offered an alternative perspective—both to Rowse's earlier, rather melancholic experience of the emigration phenomenon at home in Tregonissey, and to the wider sense of Cornish failure that had engulfed Rowse and had influenced him profoundly as social commentator and as a political candidate. For Rowse now, the Great Emigration had become, in the words of John Pearce, the Cornish Methodist historian, 'the crown of Cornish accomplishment',[46] with America its brightest jewel. As Rowse himself put it: 'For a small people the Cornish have been a great emigrating folk. . . the story of the Cornish emigration overseas is the biggest and most significant of Cornish themes.'[47]

Moreover, the Cornish experience overseas, in America and elsewhere, had alerted Rowse to the fact that notions of Cornish ethnicity were not mere affectations, self-indulgent or sentimental flights of fancy designed to give colour to an oft-expressed local patriotism, nor even devices to be deployed by the tourist industry at home to create the *frisson* of 'difference' that enticed the visitor. Rather, Cornish ethnicity was a real force, one that needed to be recognized and understood by historians intent on chronicling the modern world, not least the international mining frontier where Cornish ethnic identity had had an important bearing on behaviour and events. As Rowse explained in his Preface to *The Cornish in America*, '[t]he Cornish have always had a sense of their own distinctiveness. . . but it is only today—perhaps paradoxically, if understandably—that the outside world is becoming aware of it'.[48] At a time of his growing disillusion with England and Englishness, Rowse's renewed conviction of the significance of Cornish ethnicity, and of its role in shaping America, began at last the rehabilitation of Cornwall in his estimation, the happy conjunction of the Cornish as a people and America the place providing a fresh focus for his energies, affections and enthusiasms. Indeed, there was not a moment to be lost in applying this new effort, Rowse thought, for while other ethnic groups in America had had their literary champions, the Cornish had been all too often overlooked:

> Americans are hardly at all aware of the contributions made by Cornish folk to the making of the greatest of modern nations. . . Much has been written of other elements entering into the make-up of America—the Scandinavians, the Dutch, the Italians, the French Huguenots, the Irish, the Jews, the Germans of Pennsylvania. . . but no one has written about the Cornish in general.[49]

Taking up the Cornish mantle with alacrity, Rowse in *The Cornish in America* left no stone unturned in his relentless pursuit of the Cornish, scrutinizing genealogies for hints of Cornish links, scouring documents for give-away Cornish surnames. The Cornish were everywhere, he thought, in all walks of life, in every State, their impact and influence traceable from the earliest days of European settlement through to the present time:

> names like Penhallow, the old New Hampshire family going back to the colonial Chief Justice, the two families of Penrose and Rawle, both famous in the history of Pennsylvania; the Pendarvis family which preceded the Pinckneys in possession of their delectable estate on the river at Charleston in South Carolina. A Pearce, a Penrose, a Vivian in the life of Colorado, a Richard Trevellick or

a John Spargo in the history of the labor movement, a Trelease in the botanical history of Missouri, creator of the famous garden at St Louis, for whom Mount Trelease in Colorado is named, a Tregaskis to the fore in journalism today, a Coon in the academic field of anthropology, a Trebilcock eminent as portrait-painter.[50]

But it was the miners who had left the enduring Cornish impression upon America, Rowse thought, their influence indelible upon:

[s]uch places as the Upper Peninsula of Michigan, the coppery shores of Lake Superior; Mineral Point in the southwestern corner of Wisconsin, lead country to which they came across country from the Great Lakes, or up the Mississippi and Fever rivers; beautiful Grass Valley and Nevada City, neighbouring towns in California; over the Sierra to Virginia City, Nevada, not far from lovely Lake Tahoe; Central City, Colorado, in the mountains not far from Pike's Peak; Butte, Montana, with its lurid reputation, still producing copper, with a cloud of dust hanging over it; or remote Bisbee in Arizona, right down to the Mexican border. (Or across it, for at Pachuca, north of Mexico City, is another Cornish community).[51]

'A marvellous book—something nobody else could have written'

Here were names to conjure with, repeated time and again in essays and lectures as Rowse rehearsed and re-rehearsed his litany of the Cornish overseas, crafting as he did so a renewed, revitalized narrative of the Cornish people, one which allowed him simultaneously the discarding of England, the embrace of America, and the replacement of the Cornwall he had loathed with a re-invented Cornishness with which—enthusiastically and unequivocally—he could claim common cause. To that extent, *The Cornish in America* was as much an ideological project as it was a historiographical one, enabling Rowse to create the personal space in which he might reject England, adopt America, and refashion Cornwall, at the same time pursuing his aim of securing for the Cornish their place in the pantheon of American ethnic groups, illuminating for all to see their distinguished contribution to the creation of the United States. John McManners, in his obituary of Rowse in the *Proceedings of the British Academy* in 1998, thought that the book had been 'breaking new ground',[52] and in many ways it had. Rowse was conscious of the volume's potential as an original contribution to American historiography, as well as its value as a personal statement—the saga by proxy of a latter-day Cornish-American (as Rowse now saw himself). And as well as ensuring its simultaneous publication on both sides of the Atlantic, he had gone to considerable lengths to ensure its 'definitive' qualities.

As Rowse had recognized swiftly, distinctive Cornish surnames were an important indicator of Cornish presence in America, and although, as he readily agreed, most Cornish emigrants had possessed common patronymics such as Williams, Thomas and Richards, there were more than enough indisputably Cornish names (usually of Cornish-language origin) to enable their continental dispersal to be tracked. He had compiled a list of the more exotic surnames he had encountered during his research, submitting examples to Professor Charles Thomas, the Cornish scholar, for comment and possible explanation. Many of them Thomas had not encountered before—'I suppose they do exist',[53] he wrote quizzically— and Rowse recognized that often Cornish surnames had become disguised in America, their spellings and pronunciation 'Americanized' so that, for example, Chenoweth might become 'Chenworth' or 'Chinworth', Uren reformulated as 'U'Ren', and Polmounter mangled as 'Palamountain'.[54] Richard Blewett, the amateur Cornish surname expert, helped with some of the more obscure examples, and G. Pawley White responded to Rowse's call for help by producing a *Handbook of Cornish Surnames*, which, though complemented later by more scientific scholarship, remains in print today as a popular introduction to the subject.[55] The more important surname examples he had gathered, Rowse included in *The Cornish in America* as an Appendix that indicated 'correct' spelling, pronunciation and etymology, a handy guide for those wanting to know more about Cornish surnames but also a useful research tool for those wishing to identify the Cornish in their midst.

To this concern for the minutiae of Cornish surnames was added a wider attention to detail, and in 1967 Rowse had gladly submitted the draft manuscript of *The Cornish in America* to the scrutiny of his old friend F.L. Harris, fellow Cornishman and Oxford graduate, then one of Exeter University's extra-mural tutors in Cornwall. Harris, loyal as ever, attended to his task with diligence, providing nine pages of suggestions and corrections. His conclusion was emphatic: 'It is a marvellous book—something nobody could have written in that way'.[56] Allan Nevins, the prolific American historian, Rowse's colleague at the Huntington Library, thought the same, emphasizing the contribution of the book to comprehending 'a composite nation in which a variety of stocks and peoples will hold equal dignities, repute and influence', adding that 'all lovers of America should understand how rich and varied is its heritage from other lands and peoples'.[57] When the book was actually published, there were similar accolades. A generous review in the *Western Morning News* noted in an insightful aside that Rowse 'has become almost an Anglo-American',[58] so deep now was his sympathy for and affinity with the United States.

Charles Causley, the Cornish poet, now with an enviable international reputation of his own, was likewise 'filled with admiration'. It was, he said, 'an absolutely stunning piece of work'. It was also, Causley saw, a book that would do much to reconcile Rowse to Cornwall, and vice versa:

> Only you, of course, could have written it. . . how you breathe life into the past: it's a matchless gift. Cornwall should now declare a public holiday on the appearance of each new book you now write. As the number one member of your fan club I tell you that *The Cornish in America* is one of your finest books: unforgettable, vast in conception, quite extraordinarily gripping in the telling. To keep such control on the detail of such a story is nothing short of masterly. So I salute you and thank you for another wonderful book.[59]

But not all receptions were so uncritical. Rowse had been disappointed that there were relatively few reviews in the British press, especially the more prestigious imprints, fearing that editors in the UK did not really appreciate the importance of the Cornish as an ethnic group, and when one major piece did appear—in the *Times Literary Supplement*—there was little to cheer him. This was a review by Denis Brogan, a one-time under-graduate contemporary of Rowse's at Oxford, but now in America. Brogan condemned *The Cornish in America* as 'filiopietistic' and sneered at its supposed reliance on 'telephone books and simple works of refer-ence. This is not what I would call serious research.'[60] Rowse was stung. Fretful notes of reassurance came from old friends like F.L. Harris and A.C. Todd (the latter also an Exeter extra-mural tutor in Cornwall), Todd insisting that Brogan's review was 'mean—and also meaningless', a 'futile' display of 'ignorance' and 'anti-Cornish feeling'.[61] In his fury, Rowse turned again to Causley's letter, scrawling across it 'contrast with Brogan', and he wrote directly to Brogan to tell him exactly what he thought. Brogan was unrepentant, replying from Des Moines, Iowa: 'I'm sorry to have caused you distress or anger but the gap between us is unbridgeable. I dislike, for professional reasons, the kind of book you wrote.' Indeed, '[t]he fact that you do it better than most people could do makes it all the more dangerous. I can't see any reason why the Cornish in America should not be studied in a numerate and if you like sociological fashion like other ethnic groups.'[62]

Brogan saw in Rowse's work what Glanmor Williams, the Welsh histo-rian, would later call 'the besetting sin of the historiography of American emigration: excessive praise of the feats of one particular nationality or group'.[63] This was a shortcoming that Bob Reece would dub 'contribu-tion' history. 'We study the different "contributions" of ethnic groups:

Cornishmen, Welsh and Irish', he would write, '[o]ne of the obvious hazards here is that extravagant claims will at times be made for the contribution of one group or another'.[64] This was the 'filiopietistic' dimension that Brogan so abhorred. But he also attacked Rowse on methodological grounds, identifying what he considered superficial research methods and arguing instead for a statistically grounded approach to tackling the Cornish. There was more than a grain of truth in Brogan's criticisms. When evidence ran thin, Rowse did indeed turn to today's telephone books, picking out distinctive Cornish surnames and presenting them as indicators of Cornish influence in this city or that county. Thus in Bethlehem, Pennsylvania, 'seven Trembath families appear in the telephone directory. . . and there are no less than five Pascoe families'.[65] In Philadelphia there were twenty Penrose families, he noted, together with three Pascoe families, three Penberth, three Tregear, three Trenwith, two Trevaskis, two Treherne, two Truscott, two Hender—and so on, right across America. There were also all those local and family histories upon which Rowse relied, perhaps too heavily and at the expense of primary source research, some themselves overtly filiopietistic contributions of doubtful scholarship, the end result a series of anecdotal snap-shots rather than the sustained analysis Brogan preferred.

Rowse thought Brogan's criticism nonsense: 'There is a horrid word in American historiography, "filiopietistic"—I don't know what pedant invented it: it only means loyal, nothing worse, the loyalty of the native son'.[66] And it would be wrong to emphasize shortcomings at the expense of the book's strengths. As Causley saw, *The Cornish in America* was a literary triumph, a work of immense and intricate construction that only the most gifted writer might have attempted successfully. And, as A.C. Todd added, Brogan's refusal to accept the extent of Rowse's claims for the Cornish in America reflected a wider inability among many academics to take the Cornish seriously: 'It's a hard struggle convincing people that the Cornish are quite exceptional in the way they have got around the world'.[67] Moreover, as Rowse noted in a gloss scribbled on Brogan's letter, the Cornish were routinely 'invisible' in American records, generally classed as 'English', and therefore impossible to count. Hence the reliance on local and family histories which, despite the prejudices of professional historians, were in America often of high quality, especially those produced by prestigious county and state historical societies—such as the Nevada County Historical Society, with its impressive local-authority funded library in Nevada City, California. Moreover, the synthesis that Rowse had employed was a legitimate historical form, not the 'sociological' approach favoured by Brogan but one that was academically respectable, similar (for example) to that adopted by the mining historian Roger Burt in his major book *The British Lead Mining Industry*. Here Burt pulled together the 'wide and essentially descriptive literature [that] has emerged. . . principally due to the private publishing initiative of authors and the emergence of new publishing houses', marshalling '[n]umerous monographs and specialist periodicals', and drawing 'heavily on these regional studies, supplemented by original sources to "fill the gaps" and generally elaborate the text'.[68]

This was precisely what Rowse had attempted in America, and if there was sometimes too much anecdotal material at the expense of the analytical, then there were certainly theoretical insights of significance that helped situate *The Cornish in America* as an important contribution to emigration history. For example, Rowse had tried to set his work alongside discussions of early technological transfer from the Old World to the New (noting that the emigration of Cornish miners was matched by a parallel movement of Cornish mining machinery), and he located the Cornish role in the expansion of the Western mining frontier within the general explanations expounded in R.W. Paul's classic *Mining Frontiers of the Far West*, displaying a scholarly knowledge of the existing literature and American historiography.[69] Moreover, Rowse was an early discussant of what Sharron Schwartz and others have called 'the myth of Cousin Jack', the Cornish deployment of ethnic identity to secure socio-economic advantage on the mining frontiers overseas by stressing their 'innate superiority' as hard-rock miners.[70] And, as Rowse recognized, the Cornish could have it both ways—at precisely the same moment that the Cornish asserted their ethnic distinctiveness, so they could also stress their oneness with the norms and expectations of American life. Far from posing a threat to the existing society, the Cornish in their separate identity were also well on the way to becoming model Americans:

> they got on naturally and easily with native Americans [*sic*; Rowse means Euro-Americans]; there was a real affinity of temperament, and the Cornish had no difficulty whatever in fitting into their new environment. They liked it, they were grateful—and frequently expressed it—for the better opportunities their new country gave them, and they were proud to become American citizens. At the same time, it is interesting to note, they never ceased to be loyal to Cornwall. There was no conflict. This stands out in marked contrast with some other groups in the variegated great nation.[71]

'A portrait of the Cornish diaspora'

The Cornish in America spawned a series of both popular and scholarly Cornish emigration studies on both sides of the Atlantic, catching the mood of the moment as people in Cornwall became increasingly interested in the phenomenon, and as Americans—and others elsewhere in the New World—began to look beyond the superficial homogeneity of American (or Canadian, or Australian, or New Zealand) society to discover afresh the diverse ethnic roots of their nations. The great flowering of Cornish Associations in America (and elsewhere) from the 1970s onwards was in part a response to the interest stirred by Rowse's book, and in this and in the sustained scholarly activity that Rowse had provoked, we see the real answer to Brogan and other critics.[72] Rowse himself, buoyed by those who had come to his defence and encouraged by the burgeoning interest in the Great Emigration, retained a life-long interest in the subject, returning to it time and again in lectures and articles—sometimes in the most unlikely of places, as in his 'Saturday Essay' in the *Birmingham Post* in December 1979 where he told the unusual but engaging story of Jim Baragwaneth. Jim, as his name suggested, was a Cornishman (Baragwaneth meant 'wheaten bread', Rowse explained), but in South Africa, where he worked in the mines, his unfamiliar surname went unrecognized by the English and he was apt to be taken for a Boer or similar. As the South African War raged, Jim Baragwaneth was arrested by the British Military Police and, ajudged to be a Dutch spy sympathetic to the Boers, was promptly deported to the Netherlands. Of course, the mistake was eventually discovered and Jim was released and compensated handsomely, allowing him to retire in comfort to Cornwall and 'to acquire for [a]wife the elegant, lady-like ex-housekeeper of an old sea-captain, and her beautiful daughter'.[73]

Rowse continued to collect such stories, hoping to put them to good literary use some day, and after the success of his *A Cornish Anthology* (published in 1968, with precious little emigration material, which he later regretted), he planned a second volume, this time with far more on the Cornish overseas. The book was never published but the contents were researched and marshalled, including a variety of emigration extracts: Wilfred Grenfell in Labrador, William Sleeman in India, Bob Fitzsimmons in America, William Colenso in New Zealand, Richard Trevithick in Peru, and a piece from J.H. Williams's *Elephant Bill*.[74] Rowse had also planned to include an extract from Oswald Pryor's delightful *Australia's Little Cornwall*, published in Adelaide in 1962, selecting one of the many 'Cap'n 'Ancock' yarns about the formidable manager of the Moonta Mine in South Australia, the legendary Henry Richard Hancock. Asked about the provenance of a newly-invented piece of machinery, a Cornish mechanic comments dryly but philosophically on the power relationships within the mine: '"S'like this", the fitter replied. "If 'ee works, 'tiz Captain 'Ancock's—but if 'ee doan't work, 'ees mine"'.[75] Rowse recognized the authentic Cornish voice in Pryor's writing, and he had already, in 1950, written to him to express his admiration for the manner in which

Pryor, in prose and in his inimitable cartoons, had captured the elusive quality of Cornish humour: 'It is extraordinary how true to type your Cornish characters are'.[76] This was an opinion shared by Rowse's friend, Claude Berry, who was also prompted to write to Pryor. 'It is extraordinarily refreshing and comforting, you know', said Berry, 'for us stay-at-home Cornish folk to realise that thousands of miles across the ocean there are Cornish communities who share to the full our love of Cornwall and Cornish traditions and the Cornish humour.'[77]

Oswald Pryor had introduced Rowse to the possibilities of the Cornish in Australia but when Rowse again ventured to write a major book on the Great Emigration he turned to South Africa and to New Zealand, in the evening of his life (in 1989) producing his *Controversial Colensos*, a sympathetic treatment of two emigrant cousins—John William Colenso (from St Austell) and William Colenso. The former, John William, arrived in Natal in 1855 to become the colony's Anglican Bishop, while William went to New Zealand as a missionary. Both, in their separate ways, were indeed controversial figures, and this no doubt was the root of their appeal to Rowse. The Bishop courted controversy from the start, emerging as a tireless champion of Black rights, and in his published work on Biblical criticism managing to enrage evangelical fundamentalists and Anglican conservatives alike. The missionary courted a Maori woman, with whom he had a child, a situation calculated to arouse Rowse's interest, and became a noted botanist, sending home from New Zealand hundreds of plants and seeds for Kew and Cornwall's burgeoning semi-tropical gardens. William Colenso also compiled a dictionary of the Maori language, just as his cousin had done for Zulu, for Rowse an intriguing activity worthy of commendation.[78]

Rowse recognized that he alone could not do justice to so vast a topic as the Great Emigration, and from the beginning encouraged others to become active in the field, positively cajoling friends and colleagues who might be persuaded to take an interest in the subject. In *The Cornish in America*, Rowse had noted that the Cornish 'mark is strong upon South Africa and Australia (particularly South Australia), and is observable in Canada and New Zealand', expressing the hope that 'others may follow me with volumes on the Cornish in Australia, New Zealand, South Africa, Canada, and then we shall have a fairly complete portrait of the Cornish diaspora'.[79] Foremost amongst those so encouraged was A.C. Todd, 'Toddy' to his friends, who had in fact pipped Rowse to the post with his *The Cornish Miner in America*, published in 1967.[80] In other circumstances, Rowse might have been piqued but on this occasion he did not mind. He had been introduced to Todd by their mutual friend, F.L. Harris, and had encouraged his research on the American mining frontier, considering Todd's prospective book to be more modest (and more specialist) than his own panoramic project, confined as it was to one occupational group, a discrete collection of geographical localities, and a period of little more than a hundred years. Moreover, Rowse suggested that Todd should next turn his attention to Mexico, a natural extension of his work on the United States, and thereafter to South Africa and Australia.

Relieved that he was considered accomplice not competitor, in early 1968 Todd wrote to Rowse to say that *The Cornish Miner in America* was now in the bookshops, adding that 'you have encouraged me enormously'[81] and outlining plans for Mexico. Rowse was delighted, both by the way in which Todd had found himself in print so expeditiously (Rowse had no time for researchers who could not deliver) and with the seriousness with which Todd had responded to the Mexico suggestion. Promptly, Rowse offered to underwrite the Mexico project. By return, Todd wrote to thank Rowse for 'your generous gesture and offer of financial help for my excursion into Mexico in search of the Cornish there',[82] and the project was born. It would be almost a decade, however, before Todd's subsequent research would see the light of day as *The Search For Silver: Cornish Miners in Mexico 1825–1948*. More costly than he had expected, research was delayed by financial constraints, and again Rowse intervened with timely support, Todd writing from Tuscon, Arizona, in March 1969 to express his thanks: 'I was most grateful to receive your cheque for $500 this morning and I hasten to acknowledge your overwhelming generosity. . . It will allow the work to proceed without hindrance and worry.'[83] Later, when the book was published finally, Todd in his Preface placed on public record his indebtedness to Rowse's unstinting support: 'I doubt whether this study would have been completed but for the splendid encouragement and advice given to me by Dr A.L. Rowse, who came to my rescue with substantial financial aid when my own private funds had almost disappeared.'[84]

Finding a publisher also caused delays. Initially, D. Bradford Barton, based in Cornwall, had taken the book on, with Todd writing to Rowse in June 1972 to say that he expected proofs within the next four weeks.[85] Two years later and the book had not progressed beyond typesetting—but there was worse news to come, because the publishers had decided after all not to proceed with the title, while the printers were going out of business, with the prospect of the typesetting being destroyed.[86] Rowse suggested Anthony Adams as an alternative publisher, and also thought Todd might approach the newly-created Institute of Cornish Studies—a collaborative venture between the University of Exeter and Cornwall County Council, whose foundation Rowse had endorsed enthusiastically—for financial support.[87] Neither alternative proved viable, however, and it was not until 1977 that *The Search For Silver* was published, by Lodenek Press of Padstow. Todd had kept Rowse informed of developments:

After the failure of Barton and Anthony Adams to publish *Cornish
Silver Miners in Mexico* [*sic*], and after another year of hawking it
around, I have at last found a publisher in Cornwall who will take
it on. I think you may know him, Donald Rawe of Padstow. And
I am glad that it is to be in Cornish hands, for most of the bigger
houses, while praising the research etc etc, did not have faith in a
public demand for a topic about a region so geographically remote
as Cornwall.[88]

Rowse, however, had no such reservations, and had also hoped that
Todd might tackle the Cornish in Australia. His appetite whetted by
Oswald Pryor, Rowse had earlier corresponded with others of Cornish
descent in Australia, trying to find someone to adopt such a project. One
correspondent was Judith Wright (McKinney), the noted Australian poet,
who admitted a slight Cornish inheritance ('my grandfather Albert, who
had curly black hair and dark brown eyes, always claimed he had them
from the Cornish in him') and who, writing from her home in Queensland,
agreed that the Cornish in Australia would be a fine subject for someone.
'Yes, there are plenty of Cornishmen and men of Cornish descent in
Australia', she wrote, 'no doubt you know of the Moonta copper mine
settlement in South Australia, for instance, and Oswald Pryor's cartoons
of life there.' She was also aware of 'the Dangar family [who] were very
early pioneers of New England, in N.S.W., where they still live. And of
course there was Bligh of the *Bounty*, very early on!'[89] But for all her enthusiasm, it was not a task that Wright wished to attempt, and Rowse turned
next to Professor Geoffrey Bolton, a distinguished Australian historian
who had become familiar with the Cornish in his own work on the Western
Australian goldfields in the 1890s. But Bolton was lukewarm, and in
December 1970 Todd wrote to tell Rowse that *he* would be happy to rise
to the challenge: 'It is almost two years now since you told me that
Geoffrey Bolton was going ahead with Australia and New Zealand. If
he has abdicated, I would like to stake out a claim for the Pacific area of
migration.'[90]

However, the delays with the Mexico project had meant that Todd had
not progressed as swiftly as he had hoped, while a spell in the early 1970s
at the University of Witwatersrand had diverted his research attention to
Lewis Michell, producing a biography (as yet unpublished) of this nineteenth-century Cornish entrepreneur in South Africa. In March 1974
Todd wrote to reassure a now impatient Rowse that '[a]s soon as Michell
is finished, I'll begin with the Australian side of the story'.[91] But he was
palpably relieved when others ventured into the field instead, writing to
Rowse in June 1977: 'it is grand to hear that you have two historians tackling Australia—is one of them young Philip Payton?'.[92] It was. The other

was John Tregenza, an academic at Adelaide University, who had recently journeyed to Cornwall, meeting Rowse and collecting a number of important Cornish emigrant letters which he deposited in the State Archives in Adelaide.[93] Todd, meanwhile, had seen his Mexico project come at last to fruition, and to Rowse's evident pleasure produced a further volume on the Cornish overseas, in 1986 publishing *Ever Westwards the Land*, the tale of a Cornish family on the Oregon Trail and the Pacific North West in 1842–52.[94]

'I am a very patriotic Cornishman'

A.C. Todd was not Cornish—though he claimed a Celtic affinity through Scottish roots—but years in West Cornwall as Exeter's resident tutor, together with extended immersion in Cornish research (he was also the biographer of Davies Gilbert, the Cornish nineteenth-century technocrat), had given him a keen insight into things Cornish, a deep feeling for the Cornish people and their identity. As much as any Cornish man or woman, he understood the powerful bitter-sweet emotions unleashed by Cornwall's extraordinary experience of emigration, sharing the Cornish pride in their achievement but also lamenting their loss, and intellectually he was close to Rowse in their mutual enthusiasm for the subject. When he was in Mexico, seeking out the places the Cornish had settled and meeting their descendants, Todd felt as Rowse had done when he had visited places such as Grass Valley and Butte, Montana, experiencing his own Cornish reaction to what he had found, the same poignancy and humility. He wrote to Rowse:

> I understand what you mean when you say that you are writing about your own people. On Christmas Day we visited the Cornish cemetery at Real del Monte, 10,000' up in the mountains and ringed by pines. An old Mexican woman tends the grass. She took us into a clean but inadequate cottage—no light, no water. On the walls were photographs of her ancestors and, in striking contrast, propped up in a corner the iron cross of a Cornish miner that she had brought out of the cemetery—why? I don't know, but I felt that there was some connection between RABLING [the well-known Camborne family, made rich from Mexican silver] and this dear old lady who had no meat to put in her tacos.[95]

No doubt, Todd brought a tear to Rowse's eye. But it was not merely a case of momentary affectation, a passing nostalgia, for Rowse's increasing preoccupation with the Great Emigration had marked a shift in his world view, not only the embrace of America and the rejection of

England, the product of those post-war years, but a rapprochement with Cornwall itself. Quietly, almost imperceptibly, Cornwall had been rehabilitated in Rowse's estimation, no longer the despised paralytic society of his childhood and youth, but now the focus of international triumph—of Cousin Jacks, the skilled, mobile, tenacious people who had taken their unrivalled talents to the four corners of the globe. In expressing his enthusiasm for the Great Emigration, Rowse had rekindled his Cornish patriotism, finding a people to be proud of, and had rediscovered a sense of Cornish duty that had eluded him ever since he had resigned his parliamentary candidature in 1942. In an interview with Sydney Cauveren, his bibliographer, in 1993, Rowse explained how he thought it now his patriotic duty to encourage others to follow his example in the study of Cornish emigration. 'I am a very patriotic Cornishman', he insisted, unequivocal in this return to his allegiance, and he thought other Cornish scholars should be likewise motivated in their work: 'I've got a friend of mine whom I've encouraged to write several books about the Cornish in Australia. Because it's very remarkable—the Cornish contribution. You know, there's a Cornish area in South Australia where the Cornish miners went.'[96]

Oddly, all this presented Rowse with a difficult choice. As the *Western Morning News* had observed, Rowse had become to all intents and purposes Anglo-American, and in 1968, under investigation by the Inland Revenue and complaining loudly about the levels of British taxation, Rowse had contemplated applying for American nationality, writing to the United States Embassy to ask about procedures. As he recorded grandly in his diary, '[t]his summer. . . I have tried the first steps to becoming an American citizen'. However, despite the seriousness of this move, he sensed that it was already 'too late', though 'I have the fiercest objection to having my hard-earned earnings confiscated for the benefit of slackers and strikers. What I have built up here at Trenarren is very beautiful, but I get little enjoyment out of it—everything has been made too difficult.' At the very least, he determined, he would alter his will—'I don't want this filthy country to get anything'—making sure that his personal effects would go to American institutions: 'I don't any longer want any of my pictures to go either to the Ashmolean or the Museum in Truro. I would *rather* that the U.S. got what I have.'[97]

In the end, however, Rowse relented. He abandoned the pursuit of American citizenship and, enlivened by the sense of Cornish resurgence in the late 1960s, evident in the emerging profile of Mebyon Kernow, the Cornish nationalist movement, he flirted with the idea of Cornwall becoming a semi-independent tax haven—something like the Isle of Man or the Channels Islands. In a self-governing statelet, he imagined, he could enjoy the fruits of his labour and rest confident in the knowledge that

Cornwall at least had escaped the worst of what he now despised in England. Rowse was coming home to Cornwall, both literally and metaphorically, but in deciding against America it was, paradoxically, his experiences in that country that had convinced him of the worth of Cornwall and the Cornish, reminding him where his duty lay.

9

'I Have Been "In Love" with Cornwall All My Life'

Reclaiming the Cornish Past and Future

In the spring of 1960, unexpectedly, Rowse broke free briefly from the punishing regime that he had set himself, with his continual travelling to and fro between Britain and America, governed by the seasons and the terms, and made his way down to Trenarren, his home in Cornwall. It was to be an astonishing revelation that he never forgot, a turning point, a prelude to the years ahead as, little by little, he sought to reconcile himself to his native land. He began to realize what he had been missing.

Here at Trenarren, in glorious May, an overwhelming sense of nostalgia was combined with wonderment at an exoticism that he had not before experienced. Here was exposure to a Cornwall that was suddenly familiar from the long-ago, set alongside scenes, sights and smells that seemed not of this land but distinctly Iberian in their sunny, pungent, multi-coloured brilliance:

> Here I am at home in Cornwall in May for the first time for many years. Not since my boyhood days, not since I left home for Oxford in 1922, have I seen Cornwall in May time. It has been worth coming all the way down for. . . Entering Cornwall by the bridge over the Tamar at Launceston and crossing Bodmin Moor, I was excited to see the snowballs of may along the hedges, the sprays weighed down with blossom. . . White may running all along Cornish hedges—something I had forgotten; and from my bedroom window I see the white hedges running out to sea. I had never seen the ordinary purple ponticum in bloom at Trenarren; looking up from the lawn, one sees the grey stone of the house flanked by purple splendour, the mounded rhododendrons on either side. It reminded me of Portugal; I have kept going out to see the spectacle, up in the field on Sunday evening to look at the

purple masses enclosing the house on the west, and through the beeches the blue of the bay. I had never seen the gold of broom in flower, the laburnum out or the rare tall shrub that has a flower like orange-blossom (drymis winteri), or the syringa the scent of which now fills the hall on entering.[1]

It was less than a decade earlier, in 1953, two years after his first visit to America, and just months before his mother's death, that Rowse had at last realized his childhood dream—the acquisition of Trenarren. Hitherto the house had represented the unobtainable in his life, symbolic of a Cornwall far removed from the working-class existence in austere Tregonissey. But now that it was in his grasp, there was, in his fiftieth year, a long overdue sense of achievement, of fulfilment almost, or at least self-satisfied reflection. The possession of Trenarren was a metaphor for the literary and financial success that he now enjoyed, the first inkling of a 'coming home' in which—released from his mother's grip, removed from the politics of the 1930s, and now so well-off that he could happily ignore detractors and critics—he might begin a rapprochement with Cornwall.

However, as we have seen, it was not to be an easy process, the tortuous road to his rekindled enthusiasm for Cornwall and the Cornish being by way of America and the 'Great Emigration', culminating in 1969 in *The Cornish in America*. He was by then increasingly appalled by what he saw as the degenerate state of England, but psychologically, with a little help from America, he was correspondingly able to separate his estimation of 'Cornwall' from that of 'England'. Significantly, the 'Cornwall' of the mind that he was now busily creating for himself was not of the present, integral to all of England's ills, but one that existed in the past and in the future—a 'past' that encompassed the global triumph of the Cousin Jacks and stretched back to his favourite Tudor times and beyond, and a 'future' that hinted at a Cornwall somehow semi-detached from England, a tax haven like the Isle of Man, perhaps, already a semi-independent Celtic nation within these islands. Conveniently, the 1930s, the political career, the Nonconformists, the 'rejections' by Cornwall, and much else could all be consigned to the 'present', unnecessary baggage to be disowned, disparaged and, for the most part, ignored.

'Cornwall is to me a country of the mind'

The Cornish past seemed an obvious refuge for Rowse. Just as he had sought solace in his own mythical construction of Elizabeth I's England— so robust, innovative and courageous when compared to its late twentieth-century namesake—so he had enveloped himself in his Tudor Cornwall, writing a classic book of that title and steeping himself in a

28 The view from Trenarren, out across the Cornish garden to Black Head and the sea beyond. *Courtesy Royal Institution of Cornwall.*

29 Rowse at work in the upstairs study at Trenarren, with Black Head beyond visible through the window. *Courtesy Royal Institution of Cornwall.*

Cornish world that stretched from Richard Grenville's exploits in the *Revenge* to the Stuarts and the heady days of the Civil War. In 1981 Rowse admitted the process: 'Cornwall to me is a country of the mind, a construct of the historical imagination in which I live'.[2]

However, that had not always been the case, and, long before the estrangement from Cornwall that he sought now to reverse, Rowse had held a distinctly opposite view. In the 1920s and 1930s Rowse had drawn a sharp line between the study of the past and the demands of the present. Far from taking refuge in the past, he had insisted then that, while the study of Cornish history was of course a legitimate activity, this did not relieve its practitioners (himself included) of their responsibility for the Cornish present. On the contrary, whilst one might feel a historian's empathy with the days of pre-Reformation, Celtic-Catholic Cornwall, Cornish-speaking as it was, with its own culture of saints and legends, this should not be allowed to become a sentimental yearning for the past. Instead, a reading of the Cornish present (according to his socialist lights) demanded acceptance of that fact that Cornwall had been absorbed by the English state, for better rather than worse, and that, happily, the Cornish language had been supplanted by English.

Although, as his political skills had matured, Rowse had modified this position, courting the cultural nationalism of Tyr ha Tavas and activists such as E.G. Retallack Hooper, he had remained suspicious of the Cornish-Celtic Revivalists throughout the inter-war period, and indeed until at least as late as 1948 when he discovered to his dismay that the Gorsedd was to hold its 'idiotic' bardic ceremony in the field next to his house. He was especially hostile to attempts to revive the Cornish language, opposed to the work of Robert Morton Nance (who had constructed the 'Unified' Cornish of the Revival) and was dismissive of early invitations that he had received to join the Gorsedd.

In 1938, in a talk at Penzance on Tudor Cornwall, Rowse had crossed swords with W.D. Watson, head gardener of the Morrab Gardens and a leading figure of the Revival, who as early as 1926 had insisted that 'a great renewal of Celtic thought and feeling is taking place, and although we Cornish have but relics of our language, and are small in numbers, yet we have our part to play in the movement'.[3] Rowse considered this wrong-headed, and said so, much to Watson's annoyance. 'I am not opposed to scholars studying the language as a special study', said Rowse, 'but it seems to me that no useful purpose is served by endeavouring to make a more popular feature of it. In any case it is hopeless to attempt it, and therefore, it is rather a waste of time.' Moreover, he continued, 'it is very romantic and unrealistic to deny that Cornish people speaking the old language did confine their opportunities', and, warming to his theme, he was adamant that '[t]he learning of the English language redeemed the

Cornish from being cooped up in their Celtic dialect, and enabled them to take part in the whole conversation and thought of the English nation'. Rowse's conclusion, reflecting the conventional (English) academic opinion of the time, was that Cornish was an inferior language compared to English, and that its literature was of no great originality or merit: 'English is one of the most superb of the world's languages—athletic, vigorous, and concrete. It has a magnificent literature. There is hardly any literature to speak of in Cornish, and what there is has been translated, so that we can read the miracle plays.'[4]

In case anyone should be left in any doubt where he stood on the language issue, Rowse spelt out his position in the *Cornish Guardian* in January 1939:

> We have to remember when thinking of the past of Cornwall that we were a Cornish-speaking people right up to half-way on in the 17th century. And I think the fact that we spoke a language different from that of the main bulk of the people of England operated as a drawback. When you consider the total output of the genius of this county, it does not begin to be very remarkable until the period when we ceased to be Cornish-speaking.
>
> And for my own part I am only too grateful that we did begin to speak English. It is a great disadvantage for any community that it should be cut off from the main stream of national life by a language disability.[5]

On the eve of the Second World War, with the Appeasers apparently dominant in British political life and voices like Rowse's unheeded as they warned of Hitler's threat, anything—like Cornish language revival—that to Rowse smacked of fiddling while Rome burnt was liable to attract his criticism. Moreover, when war did break out, then Rowse's passionate devotion to Churchillian Englishness allowed no room for even a whiff of what might be construed as dissent. His attacks on the Revivalists had continued, rather to the exasperation of the *West Briton*, which in an editorial in August 1941 (probably by Claude Berry) agreed that the Cornish language was 'a corpse moribund' and 'beyond preservation', and wondered, therefore, what all the fuss was about. 'Mr A.L. Rowse's vigorous stand against a popular revival seemed vigour misdirected', the paper thought, 'since there will be no popular revival.' There was also a wartime admonition for those Revivalists who persisted with their aims, the *West Briton* insisting that '[t]he Cornish personality has been strong enough to withstand the influence of the summer visitor. . . [and] the mass disseminated culture of the B.B.C. It does not need, therefore, to be bolstered up by a resurrected language, of which even the pronunciation lies in doubt, to foster its patriotism and remind it of Cornwall's long and honourable history.'[6] Here we can detect Berry's influence, a perspective that was rearticulated in 1948 in his book *Cornwall* where he questioned the authenticity of both language revival and the Gorsedd itself.[7] As he admitted shortly after in a letter to Rowse:

> An odd result of the book was a long letter from Morton Nance. I thought what I'd said about the Cornish Gorsedd and the Cornish language would have made him (and others) angry; but instead he wants to make a bard of me in September. I've written the old man tactfully and pushed off the evil day.[8]

'The brimstone in the treacle'

If Morton Nance had not taken offence at the line adopted by Berry and Rowse (in 1953 Rowse and Morton Nance were even corresponding, on the meaning of Cornish place names, such as 'ledra'—a slope[9]), then there were others who did. Edwin Chirgwin, a leading figure in the Gorsedd and a committed Revivalist who wrote poetry in the Cornish language, had already expressed deep misgivings about *A Cornish Childhood* (see Chapter 6), reservations that extended to Rowse's other work and pronouncements. As Rowse had remarked, the medieval Cornish-language miracle plays existed in English translation (such as those by E. Norris in 1859 and Whitley Stokes in 1864 and 1872), making them accessible for the general reader and scholar alike. He had used these in *Tudor Cornwall*, published in 1941, devoting several pages to discussion of the *Ordinalia*, *Gwreans an Bys* (The Creation of the World) and *Beunans Meriasek* (The Life of St Meriasek). But Chirgwin was not impressed. Rowse had even managed to misquote an important Latin stage-direction in one of the plays, he said, and the reliance on out-dated secondary translations seemed careless and lazy when the originals were within Rowse's reach. 'One might well wonder why Cornish manuscripts should remain at the Bodleian', protested Chirgwin, 'if this scholarly Cornishman of 39 summers is to write about them without troubling to turn a page of them.' For Rowse 'a little knowledge of Cornish would have been a useful acquisition', Chirgwin added, but the language was 'another of his anathemas' and so unlikely to command his serious attention. Indeed, Rowse's account of the language in *Tudor Cornwall* would 'grate on many palates. . . anyone who knows the language will taste the brimstone in the treacle'—for had not Rowse written that the demise of Cornish was 'natural. . . inevitable'?[10]

Rowse's hostility to the Revivalists had extended to his bumpy relationship with the Royal Institution of Cornwall, the learned society at the

Museum in Truro, in that period heavily influenced by Revivalist personalities and ideas.[11] When, in the inter-war years, both Charles Henderson
and A.K. Hamilton Jenkin had been invited to join the Institution's
Council, Rowse had been passed over—a 'snub' (as he interpreted it) that
reflected his status as a Labour candidate (or so he thought), similar to
the cold-shoulder that he had received from other 'establishment' groups
in Cornwall. When, years later, and no longer a candidate, he was invited
to join, he took great delight in refusing. And later still, long after he had
made his peace with the Royal Institution, something of the rancour
remained. His apparently good-natured banter with the Museum's
curator, the amusing and much-loved H.L. Douch, concealed sometimes
a lingering bitterness. In April 1973, for example, Douch followed up a
typically lively telephone call with a short letter: 'It was a pleasure to hear
you this morning. Conversation with you is, to say the least, stimulating
in both its content and character. I can see the hackles rising and the wattles
quivering.'[12] Earlier, in 1968, an informal suggestion from Douch that the
Institution's new library be christened the 'Alfred Leslie Rowse Library'
had, characteristically, received short-shrift from Rowse himself.[13]

And yet, despite this suspicion of Revivalist intentions, Rowse's
instincts as an historian ensured at least some common ground. Moreover,
his friendship with Charles Henderson had formed a conduit of sorts with
Henry Jenner, the Father of the Revival and Grand Bard of the Cornish
Gorsedd, whose *A Handbook of the Cornish Language,* published in 1904,
had led the way for the Cornish-Celtic Revival.[14] Henderson and Jenner
shared similar antiquarian interests, and thus it was Jenner the antiquarian
rather than Jenner the language Revivalist who had first attracted Rowse's
interest and respect. As we have seen (in Chapter 4), it was Henderson
who had introduced Rowse to the antiquarian delights of the Cornish
countryside, building upon Rowse's earlier, more limited excursions
about his hinterland at home, to encompass expeditions to the most far-
flung extremities of Cornwall. In this way, Rowse had become an
inveterate church-crawler, like Henderson himself, and a seeker of ancient
Cornish manor houses tucked away down dark lanes in the remotest of
parishes.

His journals are full of notes from such expeditions. There was a visit
in 1929 to St Enoder, the church there with its 'elaborate parapet with
stone panels W.V.S. 1686; 17th century windows carry on Gothic tracery;
tower remodelled with classic moulding'. Especially intriguing was a
'[s]late monument to Tanners, of 1634; I recognise the same rustic hand
as on the Dart slab at Mevagissey; decorative Jacobean dresses, by then
out of fashion'. There was an identical antiquarian eye for detail at St
Gluvias, Penryn: 'skied high up on north wall a William-and-Mary gent
in full-bottomed wig, under a billowing curtain; winged skull and

pineapple, improbable combination: Samuel Enys of Enys, 1697'.[15] Later,
there was a trip to Constantine, to 'Trewardreva, 1701 house still
following Elizabethan pattern, central porch with extending wings. . .
Good broad staircase, dark oak panelling in dining room, plaster ceiling
in front room.'[16] At St Stephen's church, Launceston, there was 'an elaborate classical slab, a rarity in slate: John Bewys 1675'; at Laneast there
were 'medieval bench ends of simpler type', and at Stratton 'a fine plaster
Royal Arms, like Launcells, colouring still remaining'. Occasionally there
were edifices to offend Rowse's eye, such as the sinister nineteenth-
century Gothic-revival Flexbury Park Methodist chapel at Bude:
'appalling design, atrocious taste'. And sometimes there were snippets of
folklore encountered on these travels: 'two German officers landed from
a submarine, made their way to Penzance, dined at the Queen's hotel and
left a note to say so. Returned to sub concealed in remote cove.'[17]

Such expeditions typified the relationship of Henderson and Rowse,
and remained Rowse's habit long after his friend's tragic death. In his 1938
review in the *Spectator* of Henderson's posthumously published *History of
Constantine*, we glimpse the shared enthusiasm that had bound the two
men so closely together:

> visitors to Cornwall must know the parish of Constantine, for you
> pass through it on the way to the Lizard and it lies beautifully placed
> upon the north bank of the Helford River. Part of it is high stony
> moorland; and it was here that stood the great Maen Rock, one of
> the chief sights of Cornwall until it was destroyed in the last
> century. . . The rest of Constantine is good fertile land sloping
> down to those charming places upon the Helford River, Port Navas
> and Gweek. Here stand the old farms, some of the houses still
> containing Elizabethan work; details of gable and finials and
> mullioned windows. . . The chief of them is Merthen where lived
> the Reskymers.[18]

But Rowse had decided long before that he was a historian, not an antiquarian, something different entirely, the former a profession, the latter a
hobby, albeit an honourable one. Nonetheless, it was through Henderson
that Rowse had come to Jenner's attention (though as a schoolboy he had
written to the great man about Cornish place names), and after
Henderson's untimely death in 1933 Jenner had looked to Rowse to carry
on the tradition of Cornish antiquarianism. As Rowse acknowledged, 'I
had my own ideas as to the course I should pursue', but he was flattered
enough to answer the call, and in 1934 'was summoned to his death-bed—
he looked like a Hebrew prophet with his magnificent profile and long
beard—to receive, in a manner, his blessing and the word to carry on the

work, since Charles, on whom it should have rested, was already dead'. Although there was, for Rowse, mild embarrassment at this 'sort of ceremonial laying of the mantle on my shoulders', he was again flattered when in 1941 the Royal Institution of Cornwall (of all bodies) awarded him its Jenner Medal for his *Tudor Cornwall*.[19] But in receiving the honour, bestowed by the Bishop of Truro, the Institution's President, Rowse told the assembled members that although he was all in favour of people working on the history of Cornwall, as Henderson had begun to do on the medieval period and as Mary Coate had done for the Civil War, 'he would not mortgage his future to write that history himself'.[20]

This was in December 1941, approaching the moment of Rowse's crisis, and although he had not yet resigned his parliamentary candidature, his disillusion with Labour and the political process had already passed the point of no return. His resolve, as we know (see Chapter 6), was to turn his back on Cornwall completely, and in so doing he not only revised his opinion about his commitment to the Cornish present (which he now emphatically eschewed) but also had decided that the Cornish past was no longer worthy of his detailed attention. This was shocking news for those Institution members who had gathered loyally to hear his acceptance speech. As the months unfolded, there would be further shocks—the débâcle of his resignation and its unpleasant aftermath, the controversy and bad publicity surrounding *A Cornish Childhood*—but for Rowse there were other pressures, notably the pressure from academic peers to lift his sights from purely Cornish concerns to those of 'national history'. This, in part, explained his comments at the medal ceremony. G.M. Trevelyan, the distinguished historian whom Rowse admired above all others, had welcomed *Tudor Cornwall* but, as he was to explain elsewhere, felt that Rowse should now aspire to greater things—putting mere 'local history' (where novices learned their trade) behind him and focusing instead on 'national' history on the grand scale, the preserve of the accomplished historian.[21]

Decades of transition

This, henceforth, was what Rowse determined to do, at least for the next two decades, as he embraced—as Trevelyan had hoped he would—the national and international dimensions of Elizabethan English history. Suspicious already of Revivalist readings of the Cornish past, and of Revivalist aspirations, and abandoning now the wants of the Cornish present, Rowse was by the early 1940s ready to respond to the (wartime) demands of the academic community—a focus that would in any case complement his commitment to Churchill and to England's cause. Paradoxically, insofar as Cornwall remained in his purview, his activities were of the private, antiquarian sort that he had enjoyed years before with Charles Henderson, exploring distant, sparsely inhabited hamlets along lonely, high-hedged lanes, seeking out architectural gems for his personal enjoyment and hoping all the while to remain anonymous, that no one would recognize him.

The 1950s would see the first major fruits of his embrace of 'national history'—*The England of Elizabeth* was published in 1950, with *The Expansion of Elizabethan England* following in 1955—but this was, for Rowse, a difficult, complex decade. The Coronation in 1953, already a significant year for him, had prompted his fleeting faith in the possibilities of a new Elizabethan Age, one that might perpetuate Churchillian values and restore England's glory, though even at the time he had recognized that the aspiration was probably in vain, notwithstanding his own efforts to cultivate a 'Westcountryman' affinity with his wartime hero. Indeed, thereafter there was only disillusion with England and the English, while even Oxford—in failing to elect him as Warden of All Souls—had let him down. The 1950s, therefore, was an ambivalent decade. Rowse fashioned a contingent existence that saw him divide his time between Oxford, Trenarren and America. Oxford remained the linchpin, the source of scholarly status, while Trenarren was the bolt-hole, with America now the fount of inspiration, money-making and celebrity. It was a balance that Rowse was to maintain for twenty years and more. Finally, he was forced by age and circumstances to choose between the three. He flirted briefly with the idea of becoming an American citizen, of settling permanently in the United States, but decided he was too old to take the plunge. All Souls extended his half-time Fellowship until 1973—by which time he was seventy—but declined to renew it thereafter (another 'rejection'), Rowse retiring in December that year as Fellow Emeritus. It was, of course, to Trenarren that he retired.

By then, enlivened and encouraged by his experiences of the Cornish in America, he had begun his re-engagement with Cornwall. When in 1964 the historic Red Lion hotel in Truro was threatened with demolition to facilitate redevelopment of the city centre, it was Rowse who wrote to the *West Briton* to protest at this wanton assault on Cornwall's heritage: 'All people who love Cornwall and are proud of Truro, all people of any taste or education, will be shocked that such a piece of vandalism should even be considered'.[22] Shortly afterwards, when a runaway lorry had conveniently crashed into the hotel, rendering it structurally unsound and therefore making demolition 'inevitable', Rowse vented his frustration in his diary: 'Everybody said how wonderful that *he* [the lorry driver] wasn't hurt. I said that he was easily replaceable—Samuel Foote's birthplace never.'[23] This was vintage Rowse, outrageous as ever, but there was something new—a rekindling of enthusiasm for Cornwall, or at least for

Cornwall's past. Increasingly, too, he felt it difficult to pull himself away from Trenarren at the end of the summer, noting in his diary in September 1967, as the time came for him to return to All Souls, that 'I am sad. Only a week left—here in the garden where I have worked so hard this summer.' This was a new emotion, he admitted, for '[h]ow I used to love the thought of return to Oxford in earlier years'.[24]

More remarkable still, he had returned to the Cornish language, if not actually to learn it, then at least to understand some of its grammatical structures, in his diary in 1971 carefully demonstrating the conditions in which certain consonants mutated (such as *b* to *v*) in Cornish. Similarly, he was interested now in how the element 'ow' in certain Cornish surnames was apparently a Cornish-language adaptation of the English genitive form. Thus, he said, English 'Higgs' became Cornish 'Higgo'; other examples, he noted, included the common mid-Cornwall surnames Bennetto, Clemo and Varcoe, familiar from his boyhood days.[25] But this was not merely a scholarly interest, for by now Rowse, extraordinarily, was a bard of the Cornish Gorsedd—something that had been utterly unthinkable even a decade before—a convert at last to the Revivalist cause, or at least persuaded of the relevance of the Gorsedd to the future of Cornwall. Flushed with the excitement of his Cornish research in America, and on the eve of the publication of his great book on that theme, he had in 1968 relented in the face of the latest invitation from the Gorsedd to join its ranks, flattered to be asked again and now predisposed to lend his weight in support of its activities.

'We were prepared to find the show absurd'

The Gorsedd ceremony, held on 7 September 1968 in the medieval plen-an-gwarry (playing place) at St Just-in-Penwith—an open air amphitheatre where once the Cornish-language miracle plays were performed—was to prove a rite of passage for Rowse. Not only was it a belated and very public reconciliation, a personal affirmation of Revivalist aspirations (including, as we shall see, some political ones), but also an opportunity for private reflection, even a little recanting. Rowse wrote it all up in his journal, explaining in detail how he had teamed up for the day with the sculptor Barbara Hepworth, also a new initiate, arriving together at St Just to be met, much to his surprise, by the smiling welcome of old friends. This was not to be the alien trial he had feared he might endure but an altogether happier occasion:

> I ran first into John Rowe [the historian] and a few faithfuls who directed me to the new school where we all dressed up in our blue robes. As the place filled up I recognised more and more old

acquaintances. Henry Trefusis I hadn't seen since his days at
Oxford; Hamilton Jenkin, thinner and more than ever like a seagull
waiting to pounce on a bit of garbage. . . nice Charles Woolf, good
man, excellent photographer. . . P.A.S. Pool, who wrote such a
good article about Dr William Borlase—I have been pressing him
to write a full biography.[26]

The ceremony itself was more impressive than he had expected, more
moving, with a *gravitas* that hushed both bards and crowd:

> We were prepared to find the show absurd, but in fact were
> impressed: in forty years the ritual had settled into a familiar
> routine and everybody knew his part, without much
> rehearsal. . . The Grand Bard spoke his Cornish very well. . .
> Barbara and I marched up to the head of the initiates—her pres-
> ence somehow made it respectable (like Charles [Henderson]
> and Q. [Quiller Couch] my feelings were ambivalent). There
> was a large crowd, patient and quiet, considering how little they
> understood of it all. . . and [I] joined in the hymn singing in
> Cornish as best I could.
>
> Beside civic dignitaries from St Just, St Ives and Pz
> [Penzance] were 'four splendid upstanding' American naval
> officers from the battleship *Mount's Bay*. There were Cornish
> from New Brunswick, Australia, New Zealand, and even a little
> boy from Nigeria, who had won a prize.

All this was in contrast to what he had been led to expect, to what he
had imagined the Gorsedd to be like:

> I remembered Charles Henderson's description of the first Gorseth
> in 1928, when the large horn emitted three feeble hoots and the
> audience laughed. Q. was barded at the same time—he swore his
> family not to come within five miles of the ceremony; Foy Q. [his
> daughter] tells me that the Fowey story is that he locked them in
> the cellar.
>
> That was rather our attitude to the Gorseth in the early days—
> as something rather bogus and comic with its insistence on reviving
> a language already dead. I was really an opponent, with my fanat-
> ical concentration on politics; I thought Cornish history and
> archaeology genuine subjects, talking Cornish bogus. So I refused
> to become a bard, when they even offered to put me in a special
> class along with De Valera. Thirty years later, I consented to go in
> along with the rest.

30 A.L. Rowse—*Lef a Gernow: Voice of Cornwall*—and Barbara Hepworth about to be barded at St Just-in-Penwith in 1968. *Courtesy David Wills and the Royal Institution of Cornwall.*

What had happened to account for this change of heart? Candid now in his free-flow confession, Rowse admitted that just as he had been mistaken in what to expect at St Just, so he had come to recognize that the Gorsedd was not the marginal eccentricity he had suspected but was an important contributor to the cultural life of Cornwall. It was a rare admission:

> I was wrong again. In the interval the Gorseth and its bardic organisation had held on, taken root, done good work and spread. All this was largely due to the remarkable work of a man whom I greatly underestimated: Morton Nance. Charles [Henderson] used to laugh at Nance talking Cornish with his family at home, and I belonged to Charles's grouping—my own exemplar and hero was a literary one, Q., whom I hoped to follow.
>
> I had always respected Nance's maritime scholarship—he wrote the standard book on Sailing Ship Models, and advised on the collections at Greenwich. But his enthusiasm for the Cornish language—I drew a line at that!
>
> He was right and I was wrong—and I had no business to be

discouraging. . . Morton Nance did a pile of work on every aspect of Cornish, language, literary remains, folklore, drama, sea-terms, place-names—and it was all scholarly. I gradually came to realise that—but slowly, unhelpfully.

My attitude was a mistaken one, compounded by resentment at the old fogeys of the Royal Institution never making me a member of their Council, when Charles and Hamilton Jenkin were members at 30. When they eventually got round to inviting me— in the 1940s, after I gave up being a Labour candidate. . .—I replied that they were too late by just 12 years. *This* year I have given them £100 a year for 7 years—which, with tax, makes £1090. Nobody else has done.

Remembering again those years, so long ago now, when Charles Henderson was still alive, Rowse thought once more of Henry Jenner and the antiquarian succession that the great man had sketched for his disciples:

Actually, the initiatior of the Cornish Revival was Henry Jenner, and Charles was his *protégé* in antiquities, not the language— Charles had no gift for languages. Morton Nance was another, older, protégé, of Jenner, and a better scholar. Jenner was the venerable patriarch—he looked the part, with his flowing beard; he started things, the contacts with the Welsh and Breton Gorseths, the initiation of the first Cornish Bards in Wales, transplanting the ritual, ceremony, etc.

As he contemplated all this exemplary work, Rowse could not escape a fleeting sense of guilt, and thought for a moment to make good his excuses. He had not been idle, he assured himself, nor neglectful of encouraging others to get to grip with Cornish subjects, despite his erstwhile disdain for the Revivalists:

I have gone on my own way encouraging good work—John Rowe's on the Industrial Revolution, Fred Harris's on Francis Basset, Amos Miller's on Sir Henry Killigrew and now his Sir Richard Grenville of the Civil War. All round U.S. I have tried to get university scholars to take up Samuel Foote, the 2nd Lord Robartes, the 1st Lord Eliot. Then there is my campaign to get scholars to write up the Cornish in Australia, N.Z. and South Africa, so that we have a complete picture of the Cornish Emigration.

Moreover, he assured himself, as a mid-Cornishman, from the St

Austell district, he had been far removed from all that activity down west, and could be forgiven for missing or misunderstanding those agendas formulated in Truro and beyond:

> It has all been the work of those people in West Cornwall—*la Bretagne bretonnante*—who have brought these things together. Naturally enough, they could be forgotten easily: Nance at St Ives, Jenner at Hayle, Hamilton Jenkin at Redruth, Charles Thomas at Camborne, Pool at Penzance, etc. Here in mid-Cornwall one has been out of touch—Charles [Henderson] at Truro was nearer: Truro is really West Cornwall. . . you feel different beyond Truro—anything might happen.

Indeed, so remote was the far west that there was a positive advantage in being isolated there, unlike more urbane St Austell, the disconnect between the normal bounds of civilization and the creative spirit an impetus to scholarly activity:

> Charles's friend, old Tommy Taylor, excellent scholar that he was too: marooned in that wild outlandish parish [he was vicar of St Just-in-Penwith], with the ex-miners stealing his chickens etc and nobody civilised to speak to within miles. So he gave himself up to writing his books: *The Celtic Christianity of Cornwall*, a history of St Michael's Mount, a life of St Samson of Dol. . . then, over the hills, was old Doble at Wendron, with all the work he did on the Cornish Saints, with his scholarly forays into Brittany and Wales.

'I am a Celt: I retreat within myself'

But now, in 1968, there was no use in hiding his regret. Rowse had deliberately shunned the work of the pre-war Revivalists, obsessed as he had been with his Labour candidature. In turning his back on Cornwall after the crisis of his political career and the furore over *A Cornish Childhood*, he had with determination distanced himself from those who might have been his friends, colleagues, collaborators, those in Cornwall with whom he might over the years have spent a great many golden hours convivially exchanging ideas and enthusiasms, and planning for the future: 'What an interesting circle it was that I had been kept out of! But I couldn't have taken on any more lives than I had. If only I hadn't wasted them on politics, creating all those enmities and making myself so ill with misery!'[27]

Oddly enough, despite these regrets at the time spent on politics, Rowse's re-engagement now with Cornwall led to a renewed interest in political activity, for while his new understanding with the Revivalists had confirmed his intellectual location in the Cornish 'past', so it had focused his attention on the possibilities of the Cornish 'future'. His disillusion with England complete, and his perspectives now partly American, he could begin to sympathize with the claims of Cornish nationalism, and indeed those of the other Celtic peoples, as well as taking a more academic interest in the upsurge of sub-state nationalist and regionalist sentiment that was apparent in many Western states by the late 1960s. In 1963 he had reacted with a mixture of amusement and annoyance to a report in the *Irish Independent* newspaper that he had become a *de facto* 'official English historian', objecting strongly to the description 'official'—'anyone who knows me knows that I do not subscribe to any official point of view'— and bridling even more forcefully at the suggestion that he might be 'English': 'As for being English, I have not a drop of English blood in my veins, so far as I know, but am 100 per cent Cornish—much more of a Celt than most Dubliners'.[28]

The Celtic dimension was important to Rowse, including its political implications—'I look with interest towards Dublin as the seat of the only Celtic state'[29]—and in emphasizing his Cornishness he was keen to explain it as part of a wider Celticity. Indeed, as early as 1952 the same *Irish Independent* had warned that 'Mr Rowse, who is a Cornishman, is very proud of his Celtic blood',[30] while Rowse himself had explained that 'I am Celt: I retreat within myself and get on with myself'.[31] Such protestations came thick and fast over the subsequent decades, the *New Statesman* in February 1953 reporting wearily Rowse's speech at a Foyle's literary lunch at the Dorchester in honour of Dylan Thomas. Rowse was a 'much-professed Celt', the journal observed, who 'told us that he was a Cornishman' and who 'sometimes found his Celtic temperament a nuisance'.[32] The *Sunday Times* was similarly brow-beaten, complaining in 1976 of 'Dr Rowse's Celtic blood pressure'.[33] But in his quest to self-ascribe Celtic characteristics—one skin too few, second-sight, feminine intuition and sensitivity, dark moods, bouts of melancholy, and so on— he was also anxious to identify such characteristics in others, especially if these 'un-English' attributes might in those individuals be deemed the source of genius or profound creativity. Thus, for example, as Rowse wrote in the *Kipling Journal* in March 1960, 'Kipling was not essentially an Englishman: he was in the manner of his mind and being—that part from which he created his work—a Celt'.[34]

Rowse detected in Rudyard Kipling some of the ambivalences that he acknowledged in himself. In 1960, as he wrote his Kipling article, Rowse had all but given up on England but the memories of the Churchillian war years had not yet dimmed, and his literary outpourings were alive with the glories of the Elizabethan Age and, increasingly, of William Shakespeare. But he had also become partly American, and in so doing had re-burnished his Cornishness and his Celticity. At the heart of it all, as he increasingly admitted in the 1960s, was the tension between 'Englishness' and 'Cornishness'—and his growing conviction that his uncritical enthusiasm for all things English had been misplaced. Kipling, of course, had been born in India—a son of the British Raj—but, as Rowse explained, he was on his mother's side a Scottish Highlander, while on his father's there was Welsh blood. His wife was also American—with all that that meant to Rowse—and for good measure his uncle by marriage was Sir Edward Burne-Jones, the Pre-Raphaelite painter with a penchant for Celtic-Arthurian themes.

This was a subtle Celtic blend, Rowse thought, which lent Kipling an 'instinctive sympathy' for the Celtic peoples—such as that displayed in his history of the Irish Guards, in which regiment his son had fought and died—and accounted for his sense of humour that was 'like the Irish'. But, for all this Celticity, Kipling was first of all an anglophile, though, unlike Rowse, and notwithstanding his 'recessional' fears, he had luckily not lived to see the full extent of England's fall from grace.

> It is clearly a Celtic trait to be so much in love with the English. . . And Kipling had all the stigmata of the Celtic temperament: an extraordinary gift of intuition, the quick inner sympathy that enabled him to enter the lives of all sorts and conditions of men— he had even the Highland gift of second sight. It was all this that enabled him to penetrate the *inner* experience of India.

There was more. There was 'the prophetic, the *bardic* note' in Kipling's work, and the quality 'I like to think of as especially strong among Celts. . . an intense feeling of place'. Also, 'a good deal of Kipling is rhetorical in expression—not all the English like that', and then there was the quirky personality that sometimes upset the English too. 'Why should we Celts be expected to conform?', Rowse demanded to know, 'We have our own idiosyncrasies. . . The English world would be much duller and less coloured without us.' Like Kipling, Rowse shared in the Celtic person-ality—a 'combination of an extreme sensitiveness with an acutely personal pride'—but he shared too in the fate that had awaited Kipling and any other Celt of genius: 'it was England that conquered and annexed the Celt, as is the way—to become one of its brightest and proudest luminaries'.[35]

'Celts are good haters'

As the post-war years drew on, Rowse reflected increasingly on his own 'annexation'. The division between the 'Englishness' that he had been 'forced' by circumstances to acquire and the innate reality of his 'Celtic' genes emerged more and more as an explanation—for both his triumphs and his failings, and for the ambivalent treatment he had received at the hands of the English. As he mused in 1979: 'By education and intellectually I am English, but by temperament and heredity a complete Celt. My temperament gives me as much trouble with the English as Aneurin Bevan's gave him', he added, 'but then there are things about the English I don't like: their laziness and slackness for one thing.'[36] When John Mander had the temerity to publish a book entitled *Our German Cousins*, Rowse was quick to issue a disclaimer. The Germans might be related to the English but '[t]hey are certainly not cousins of mine. I am one hundred per cent a Cornish Celt.' And Mander should have known better, 'for on his mother's side he is Cornish too'.[37] Gavin Kennedy had also slipped up in his book on Captain Bligh, imagining him to have been born in Plymouth (and therefore England). 'But', Rowse interjected, 'Richard Polwhele the Cornish antiquary, who knew Bligh, says Tinten [St Tudy, Cornwall] on the authority of the Admiral himself.'[38]

And then there was Rowse's poetry and his fiction. Rowse considered himself in the front rank of contemporary poets and as a good writer of short stories, and he thought himself as much a man of letters as he was a historian. But while the English might grudgingly respect his historical skills, they combined to ignore his poetic and other literary accomplish-

31 Rowse amongst his books in his downstairs study at Trenarren.
Courtesy Special Collections, University of Exeter Library.

ments: '[a] mere Celt and accepted as a historian, I am not allowed to write poetry, let alone stories'.[39] It was, however, a mutual antipathy, for 'of the English of today I have less than no admiration, little indeed but contempt'.[40] Darkly, he remembered that 'Celts are good haters'.[41]

As early as 1957, in an article in *London Calling*, the journal of the General Overseas Service, Rowse had spelt out for his readers the difference between being English and being Cornish, and how the distinction remained important today:

> I suppose most people when they think of Cornwall, think of the magnificence of the coast. A Cornishman myself, which is a very different thing from being an Englishman, I think of something else: the very difference of Cornwall, its idiosyncrasy, its individuality so strongly marked that most English people crossing the border into Cornwall have no doubt that they are entering a foreign country.[42]

In elaborating this difference, Rowse drew upon the imagery of the Cornish-Celtic Revivalists, 'of Celtic saints crossing the western seas, leaving holy wells and stone crosses. . . [t]he dedications of the churches'. And then there was the Arthurian tradition: 'the mighty memories of King Arthur, of Tristram [*sic*] and Iseult, which have made such a mark upon the literatures of Europe, all point their fingers to Cornwall, somehow anchored there'. But Cornishness was not lost in some dim and distant Celtic-Arthurian past; it was embodied in the emblematic River Tamar— 'that frontier between the West Saxons and the ancient Cornish that still retains its validity and keeps us separate'.[43]

'Towards self-government for Cornwall'

The Tamar as a bulwark against England was an idea that appealed to Rowse. The fact that the parishes of Werrington and North Petherwin were administered as part of Devon, though lying west of the river, infuriated him, and he was much pleased when in 1966 they were 'restored' to Cornwall:

> Everybody knows that this [the Tamar] is a real frontier: you certainly feel it—if you are capable of feeling anything—when you cross from Devon to Cornwall. Nearly the whole of the way the frontier follows the course of the Tamar. But near Launceston there is a deviation: some nineteen square miles—virtually three [*sic*] parishes—on the Cornish side of the Tamar belong to Devon. Very improperly, as all right-thinking Cornishmen consider: it

maddens me and my Cornish friends as we tramp about there and find ourselves in Devon on the *Cornish* side of the Tamar: it is our Irridenta.[44]

Rowse recalled how, before the war, Cornwall County Council had spent £30,000 (money it could ill afford) trying to wrest this territory from Devon's grasp, only to fail before the House of Lords: 'it is very inconvenient administratively and Devon ought to let go of it'.[45] When, in the mid-1960s, it did, Rowse was already taking an increasing interest in Cornish nationalism—imagining his Cornwall of the 'future'. The preservation and enhancement of the Tamar border, and with it the territorial integrity of Cornwall, was an important part of the emerging nationalist agenda espoused by Mebyon Kernow (MK) and other groups. Local government reform immediately after the war, and again in the 1960s and early 1970s, had threatened to allow the administrative expansion of Plymouth westwards across the Tamar, while the debate surrounding the Crowther-Kilbrandon Commission on devolution in the 1970s acquired a Cornish dimension as Cornish interests determined to make themselves heard.[46]

Mebyon Kernow, formed in 1951, initially as a pressure group, was by now transforming itself into a political party. It had already won seats on local authorities in Cornwall—including the St Day and Lanner seat on Cornwall County Council in 1967—prompting the (Manchester) *Guardian* to muse on the 'growing support in the movement towards self-government for Cornwall. . . there are some signs that Mebyon Kernow could become an organisation to be reckoned with'.[47] MK submitted a lengthy submission to the Crowther-Kilbrandon Commission, emphasising Cornwall's distinctive constitutional history and seeking 'recognition for Kernow [Cornwall] as a member nation of a British federation. The fact that we are a nation should be written into the constitution and the Tamar border guaranteed by statute.'[48] Although, when it did report, the Commission did not recommend a Cornish devolutionary assembly, it did acknowledge the strength of Cornish feeling. It noted widespread concern in Cornwall that 'its traditional boundaries be respected', and, accepting that the institution of the Duchy of Cornwall represented 'a special and enduring relationship between Cornwall and the Crown', argued that '[u]se of the designation [Duchy] on all appropriate occasions would serve to recognise both this special relationship and the territorial integrity of Cornwall'.[49]

Like the *Guardian*, Rowse was prepared to take this upsurge of activity seriously. In earlier years, if only for political expediency, he had sought dialogue with the cultural nationalists of Tyr ha Tavas but, as we have seen, was suspicious of, even hostile to, the wider Cornish-Celtic Revival.

He had, however, developed a soft-spot for John Legonna, one Revivalist with a distinctly political agenda, smiling upon him with a patronizing tolerance as the young half-Cornish/half-Welsh radical nationalist railed against the iniquities of English rule in his two countries. Legonna had also helped Rowse with his political campaigning in the 1930s—having developed a passion for Kathleen Tremewan, a Cornish socialist activist who had encouraged Legonna in his political enthusiasms. He had sought Rowse's opinion on a range of issues—including advice on his academic career—a course of action that had endeared him to his 'mentor', as Rowse had by then become. In the war, Legonna had tried to avoid conscription—his version of the story has him cycling from Land's End to Morwenstow, pursued by the police—and although Rowse did not approve, he was impressed. Later, in a thinly veiled reference to Legonna, Rowse wrote, only slightly tongue-in-cheek, that 'I haven't a drop of English blood myself, but I do not go as far as an inter-war pupil of mine, half-Welsh, half-Cornish. . . [who] wanted to blow up the Saltash Bridge'. This was the time when Saunders Lewis, the Welsh-language militant, 'was trying to blow up the aerodrome on the Lleyn Peninsula' in Wales. But 'the young man [Legonna] married, and that settled his hash'.[50]

In fact, Rowse had been remarkably accommodating of Legonna, grateful no doubt for his help in campaigning but genuinely intrigued, if sometimes rather amused, by the strength of his political belief. Legonna wrote to Rowse at extraordinary length, pouring out his political creed and his views on human nature—some of which bore the mark of Rowse but most of which was a highly individualistic doctrine synthesizing various strands of socialist and nationalist thought. 'I am still a nationalist, Welsh and Cornish, but in a slightly different sense', he wrote, '[m]ore nationalist than ever and yet more aware of the unique foolishness of regarding the common people as a body capable of bettering their own wishes'. Hope for the future, then, depended on understanding the past: 'the sweat, the effort, the failure of past generations of Cornishmen is the present Cornish generation's heritage', he argued, 'and it should be appreciated deep in the heart and should, I believe, be one of the most potent incentives to this generation, and the halo to the next'. A better knowledge of the Cornish past, insisted Legonna, 'should give us the understanding and the grit whereby we become better Cornishmen, more useful-to-Cornwall Cornishmen today'. Moreover, England's hegemony was already waning, and in this lay Cornwall's hope: 'England's might, it is certain to me, will pass calmly back to its small starting point. . . To me Cornwall shall live, because there is worth in her life.' And yet, even as he expressed it, his optimism and confidence faltered: 'To you, maybe, Cornwall no longer exists: perhaps you are right: perhaps, alas, you are right'. And then there were apologies: 'I know that you regard much of my attitude as a type of irrelevant uselessness. Maybe there are good grounds for supposing it to be so.'[51]

Rowse endured—and responded to—Legonna's outpourings with patience and equanimity, a sympathy that went further than passive understanding and bordered sometimes on embrace, or so it seemed. In 1944 (or thereabouts) he had told Legonna that 'I really think in my heart I understand you and what I call your "dream" better than any of them'. Indeed, 'I'm not sure that very deep down, buried underneath all the virtuosity and the talents, the intellectual sophistication and the rest of it, I haven't something of "the dream" too'. Then, in the 1940s, the decade of Rowse's 'rejection', it was a case of 'you and I—against the rest'; and if this 'dream' of Cornwall had any meaning at all for Rowse, it was an angry, introspective one.[52] But twenty years later—in the mid-1960s, with all that had come to pass in his life, and with the new-found credibility of Cornish nationalism—there was suddenly a relevance to John Legonna's meanderings.

In June 1968 Rowse addressed the Royal Institution of Cornwall on the occasion of its 150th anniversary. He observed that 'it was interesting to see the reactions against the nationalists in Cornwall'.[53] But instead of adding his voice to those criticisms and objections, he insisted that to evaluate the nationalist case one had to consider first whether the Cornish were a separate people. For his part, he was clear that they were. He was 'convinced. . . that the Cornish could claim to be an original people from the evidence of their racial stock, Celtic language, history and distinctive place names and surnames'. Besides, '[t]he fundamental answer is that if we think we are a people, then we are'.[54] In 1968 Mebyon Kernow had published *What Cornishmen Can Do*, an important policy document that carefully outlined a plan for the economic future of Cornwall, evidence of a new sophistication that had propelled the movement from its erstwhile preoccupation with Cornish-language serviettes and calendars into the realms of serious political debate. Rowse was impressed. In the December he thought of writing an article on '[w]hy there is this present growth of Cornishness, of Cornish national feeling',[55] and in the following year he explained to one American newspaper that the upsurge of nationalist and regionalist agitation in modern Western states was the function of both the breaking down of the unifying influence of the old governing classes and the effects of what today would be called 'globalization': 'Ah, the cosmopolitan sameness of life. . . It's responsible for the recrudescence of nationalism among the smaller peoples—the rise of Brittany against de Gaulle, the trouble brewing for England in Wales, the revival of the Cornish language in Cornwall.'[56] A decade later and his opinion had hardened:

No wonder there has always been a residual hatred of the English among the Welsh—and, as a pure Cornishman, I am certainly not starry-eyed about the English or very sympathetic about the fate they have called down upon themselves. . . Today they are receiving their comeuppance; the unity of the island, or islands, which was the achievement of the governing class, is caving in with the caving in of that governing class.[57]

'A wonderful opportunity. . . and an important job to do'

In August 1967 Rowse had reviewed Daphne du Maurier's *Vanishing Cornwall*. The book vacillated, he thought, between 'Cornwall as it is and the romantic land of Miss du Maurier's imagination', and although she 'has done her homework', he said, 'the dull historian cannot always see eye to eye with what she has fished up'. However, it was with the general thesis of the book that he really took issue: 'She fears for the future and the possible vanishing of Cornwall as she knows it. An addict of the past myself, I yet question that.'[58] There *was* a future for Cornwall, he insisted, in November 1968 congratulating Mebyon Kernow on the production of its journal *Cornish Nation* and offering encouragement for the party's endeavours: 'There is a wonderful opportunity for *Cornish Nation* and an important job to do'. Earlier, in October 1966, Rowse had been invited by Mebyon Kernow to the unveiling of the plaque at St Keverne commemorating Michael Joseph 'An Gof' ('the Smith'), one of the leaders of the great Cornish rebellion of 1497, a revolt precipitated by the increasing intrusion of the English state in Cornwall's affairs, most especially taxation to finance a war against Scotland. Rowse regretted that he could not attend—he would be in Michigan pursuing his research on the Cornish in America—but 'I shall be with you in spirit', he said, for '[a]ll good Cornishmen must sympathize with the Smith's revolt against taxes imposed by the English!'. Indeed, 'so much of the County's wealth was drained away through centuries by the Duchy for the upkeep of the English crown'. Perhaps, he ventured, 'we need the spirit of the Smith today to raise the standard against predatory over-taxation by the English state. . . If only the Tamar boundary were a real [political] frontier!'[59]

These were themes to which Rowse returned time and again in the years ahead. In his collection of essays *The Little Land of Cornwall*, first published in 1986, he reaffirmed his faith in a vision of Cornwall for the future, a vision in which Cornwall would remain firmly rooted in the reality of its past, obstinately refusing—as Rowse himself had done—to bend in the face of the depredations of the present:

Today appearances are rather against us, with the swamping of Cornishry by the hordes of holiday makers, trippers, immigrants from England. . . But that is just to look at the surface of things. It is the business of the historian and the poet to look beneath the surface. . . . To the historian there is something continuous and permanent in the Cornwall of his knowledge and imagination. A little land of historical fact—as to the poet, of vision and consolation: places alive to the discerning mind in tune with their memories, even when in ruin or vanished in the appalling, over-trampled society we live in. We can turn our backs on that, as I do, withdraw as Celts are supposed to do into ourselves, into the living past which is history, or the lore which is the silted-up life of a people.[60]

Such obstinacy, such recalcitrance would be the saving of Cornwall, as society generally disintegrated: 'A feature of the twentieth century has been the resurgence of the Celtic peoples, now that the unifying influence of the old governing class has broken down: one sees it in Ireland and Gaelic Scotland, Wales and Brittany, even in my own "little land" of Cornwall'.[61] Cornwall as a tax haven was an especially attractive idea. 'I have enough atavistic sympathy with Cornish nationalism to wish that we could loosen our subjection to the mainland sufficiently to enjoy a reasonable system of taxation', he wrote, 'Wouldn't it be nice if Cornwall could stop penal English taxation at the frontier, with a sensible five bob in the pound.' But there would be one drawback: 'I fear we should have to mount machine-guns along the frontier to prevent the hordes of English. . . fleeing from the flaming injustice they put up with, in such numbers as to submerge us'. Put like that it all sounded rather fanciful, he sighed, and he remembered the days when, jokingly, he had assured Princess Marthe Bibesco 'that she would make a splendid *Madame la Presidente de la Republique Cornouaillaise*'.[62] But 'was it all fantasy', he asked himself, was it all so unrealistic an aspiration? The answer lay in an article he had come across by Dr Samuel Johnson, famed eighteenth-century man of letters, in which the case for American independence had been discredited through a *reductio ad absurdum* wherein American claims were ridiculed in a supposed comparison with Cornish aspirations for self-government:

We the delegates of the several towns and parishes of Cornwall hold it necessary to declare the resolutions which we think ourselves entitled to form by the inalienable rights of reasonable beings, and into which we have been compelled by grievances and oppressions. . . . Know then that you are no longer to consider Cornwall as an *English* county, visited by *English* judges, receiving laws from an *English* parliament, *or included in any general taxation of the kingdom,* but as a state distinct and independent, governed by its own institutions, administered by its own magistrates. . . We are the acknowledged descendents of the earliest inhabitants of Britain. . . Of this descent our language is sufficient proof. . . Every Cornishman is a free man. . . Our union with the *English* counties was either compelled by force or settled by compact. . . . From the *Cornish* Congress at Truro.[63]

As Rowse reflected, 'Dr Johnson thought all this was a joke. . . [b]ut in human affairs, historians know, the absurd sometimes becomes real'. Thus:

The Americans turned the joke against the Doctor by winning their independence. An old American fan of mine was in college with De Valera in New York; they all thought his Irish nationalism a joke, but the joke came true. And the funny thing here is that the English Doctor, without meaning to, wrote a very reasonable Declaration of Independence for the Cornish, who share the odd Celtic sense of humour about the English.[64]

In March 1974, when he addressed the 88th Annual Dinner of the London Cornish Association, Rowse had dwelt on such things. The Cornish were 'different emotionally at a deeper level', he explained to his audience, though they (including himself, in his younger days) had been 'brainwashed by the English'. The Cornish were 'not so *nice* as the English—and thank God not so easy-going', he thought, for 'that's going to be the end of the English'. But 'I don't see why we shd [*sic*] go down with them', he added, and he looked forward to a 'Cornwall independent' and a *'Barrier at the Tamar'*.[65] Increasingly determined in these views, he was fiercely critical of all attempts—for whatever purpose—to lump Cornwall and Devon together. In 1979 he published a strongly worded review of Denis Kay-Robinson's recent book *Devon and Cornwall,* a volume that in Rowse's opinion played down the differences between the two and amplified the similarities. 'Devonshire and Cornish folk are distinguishable and recognisably different', Rowse fumed, 'The Cornish descry dominantly English characteristics among Devon folk: they are more placid and easy to get along with, less mercurial and more stolid than Celts, less clannish and not so individualistic and touchy.' And then there was the Cornish language. 'Now we are learning it up again. You see, Mr Kay-Robinson, how different we are from Devon?'[66]

Subsequently, into the 1980s and 1990s, Rowse continued to assert this quasi-nationalist line. He contributed frequently to *An Baner*

Kernewek/Cornish Banner, the journal of the Cornish Nationalist Party (itself a splinter group that had broken away from Mebyon Kernow) with book reviews, historical articles, new poems, and essays on what it was to be Cornish. He was intrigued by attempts to revive Cornwall's old Stannary Parliament and to float a Cornish currency. 'And why not, indeed, our own stamps?'[67] New contacts were made with the Revivalist movement. He was persuaded by his friend Paul Smales to speak on 'Dr Johnson and Cornish Nationalism' at the bi-annual Conference on Cornwall at Perranporth, a symposium for groups and individuals with broadly nationalist leanings. Similarly, in 1989 he allowed himself to be appointed Patron of the Cornish Literary Guild/Cowethas Lyenak Kernewek, an organization with strong Revivalist sympathies led by Cornish language enthusiasts such as Donald Rawe (who had published A.C. Todd's Mexico book in 1977) and the former Grand Bard, Richard G. Jenkin. When the language movement split in the late 1980s into three competing camps, Rowse—taking his cue from his old friend, P.A.S Pool—was appalled at what he saw as a threat to all the good work of Robert Morton Nance. Yet he was also attracted by the 'Modern Cornish' advocated by Richard Gendall, based on the language as it was last spoken traditionally, visiting Gendall's study centre at Menheniot, near Liskeard, and speaking there in his support.

Rowse had also struck up a strong working relationship with Leonard Truran, one-time chairman and secretary of Mebyon Kernow, who in his retirement had become a publisher of note. His Dyllansow Truran imprint reissued a number of Rowse's classics in the late 1980s and early 1990s, including *Tudor Cornwall* and *The Cornish in America*. In his own 'retirement', Rowse reflected, he was now even busier than he had been before, producing a steady stream of books, articles, poems, reviews and lectures. 'Retired?', he asked rhetorically in his diary, 'Actually I am busier than ever. . . in this last phase of my life—too, too busy'.[68] And in among all this hectic activity, there was his renewed on focus on Cornwall. As we have seen, he insisted ever more loudly on his quintessential Cornishness, of Cornwall as the central factor in his existence, and he protested a devotion to his native land that was unequivocal, had never been in any doubt, and was permanent. All the old ambivalence was shrugged off, the bitter hostilities forgotten—as if they had been of no consequence, almost as though they had never happened. 'I can honestly claim', he wrote, without a hint of irony, 'that I have been "in love" with Cornwall all my life.'[69]

10

'Marooned on My Headland'

Retirement, Isolation and Loneliness

James Whetter, in his affectionate memoir of A.L. Rowse, thought that '[i]n many ways. . . his later years may have been his happiest'.[1] These were the years from Rowse's retirement to Trenarren at the end of 1973, through to the 1980s and especially the 1990s, when he was visited regularly by a small group of devoted friends who took him on outings, arranged visits and treats, or simply passed the time of day as the great man lay resting in bed. Perhaps these were his happiest times, and Rowse himself was keen to present his followers with a picture of peaceful contentment in his retirement in his native Cornwall.

In 1978, for example, BBC Radio 4 broadcast 'My Delight', a short piece by Rowse in which envious listeners were invited to share in his Cornish idyll, to imagine the joy of living in an exotic Cornish garden, full of Asiatic and Antipodean rarities, within sight and sound of the Cornish sea in all its moods. '[T]he fresh air down here at my place in Cornwall is wonderful', he told his jaded suburban audience, '[w]hen I put my head out of the window I sniff pure air coming off the sea, but I smell the delicious green scents of the garden, the lawn and the steep banks with a tang of camomile in it, the trees all speaking to each other. . . a touch of eucalyptus, always the aromatic fragrance of pines.' Being 'no good at anything mechanical', he employed a gardener for mowing and for complex tasks, 'but I *love* trundling around with wheelbarrow, spade and rake, fork and hook. I'm just a handyman. . . That means that I like clipping and pruning. . . And, my goodness, doesn't a Cornish garden need it!' Sometimes he worked 'stripped to the waist', he said, 'scratched all up arms and legs, stung by stinging nettles'. But it was worth it:

> You should see the pickle I get into! Pouring with sweat, tangled up in brambles, chased by angry bees, my head bloody but unbowed—I go to bed early, after a blissful day in the garden, completely happy, limbs stiff at my advanced age, heart beating

out of my body, to sleep the sleep of the just, entirely satisfied.[2]

The self-image of a playful, happy, almost frivolous Rowse, impishly having fun, was also conveyed in the various Cornish place-name rhymes he composed in later years, some of which appeared in issues of *An Baner Kernewek/Cornish Banner*, the whole collection published posthumously in 1997. '[W]hen I can't get to sleep I take to making rhymes on Cornish place names', he explained, 'these Place Names give us a rich harvest to learn from or to play with'—especially those 'that are hardly explicable [and] may serve their turn for Cornish Quizzes'.[3] Thus, for example:

> There was sometimes a rumpus
> At Gwennap's Goongumpus.

> The Furry dance makes merrier
> The ancient Hundred of Kerrier.

> What can be said of Constantine?
> —More given to cider than to wine.

> Treviades is pronounced Trevizzes—
> A useful tip for Cornish quizzes.

> The Cornish Institute at Pool
> Is where we need to go to school.[4]

'My cat and I grow old together'

Another work of nostalgia calculated to gladden the suburban heart was Rowse's *Peter: The White Cat of Trenarren*, a biography of 'a little Cornish cat', first published in 1974, and brought out again in 1992 as *A Quartet of Cornish Cats*, including now further stories about his other feline pets.[5] It was a book, according to its promotional blurb, that would 'appeal not only to friends of cats, but to lovers of Cornwall and literature', an 'account of a cat' and 'an evocation of the beautiful place in Cornwall where he lived', as well as 'a revelation of an unknown side to the well-known historian'.[6] The book's preface, a poem, was decidedly revealing, recalling distant times 'When as a child I played all day/With only a little cat for companion/At solitary games of my own invention', a solitude re-echoed now when:

> Careful of his licked and polished appearance,
> Ears like shell whorls pink and transparent,

White plume waving proudly over the paths,
Against a background of sea and blue hydrangeas—
My cat and I grow old together.[7]

If there was a suggestion here that Rowse preferred animals to people, then he was happy to confirm it: 'within their own terms, they were more satisfactory, less bumbling and confused and ugly. Cats, for example, were a) perfect and b) comic.'[8] But there was also in the book a suggestion of inner loneliness, not just that Rowse might prefer feline company to human, nor that cats were easier to make friends with, but a sharp lingering sense of loss when these animals passed on—an acute pain more deeply felt, perhaps, and for longer, than the normal mourning for a family pet. There was Chalky Jenkins, a stray that he had befriended but had not allowed in the house, a 'betrayal' that he regretted when the cat disappeared for good: 'I at any rate have paid the penalty for my betrayal with an aching heart and many tears. . . Nothing can console me for my failing him, or to think that I shall never see him again—never, never, never.'[9] Then there was Tommer, the black farm-cat—'[h]ow we miss his little black mug, dear Tommer, dear little soul!'[10]—and Flip, his last cat, who disappeared suddenly one night. '[W]hichever way I turn my mind', Rowse wrote, 'I find no consolation for that engaging little presence, who brought companionship and merriment, gaiety and occupation, into my last years.' There was now a gap in his life, or what remained of it; it 'leaves an aching void where he was, though his constant memory and image accompany me, wherever I am'.[11]

Sometimes, when it was not spring or summer, and the garden at Trenarren was not a radiant, sun-lit picture of exotic colour and fragrance, Rowse would look out from his window at the rain sheeting across Black Head. It was then that he felt 'marooned on my headland',[12] alone in 'this melancholy Celtic world'[13] of his own making. There he was, he pondered sadly, in a house that he did not own, unsure of his paternity—'heir to nothing. . . a cuckoo in every nest, not belonging anywhere'.[14] It was at such times that he felt isolated, unloved, neglected by fair weather friends, and derided by those 'second-rate' academics and literary critics who either did not have the wit to appreciate the scope of his achievements or were insanely jealous of his intellect and abilities. There were moments of deep introspection, liable to assail him at any time, triggered by events that set his thoughts running, a dark contemplation that could border on despair. In November 1982, for example, with winter approaching, he made the short journey to Bodmin, where he was to address the congregation at St Petroc's church on the occasion of a service of thanksgiving for the life of Marika Hanbury-Tennison, wife of the well-known explorer and adventurer and herself a writer of distinction, who had died recently

32 A.L. Rowse celebrates his 86th birthday in bed at Trenarren in 1989. *Courtesy Special Collections, University of Exeter Library.*

33 Rowse, with his cat, contemplates the advance of old age. *Courtesy Special Collections, University of Exeter Library.*

34 Rowse in his later years on an expedition in Cornwall with his old friend, David Treffry. *Courtesy Special Collections, University of Exeter Library.*

35 Rowse in quiet contemplation in the drawing room at Trenarren. *Courtesy Special Collections, University of Exeter Library; photo by John Herzecol.*

of cancer. 'I have never wanted people to know the real me, or to know them', he confided in his diary, 'I felt that loneliness in Bodmin Church on Thursday, when I had to give the address at Marika Hanbury Tennison's memorial service.'[15]

'Loneliness is everywhere'

For those who cared to look, there was evidence enough of this loneliness: not least in his poetry, always the vehicle for his innermost thoughts. When Rowse's collected poems, *A Life*, appeared in 1981, Keith Brace, the literary editor of the *Birmingham Post*, observed that in this poetry 'loneliness is everywhere'.[16] Colin Wilson, a writer whom Rowse greatly admired, and who lived close by at Gorran Haven, agreed, noting 'Rowse's peculiar quality, the ability to conjure up silence and loneliness'. Rowse's best work, Wilson argued, 'has this still, contemplative quality, like something overheard in the silence', and there was 'often a quality of sadness', for Rowse was a 'poet of a single mood, an unchanging outlook'.[17]

Best known of all, perhaps, is Rowse's early poem 'How Many Miles to Mylor?', a poem which manifests all the attributes that Wilson described. Published originally in *Cornish Labour News* in January 1934 as 'Walking to a Meeting: A Christmas Ballad', it was a product of those desperately lonely days when Rowse had been a Labour candidate. It was also to become iconic of Rowse's *genre* in the years ahead.

> How many miles to Mylor
>   By frost and candle-light:
> How long before I arrive there,
>   This mild December night?
>
> As I mounted the hill to Mylor
>   Through the dark woods of Carclew,
> A clock struck the three-quarters
>   And suddenly a cock crew.
>
> At the cross-roads on the hill-top
>   The snow lay on the ground,
> In the quick air and the stillness,
>   No movement and no sound.
>
> 'How is it?' said a voice from the bushes
>   Beneath the rowan-tree;
> 'Who is it?' my heart re-echoed,
>   My heart went out of me.

I cannot tell the strangeness
   There lay around Carclew:
Nor whatever stirred in the hedges
   When an owl replied 'Who-whoo?'

A lamp in a lone cottage,
   A face in a window-frame
Above the snow a wicket:
   A house without a name.

How many miles to Mylor
   This dark December night:
And shall I ever arrive there
   By frost or candle-light?[18]

Rowse's Cornish poems, at their very best, combined the loneliness, silence, sadness and quiet contemplation identified by Colin Wilson with an exquisite tenderness for his native land, as though real love for Cornwall would always be painfully personal, reclusive even, deeply felt and perhaps not understood by those insufficiently sensitive to the subtlety of his Cornish mood. At such times, Rowse's poetry reached a lyrical quality reminiscent of 'Q', his mentor all those years ago, evident for example in 'Ardevora Veor', a poem bringing to mind (perhaps intentionally) Quiller Couch's well-known and much-loved 'Helford River':

At turn of tide, clear sky,
Seventh September morn,
A boy goes sculling by
Down river from Ruan Lanihorne.

The secret flats of the Fal
Reveal unnumbered birds
Mirrored in quiet waters:
A world beyond words.

Behind a screen of elms
A deserted house is there,
Haunted by its echo—
Ardevora, Ardevora Veor.[19]

There was an identical mood in Rowse's 'Cornish Landscape', again intensely personal, full of introspective feeling:

> The rich evening sun on the harrowed field,
> The chittering of birds,
> The insistent drone of planes out at sea,
> The scolding of rooks,
> The colder tones of the water;
> What is there in a Cornish hedge,
> The herring-bone pattern of stones,
> The gorse, the ragged rick,
> The way the little elms are,
> Sea-bent, sea-shorn,
> That so affects the heart?[20]

And sometimes the loneliness was palpable, giving voice to the marooned soul, as in 'Winter at Trenarren':

> Make my chair a refuge
>   From the winter's rage,
> And the room a fortress,
>   Firelit, from old age.[21]

A circle of Cornish friends

Rowse's 'Celtic melancholy' was never far from the surface. But such moods passed, and in the 1980s and 1990s, as he grew yet older and became less mobile, and when trips to America had become a thing of the past, Rowse had the redeeming consolation of his small circle of friends locally. They included such as James Mildren, the broadcaster, over the border at Devonport; Raleigh Trevelyan nearer at St Winnow; James Whetter across the bay at Gorran; Donald Adamson along the coast at Polperro; Caroline White the 'Tabb House' publisher up at Padstow; and David Treffry at Place, the ancient seat of the Treffry family at Fowey. At Trenarren there was the constant attention of his aged housekeeper, Phyllis Cundy—who years before had replaced her sister, Beryl Cloke— and when she retired in late 1995 she was replaced in turn by the vivacious Valerie Brokenshire (later Jacob), a local historian whom Rowse much admired.

James Whetter, a key member of this Cornish circle on which Rowse relied increasingly for entertainment and stimuli, recalled the trips he arranged for Rowse in those years, taking him out and about across Cornwall to favourite locations—lunch at the Metropole Hotel at Padstow, for example, or a detour around the new Wadebridge bypass, slowing on the flyover to allow Rowse a panoramic view over the old town. The author of numerous Cornish books—including his well-regarded

Cornwall in the Seventeenth Century and an important history of the notorious Bodrugan family—James Whetter shared Rowse's historical tastes and made an ideal travelling companion as together, Henderson-like, they sought out remote and ancient places.[22]

David Treffry was a friend of longer standing. He belonged to an ancient Cornish family and counted amongst his forebears both John Treffry, who had fought at Bosworth Field under Henry Tudor, and William Treffry, who under the same Henry VII had become Comptroller of Tin Coinage for the Stannaries of Cornwall and Keeper of the Stannary gaol at Lostwithiel. This was an illustrious lineage that could not fail to impress. Thinking, no doubt, of the qualities of his friend today, Rowse described that William Treffry of long ago as a kind and generous man, who had no children of his own but who provided for his nephews and servants and left money for the poor of Fowey.[23] Certainly, Rowse thought David Treffry 'the one intelligent person the Treffry family has produced since the days of Henry VIII',[24] and in their relationship we can detect the elusive quality that Rowse reserved for so very few of his social contacts— a friendship based on mutual deference and respect. Where the quality existed, there was warmth and empathy, good humour and fun to be had. But Rowse was sparing in his friendships, especially in his retirement, and his relationship over many years with David Treffry stands out as the exception rather than the rule, a respite from a world of loneliness rather than just one thread in a rich social tapestry.

Treffry had worked for a time for the International Monetary Fund, and when Rowse visited him in Washington DC he would stay at Treffry's 'charming Georgetown house'.[25] But Treffry's heart was in Cornwall, and it was this that bound him ever closer to Rowse as the years passed. In the 1950s he and Rowse had explored what the latter described as 'the unknown country the Treffrys sprang from in the middle ages'[26]—Higher and Lower Trefrize, near North Hill in East Cornwall. He had also, as Rowse put it, 'an unappeased passion' for the locality around the River Fowey, for this too was 'Treffry country' and it was 'in his blood'. Treffry had a particular fixation on the vicarage at St Winnow and, Rowse said, 'David was sad to think he would never occupy his Naboth's Vineyard, nor perhaps anywhere in his Treffry country'.[27] In fact, by an extraordinary stroke of fate, David Treffry came to inhabit Place, the ancestral home of the Treffrys at Fowey, overlooking the harbour. This was to Rowse's great delight and somehow put a permanent seal of approval on their friendship, especially in their later years when they spent much time together—a friendship based even more firmly now on mutual deference and respect: Rowse for Treffry as the fitting inheritor of an ancient Cornish name and seat, Treffry for Rowse as a distinguished Cornishman of great learning.

There was in this relationship an echo of an earlier, though certainly less close, relationship based similarly on deference and respect—that between Rowse and G.M. Trevelyan, the great Whig historian whom Rowse strove to emulate. He deferred to Trevelyan as a scholar of distinction but he was also drawn by the illustrious Cornish name, for although the Trevelyans had several centuries before migrated to Northumberland by way of Somerset, they had remembered their Cornish origins. In 1942 Trevelyan had admitted to Rowse his 'very strong Cornish feeling', revealing that he had 'walked around the whole of the coast of Cornwall twice', and opining that 'I should be quite a good guide to the old Trevelyan places near Fowey'.[28] Almost twenty years later, he was thanking Rowse for his birthday message, 'which gave me special pleasure because it hailed me as a Cornishman'.[29] Trevelyan could be equally complimentary, writing to Rowse in terms that were amusing as well as flattering and encouraging: 'But though Cornwall's / and fortune's son / March indefatigably on, / And for the best effect / Still keep the pen erect'.[30] However, unlike the burgeoning friendship with David Treffry, at its strongest in the 1980s and 1990s, this was a great many years before Rowse's retirement. Trevelyan died in 1962, and as old friends like Trevelyan passed away, so Rowse had fewer relationships of quality on which to draw. Indeed, as Rowse grew older, he found it harder than ever to take people at face value, to construct that bond of mutual deference and respect. He became increasingly suspicious and disparaging of those whom he feared might take advantage of him, or, worse still, seek to disagree or compete with him.

Although, as we have seen in Chapter 4, Rowse tried hard in later life to admire the work of Daphne du Maurier, and thought to construct a closer relationship with her, he had never really deviated from his view that it was '[p]erfect shopgirls' literature' and that, unfortunately, 'there is no doubt that the people see Cornwall through the eyes of Miss du Maurier'.[31] But then, she was not Cornish. Nor was F.E. Halliday, author of the accomplished *A History of Cornwall*: 'When my *Shakespeare* came out, F.E. Halliday of St Ives—to whom I had been helpful—attacked it. He was mildly Shakespearean himself, and evidently dog-in-the-manger. I have survived him.'[32] Similarly, when Denys Val Baker wrote tactfully to Rowse to say that he had detected some antipathy in their relationship, and that perhaps this was 'partly because we once published a critical book review'[33] in his magazine, Rowse scribbled across the letter: 'mere abuse by a 3rd rater'—a rebuttal aimed as much at the unnamed reviewer as at poor Val Baker himself.

Even impeccable Cornish credentials were not always enough to win Rowse's approval. When D.M. Thomas's internationally acclaimed novel *The White Hotel* was published in 1982 Rowse thought it 'appalling. . .

quasi-pornographic rubbish',[34] and a dozen years earlier he had refused Thomas permission to reproduce some of his poems in an anthology, *The Granite Kingdom*—much to Thomas's regret.[35] Years before that, Anne Treneer too had felt the sting of Rowse's pen. He never did approve of the cosy affectation, as he saw it, of her *School House in the Wind*, an auto-biographical rival to his *A Cornish Childhood*, and his antipathy became apparent when she wrote to ask for his help in the book she planned to write about Sir Humphry Davy.[36] Rowse replied that she was not equipped to attempt it—because she was not a scientist and because she was a woman. Bravely, she responded that his was a letter 'I didn't exactly enjoy' and that 'I certainly felt red in the ears'. But 'I've made up my mind to try', she wrote, even though 'not being a man will be a drawback'[37]—a determination that led eventually to her successful book *The Mercurial Chemist*.[38]

Later, F.L. 'Fred' Harris, Rowse's erstwhile political ally, was similarly the butt of Rowse's discouragement. For years, Rowse had badgered Harris to produce a history of the Bassets of Tehidy, the family that had made its fortune from the mines of Camborne and Redruth. At last, in March 1973, Harris announced that 'Basset is finished', and he sent the manuscript to Rowse: 'The question is whether it is publishable'.[39] The answer, alas, was that it was not, at least in Rowse's estimation. 'My modest attempt turns out to be a horrid monstrosity', wrote Harris, though '[a]s far as I'm concerned the loyalty goes on'. But there was much pain: 'will you do me one more favour, if you can?', Harris asked, '[y]ou would save me from some damage, I guess, if you let your judgement, and rejec-tion, be confidential to me alone. . . [a]fter your rejection I won't get anyone to publish the thing as it stands'.[40] Eighteen months later, Harris wrote to Rowse to inform him of the death of his wife, Gladys. 'Poor Fred!', Rowse wrote in the margin of the letter.[41] 'Basset' never did see the light of day, but a year later, in 1976, there appeared *The Making of a Cornish Town: Torpoint and Neighbourhood through Two Hundred Years*, by F.L. and Gladys Harris, a model of local history research and writing.[42]

Of course, there were some with whom Rowse was capable of co-oper-ating: when Charles Causley had written in a review that 'those who see the eminent historian and ignore Rowse the poet will miss a voice that is rare and wholly individual in modern verse',[43] he struck exactly the right note and instantly became a friend for life. But as the years passed Rowse became increasingly territorial, even proprietorial in his suspicion of those who might be moving onto his 'turf'. This was evidenced in his increas-ingly shrill defence of his Shakespearean work, especially his alleged discovery of the identity of the 'Dark Lady' of the sonnets, but it was also apparent in his ever more strident 'ownership' of Cornwall and things Cornish. 'Nothing Cornish is alien to me!',[44] he declared in 1979, with a defiance that bordered on menace, a warning for others to watch their step.

At the same time that Rowse was effecting his 'rehabilitation', consenting to become a bard of the Gorsedd and striving to build bridges with the cultural and political nationalists of the Revival, so his increasingly assertive Cornishness left little room for those with alternative perspectives or different ideas about Cornwall, and absolutely no space for those who might challenge or usurp his role as 'the greatest living Cornishman'[45]—as he was now routinely hailed by admirers and apologists. For those able to defer unquestioningly to his superior authority, there was still the opportunity for encouragement, support and a helping hand, and for his inner circle of friends there remained his familiar generosity (though even here, as Whetter noted, he found it difficult to accept dissenting views).[46] Even in the last weeks of his life Rowse was helping Raleigh Trevelyan with ideas for his then forthcoming *Sir Walter Raleigh*.[47] Others, however, beyond his confidence, were 'buggers', 'bloody idiots' and 'ignorant third-raters'—to be kept at arms length, and preferably ignored altogether.

Jan Killigrew Trebetjeman

In 1988 *A.L. Rowse's Cornwall* appeared, in many ways the literary high-point of Rowse's renewed embrace of Cornwall. A profusely illustrated and highly personal survey of his 'little land', *A.L. Rowse's Cornwall* was presented as something entirely different from the normal run-of-the-mill books on Cornwall. As he explained to his readers, '[m]any illustrated books are devoted to Cornwall—mostly by "foreigners" as we call them'. He went on: 'Naturally they are taken by the surface of things, the cliffs and beaches, headlands, rocks, the sea spilling over them. That is not my Cornwall, or at any rate only a small part of it'. As he re-emphasized, in case people had forgotten, 'I am 100 per cent native, irremediably Cornish, and I offer something different, more deeply Cornish. An historian, as well as poet, seeks to look under the surface of things, to see the past continuous with the present, and perhaps the past more truly and faithfully Cornish.'[48]

Here again was Rowse asserting his proprietorial credentials, insinuating a profound degree of ownership, insisting upon his unique qualification to write about his 'little land' and questioning the ability—and indeed right—of others to attempt the same. It was an attitude that could bring him dangerously close to conflict with old friends, sometimes introducing a sour note in his relationships in those later years. John Betjeman, for example, was a friend of long standing, and although he had not known Rowse during his undergraduate days at Oxford, by the mid-

1940s they were well acquainted. In 1979 Rowse reflected that he had 'lived much of my life on the margins of John's acquaintance',[49] and indeed he had. When Betjeman had worked for the British Council at Oriel in 1945 he would call often at All Souls to take tea with Rowse, and in 1954 they appeared together with Lord David Cecil on the BBC television programme *Conversation Piece*. Three years later, Rowse and Betjeman were both supporting efforts by the Old Plymouth Society to avert the demolition of 'Plymouth's heart' in the post-war redevelopment of that much-blitzed city, and to advocate the restoration of the old Barbican area.[50]

They were also mutually supportive of each other's work. It was Rowse who suggested that Betjeman bring together as a book his articles and broadcasts on topography and architecture, leading to the publication in 1952 of *First and Last Loves*. In the opinion of Bevis Hillier, Betjeman's biographer, this was his best prose book: a volume that included—amongst other things—Cornish pieces on Blisland, St Endellion, Looe, Port Isaac and Padstow.[51] Much later, it was Betjeman, when Poet Laureate, who suggested that Rowse produce a definitive collection of all his poetry, thus prompting the appearance of *A Life* in 1981.[52] Always adept at flattery, Betjeman recognised this as Rowse's Achilles' heel, and was sure to try to say the right thing at the right time. When Rowse's *West Country Stories* came out in 1944, Betjeman in a review wrote that 'I had the inestimable privilege of spending most [*sic*] of my childhood in Cornwall, and I do not recollect reading better descriptions of the county than those of Mr Rowse'.[53] Private correspondence was similarly effusive. 'God bless you dear a great Cornish writer',[54] he wrote in 1967. In 1975, knowing Rowse's desire for recognition as a serious poet, he exclaimed that '[t]here are no things more enjoyable than a good poet in an old friend', opining two years later that '[y]ou must be the only historian who has written truly topographical poetry'.[55] Similarly, in 1980: 'Your road to Oxford poems are a constant pleasure to me: so are your vigour and Cornishness'.[56]

This was a Cornishness that Betjeman was careful to evoke in his letters. He was unwittingly sailing close to the wind when he hailed Rowse as 'My dear St Austell', and signed himself off variously as 'Jan Trebetherick'—reflecting his part-time domicile at Trebetherick, on the north coast—'Jan Killigrew Trebetjeman', and 'St Enodoc and Trebetherick'.[57] In 1971, aware of Rowse's passion for the epic tale of the Cornish overseas, he enthused: 'I've just come back from Australia where Cornwall meets one at every turn in place names and mining. . . I am dotty about Australia'.[58] Rowse, for his part, returned all the compliments, or most of them. In 1978 he showered praise on the *Shell Guides*—including that to Cornwall—the work of 'those apostolic twins, John Betjeman and John

Piper. . . my favourite reading'.[59] In the following year Rowse was to write at length about Betjeman in his *Portraits and Views*, informing readers that Betjeman's 'Cornish poems—and there are many of them—are amongst his most moving'.[60] However, Rowse did issue a mild disclaimer—'lest anyone think that my love for Betjeman leaves me incapable of criticising'[61]—and he rebuked Betjeman for failing to appreciate the quality of the Elizabethan poets whom, of course, Rowse much admired. Publicly, Rowse and Betjeman were the best of chums. But here was an intimation that, privately, their relationship was more complex, that beneath the veneer of genuine mutual affection there were important differences in character and temperament, and occasionally hints of rivalry. Betjeman, for example, had once confided to a close friend that Rowse 'is a very strange character',[62] while Rowse had made no secret of his disapproval for Betjeman's partying and frivolity, his inability sometimes to take work seriously.

During the 1940s Rowse had suggested, rather cynically, that Betjeman composed so many glowing book reviews, with rarely a bad word to say about anyone, because '[h]e didn't want to make enemies in the literary world'.[63] In other respects he also found Betjeman vaguely irritating, especially when John and his wife Penelope came to stay at Trenarren. Penelope, a Roman Catholic convert, insisted on attending Mass on such occasions, as in August 1956 when Rowse found himself driving her one Sunday morning to 'the little RC church on the Bypass at St Austell'. As Rowse recorded in his diary, 'Penelope has arrived early to make her confession before Mass, the silly. I hope she enjoys it as she enjoys food, everything: what a rigmarole.'[64] Rowse's irritability with Penelope tended to rub off on his relationship with John, not least when Penelope wrote to him—'My Dear Leslie'—to ask for a loan to finance her son's travels in the United States. 'I won't beat about the bush', Penelope wrote, 'but say straight out I WONDER whether you would consider giving our Paul a loan of £400 in American dollars *repayable within three years??*' Rowse scribbled across the letter: 'Certainly not—for this nasty young master!'.[65] He never had liked children, and was not going to make an exception for the Betjemans' offspring.

But there were more significant frictions. In 1974 Rowse had collaborated with Betjeman to produce *Victorian and Edwardian Cornwall from Old Photographs*, one of the successful Batsford series of illustrated histories. Betjeman and Sam Carr, his editor at Batsford, had already chosen the relevant photographs and they approached Rowse, asking him to contribute an appropriate text. He was happy to oblige. However, when the book appeared, the introductory material explained that: 'Sir John Betjeman and Dr A.L. Rowse are the two most eminent living Cornishmen—the one by adoption, the other by birth'.[66] The knighthood took precedence over the honorary doctorate, the foreigner over the native. Rowse was livid, Betjeman mortified. Betjeman sent a placatory, if panicky, note to Rowse: 'I wish they hadn't said I was a Cornishman in the blurb. I have always been a furriner. But I am v. proud to be linked to you.'[67] Rowse bided his time but in 1986 (two years after Betjeman's death) let the world know what he thought of such presumption. He was, he said, greatly irritated by the general 'assumption of [Betjeman's] Cornishry. Some public prints would refer to him as Cornish—fancy the idiocy of anyone supposing that a name like Betjeman could possibly be Cornish!' And while he acknowledged that 'Betjeman was passionately devoted to that bit of Cornwall around Padstow, Trebetherick and Rock', he went on to insist that '[t]hat is not the same thing as being Cornish, though we are grateful to him for his love of Cornwall'.[68]

To make amends for the publisher's gaff, Betjeman had in 1978 decided to leave Rowse 'a shell model of St Mary's [church], Penzance, in my Will, if you survive me—which I hope you do'.[69] And Rowse, equally magnanimously, wrote to Lady Elizabeth Cavendish—Betjeman's constant companion in those later years—to express his condolences when John Betjeman died at Trebetherick in May 1984.[70] But there was no hiding Rowse's annoyance at those individuals who might try to affect Cornish credentials: to suggest intimate Cornish connections when in fact there were none, or to threaten or usurp his position as the ultimate authority on things Cornish and on what it was to be Cornish:

> We have had Daphne du Maurier's *Vanishing Cornwall*, Winston Graham's *Poldark's Cornwall*, and eventually *Betjeman's Cornwall*—none of them Cornish, all of them having adopted Cornwall. I am the real thing, 100 per cent Cornish: when is someone going to see that a 'Rowse's Cornwall' would be a different matter—history, antiquities, villages, crevices, holes and corners, relics, what is beneath: the *real* Cornwall.[71]

'Gaity and sparkle on the surface, an inner melancholy and pessimism below'

This was in 1986. Two years later and *A.L. Rowse's Cornwall* had indeed appeared, delivering at last, Rowse thought, the native's superior, definitive, more authentic view. The book was part of his urgent engagement now with Cornish themes but also further evidence of his anxiety to express a defiant Cornishness in the face of all-comers—especially the counterfeit and the imitator. In this renewed embrace of Cornwall, Rowse had returned with redoubled and determined energy to the production of books on Cornwall and the Cornish, the sheer volume of his output establishing his credentials for all to see and pushing potential rivals into the shade. His *Cornish Anthology* had appeared as far back as 1968, with the milestone *The Cornish in America* hot on its heels in 1969, and other volumes set to follow, though a second anthology of Cornish material was completed in draft but never published.[72] He was especially keen to draw attention to the little-known Cornish connections of famous literary folk such as Matthew Arnold and Lord Byron, arguing from his fiercely Cornish perspective that one could not really begin to understand these complex personalities until one had assessed the Cornish dimensions in their lives, and hinting by association at the significance of his own Cornishness in determining *his* literary success. For Arnold and Byron, read Rowse.

In his biography of the former, published in 1976, Rowse attributed Arnold's enthusiasm for Celtic literature to his Cornish descent (he was Cornish on his mother's side; she a Penrose from Carwythenack—pronounced 'Crannick'—in Constantine) and argued that his temperament was essentially 'Celtic', like his own: 'gaity and sparkle on the surface, an inner melancholy and pessimism below'.[73] Especially moving, he thought, was the story of Arnold's grandmother and her departure from Cornwall, as she accompanied her clergyman husband to his new living in Nottinghamshire: 'When the carriage came to cross the boundary between Cornwall and Devon, Mrs Penrose. . . got down and kissed the dust on the road, as her "tender farewell to the land she loved"'.[74] Equally telling, Rowse thought, was the letter Arnold had written to his mother from Paris in 1859: a letter which revealed his understanding of the ancient kinship of the Cornish and the Bretons. 'I could not but think of you in Brittany, with Cranics and Trevennecs all about me', Arnold observed, 'and the peasantry with their mournful faces, long noses, and dark eyes, reminding me perpetually of dear Tom [his brother] and Uncle Trevenen, and utterly unlike the French.'[75] There was also an element of Celtic tragedy and romance in Arnold's own life, Rowse detected, such as his unfulfilled—if not unrequited—love for the enigmatic Margueritte celebrated in his poetry. In Arnold's life, perhaps, Rowse saw reflections of his own.

Similarly, in his *The Byrons and Trevanions*, published in 1978, Rowse illuminated the series of Byron–Trevanion marriages—'besides their extra-matrimonial intermixings'—over three generations in the eighteenth and nineteenth centuries. Once again, this book emphasized the importance of the Cornish dimension, including Byron's sojourn at Falmouth where, among other things, he described the port's 'capabilities or incitements to the *plenum* and *optabile coitum*'.[76] Dedicating the book to 'Rosalie Glyn Grylls (Lady Mander) in constant affection and faithful Cornishry', Rowse opined that 'people are unaware of the Trevanion element in the poet Byron's make-up as they are of the significant Penrose inheritance in Matthew Arnold's'.[77] But they should be made aware, and it was Rowse's job to make sure that they were.

The culmination of this intense 'Cornish' biographical treatment was Rowse's *Quiller Couch: A Portrait of 'Q'*, which appeared in 1988 and was dedicated, interestingly enough, to 'Daphne du Maurier in common admiration of our old mentor and friend'.[78] The book was in part an attempt to achieve greater recognition for Q: to restore him to the literary heights he had enjoyed in his lifetime. Rowse insisted that 'Sir Arthur Quiller Couch is apt to be overlooked these days. This book will help put that right.'[79] But it was also part of Rowse's Cornish 'rehabilitation'. It was the premier volume, as far as he was concerned, in his string of biographical works: a book that he had always meant to write but had put off until now—well into his 'eighties'—he at last felt distanced enough from the difficult years of his youth to turn to the subject. That the book was written in old age is telling. The passage of so many years since the traumatic 1930s and 1940s allowed him now to return to the themes of his early life, to produce the tribute and memorial that he had always planned to the man who, more than anyone, had set him on the road to Oxford and literary distinction. But still, forty-four years after Q's death, he felt the loss of his mentor keenly: 'he was irreplaceable; I have never felt Cornwall, in particular Fowey, to be the same without him'.[80] Now, however, Rowse could at least claim common ground, as well as common cause, with Q, if not actually aspiring to the hallowed reputation of Sir Arthur Quiller Couch—and challenging his position at the head of the pantheon of Cornish writers—then certainly claiming to be his legitimate literary heir. It was a mantle that Rowse wore with pride; in a hostile post-Q world he was his late master's protector, his advocate in uncouth, dangerous times.

Stories from Trenarren

As well as biography, there was a return to the genre in which Rowse thought himself especially accomplished: the short story. *Night at the Carn*—dedicated 'For Foy Quiller-Couch in memory of dear Q'— appeared in 1984, and *Stories from Trenarren* was published in 1986.[81] The collections included some old favourites, notably 'When Dick Stephens Fought the Bear', published years before, but there was much new material as well, including stories with a contemporary or near contemporary theme—set in the Cornwall (and Oxbridge and America) of his lifetime. But lest it appear that his 'rehabilitation' had gone too far, Rowse was careful to remind his readers that actually 'I am not in the least interested in contemporary demotic society, or its characteristic stories of drinking and drugging, thugging and mugging—too boring and common, like the daily newspapers'.[82] The main purpose of his collections, he explained, was to perpetuate the tradition of Cornish short-story writing that had been brought to perfection by Sir Arthur Quiller Couch. He was 'a first-class story teller', wrote Rowse, 'absurdly under-estimated and overlooked today, by people who have no idea of good writing, as he had and exemplified'. Unfortunately, Rowse continued, '[i]n a period of social revolution the first thing that goes is quality, good standards. . . one has only to look around today'. Nonetheless, 'there will always be the few, the elect [such as himself], to set store by them and maintain them for themselves':[83] hence the current collections.

There was, however, another, more intriguing, more revealing dimension to these stories. There was an echo in their plots of events from Rowse's own life, entwining enigmatic hints of autobiographical insight with fiction. This, in turn, was evidence of a curious process in Rowse's later years in which he picked over his life: re-arranging it for posterity, annotating his own diaries at length and musing on the salient features of his career in an attempt to make sense of it for himself. This was introspection in depth and at length, identifying telling incidentals as well as grand themes, alighting on fragments as well as key events. Sometimes there were merely fleeting glimpses in these stories, as in the tale of a visitor to America [a thinly disguised Rowse] who was being taken to an ancient Native American site by an enthusiastic professor. The professor braked hard at the cliff edge as they arrived, and the visitor was 'alarmed and inwardly angry [as Rowse would have been]. Good manners forbade that he should show it, especially to an American who had been so good as to bring him to the pueblo he so much wanted to see'.[84]

There was a hint of his old friend David Treffry, perhaps, in 'Naboth's Vineyard', another of the stories. This was a tale of a 'young man [who] had several Naboth's Vineyards, as he called them to himself, in Cornwall', the young man in question being partly American—as Treffry was, arguably, by residence. But the 'ancient little rectory', one of the places that so appealed, 'was a sequestered inland place at the head of a valley of rocks'. This was suggestive not of St Winnow—Treffry's personal fixation—but of Rowse's own delight: Luxulyan. Rowse, too, thought himself partly American, so here was another glancing reference to his own life, as there was later in the story when another of the 'vineyards' was revealed. This was Treneglos, for which read Trenarren, a 'house [that] belonged to an ancient West Country family that. . . leased it to a succession of tenants'.[85] In his inner consciousness, expressed now in prose, the mutual deference and respect that he and Treffry had felt for each other had somehow coalesced: their yearnings congruent, inextricable.

More complex still was 'Pinetum', a story that appeared to conflate Tregrehan, the home of the Carlyons near St Austell, with aspects of St Michael's Mount, seat of the St Aubyns. 'The clever young grandson of the lodge-keeper' was clearly Rowse—his Vanson grandparents had been lodge-keepers at Tregrehan—and the local pub, the Penvanson Arms, was a scarcely veiled play on words. And references to males of the gentry family who 'had certainly left a penumbra of illegitimates about the purlieus of the estate' may have been an allusion to his own mother's experience when in service at the Mount. Certainly, the young grandson, 'inquisitive as all Cornish folk are', who 'sometimes ventured into the formal Italian garden below the terrace of the big house'—just as Rowse had done at Tregrehan as a boy—divined that there was a dark, hidden secret, and in the story he determined to find out what it was.[86]

'The Doctor's Family', another story, revealed a further aspect of his mother's experience. Just as Rowse's mother, made pregnant at the Mount, had been whisked away to the protective guard of a doctor's household near St Austell, so too was the young woman in the story. There had been an arrangement, just as there had been for Rowse's mother, 'for the child to be adopted by its grandmother'. The young woman was 'remarkably handsome', and needed to be married off before further trouble might ensue, and so the good doctor made a match for her with his favourite groom, one Rawe (for Rowse). Already '[h]opelessly enamoured' of the young woman, Rawe needed little encouragement: 'Rawe thought of nothing better than having this handsome piece, if only of "damaged goods", as they put it in the stable-yard, for his own'. The young woman herself was not in love with the groom—she had 'fancied something higher for herself in submitting to her lover's embraces, the Squire's younger son'—but '[w]ith her experience, a vein of iron was to show itself in her life: no illusions'. Given that '[b]eggars can't be choosers', she agreed to the wedding and—just as Annie Rowse had said in real life (p. 58)—she explained that she did it 'to cover up me shaame'. And, like Annie and Dick Rowse, the young woman and Rawe 'made a respectable couple'; he, 'a simple, kindly soul, adored the wife he had not expected to achieve'; she 'put up a brave face to the world. . . encouraged no confidences'.[87]

Autobiographical fragments also litter the tale of 'Kellow's shop. . . the hub of the universe at the cross-roads at the upper end of our straggling china-clay village'. In this story there is a 'Mrs R' (for Rowse) who 'ran the little sweet-shop which made no such fortune as Mr Kellow's up along'. There was also a young man who, as Rowse had done in his youth, made the local Carn (Grey) a place of personal pilgrimage. The story described the Carn in loving detail, that 'pile of flat altar-shaped rocks. . . which dominated all that landscape for miles', with 'views extended in every direction'—across the Bay towards the Gribbin, out over Hensbarrow and to distant Brown Willy and Rowtor, and nearer 'the grey tower of Luxulyan church, the westering sun lighting up the western face'.

Here was that magical, romantic spot, described exactly as Rowse remembered it from all those years ago, but there was a twist. It was on the Carn that the young man of the story exchanged his first kiss with his first love, a girl he had known for years and had gone to school with. 'One way or another they never forgot that evening', but through a series of unfortunate events, compounded by the young man's irresolution, they then went their separate ways and did not meet up again until their lives were nearly over, when it was all far too late.[88] There were shades here, perhaps, of Noreen Sweet (when *A Life* had appeared in 1981 Rowse had dedicated it to 'N.S.'), as maybe there were in another of Rowse's tantalisingly autobiographical stories, that of 'Miss Pengrugla and Mr Roseudgeon'.

Mr Roseudgeon was—just like Rowse—'an irritable man', a 'teetotaller', 'politically on the Left', a 'fussy bachelor' who 'hated anything out of its place, particularly books he might want to consult at any moment'. He also hated his first name, as Rowse did, 'it represented the taste of his sister aged ten, when he was born'. Moreover, '[h]e *looked* masculine enough, but was not responsive to women, at any rate sexually. In fact he was a complex character, whom people could not quite make out.' On top of that, he 'was of lower-class stock, but—very much an intellectual, and ambitious—was bent on raising himself into the class with which his tastes had most affinity—the old country gentry'. Miss Pengrugla, meanwhile, had 'personality and initiative' and 'she knew how to run things', and though not at all literary had an interest in 'old Cornish history and folklore', and so 'their [mutual] interest in local history made a bit of a bond'. They also both hated the Germans: 'the writer [Roseudgeon] hated their guts for ruining the age he lived in'. But Miss Pengrugla irritated Mr Roseudgeon, borrowing his books and failing to return them, and taking the liberty of shortening his name to 'Mr Rose'. She was also jealous when Mr Roseudgeon took an interest in a woman who 'lived in the house where Kilvert had visited in the Victorian age'—an allusion to Marthe Bibesco at Tullimaar?—and from then on things went from bad to worse, she marrying another, though they kept in touch thereafter. Years later, reflecting on their relationship, Mr Roseudgeon knew that he could not have married her but he admitted that he had underestimated her qualities. He had dismissed her as merely middle-class. But '[s]he was a lady—and he was not a gentleman'.[89]

Tinged with regret, this and other stories were evidence of an increasingly introspective Rowse, who had moved from the more extrovert medium of autobiography proper to the diffuse, complex vehicle of the short story. The short story provided a world where truths might be subtly alluded to, the shocking hinted at without embarrassment, clues left enticingly for the discerning reader to ponder, trails—false as well as true—laid for the literary detective determined to know more about the elusive author. Less egotistical, perhaps, certainly more self-critical, with a greater willingness to admit error, misjudgement or opportunities missed, and written sometimes with a new-found humility, Rowse's stories—like his poems—were also testament to an underlying loneliness and a profound sense of isolation and frustration. That they appeared in the mid-1980s is telling, marking a period of honest reassessment in his life, now that it was beginning to draw to a close. Their collection and publication was of considerable therapeutic value to Rowse himself, allowing things which had been bottled up for years to be spilled out across the pages.

'Do you think I'd be such a fool?'

As well as allowing him to explore, through fiction, new autobiographical perspectives, the stories—a number of these with considerable erotic content, sometimes explicitly so—enabled him to return to the subject of sexuality: his, and other people's. Familiar concerns reappeared in old age—his lack of response to women, his sexual ambivalence, the unequal power relationships that often lay behind heterosexual relationships, whether it was predatory women trying to ensnare their men (which Rowse feared) or predatory men preying on vulnerable women (which he loathed). Sometimes there was the raw sexuality of the landscape, as in his story about Phernyssick where 'half the population of the village below had been conceived in the shelter of the furze bushes on hot summer nights', and 'Look-out Lane, where girls not on the look-out got pregnant in the spring'.[90]

In 'Polly of Trethurgy' Rowse elaborated on one of his stock themes—that of the young school mistress attracting the attentions of her male superior, with illicit pregnancy as the inevitable result. Mr Brenton, the School Attendance Officer, in 'his later, seedy days. . . had more sex on him than he knew what to do with. . . [s]o he played around with Polly'. Of course, 'Mr Brenton's job gained him regular entrance into the Infants' School, and not only the school'.[91] In another story, there was the Headmaster of the Senior School, 'married to a sourpuss of a wife twenty years older than himself', and Miss Margaret Tregenza, Headmistress of the Infants, who was his 'fancy woman'. When an envious female colleague asked what Margaret had that she didn't, he replied silently to himself: '[b]reasts—a full bosom'.[92] In another variant, there was the Master and his newly appointed pupil-teacher, Lily Angwin: 'he had made an opening for her. In return, she made an opening for him.'[93] A yet further version saw a Rector and a new parishioner '[u]p in the Rectory glebe. . . haycock, which provided a comfortable bed for assignations; the Rector and the buxom newcomer made considerable use of it'.[94] Then there was the mining magnate who was also a Methodist local preacher—'M.P.' as 'he was always known somewhat pompously, and pomposity was his *faible*'—who hailed from St Ann's Chapel and preached regularly in the little bethels of that locality: Harrowbarrow, Calstock, Gunnislake, 'the Tamar frontier that divides Cornwall from England'. As Cornish tin had declined, so 'M.P.' had shrewdly invested in buoyant Malaya: Kuala-Lumpar Consolidated, Koh-i-Nor United, Penang Rubber and Tin Associated. However, although he was 'very strong in the pulpit on morality—by which the Cornish always mean sex', he was a veritable wolf in sheep's clothing and 'made a regular thing of taking the Bible classes at Sunday Schools with senior girls, whose breasts were beginning to show'. But when he asked one of the girls for an evening stroll in the woods, she replied: 'Do you think I'd be such a fool?'.[95] It was a phrase that Rowse had heard his mother use years before (see p. 67).

Power relationships could be reversed, it seemed, with predatory men like 'M.P.' put firmly in their place, but for Rowse there had been the constant 'danger'—as he saw it—of himself getting caught out, of being manoeuvred one way or another into marriage. This fear informed 'The Collaborator', another of his stories, in which a 'famous novelist'—who exhibited Rowse-like characteristics, including resistance to women—fell victim to a young woman of 'boyish charm' who 'looked like a beautiful boy' and was 'on edge with desire to produce a child by the famous writer'.[96] This may have been Rowse writing with his heart on his sleeve, reconciling fear of being trapped with a need now—again, far too late—to address his sexual repression. It was a decade and more since his fantasy (if that is what it was) about a relationship with Daphne du Maurier but probably not long after his nostalgic yearning for Noreen Sweet and the thought that she should move to Cornwall to be near him:

> Arriving at middle age [*sic*] he [the 'famous novelist'] felt a stirring of interest in the opposite sex. Was he undergoing a change? Earlier, bent on fulfilling himself in his work, an absorbed egoist, he had rigidly repressed such leanings. Now, more fulfilled, having acquired something like fame and fortune, he felt safe, and consequently more responsive—at any rate, more ready to respond. Perhaps less unready.[97]

'The greatest living Cornishman'

This may or may not have been Rowse speaking for himself. But what is clear is that, as the 1980s drew on, such introspection became increasingly characteristic of his life at Trenarren. He continued to write prodigiously but—notwithstanding the cathartic short stories of the mid-1980s, which had been aimed at laying so many ghosts in his long life—there remained an inner discontent. He might have taken comfort in his popular reputation as 'the greatest living Cornishman', and in the fact that in Cornwall he had become the people's historian, his name almost synonymous with the 'little land' about which he wrote so energetically and effectively, his Cornish books perennially lively, entertaining, accessible. In this respect, he was comparable with similar writers elsewhere who, like him, had emerged from impeccable academic backgrounds to become popular icons of their national histories, in the process courting controversy and winning devotees and detractors alike.

In Wales, for example, there was Gwyn 'Alf' Williams. As Geraint H. Jenkins wrote in his penetrating memoir of Williams's life and work, he was a 'wayward genius', a 'gifted, pugnacious and seemingly indestructible personality [who] had acquired a reputation as the most passionate and controversial Welsh historian of modern times'.[98] From a lower-middle-class background in a South Wales industrial town, Williams was a grammar school boy who won a scholarship to attend university. Like Rowse, Williams was an ardent Marxist in his younger days, but ended up a Welsh nationalist and a member of Plaid Cymru (the Party of Wales), though never abandoning his left-wing credentials. He wrote furiously, straying from the strictly academic into popular history and into broadcasting (including some memorable television performances), enthusing over the history of the Welsh people and forever playing to his popular audiences—to the dismay of his more conservative colleagues, even at Cardiff where there were those 'who had long believed that the study of Welsh history belonged to a lesser plane'.[99]

Further afield, there was Geoffrey Blainey, 'certainly the most controversial member of the Australian historical profession',[100] as he was described by academic peers in 2003. Born to an Australian family with Cornish-Methodist antecedents, Blainey was the first scholar to chronicle in detail the continent's mining history—so central to Australia's national story. From mining, he ventured into other themes vital to Australia— from colonial settlement policy to the experiences of the Aboriginal peoples—in the process drawing a strong popular following. His books were eminently readable and often dispensed with what he considered tedious academic conventions. But he also provoked the suspicion of more cautious colleagues. According to one observer, 'Blainey has determinedly set himself apart from those whom he regards as conventional historians. He is the individualist, the solitary prospector who searches in magpie fashion across the terrain of Australian history looking for a pattern in the landscape which others have missed.'[101] Here was an echo of Rowse: similarly 'individualistic' and 'solitary' in his scouring of the Cornish terrain. Moreover, when in the 1980s Blainey began to express fears on a range of contemporary issues—including multiculturalism, Asian immigration, and Aboriginal land rights—he outraged the liberal-left in Australia just as Rowse had done in Britain.

However, despite the obvious similarities between Rowse on the one hand, and Williams and Blainey on the other, there was an important, vital distinction. Notwithstanding the objections and even the outright hostility of their detractors, Gwyn A. Williams and Geoffrey Blainey retired with their academic reputations solidly intact. Both men were popular icons of their countries' national histories but also admired and respected across the academic world for their scholarly achievements and their contributions to their national historiographies. For Rowse in his retirement, by contrast, there was only academic isolation, at best the ignominy of being ignored, at worst the pain of ridicule. His bid to be recognized as a leading—*the* leading—Shakespearean scholar had foundered on the rocks of the Dark Lady and 'her' sonnets. This was not only because of flaws in his argument and evidence but as a result of the perfunctory and uncharitable way he dealt with critics, his unwillingness to engage in serious debate, and his inability to admit shortcomings in his own work. Lampooning his Shakespearean pretensions had become a favourite pastime for journalists, who took their cue from his academic critics. A satirical piece in the *Spectator* in February 1973 hit its target with mock Shakespearean verse that also made fun of Rowse's much-protested Cornishness:

> 'Th' famed researches of this Dr Rowse
> Who burrows in the secrets of my dayes,
> Hot on the scent as beagle after hare
> Or beaver, eager in Hibernian bogge
> To aedifie its damme, concerne me much
>
> 'Thicke sette, full armoured, see he comes apace
> With measured treade, and formidable front.
> 'Tis Cornish Rowse, for sure!'[102]

The sting of such attacks nearer to home was felt even more keenly, no doubt. In the same month John Pardoe, Liberal MP for North Cornwall, contributed a similarly fun-poking article to the Plymouth *Sunday Independent*. 'Well done, Doctor Rowse', he wrote, 'You've made one half of the [dark] lady Italian. Could you stretch a point and make the other half Cornish?'.[103]

Being held up to public ridicule was upsetting enough, but worse still—in Rowse's estimation—was the failure of the Establishment to honour him with any kind of public recognition. He had been elected a Fellow of the British Academy, was a Benson Medallist of the Royal Society of

Literature, and had been awarded an Honorary Doctorate by the University of Exeter. But the Order of Merit that he had once expected had gone to C.V. Wedgwood, and thereafter there was nothing. John Betjeman's knighthood hurt. 'All my contemporaries have had recognition. . . [even] John Betjeman',[104] he wrote in his diary in November 1982. An invitation in February 1988 to dine at No. 10 with Mrs Thatcher—whom he much admired, wondering whether at this eleventh hour she could save England from final degeneration—might have been a prelude to an imminent Honours List appearance. But, as Rowse readily admitted, he had rather blotted his copy-book at the dinner, for he had berated loudly the woman who had had the misfortune to be seated next to him (wife of a senior military officer) for her ignorance of the historic houses and churches of East Anglia, where she lived. Moreover, '[s]he came from New Zealand. So I held forth about the leading New Zealand poet, Alan Curnow, she had never heard of; William Colenso, the great N.Z. naturalist she had heard of neither. . . And I deliberately said I had tried again and again to get some third-rate professor there to write up the N.Z. Cornish.'[105]

'Outrageous and wounding'—a Companion of Honour

As Rowse moved into advanced old-age his friends waged something of a campaign to achieve public recognition. In November 1993, A.N. Wilson reminded his readers in the London *Evening Standard* that 'Dr A.L. Rowse will be 90 years old on 4 December', insisting that 'Rowse should be knighted to mark his 90th birthday and the Duke of Cornwall should go down to dub him'.[106] Two years later, Wilson again pressed Rowse's case, opining that '[t]he redoubtable 92-year old Cornishman A.L. Rowse is, beyond question, the most distinguished popular historian still alive'. He was comparable to Lord Macaulay, he said, but 'he is not Lord Rowse'. Why?—because the Establishment had blocked all moves to honour him: 'They don't like being dismissed as third-raters'. Recalling that the Duke of Cornwall ('aka Prince Charles') admired Rowse's Shakespearean work, he demanded that '[t]he Prince should ask the Queen to overrule the stuffpots and give Leslie Rowse the knighthood he deserves'.[107] For his part, Rowse had never really thought much of the Royal Family—'except the Queen Mum'—and had never looked in that direction for preferment, refusing all invitations to meet its members: 'they should not meet me', he insisted in 1988, 'the foremost Cornishman in Cornwall'.[108]

However, in the final years of his life, Rowse struck up a friendship of sorts with Prince Charles and even dedicated his last book to him, telling James Whetter that '[h]e seems to have a thing about me'.[109] And in 1997, the year he died, Rowse did at last appear in the New Year's Honours List, being appointed a Companion of Honour, the highest honour available, with the exception of a knighthood ('which he never coveted'[110]) and the exclusive Order of Merit. A telegram was received from Prince Charles— 'I was so delighted to hear the splendid news. . . and wanted to send you my warmest possible congratulations'[111]—and in the following June the Duke paid a visit to Trenarren to see the by now very ill old man, debilitated by the stroke he had suffered in October 1996. There was no doubt that Rowse was delighted with his CH, but at the party at Trenarren to celebrate the award, he whispered to his old friend Donald Adamson that he 'would have preferred something more academic'—by which, according to Adamson, 'he meant the Order of Merit'.[112]

Academic recognition had, Rowse feared, eluded him. And, alas, he was right. John McManners, a colleague at All Souls, thought Rowse 'impossible', 'outrageous and wounding', 'eccentric', and in his obituary of Rowse in the *Proceedings of the British Academy*—that inner sanctum of the academic Establishment—he wrote of the 'deterioration' over many years of Rowse's work and scholarly conduct, with his reputation 'tarnished' by his 'spleen', 'selfishness', 'ranting' and 'blinkered self-importance'. During that time, '[h]is mind retained its acuity, but his lunatic self-importance was subverting his scholarly judgement'.[113] David Loades, the distinguished Tudor historian, agreed. 'Thirty years ago he stood alongside J.E. Neale and G.R. Elton in the Tudor pantheon', Loades wrote in an obituary in the scholarly journal *Renaissance Studies* in 1998, '[t]ime, however, has not handled his achievements sympathetically, and few teachers of the period would now guide their pupils to his work as preferred reading'. Moreover, 'Rowse throve on controversies, which he sometimes seems to have provoked deliberately', and, unlike Elton and other scholars, would not modify his views in the face of criticism: 'It was not so much that he was angered by criticism as that he considered it to be beneath contempt. This characteristic became more pronounced with age, and as his own work became more vulnerable.' Given to unsound generalizations, cutting corners in research, and preferring literary sources to more mundane archival records, Rowse was 'the antithesis of the modern professional historian', Loades thought, adding that '[l]yrical descriptions of Roanoke Sound or sunset over St Ives are no substitute for the investigation of taxation returns or serious critical analysis'. As for Rowse's monumental three-volumed work on the Elizabethan Age, Loades went on: 'after reading his trilogy on the England of Elizabeth, we know more about the author and his idiosyncratic vision than we do about Tudor England'.[114]

Christopher Haigh—like Loades, a distinguished Tudor scholar—has in his excellent Introduction to the 2003 reprint of Rowse's *The England of Elizabeth* (the first of the trilogy) sketched with consummate skill the complexities and contradictions of Rowse the man. Recognizing Rowse's achievements, even to the extent of deciding that '*The England of Elizabeth* has not been surpassed' in the half-century since it first appeared, Haigh has also highlighted the failings that had 'made [Rowse] a cantankerous fool' in the eyes of his critics and led to his unfortunate reputation amongst fellow academics as 'bloody Rowse'—or even 'bloody, bloody Rowse'. Haigh is kinder in his own assessment but is critical nonetheless. His principal charge is that, at a time (the 1950s and 1960s) when the divide between academic and popular history had become increasingly apparent, Rowse did not deploy his considerable skills in the writing of both to build bridges between them. Instead, 'he became part of the problem', and 'faced with a choice between academic reputation and the rewards of commercial success, Rowse went for the money: in the 1960s he turned to sex, Shakespeare, literary biography, and picture-books'. Inevitably, '[w]hen scholars sneered at what he was doing, he derided "intellectuals" and mocked them—they couldn't understand the real world, they couldn't write, and they couldn't make money'. Thus it was that 'among academic historians he became a joke'.[115]

In Rowse's last years, as John McManners noted with more than a hint of pity and regret, this diminished academic reputation added to the isolation he endured at Trenarren. Rowse had effected a 'withdrawal into his fortress of pride' and '[s]uch academic friends as corresponded with him put up with his overweening self-esteem and denigration of others because they sensed his inner loneliness and saw that he himself was the chief victim of his outrageous performances'.[116] The tragedy was that Rowse sensed this too. As he had once complained in a newspaper interview with Lynda Lee-Potter: 'Underneath, I have a very affectionate nature, but it's perhaps been rendered rather sour by so much misunderstanding from second-rate professors in literary and academic circles'. And yet, in his bitter isolation, he remained driven to confound his critics, and to scale yet further heights. 'I'm possessed by the spirit', he admitted, 'I'm obsessed with work, which is why I am so prolific. Ultimately, it could really force me over the edge.'[117]

36 Rowse at the nadir of his academic reputation, in advanced old age.
Courtesy Special Collections, University of Exeter Library.

11

'All the Island Peoples'

Writing British and Cornish History

When A.L. Rowse died on 3 October 1997 his academic reputation was at its nadir. Even in the 1950s and 1960s, the heyday of his great Elizabethan works, so popular with the reading publics of Britain and America, Rowse had been seen by many academic colleagues as increasingly old-fashioned: out of touch with contemporary trends and concerns. As James Whetter recalled, when he read History at Birmingham in the 1950s and graduated to work on a doctoral thesis at the London School of Economics, '[w]hile Dr Rowse's scholarship was respected, his literary skills admired, it was felt that he was not part of the modern scientific school of history, a brilliant individual out on his own'.[1]

Thereafter, Rowse's scholarly reputation declined still further, a slide that accelerated after his retirement from All Souls in 1973 and his subsequent retreat to Cornwall. It is only now, in the early twenty-first century, that there are the first signs of his rehabilitation in the eyes of academic commentators. It is not so much that the intrinsic value of his sizeable corpus is being systematically reassessed. Even if it were, much of it would still be considered dubiously ephemeral, no doubt. Rather, it is that there is now emerging a clearer understanding of Rowse's early contribution to what is known today as 'the new British historiography'. This understanding has arisen, not from Richard Ollard's biography and edited diaries, significant as these are, but from a new mood in the academic world itself.

First of all, and coincidently, the year 2003—the hundredth anniversary of Rowse's birth—was also the four-hundredth anniversary of the death of Elizabeth I. Inevitably, the academic community took notice of the latter, and in so doing could hardly avoid noticing Rowse. The Royal Historical Society, for example, organized a commemorative conference 'Elizabeth I and the Expansion of England', a title that, as the society's *Newsletter* acknowledged, 'was shamelessly borrowed from A.L. Rowse's *The Expansion of Elizabethan England* of 1955'.[2] A further coincidence was that 2003 was also the fiftieth anniversary of the Coronation of Elizabeth II, and in its May 2003 edition the magazine *History Today* reprinted an article by Rowse from 1953 on the Coronation of the first Elizabeth, together with an appreciation by Christopher Haigh of Rowse's contribution to the study of Elizabethan history.[3]

The latter was an abridged version of Haigh's masterly Introduction to a new commemorative edition of *The England of Elizabeth*, first published in 1950. It was a significant critical assessment of Rowse's major work. Haigh readily acknowledged Rowse's shortcomings, and the fact that *The England of Elizabeth* '[i]nevitably, and splendidly. . . is a book of its time': a volume that had wrestled with what were then current historiographical problems, but which were now dated and outworn. But, as Haigh also acknowledged, Rowse was in several respects 'path-breaking—or at least path-pointing': not least because 'he was one of those who moved away from the narrative of high politics and helped to refocus English historical studies for the later twentieth century'. Moreover, '[m]uch of Rowse's material came from the localities. . . he. . . sought to marry national and local history', and in achieving this his *The England of Elizabeth* was a 'huge advance on [G.M.] Trevelyan's *English Social History* (1944): in its range of sources, in its conceptual sophistication, in its intellectual precision and mastery of detail, and in the interest and significance of what it had to say'. Rowse was, Haigh concluded, 'certainly (if rather briefly) a significant academic historian'.[4]

In reaching this assessment, Haigh recognized that *Tudor Cornwall*, Rowse's earlier and 'ground-breaking' book, had pioneered the method made plain in *The England of Elizabeth*—namely the use of local sources, and the fusion of the 'local' with the 'national'—and he also saw that in his later volume, *The Expansion of Elizabethan England* (1955), Rowse 'had almost invented a new subject'.[5] Indeed he had. But it is only very recently that historians have come to understand the extent to which this was so. And fittingly, and not entirely coincidently, it is historians of Cornwall who have largely led the way in this new appreciation of the important contribution by Rowse to the writing of British (and Cornish) history.[6]

The new British historiography

Central to the thesis of *The Expansion of Elizabethan England* was Rowse's argument that 'the sixteenth century saw the great awakening for all the island peoples'.[7] Today, in the early twenty-first century, this view is at the heart of the 'new British historiography': the new approach to the writing of British history that eschews hitherto dominant Anglocentric perspectives and stresses instead the individual but complementary roles of the constituent territories of the British Isles—or rather, in the parlance of the new British historiography, of the 'Atlantic Archipelago'. Nowhere has this approach been more significant than in the study of the early modern period, the years from the end of the fifteenth century until the late seventeenth or thereabouts, when—as Rowse suggested—the state-building activities of England (and, to a lesser extent, Scotland) brought the several peoples of these islands into vigorous contact as they coalesced and reacted to the processes of state formation.

In tackling this era, historians such as John Morrill and Steven G. Ellis have abandoned the old Anglocentricity but have also sought to transcend the limitations of compartmentalized English, Welsh, Irish and Scottish histories by taking a 'holistic' view of the development of the Atlantic Archipelago.[8] Although the resultant 'four nations' (England, Wales, Ireland, Scotland) view of British history has to some observers appeared unnecessarily simplistic and constrained, in practice it has proved sufficiently flexible to accommodate, and indeed to encourage, new approaches to regional history, enabling historians to set regional distinctiveness within the experience of the Archipelago as a whole. Helen M. Jewell, for example, in her *The North–South Divide*, has examined the origins of Northern consciousness within the English state, arguing that the North existed as a distinct culture zone long before the industrial revolution re-invented its separate identity.[9] Closer to home, and even more profoundly, Mark Stoyle's *West Britons: Cornish Identities and the Early Modern British State* has fundamentally subverted the 'four nations' approach by establishing Cornwall incontrovertibly as one of the component territories and the Cornish as one of the constituent peoples of the Atlantic Archipelago.[10] But, far from refuting the basic tenets of the new British historiography, Stoyle's intervention, in revealing the limitations of an assumed 'four nations' history, has brought a renewed freshness, subtlety and vitality to the Archipelagic debate.

And yet, there was a certain paradox in Stoyle's contribution. As Stoyle himself remarked, Cornwall has come late to the current Archipelagic debate, for too long hidden from the historian's gaze by the 'four nations' paradigm. Geraint H. Jenkins, a distinguished historian of early modern Wales, agrees: Stoyle 'deserves high praise for rescuing the descendants of Corineus [the Cornish] from the marginalizing effects of Anglocentric historiography'. Moroever, 'it is a measure of his achievement that no self-respecting early modernist can afford any longer to ignore the contribution of one of the component territories and constituent peoples of the British Isles to the current debate on "Britishness"'.[11] But, as we have seen already, almost fifty years earlier Rowse was busy 'inventing' his new subject, the forerunner to the great 'Archipelagic' debate of the last decade or so, and in so doing he had already placed Cornwall and the Cornish centre-stage, describing the intrusion of the Tudor state into Cornish affairs as characteristic of English expansionism in that period. So what had happened in the half-century since the crafting of *The Expansion of Elizabeth England* to render Rowse's pioneering work invisible, and with it the role of Cornwall and the Cornish in the fashioning of the modern British state? The answer lies partly in the long decline of Rowse's academic reputation, accelerated by his turning away from serious to popular history and his growing obsession with Shakespeare, ensuring that his contribution would be routinely ignored or even denied. But it lies also in the fact that—as Whetter has observed—Rowse was out on his own, forging ahead with new ideas that would be not become fashionable until the late 1980s and 1990s.

Detecting Rowse's legacy

It is time, therefore, to return to the work of A.L. Rowse: to rediscover his early and tentative, yet vigorous and in several respects crucial contributions to the formulation of the new British historiography. His prophetic volume *The Expansion of Elizabethan England,* published in 1955, is key to this voyage of rediscovery, but there are other significant books to be revisited too, most notably *Tudor Cornwall.* In these works are revealed not only Rowse's role as one of the progenitors of today's Archipelagic debate but also his parallel concern for history that was 'holistic', able to reconcile the 'local' with the 'national', written from the 'bottom up', and which recognized the 'Celtic' component in Britain and its diaspora overseas—concerns that also anticipated many of today's scholarly pre-occupations.

Ironically, notwithstanding Haigh's recent intervention, many of those who are sympathetically predisposed towards the current Archipelagic debate—and even to Cornwall's accommodation within it—are unaware or dismissive of Rowse's early role. As we have seen in Chapter 1, Norman Davies, architect of the monumental Archipelagic tome *The Isles,* has dismissed Rowse as an 'Anglocentric' historian who did 'little to further the cause either of Cornwall or of non-English perspectives' in the writing of British history, and who seemed to 'thank God for [Cornwall] being overrun by the English'.[12] More generally, there has been a great silence in the academic world and beyond, with only occasionally a glimmer or hint that the name of Rowse might be relevant in such discussion. Even Michael Portillo, in his Foreword to the new edition of *The Expansion of Elizabethan England,* rather missed the point, noting merely that the book was written when Britain was still conscious of its global position 'and in an age before political correctness', allowing Rowse 'to describe England's push into Cornwall, Wales and Ireland without pussyfooting. . . without embarrassment'.[13]

Worse still are those who imagine that they are emulating Rowse's achievement, or following in his footsteps, yet who are either unaware of the particular nature of his contribution or are actively hostile to Cornwall's accommodation within the Archipelagic debate. In 2002–3, for example, there was the amusing if unedifying spectacle of two newly published volumes vying to be considered as Rowse's successor. First was John Chynoweth's unimaginatively entitled *Tudor Cornwall*, a culturally blind local history that hardly ventured beyond consideration of the gentry, exhibiting none of the strengths of Rowse's original and unaware of the wider historiographical context, yet asserting boldly in its dustcover notes that it was 'the first major book on the subject since the late A.L. Rowse's pioneering book of 1941'.[14] Bent on dismissing Cornish distinctiveness, Chynoweth ignored recent advances and discoveries in Cornish-language scholarship, while downplaying the significance of Cornish religious pilgrimages to Brittany and the fact that Cornish saints were routinely imagined to have had Welsh or Irish origins, thus seriously underestimating the popular consciousness of ordinary Cornish people. As Nicholas Orme has remarked in his review of Chynoweth's book: 'People [in Tudor Cornwall] seem to have believed (or been told) that their Christian origins lay with these nations [Brittany, Wales, Ireland] rather than England or Rome'.[15]

J.P.D. Cooper's *Propaganda and the Tudor State*, the second of the recent volumes, was trumpeted by its marketing literature as a timely successor to Rowse's *Tudor Cornwall*, but was in fact a surprisingly confused book that, like Chynoweth's volume, attempted to undo the Cornish particularism emphasized by Rowse.[16] Adopting instead a Devon-and-Cornwall model, Cooper was confronted time and again by inconvenient evidence that did not fit his thesis, and was reduced to either downplaying its significance or admitting a grudging acknowledgement of Cornwall's distinctiveness. Reliant, like Chynoweth, on outdated and long-discredited work on the history of the Cornish language, Cooper was similarly light on recent Cornish scholarship and his book has been the subject of a devastating critique by Bernard Deacon. Errors of fact, flawed judgement, and interpretations that are awry, combine with 'a serious lack of historical imagination' to ensure that this book is not a convincing successor to Rowse let alone a persuasive engagement with current historiographical debate.[17]

Paradoxically, despite these unpromising attempts to follow where Rowse had led, it is where Rowse's influence is unspoken, unacknowledged, uncited that it is best detected and is at its most profound. Indeed, beyond the silence, for the discerning observer the continuing influence of Rowse is unmistakable. Such acknowledgement as there was before Stoyle's intervention of Cornwall's place in the Atlantic Archipelago was due almost entirely to Rowse's elaboration of the Cornish experience—in his *Tudor Cornwall* and in its wider contextualization in *The Expansion of Elizabethan England*. How else, for example, would one explain Steven G. Ellis's confident assertions regarding Cornwall in his pathfinding article 'Not Mere English' in 1988, where he described 'the extension of English law and language in Ireland, Scotland, Wales and Cornwall from the mid 1530s onwards' and noted that within the Tudor state 'Cornwall, with its separate language, exhibited special features'?[18] Equally, Hugh Kearney's treatment of Cornwall in his 1989 book *The British Isles*—where he observed that 'Celtic-speaking Cornwall. . . was incorporated into "England", governmentally if not culturally'—smacks strongly of Rowse's influence, though one searches in vain for mention of Rowse in the notes and 'Selected reading list'.[19]

Mark Stoyle, more explicitly, in his 1997 article on 'Cornish Rebellions 1497–1648' recalled the comparative importance of Rowse's work, noting that 'A.L. Rowse has described the 1549 rising as Cornwall's equivalent of the Scottish '45 and the comparison seems an apt one'.[20] More significant still, Michael Hechter in his *Internal Colonialism: The Celtic Fringe in British National Development*, published in 1975 before the current rush of Archipelagic history, observed that the territorial extent of the United Kingdom had occurred through a lengthy period of territorial interactions and annexations. Rowse, he considered, had enjoyed an early and pivotal role in elucidating this process, and he cites a telling article in a 1957 edition of the *William and Mary Quarterly* by Rowse and remarks with considerable insight and historiographical sophistication that 'Rowse is quite well aware of the fact that his own Cornish origins were indispensable to this view of British history'.[21] But although, like Rowse, an early advocate of what we would recognize now as an Archipelagic approach to British history, Hechter has—again like Rowse—not been generally accepted into the community of Archipelagic writers, partly because his own academic domain is sociology and political science rather than history proper, and partly because his 'internal colonialism' thesis has endured sustained savaging from other scholars, notably Jim Bulpitt in his masterly *Territory and Power in the United Kingdom*.[22] Rather like Rowse, Hechter has been seen by many as a maverick and an outsider, and his identification of Rowse as a forerunner of the new British historiography has, therefore, gone largely unnoticed and unremarked.

That Hechter was writing from America may have influenced his work's cool reception in Britain, and it almost certainly accounts for Hechter's selection of Rowse as a historian worthy of note: for Rowse's reputation had declined less quickly on that side of the Atlantic. It was in the United States, indeed, that Rowse had acquired one of his most devoted academic adherents, Amos C. Miller. Miller's *Sir Henry Killigrew*, a biography of the Elizabethan Cornish diplomat, appeared in 1963. In the book's Acknowledgements, Miller recorded his debt to Rowse's encouragement, and Rowse himself contributed an Introduction. Rowse praised 'Dr Miller's excellent book' and 'his contribution to our joint [British and American] historiography', adding that Miller 'has got the Cornish background of the Killigrews accurately and well—which is not easy for those who do not belong here'. Rowse hoped 'that more young Americans will follow Dr Miller's example. . . I not only commend his book but congratulate him on his achievement'.[23]

Suitably encouraged, Miller proceeded with a second book, published in 1979, *Sir Richard Grenville of the Civil War*: a curious title, until one recognizes that Miller was deliberately echoing that of Rowse's earlier volume, *Sir Richard Grenville of the Revenge*. Again, Miller acknowledged 'a special debt of gratitude to Dr A.L. Rowse'—for first suggesting the topic and for scrutinizing the manuscript before publication—and Rowse's influence may be detected in Miller's nuanced and original treatment of the Cornish context. In particular, it was Miller who pointed out Grenville's attempts, in the closing acts of the Civil War, to secure a separate peace for Cornwall. According to Grenville's plan, the Prince of Wales—Duke of Cornwall—would head this independent Cornish statelet. The Prince would thus, according to Clarendon, the contemporary observer, 'sit a neuter between King and Parliament' and, as Miller observed, Cornwall would be permitted by treaty to conduct its own trade with foreign countries, with the Prince allowed for his own maintenance the surpluses from Duchy estates beyond Cornwall in Parliamentary England.[24] Miller's insights, sanctioned and possibly prompted by Rowse, amounted to an extremely important contribution to what would become shortly an animated debate about the significance of peoples and territories in the Civil War. But, published by a local history imprint in England, Miller's book failed to gain the attention of the new British historiography as it developed in the subsequent decade or so. It was not until Mark Stoyle's much later intervention in *West Britons* that Grenville's plan for a separate Cornish peace—and thus the importance of Cornwall and the Cornish in the territorial complexity of the Civil War—was given due prominence on the academic stage.

And so despite these fleeting and fragmentary evidences—implicit and very occasionally explicit—of Rowse's influence, there has been no place for him and no acknowledgement of his contribution in the principal historiographical texts of recent years. For example, there is no mention of Rowse in Glen Burgess's lengthy and otherwise illuminating Introduction to his important collection *The New British History*, published, like Davies's tome, in 1999. Ironically, looking back to try to identify the founding fathers (or mothers) of the new British historiography, Burgess alighted briefly on the work of Veronica Wedgwood, who '[i]n one of her essays. . . managed deftly to weave a British dimension into an account of the causes of the English Civil War'.[25] The irony is that Wedgwood and Rowse, as we have seen in Chapter 4, were once close friends and collaborators; she, when an undergraduate student at Lady Margaret Hall, was one of his first and (he averred) best pupils. They saw each other frequently when Rowse was in London during the 1930s (she even encouraged him to write a play about Elizabeth I and was complimentary about his poetry), and she wrote an enthusiastic review of his *The Spirit of English History*, published in 1943.[26] As an editorial assistant at Jonathan Cape, Rowse's first publisher, Wedgwood remained in almost constant contact with her former mentor, nurturing a friendship that did not turn sour until 1969.[27]

In their closeness over many decades, as like-minded friends and as professional historians with similar interests, it is almost certain that some of Rowse's early ideas about a 'British dimension' might have rubbed off on his erstwhile student, especially on occasions such as those when together they visited Boconnoc and the Civil War sites of East Cornwall. In the academic world of today, or at least until very recently, it is, as Burgess has evidenced, Wedgwood and not Rowse whom historians have chosen to remember and respect. This helps to explain why Steven G. Ellis in his otherwise excellent article 'Tudor Northumberland: British History in an English County'—a contribution to a recent collection of Archipelagic essays—failed to note the compelling comparative relevance of Rowse's *Tudor Cornwall*: an omission which was echoed elsewhere in his chapter 'The Tudor Borderlands, 1485–1603' in John Morrill's *The Oxford Illustrated History of Tudor and Stuart Britain*.[28]

From Pocock to *The Isles*

In searching for the origins of the new British historiography, Burgess and others like him have settled almost unanimously upon the New Zealand historian J.G.A. (John) Pocock, who in an address to the New Zealand Historical Association in 1973 made 'a plea for a new subject', a plea that was published subsequently in New Zealand, British and American academic journals over the next decade.[29] Notwithstanding the brief acknowledgement of Wedgwood's earlier influence, this posits the new British historiography as a remarkably recent phenomenon, still hardly more than a quarter of a century old. From this perspective, it had begun hesitantly in the mid-1970s, finding its feet in the late 1980s in contributions such as Steven G. Ellis's article 'Not Mere English: The British Perspective 1400–1650' and Hugh Kearney's *The British Isles: A History of Four Nations*, gaining maturity in collections like Bradshaw's and

Morrill's *The British Problem c.1534–1707: State Formation in the Atlantic Archipelago* in 1996, and culminating (perhaps) in Norman Davies's *The Isles* on the eve of the Millennium.[30]

As Burgess observed, '[t]he British history for which Pocock called was a long time in coming'. However, '[w]hen it did come, it bore only partial resemblance to the vision that Pocock's wizardry had so beguiling conjured from nothing [*sic*]'.[31] For what Pocock had envisaged was not only a new approach to the study of these islands but one which took the story of the several British peoples beyond the Archipelago to America, South Africa, Australia and (of course) his native New Zealand, a broad panorama that would first explain the coalescence of peoples in the Archipelago and then trace the export and impact of this multi-threaded 'Britishness' in the New World. As Pocock explained, the new British history 'should start with what I have called the Atlantic archipelago'.[32] But it ought not be 'confined to the island that the cartographers have called "Britain"'. Rather, he said, it should extend first to encompass the enigmatic, ambiguous, partly colonial relationship between Ireland and the several peoples of the emerging British state, and then extend still further 'into oceanic, American and global dimensions'.[33]

The archipelagic Rowse

As Burgess has remarked, the new approaches to British history that have appeared have not generally been like this. Despite the very recent emergence of a 'British world' perspective from the editorial pens of Carl Bridge and Kent Fedorowich which seeks to establish a global project much like that which Pocock had in mind,[34] the method of those Archipelagic historians who have looked beyond these islands has more often than not been to construct European comparisons—to compare the processes of state formation in the Archipelago with those on the Continent itself. While pointing to many pertinent and important comparisons between the Archipelagic and Continental experiences, this had had the effect, critics might argue, of deflecting the historian's gaze from the rest of 'the British problem'—its diasporic context. Paradoxically, just as Rowse's early contribution to the formulation of Archipelagic perspectives has been overlooked, denied or plain forgotten, so his equally early insistence on a perspective that took the experience of the British peoples first to Ireland and then on to the New World has been likewise disregarded. Here, for example, is Rowse's assessment in his *The Expansion of Elizabethan England* of the processes of state formation in the Tudor period:

> The subject of this volume is the expansion of that society, both
> by the state and by individual enterprise, first into the margin of

backward societies at home—Cornwall, Wales, the Borders, with
the sweep of a sickle on the map: into Ireland, where the process
involved conquest and colonization; then across the oceans, to our
first contacts with Russia, the Canadian North—the tenacious
search for a North-East or North-West Passage to the riches of
Eastern trade—our emergence into the Pacific, the search for *Terra
Australis* (the ultimate discovery of Australia may be seen as a
distant product of the Elizabethan age). . . the first projects and
attempts at the colonization of North America.[35]

Of course, it may be objected that the very title of Rowse's book betrays
unionist, even imperialist, predispositions, with the author's ingrained
anglophilia never far beneath the surface and his adherence to the Whig
tradition of English history worn firmly on his sleeve—all of which is
anathema to Archipelagic history as practised today. As Portillo intimates,
the phrase 'backward societies' is value-laden and pejorative, and who
today could write innocently of 'the discovery of Australia'? Elsewhere
there is language that would offend the sensibilities of Norman Davies—
and indeed many others—and give credence to his stinging criticisms of
Rowse. We learn, for example, that in Scotland the embryonic Scottish
state had to deal with 'Celtic chaos', while in Ireland there was the
'deplorable spectacle of a Celtic civilization in part medieval and in part
pre-medieval. . . in a stage of rapid social decomposition'. The Borders
of Scotland and England were characterized by 'the primitive conditions
of life'. Wales had been rescued by the Tudors 'from the disaster of Owen
Glendower's rebellion', while 'Cornwall was brought inevitably, and prof-
itably, into the mainstream of English life'. But there was Cornish
resistance to this English intrusion: 'One recognizes the familiar symptoms—how boring they are!—of anti-English feeling'.[36]

These scathing and dismissive words no doubt reflect the fact that *The
Expansion of Elizabethan England* was researched and written at the time
of Rowse's greatest disaffection and disappointment, most especially in
the aftermath of his 'failed' political career and his keen sense of 'rejection' by Cornwall and the Cornish people. It is also important to recognize
that his more assured advocacy of things Cornish and Celtic came much
later, in the evening of his career when he had retired to his Cornish home
at Trenarren. However, despite objections today to the attitudes and
language so uncomfortably apparent in his book, in the context of his time
(immediate post-war) and place (Oxford), Rowse's approach was already
a significant departure from what was then Anglocentric orthodoxy in the
writing of English/British history. Obscured perhaps by his obvious
approval of the actual process of English expansionism, was his understanding that state formation in these islands, though dominated by

English imperatives, involved a series of complex relationships between the several territorial components of the isles, not least as they coalesced and reacted to those state-forming activities. Moreover, long before Pocock's largely unheeded call for a British history that sought first to understand the Archipelago and then, armed with understanding, to proceed to 'oceanic, American and global dimensions', Rowse was already there arguing for just such a juxtaposition. There was also, long before the appearance of Mark Stoyle and others on the scholarly stage, recognition in Rowse of Cornwall and the Cornish as distinctive and integral in the Archipelagic story.

Indeed, Rowse's apparently Anglocentric title served to disguise the radical structure of his book and his method, for the crucial first four chapters were devoted not—as one would have expected of his time and place—to the English 'centre', the hub of the expansionist imperative, but rather to the Archipelagic reactions of Scotland, Cornwall, Wales and Ireland to England's state-forming aspirations and activities. Remarkably, there was brief acknowledgement, too, of the state-building efforts of Scotland, which, even as the English state looked to consolidate and secure the Borders, sought to bring the Gaelic Highlands and Islands more firmly within Edinburgh's Lowland sway. There was even a comparative word or two about Brittany, that 'Celtic duchy'[37] as Rowse dubbed it, which was increasingly the object of French state-building attentions in this period. This was a recognition on Rowse's part that Continental comparisons might be instructive but an acknowledgement too that in those days of state-building flux Brittany was still—culturally, economically, even politically—somewhere on the edge of the Archipelagic world.

'The approach through the Celtic lands was an inspiration'

Should all this seem suspiciously like an *ipse post facto* attempt to attribute to Rowse an originality and prophetic vision that in fact he did not possess, then it is useful to consider the contemporary reaction to his book. Rowse himself, in September 1944, had written to the Warden of All Souls, submitting for approval his research plans for the future, intimating the genesis of what would become his great Elizabethan trilogy (of which *The Expansion of Elizabethan England* was to be a part): 'the main direction of my reading and research', he wrote, 'continues to be the Elizabethan Age. And I want to write what will be a really big book, a kind of successor to *Tudor Cornwall*, on the whole Elizabethan Age in all its aspects, political and economic, social and literary; in fact a portrait of a whole society.'[38] Actually, what Rowse achieved was something rather more than this. His friend and mentor G.M. Trevelyan welcomed *The Expansion of Elizabethan England*, writing that 'I enjoyed it very much, particularly the part about Cornwall, which was an excellent introduction to the subject of the expansion of England'.[39] But the real significance of the work was recognized by Sir John Neale, doyen of Tudor historians, who wrote to Rowse from his home in Beaconsfield in June 1955, shortly after *The Expansion of Elizabethan England* had appeared. Neale knew at once that Rowse's approach was novel, ground-breaking, that the decision to commence his study with the Celtic lands was an insightful flash of brilliance which would change the way in which the history of these islands was considered: 'I admire its conception. The approach through the Celtic lands was an inspiration. It is fresh; it is absolutely right; and artistically it unifies the whole story. It gives one a new grasp of the age. . . You have reason to be very proud indeed.'[40]

This was high praise indeed, for Neale was then at the peak of his powers and at the very pinnacle of his profession. He had begun his career at University College London in 1919 and, by way of the Chair of Modern History at Manchester, gone on in 1927 to become Astor Professor of English History at University College. On his retirement in 1956 Neale was appointed Emeritus Professor. For many years he presided over the Tudor Studies seminar group (of which Rowse was a member) at the Institute of Historical Studies, and it was there that new ideas were raised and debated. Not surprisingly, for a time Rowse exercised some influence within the group, and when in 1961 colleagues published a *Festschrift* in honour of Neale it aimed to review 'recent trends in Tudor political and social historiography' in which, among other things, '[o]ur Irish, Scottish and Welsh contributors have enabled us to include something of the complex story of the relations between the four peoples who occupy these islands'.[41] This was proto-Archipelagic language, an indication perhaps of Neale's developing taste and of the influence of Rowse upon him, although there was in the book but one fleeting mention of Cornwall and no contribution from Rowse himself (though there was a 'Westcountry' piece by W.G. Hoskins on Exeter's Elizabethan merchants). By this time, perhaps, Rowse was already moving on: no longer the intimate of the lead thinkers in the field, no longer able to persuade and cajole in the way he had before, heading inexorably into other areas (notably Shakespearean) and—although the third volume of the trilogy was not published until 1971–2—away from serious history. The Archipelagic legacy remained, though it was not to be fully grasped until years later, but Rowse's role was already being forgotten.

However, all this lay in the future. For the moment, in 1955, there was only praise and adulation. Like Neale, the *New York Times*, sensing the novelty of Rowse's approach, thought that the general thesis of the 'English expansion in that period into [other] areas of the British Isles' and into the New World constituted an 'original contribution to historical

knowledge'.[42] The *Chattanooga Times*, equally enthusiastic but less incisive, considered this expansion England's 'manifest destiny', while the
more cerebral *Hartford Court Magazine* identified in the book 'a great
trend on the part of western European governments to amalgamate the
Celtic fringes of their states'.[43] Rowse had put 'Ireland into a generaliza-
tion that includes Brittany, another Celtic society at the same time being
subjected by the French crown, [and] the Scottish Isles'. This was 'a brilliant and refreshing interpretation', one 'which only a Cornishman' could
have conceived.[44] Closer to home, the *West Briton*—in the form of a review
from Claude Berry's pen—echoed the importance of Rowse's Cornish
insights, opining that '[o]nly a Cornishman could have exposed the real
significance to Cornwall and the Cornish people of the transition from the
county's age-old separateness and isolation from England to its post-
Reformation place in our island story'.[45] Jack Simmons, writing in *Time
and Tide*, agreed. Hitherto, he argued, the expansion of Elizabethan
England was 'far from being generally understood'. This was because, he
said, 'in England, so little attention has been paid to the history of Wales
and Ireland'. But, with *The Expansion of Elizabethan England,* this 'for the
first time' had been addressed: 'Mr Rowse has mastered it'.[46]

'Wild, unruly, un-English and defiant'

This achievement rested not only on the experience gained in the writing
of *The England of Elizabeth* but on the sure foundation of his *Tudor
Cornwall*, published back in 1941—indisputably Rowse's greatest book—
where he had first tested his ideas about the importance of 'locality' in
'national' history, and where he had first elaborated his theme of the
expanding English state and its Celtic neighbour(s). In the Preface to this
remarkable work, Rowse explained that *Tudor Cornwall*, the fruit of a
dozen years' research (interrupted, as we have seen, by political distrac-
tions when a Labour candidate in Cornwall and by illness) had been
conceived initially as a study of the Reformation in Cornwall: what it
meant, where it had come from, and how it had affected society. But these
inquiries soon led him to other fields—economic, political, military,
cultural, and so on—and to his growing conviction that 'the time has come
in our historical writing for a synthesis of local and national history'. And,
recognizing the particular value of Celtic Cornwall as a case study in
attempting this convergence of the 'local' and the 'national', he added:
'Perhaps a Cornishman may be forgiven for thinking that no area would
prove more intrinsically interesting or historically fruitful than Cornwall
in the Tudor age'.[47]

So *Tudor Cornwall* was to be much more than mere local history,
nothing less than an attempt to elucidate Cornish society in all its

complexity against the background of the influences and intrusions of 'national' (i.e. English) affairs in the Tudor era. It was, after all, a turbulent period of change, upheaval and danger, one which witnessed the growing centralization and outward expansion of the English state—both trends which impinged upon the life of Cornwall—and which culminated in the great confrontation with Spain: in which Cornwall was also to play its role. In Rowse's own words:

> From being a far-away, insignificant corner of the land, sunk in its dream of the Celtic past, with its own inner life of legends and superstitions and fears, its memories of Arthur and Mark and Tristan, lapped in religion and the cult of the saints, it was forced in the course of the Elizabethan age into the front-line of the great sea-struggle with Spain. Inevitably, the small backward-looking society struggled against the process: the Rebellions of 1497 and 1549 were to Cornwall what the '15 and '45 were to the Highlands.[48]

Behind the veneer of pejorative language that offends the early twenty-first-century eye (but is more or less symptomatic of mid-twentieth-century scholarship)—the inevitability and futility of the 'backward-looking' society's resistance to change; the implied redundancy of the old Celtic periphery, Catholic Cornwall as much as Gaelic Scotland—is the historiographical innovation inherent in Rowse's approach. The *Sunday Times*, in its review of *Tudor Cornwall* in December 1941, caught well the spirit of the book: 'He [Rowse] tells of the change from the Cornwall of the Wars of the Roses, wild, unruly, un-English, and defiant, to the Cornwall of Elizabeth's latter years, patriotic and Protestant, a bulwark of the realm, its turbulent energy pouring out through its seaports to attack the Spaniard'.[49] But the *Times Literary Supplement*, in its review, detected something more: 'A sense that Cornwall was being exploited for the benefit of foreigners runs through the whole of Mr Rowse's book, and was undoubtedly present to the Cornish mind in this age'.[50] Between them, the reviews had captured the complexity of Rowse's portrait, the transformation wrought by English intrusion but also its trauma: not only the redirection of Cornwall's 'turbulent energy' but also the lingering sense of exploitation and resentment that endured throughout the period, surviving even the Reformation and the wars with Spain. Here we see, perhaps, the influence of Mary Coate (of which more below), but what is especially apparent is Rowse's attempt to match the 'local' to the 'national', to explore the interaction of the two and the impact of the one upon the other.

Rowse was already a devotee of 'total history': the bringing together of the various strands of historical writing in the manner advocated by his hero G.M. Trevelyan. He made plain his position in his *The Use of History*, first published in 1946, where he insisted that there was now an 'impulse towards this kind of total history—giving an account of a society in all its aspects, it geographical environment, the land system and its industries, the governmental and administrative system, the social structure, the political events, the social, religious and cultural life'.[51] In the 1940s this was hardly a conservative approach to the study of history, and especially innovative was his recognition that historical writing should encompass much more than the deeds of the great men and women of the state's 'centre'. But if this was innovative in the 1940s, then it was positively radical almost two decades before when in 1927, as a young scholar still fresh to his subject, he argued for an interpretative 'total history' which would pull obsessive historians away from the minutiae of unceasing and never-to-be-written-up research and force them into wide-ranging, generalizing literary expression:

> it is apparent that the supremacy of research in schools of English history has lasted long enough, and what is needed is a return to synoptic writing. . . Research must go forward all the time, but the exigencies of research have for too long determined historical style. We must expect, therefore, from the new movement a greater breadth of conception, a nobler treatment of subject, which will restore the literary graces which have almost ceased to adorn recent work.[52]

If all this seemed somewhat obscure—the young Rowse had yet to develop the 'easy reading' style for which he was later appreciated—he went on to explain:

> It will no longer be sufficient to describe the minute happenings in the small circle of a governing class under the impression that this is the history of England; and it will become clearer that the history that we read is only the record of changes in the distribution of power within the ruling classes. We shall have to plumb the depths of society in order to reach rock bottom; and upon that foundation we must begin to rear the structure upwards, and give up the attempt to build from the top downwards.[53]

Rowse the anti-antiquarian

Here we can detect Rowse the socialist—anticipating Eric Hobsbawm, perhaps, or E.P. Thompson—but we also see unmistakable signs of the 'holistic' and 'history from below' approaches which became fashionable in the 1960s. E.P. Thompson's essay 'History From Below' in the *Times Literary Supplement* in 1966 is often credited as the 'real starting point' to this movement in historical writing.[54] But, as we have seen already, Rowse was toying with such ideas years before. Indeed, in an apparently unpublished manuscript 'Local and National History', prepared not long after the Second World War, Rowse returned to his favourite subject of the relationship between the 'local' and the 'national': arguing not only for their fusion in a 'total history' but for the relevance of this fusion in attempting history from 'the bottom upwards' (as he termed it). *Tudor Cornwall*, he thought, had provided the model and the inspiration for such work:

> What is new in all this, what is so fascinating *now*, is to watch the way in which this local material is being used to illuminate the history of the nation, of our people as a whole: we are watching the marriage of local and national history, observing the fertilisation of one with the other. It is bringing about a deepening of our nation's history: we no longer think of it as just the narrative of political events on the top surface; we try to carry along in our minds all the layers of the cake, all the strata of society from the bottom upwards.[55]

Lest this should be seen as something less lofty than traditional history, Rowse was quick to insist that this new approach to historical writing was intrinsically more difficult. 'Of course that makes history harder to write', he said, 'almost impossible on the grand scale.' The answer, therefore, was 'to portray society in miniature, to take a particular area at a significant time, a subject that has some homogeneity—like Tudor Cornwall or Wales, Reformation Yorkshire or Lancashire, Medieval Kent or East Anglia in the Civil War'.[56] In considering how such a task might be accomplished, Rowse turned to local history: a field dominated for so long by those he saw as harmless antiquarians who had done much to record in infinite detail all the incidentals of their parishes. Now, however, local history was to be called upon to fulfil an altogether more important task. Rowse smiled upon the antiquarians but he thought their time had passed:

> Local history has for long been a favourite subject of study all up and down the country. I love those generations of antiquarians who have done so much to recover and keep alive the story of their parishes, their families, their counties and towns. I see them—clergymen up from the country with their Gladstone bags. . . to work at the British Museum or Public Record Office; passionate and

often whiskered antiquarian ladies and gentlemen who cared so hotly for learned subjects that the bodies to which they belonged— like the Devonshire Association—were sometimes riven by their quarrels; or quiet county gentlemen in their gilt and calf-bound libraries looking out on the acres of their ancestors—libraries and acres now alike dispersed, the species vanished.[57]

But now local history, if it was to ensure its continuing relevance and its engagement with professional history, had to abandon its antiquarian past and participate in the grander project for which Rowse wished to prepare it:

> there is no doubt that a change has come over the study of local history—it has got a new breath of inspiration: I should say that it is the most promising field of the lot, where some of the best and most fruitful work is being done. . . In my view it offers far better returns than those over-cultivated and too much trodden areas— diplomatic history, the endless works being poured out, the interminable discussions on the history of the two World Wars. When you think of the innumerable books written about Napoleon, think of the libraries that will be written about Hitler![58]

As it happened, Rowse was to be disappointed in his aim, for there was to be no mass realignment in the writing of local history. Notwithstanding the indefatigable efforts of the local history department set up at Leicester, much of this work continued more or less as it had before. W.G. Hoskins, doyen of the Leicester school, a historian as devoted to the study of Devon as Rowse was to that of Cornwall, shared Rowse's enthusiasm for a new approach to local history—Rowse much admired Hoskins's work and Hoskins had made available his unpublished research for inclusion in *The England of Elizabeth*—and the two men corresponded on the subject. In 1960, for example, Hoskins welcomed Rowse's newly published volume on his native parish, writing that: 'Your St Austell book is a little master-piece'.[59]

However, there was profound scepticism amongst many mainstream historians as to whether such attempts were even desirable. G.M. Trevelyan, though an admirer of Rowse and of *Tudor Cornwall*, thought local history merely 'the training ground where a man could find his sea legs before launching out on the broad ocean of national history'. Indeed, 'ever since the publication of *Tudor Cornwall*, I have believed that Mr A.L. Rowse had it in him to become an historian of high rank if he would lay aside lesser activities and bend himself to the production of history on the grand scale'.[60] This Rowse achieved in *The England of Elizabeth*, much to

Trevelyan's approval, though even here, as we have seen, Rowse by no means abandoned his aim of balancing the 'local' and the 'national'— indeed, quite the reverse. There was much material from the 'localities' and an appreciation of the importance of regional diversity, such as the strength of Catholicism in Lancashire, together with—as one would expect—particular recognition of the distinctive characteristics of Wales and Cornwall. Rowse was careful, for example, to quote from Humphry Lluyd's *A Breviary of Britain* of 1568: 'the Cornishmen, being remnants of the old Britons, as they are the stoutest of all the British nations, so they are accounted to this day the most valiant in warlike affairs'.[61]

However, as Rowse recognized, there continued to be resistance from 'national' historians to such an approach, while many local historians, deeply conservative in their amassing of 'facts', were themselves suspicious of his reforming agenda. Every now and again Rowse would re-emerge to call for a study of Tudor this or Stuart that or somewhere in the Civil War but it was not until the appearance of the much later work of David Underdown—of which more below—that he felt that his urgings were at last being heeded. By then Rowse had in any case drifted away from mainstream history, so much so that later writers on local history habitually forgot his pioneering work. H.P.R. Finberg, then head of the Leicester school, had as early as 1952 regretted the attitude of Trevelyan and like-minded historians, fearing the effects their prejudices would have upon Rowse. Finberg disapproved of their view that 'if you write it [local history] as well as Mr Rowse, it is a pity you cannot find something better to do'—a regret he repeated again in 1967—and he opposed the unhelpful suggestion that it was a shame to waste promising talent on the writing of local history.[62] Later, in 1987, Charles Phythian-Adams, also of the Leicester school, recalled that *Tudor Cornwall* had been 'national history localized', a 'microcosm' of society as a whole, but his remembrance was the exception rather than the rule.[63] By the 1990s, Rowse the local historian was, by and large, forgotten.

It was John D. Marshall—in his *The Tyranny of the Discrete: A Discussion of the Problems of Local History in England*, published in the year of Rowse's death—who at last admitted this omission and belatedly restored Rowse to something like his position as a progenitor of post-antiquarian local history. Like Rowse so many years before, Marshall argued for a new direction for local historians, noting that in the previous forty or fifty years the practice of local history research and writing had not lived up to the expectations of its academic advocates. 'In standard and style of approach', he observed, 'it has clearly disappointed the proponents of people's history, history from the grass-roots.'[64] Criticizing antiquarian local historians who beavered away in local record offices with no real aim other than the amassing of 'facts' about their preferred localities, Marshall in an earlier article had regretted that 'there have been few successful attempts to look at regions holistically'.[65] There were, he noted, relatively few volumes—mostly in the area of regional economic history—that had come anywhere near the mark. In the *Tyranny of the Discrete* Marshall returned to this article, explaining that in his survey of those successful histories he had unfortunately overlooked the much earlier work of A. L. Rowse. 'One major work not there noticed', Marshall observed, 'is Rowse, A.L. (1941), *Tudor Cornwall: Portrait of a Society*, which is essentially "political" in approach, while it attempts at the same time to do justice to economic and social factors'.[66]

Rowse, Henderson, Coate and 'Q'

As reviewers and commentators had suggested, in considering his novel approach to the writing of 'local' and 'national' history, it was important to recognize Rowse's Cornish credentials and to understand their underlying influence in moulding his disposition as a historian. Significantly, Rowse's interest in local history was due in the first place to the influence of his close friend Charles Henderson, whom he had met in 1928 (see Chapter 4). In later years Rowse would insist that Henderson was really 'an antiquarian' and 'not a historian', distancing himself from Henderson's youthful enthusiasm for collecting ancient documents and enthusing over the obscure. In 1976 Rowse wrote that Henderson 'did not finish much in the way of books', his principal contribution being 'a voluminous mass of notes'. As Rowse explained, '[h]e was really an antiquary—an honourable title—rather than an historian. . . folk in Cornwall do not know that; nor that, when he died, he was actually turning away from his intense, rather parochial, concentration on Cornwall, perhaps in the process of development towards becoming an historian'.[67] However, it was Henderson who had alerted Rowse to the possibilities of local history in Cornwall. Well-connected and well-off, certainly when compared to the young Rowse, Henderson had the means to explore Cornwall and was welcomed to the muniment rooms of almost all its great houses, something impossible for the working-class Rowse until Henderson had made the necessary introductions. Thus it was, as we have seen, that Rowse had his first taste of a 'country-house weekend with Charles Henderson at Penmount' and, accompanied by Henderson, 'Sunday lunch at Killagordan, sequestered Queen Anne House deep in the valley. . . [t]ea with the Masefields at Mawnan. . . [s]upper at Lis Escop with Bishop Frere'.[68]

As we have also observed, Rowse was deeply impressed by his companion's apparent knowledge of every church, farm, lane, stream and bridge from the Scillies to the Tamar. It was this topographical intimacy, the willingness to step beyond the record office and into the field, that, Rowse considered, gave Henderson's antiquarianism its particular innovative quality: something that promised a fresh approach to local history—if only Henderson could be persuaded to write it all up. Hitherto, Rowse had not considered seriously the possibilities of Cornish research that might be significant or sophisticated enough to stand up in the national and international arenas. In any event, 'I wasn't interested; Cornish history was not my subject, history in general, literature, and politics were'.[69] Furthermore, it was Sir Arthur Quiller Couch, the immortal 'Q', who had thus far guided the young Rowse, an influence that had helped him on the road to Oxford but had also led him firmly in the direction of literature. 'My interests were as much literary as historical', Rowse wrote later, 'I thought of Q as my model and mentor.'[70] Henderson, however, emerged as a new, in some respects stronger, influence, unveiling for Rowse a hidden Cornwall that had been beyond his view and whetting his appetite for Cornish research. Henderson's main interest was medieval, so that without any sense of rivalry or intrusion Rowse could happily concentrate on the Tudor period. Moreover, Henderson introduced Rowse to the difficult but essential world of paleography. As Rowse observed: 'I came to manuscripts rather late. . . [u]nlike my early friend and mentor, Charles Henderson, the leading antiquary of his time, who was up to his knees in manuscripts from the time he was a boy'. And so, '[a]ctually I learned my A.B.C. of Elizabethan handwriting from a transcript that Charles Henderson made from a document in the City Library in Exeter, by systematically comparing the two'.[71]

When Henderson died on his honeymoon in Rome in 1933, Rowse was devastated. Already convinced by Henderson of the intrinsic value, as well as of the fascination, of Cornish research, Rowse saw it as his duty to take up where Henderson had left off: to bring the worth and international relevance of Cornish history to the academic world and to the informed reading public. 'When he died so young, at thirty-three, I was heartbroken', Rowse later recalled, adding that 'it worked out strangely that I should become his inheritor. He was essentially a medievalist, not attracted to the Tudor period. It fell to me to write *Tudor Cornwall*, and to dedicate it to his memory—since I was determined to do everything I could to keep it green.'[72] Rowse also collaborated with Charles's widow, Isobel, to publish in 1935 an edited collection of Henderson's *Essays in Cornish History*, to which Q contributed an elegant Preface, and in 1937 the Royal Institution of Cornwall published Henderson's *History of Constantine*, lightly edited by Canon G.H. Doble.[73] This latter book had been in the making for some years, Constantine being amongst Henderson's favourite Cornish parishes and easily accessible when he was living at Falmouth and later at Penmount. To the modern eye it is a strange volume. The greater part—which was no doubt the earliest to be written—is in traditional anti-quarian style, with its painstakingly detailed account of church and vicars and manors. The final, and much shorter, part ventures cautiously into the realm of social history and into the modern period, with short essays on education, Nonconformity and the several industries of the parish. But there is only one page devoted to copper mining, and there is no mention at all of Constantine's great nineteenth-century industry, granite quar-rying, or of the craft trade unionism and the emigration of skilled workers that it engendered.

However, there was perhaps just enough 'history from below' in this volume to satisfy Rowse, and he was certainly delighted when the *History of Constantine* finally saw the light of day, writing loyally and enthusiasti-cally in the *Spectator*. 'The book is a model of what a parish-history should be; it is most thorough, based at every point upon documents in public or private hands, the whole picture made living and real by Charles Henderson's genius for topography, his loving knowledge of every field and building and road, every feature in the Cornish landscape'.[74] In a sense, Rowse may have used the *History of Constantine* as a model or inspi-ration for his own *St Austell: Church: Town: Parish*, published in 1960 to the approval of W.G. Hoskins, although Rowse's book is altogether more integrated, with a leavening of grass-roots history and a much fuller picture of the modern, industrial period (not least the china clay industry into which Rowse himself had been born).[75] John McManners, in his memoir of Rowse in the *Proceedings of the British Academy*, thought *St Austell* 'a gem of local history writing',[76] but for Rowse it was a sideshow, if not a distraction, a momentary departure from other tasks to help the parish church in its fund-raising efforts. For Rowse, if local history was to be important it should be more than parish history: able to contribute to the 'national' picture in the way that *Tudor Cornwall* had.

In this conviction, articulated time and again over many years, we see the influence, not so much of Charles Henderson but of Mary Coate, who had reached much the same intellectual position during the 1930s. Coate's position was exemplified in her *Cornwall in the Great Civil War and Interregnum, 1642–1660*, published in 1933, the year of Henderson's death.[77] Mary Coate was, like Veronica Wedgwood, at Lady Margaret Hall, and was likewise an early friend of Rowse. He recalled how 'conge-nial [it] was meeting Mary Coate, who was writing her book *Cornwall in the Civil War*. A good historian, she was a dedicated Tory, a devoted teacher, who handed on pupils for me to teach.'[78] She had been his first guest at an Encaenia Luncheon at the Codrington, and when they walked together across the parks or met for tea in 'her roomy book-laden room', they were 'each of us brimming over with talk about Cornwall'.[79] He also lent her books, and a measure of their closeness was the fact that, when

Rowse lay gravely ill from a stomach operation and his mother was summoned from Cornwall, it was Mary Coate who offered to meet her from the train.[80] As Rowse recalled years later, when he was ill at Oxford, '[p]eople were very kind to my parents—especially Mary Coate'.[81] A further connection was that Noreen Sweet, Rowse's lifelong friend, had for a time taught English at Truro High School for Girls when Dora Coate, Mary's sister, was headmistress there.[82] Again, years later, Rowse chose to emphasize in his Foreword to the *History* of the school that 'I was a great friend at the University [Oxford] of her sister, Mary Coate, admirable historian of Cornwall during the Civil War'.[83]

When Coate's book first appeared, Rowse wrote an approving review for *Devon and Cornwall Notes and Queries*.[84] He thought the volume perhaps 'the most important single contribution to Cornish history that has been made'. From Rowse, this was praise indeed. Yet he went further still, adding: 'But it is more than that: it is a valuable contribution to the history of England'. Here Rowse was echoing Coate's belief in the symbiotic relationship between the 'local' and the 'national' in the Civil War, 'this dualism between the visible political changes at the centre and the unvarying life of the countryside' as she chose to describe it.[85] 'The history of Cornwall in this period has more than a local interest and importance', Coate insisted, '[i]t belongs to the realm of the historian rather than of the antiquarian'.[86] Rowse agreed entirely and was at pains to remind his readers in another review that what Coate had found in the Civil War in Cornwall was also true of the earlier period, when the intrusion of the Tudor state in Cornish affairs had had profound consequences for both Cornwall and England. That era, he observed, was 'a century that saw an army of Cornishmen march from one end of the country to the other in 1497, until it met with defeat only upon Blackheath, and that witnessed the dangerous Rebellion of 1549, which paralysed government for a time and ultimately led to the downfall of the Protector Somerset'.[87] Here there was also more than a hint of Cornish particularism, something that Coate had made plain in her own book where she sought to explain the devotion of the ordinary folk to the Royalist cause in terms of 'the passionate attachment of the Cornish to their own county and their own race' and a 'local patriotism, born of racial difference and geographical isolation'.[88]

It is not difficult to imagine Rowse and Coate—and Wedgwood too—swapping notes and exchanging ideas on such matters, the one influencing the other, and if we can detect in Rowse an early advocate of an Archipelagic approach to British and Cornish history then we must also acknowledge the place of Mary Coate in crafting his views. Indeed, so enthused was Rowse, that at one stage he even thought of writing his own book on Cornwall in the Civil War—'[w]hat will Miss Coate make of it, I wonder?'.[89] To be sure, it is the influence of Coate the historian, and not

Henderson the antiquarian nor Q the literary mentor, that we can see in Rowse's confident characterization of the Cornish at the beginning of the Tudor period. Cornwall was then, he said:

> a homogeneous society of its own, defined by language and having a common heritage underneath, like Brittany or Wales or Ireland, reaching back beyond Normans and Saxons, beyond even Romans in these islands, to an antiquity of which its people were still dimly conscious. Some memory of all this they carried in the legends of the race that haunted them. They remembered that they were a conquered people.[90]

'A Celt myself, I can rise above these prejudices'

The Cornwall that Rowse thus described was the 'Celtic Cornwall' of his historical imagination. Indeed, all the while that Rowse was writing of *English* history and extolling England's Elizabethan greatness, he was mindful of a countervailing and component 'Celtic' existence, a sensibility sharpened by his view of Cornwall as a land of 'difference' and given breadth by his Archipelagic interpretation of the processes of state formation in these isles.

Rowse was encouraged in this consideration of the 'Celtic' element of British history by Fr Dr David Mathew, one-time Bishop-auxiliary of Westminster, whose book *The Celtic Peoples and Renaissance Europe* was published in 1933, the same year that Coate's volume had appeared. Nowadays almost forgotten, Mathew's book was remembered in J.G.A. Pocock's 'plea for a new subject' in 1973. Pocock thought that—in drawing a panoramic picture that stretched from Iberia and Brittany, through Cornwall and Wales, and on to Ireland and Scotland—Mathew was 'sketching what a history of Britain might be like'.[91] Here, Pocock argued, was a history of the isles that was not Anglocentric, one that—despite its pre-war publication—pointed the way ahead for a new generation of scholars. Indeed, in a manner that anticipated the rhetoric of the new British historiography, Mathew had emphasized in his volume 'the change in the structure of life in Britain and the political influence of the Celtic fringes upon the new [Elizabethan] England'. His book, he said, explored 'those Celtic countries which were bound with enthusiasm or reluctance to the Tudor rule'.[92]

Rowse was certainly alert to the relevance of Mathew's work. Mathew had included a chapter on 'The Cornish and Welsh Pirates' in his book, arguing that the intrusion of the Tudor state in Cornish affairs had fatally undermined the independence of action—and thus profitability—of the Cornish piracy industry. 'So long as the leaders could safeguard their harbours, the working expenses were small', Mathew wrote, 'but, as soon as order was established in Cornwall, it was necessary to bribe a whole countryside and there could be no profit.'[93] Rowse was impressed, acknowledging in 1941 'the constant interest and encouragement I have received from Dr David Mathew. . . from whose own historical work I have profited greatly'.[94] The influence was twofold. Firstly, Mathew had argued persuasively for the inclusion of Cornwall in any comprehensive consideration of the Celtic world. Secondly, he had highlighted the all-pervading impact of that Celtic world—of which Cornwall was an integral part—upon the affairs of neighbouring England.

This was music to Rowse's ears. Notwithstanding his enthusiasm for all things English he was a self-confessed 'Celt', and always on the lookout for the opportunity to stress the 'Celtic' in British history. For example, in a patriotic radio broadcast in 1940, designed no doubt to evoke Britain's glory and to strengthen resolve in that darkest hour, he spoke of the 'spirit of English adventure' but immediately offered a corrective:

> That leads me to another point. We say the 'British Empire'—you know it was a Welshman who coined the phrase in the sixteenth century, the distinguished geographer, Dr Dee. And I suppose I ought to say 'the spirit of British adventure', not merely English. For I think the greatness and variety of its record is partly due to the different elements, the different contributions of temperament and character, of English, Scots, Welsh, and Irish: it has made it all the richer.[95]

Similarly, in 1943 Rowse could note that '[n]ineteenth-century historians were apt to regard us simply as an Anglo-Saxon folk; in fact we are really an Anglo-Celtic people'.[96] He also asserted that the Celtic component of English make-up was much greater than popularly imagined, making the English in 'racial' composition far nearer to the French and less close to the Germans than was generally supposed. This was, no doubt, a welcome message at the height of the War, and although it reflected Rowse's by now deeply ingrained hostility to all things German, it also revealed his genuine conviction that the 'Celtic component' of both Britain and England mattered and was important in any historical elucidation of these islands. It was a conviction that Rowse carried with him over the years. It was evidenced, for example, in an aside in his 1987 discussion of the Victorian historian James Froude, where he not only berated Froude for his 'Teutonist' [sic] and anti-Celtic sentiments—'A Celt myself. . . [I] can rise above these prejudices'—but also reaffirmed his belief in an 'Anglo-Celtic England (for we must not overlook Wales and the West of the island)'.[97] The concept of an Anglo-Celtic England, of course, was comfortable and attractive for Rowse or for any other Cornish person faced with the 'in England but not of England' ambiguity of Cornish identity, especially if they relied, as Rowse did, upon the patronage of England for their advancement.

Be that as it may, Rowse's insistence upon a 'Celtic component' represented a recognition on his part of the possibility of non-English perspectives in the writing of British history: a demand for consideration of the 'Celtic' in the make-up of Cornwall, England and Britain that complemented both his Archipelagic view of state formation in these isles and his regard for the necessary reconciliation of the 'local' with the 'national'. But this assessment is in one respect too easy, too neat, for while it gives due acknowledgement to Rowse in the development of these ideas, it avoids the uncomfortable fact that underpinning Rowse's construction of the 'Celtic' was a good deal of racial stereotyping. In the pre-1945 era, when scholars could get away with sweeping generalizations about 'national characteristics', it perhaps did not matter too much, but after the war—with the experience of the Hitler years still fresh in memory and with the emergence of more sophisticated understandings of ethnicity and ethnic identity—Rowse's continued resort to stereotypical characterizations was increasingly frowned upon. While his continual self-ascription of 'Celtic' attitudes, foibles and failings might be indulged, even enjoyed, his attempts to perpetuate outdated stereotypes were met with less tolerance. The 1971 Pelican edition of his *The Use of History* revealed the signs of what must have been an interesting tussle between Rowse and his editor, as Rowse's insistence upon the continued discussion of 'racial characteristics' was tempered by a new demand for 'scientific ethnology'. The resultant compromise is not entirely convincing:

> Nothing is more remarkable to a discerning student of British history than the dualism of English and Celtic characteristics in the people: the extremism, the vivacity and temperament of the one, the reliability, the dogged qualities, the imagination, the sense of moderation of the other. . . Anyone with discernment can observe these strains coming out in our people and their history; and we can say that without involving ourselves in the crudities of racialism. The stock counts for something, and a scientific ethnology is the way to assess it.[98]

Life after Elizabeth

By this time, however, Rowse was already a very different writer from the man who had penned *Tudor Cornwall* thirty years before. Returning to his first love, English literature, the domain of the 'dear Q' whose memory he cherished, Rowse had increasingly turned away from mainstream history and into literary work. Shakespeare, in particular, whose quintessential 'Englishness' and central place in the canon of English literature appealed to Rowse, was a favourite subject. Complementing his historical research into the Elizabethan period, Rowse's work on Shakespeare resulted in a string of publications, from his *William Shakespeare: A Biography* in 1963 to *My View of Shakespeare*, which appeared in 1996, not long before his death. The former was an instant popular success, which was massively reviewed in both Britain and America and had sold 200,000 copies in hard covers by 1965.[99] From the start, Rowse's Shakespearean following was as much popular as academic. Popular enthusiasm held up for as long as he cared to write books on the subject. But his academic credibility, as we have seen, was severely dented by the furore over his supposed discovery of the identity of the 'Dark Lady' of the sonnets, not merely because critics found flaws in his circumstantial evidence but also as a result of the way in which Rowse defended himself— denouncing his critics and refusing to acknowledge any weakness or uncertainties in his argument.

John McManners thought that Rowse's injudicious responses to the Dark Lady criticisms had 'made him a laughing stock' in academic circles, resulting in his 'frantic industry, perhaps desperate to reinforce his tarnished credentials'.[100] Part of this 'frantic industry' was the turning out of historical 'potboilers', such as his *Story of Britain* produced for the retail chain Marks & Spencer in 1979, none of which did much to restore his reputation within the academic community.[101] But there were some works of real worth amongst this outpouring. In *Court and Country: Studies in Tudor History,* for example, published in 1987, and which included some Cornish material, Rowse returned in assured manner to familiar territory.[102] Earlier, in 1969, a more radical departure had been his *The Cornish in America* (see Chapter 8), published on both sides of the Atlantic, which Rowse saw in some respects as a development of the transatlantic themes he had already identified in *The Expansion of Elizabethan England* and *The Elizabethans and America*. In fact, along with his friends A.C. Todd and John Rowe, Rowse had laid the foundation for a rich tradition of Cornish emigration studies that even today shows no sign of abating. Moreover, having in his Elizabethan volumes identified the particular place of Cornwall and the Cornish in the 'making of Britain', he was now in the manner later advocated by Pocock taking his perspective overseas, tracing in the New World the nature and impact of Cornish ethnicity transplanted. But Rowse was already fair game for academic snipers, and, as we have seen, *The Cornish in America* was the target of a devastating attack in the *Times Literary Supplement* by Denis Brogan, who condemned it as 'filiopietistic' and demanded a more 'sociological' approach to the study of the Cornish, such as had been afforded other immigrant ethnic groups in the United States.

Already scornful of 'sociological fashion' in historical writing, Rowse had had his worst fears confirmed by Brogan. Thereafter, there were to be no half-measures in his opposition to 'sociological history'. 'Why do I not subscribe to the exaggerated esteem for sociological history which is fashionable among academics today?', he asked rhetorically, 'My reason is that history is a portrait of life as it is lived, in all its subtlety, its fluidity and variableness, and this cannot be caught and rendered in sociological generalisations.' Moreover, '[t]he rigidifying of life into abstract concepts yields dubious results', for 'history is not a theoretical subject'.[103] Rowse later widened this view to include criticism of a variety of other historians of whom he did not approve or with whom he had crossed swords. Writing in *Historians I Have Known* in 1995, he remarked that he did not care for Arnold 'Toynbee's attempt to sociologise history' and that R.H. Tawney the arch 'theorist' finally tired of the conceptual. 'So much for historical theorising', Rowse observed scathingly, 'Tawney eventually gave a halt to it as serving no purpose'. And as for Hugh Trevor-Roper: 'if one is addicted to pushing forward a thesis one is liable to go wrong'.[104]

For Rowse, who had devoted so much time, even after abandoning the politics of the Left, to arguing that the rigour and clarity of Marxian analysis were indispensable to a proper understanding of history, this contempt for 'theory' was a considerable retreat from a position once stoutly defended. Moroever, despite the years he had given over to writing *about* history—calling for the reconciliation of the 'local' with the 'national', for history to be written from the 'bottom up', and so on—he was now entirely of the view that such activity was the preserve of the second-rate. 'Really distinguished historians do not waste time discussing how to write history', Rowse declared, 'they get on with the job. They leave it to the not so good at it to discuss how it should be done.'[105]

Such an attitude contributed to the prevailing conventional wisdom, made clear by McManners and others, that Rowse was now little more than a marginalized eccentric whose views were not to be taken seriously. Rowse's attitude also meant that he had intentionally distanced himself from historiographical debate, which he now saw as worthless, so much so that when Pocock began his call for new Archipelagic approaches and Marshall criticized antiquarian local history, he was not merely silent but plainly not interested. He was by then, of course, an old man. But, paradoxically, age did not prevent him from dusting off his old concerns from time to time, returning briefly to those passions of years ago, and then having made his point—often rather forcefully—retreating once more to his 'fortress of pride' at Trenarren.

For example, Rowse applauded the newly emergent 'younger (and better) historians of the Civil War, putting behind them the out-dated theses of Christopher Hill, Trevor-Roper, Lawrence Stone and company'.[106] He welcomed John Morrill's *Cheshire 1630–1660*, which appeared in 1974, but was most enthusiastic about David Underdown's *Somerset in the Civil War and Interregnum*, which had been published twelve months before. There were in Underdown's title shades of Mary Coate, but more than this: 'Mr Underdown's book on Somerset during the Civil War and its aftermath is quite first-class, a model of how these things should be done'.[107] Here, at last, was someone responding to the challenges he had set years before, reconciling the 'local' with the 'national' and dealing with his subject from the 'bottom up'. Underdown, for his part, devoted a series of books and articles to popular behaviour and politics in Civil War Somerset, Dorset and Wiltshire, culminating in his masterly *Revel, Riot and Rebellion*.[108] Even as late as 1990 Rowse was prepared to enter the fray, albeit briefly, writing strongly in support of Conrad Russell, one of the architects of the new approaches to British history, describing his *The Causes of the English Civil War* as 'original and convincing', especially in its treatment of 'the tangled complexity of the relations among the three kingdoms'.[109]

David Underdown, meanwhile, had influenced the writing of Mark Stoyle, who produced first (in 1994) his *Loyalty and Locality: Popular Allegiance in Devon during the English Civil War*, before moving more explicitly into the area of Cornish identities and the forging of the early modern British state.[110] Although Rowse did not live to see *West Britons*, Stoyle's all-important contribution that restored discussion of Cornwall and the Cornish to the Archipelagic debate, he had been much impressed by Stoyle's article '"Sir Richard Grenville's Creatures": The New Cornish Tertia, 1644–46' in *Cornish Studies: Four* in 1996.[111] In the late evening of his life he was expressing pleasure that the themes that had captivated him of old were gaining a new popularity, but he was also interested in the new approaches to the wider study of Cornish history that had by then appeared. In his Foreword to the book *Cornwall* in 1996, for example, he enthused about the new historical synthesis 'of all the latest writing across the disciplines'.[112]

Although privately expressing misgivings that *The Making of Modern Cornwall*, published in 1992, was in its embrace of social theory dangerously close to the 'sociological history' he so abhorred, he had written a favourable appreciation in the *English Historical Review*, though attributing the recent resurgence of territorial politics in the United Kingdom not to an enduring centre–periphery relationship (the overarching thesis of the book) but rather to what he considered to be the disintegration of the governing classes.[113] This view was, in effect, Rowse's last contribution to the writing of British and Cornish history, a brief flirtation with the contemporary history of the United Kingdom (and other Western states) in which he reflected upon the causes of 'disintegration' and the rise of regionalism and nationalism. Both were phenomena which—as he was well aware—threatened at least partially to undo the state-formation processes of the early modern period that he had chronicled so many years before. It was a process that would have horrified him in his glory days as an Elizabethan historian but one with which he now had considerable sympathy—at least as far as Cornwall was concerned. This growing tolerance for the aspirations of 'smaller peoples' reflected his ultimate disappointment with England and the English.[114] Having invested so much time and energy in admiring and celebrating all things English, England's loss of Empire and decline of international influence after 1945 had, as we have seen, distressed him deeply—as had what he took to be England's post-war descent into economic failure, strikes, social collapse and moral bankruptcy.

But Rowse was astute enough to recognize that the 'malaise' was not merely English: that all Western states had, to a greater or lesser degree, to grapple with a range of contemporary issues that threatened their very fabrics—including the rise of separatist sentiment from Quebec in Canada to Brittany in France. Moreover, Rowse was far-sighted enough to predict that, while Western states might be resilient enough to weather such storms, equivalent problems in the Eastern Bloc were altogether more intractable and posed a long-term challenge to the viability of the Soviet system. He said so in a letter to Richard Nixon, the former American President, in April 1988. Nixon replied that Rowse was 'right on target', and agreed with him that, while the Soviets had used nationalism as a powerful weapon against the old European powers in their former colonies, now—ironically—nationalism within the Soviet Union and Eastern Europe 'could lead to the disintegration of their empire'.[115] How right the two men were: within a few years the Iron Curtain had crumbled, and the Berlin Wall had been torn down.

'Betwixt and between'

In the end, however, Rowse had neither the inclination nor the energy to pursue what might have been a renewed contribution to the debate about the relationships between the several peoples of these islands, or indeed about the future of both Western and Eastern Bloc countries in the new Millennium. His important insights into Cornish nationalism and the resurgence of territorial politics in the United Kingdom did not go much further than incidental observation and comment—the occasional aside in an article, lecture or book review, a letter to a friend or a discussion with a visitor over tea. Ultimately, he had no desire to become embroiled in the study of contemporary history and politics, for England, he thought, had gone to waste already. In extreme old age he contented himself with his favourite subjects—especially Shakespeare, the subject of his final book, entitled, aptly enough, *My View of Shakespeare*, published the year before his death and 'Dedicated to HRH the Prince of Wales [Duke of Cornwall] in our common devotion to William Shakespeare'.[116]

By then, in any case, Rowse was retired long since from All Souls and well beyond the reach of current academic debate. Such contact as there was with that world was hostile—with the exception of the tiny group of academics who, for sentimental reasons of personal affection, went out of their way to maintain their friendships with him. It was not until 2002, nearly five years after Rowse's death, that Mark Stoyle in his *West Britons* first complained that Rowse's early contributions had not 'received the recognition they deserve from the new breed of early modern British historians',[117] and it is only subsequently that Christopher Haigh and others have begun a sympathetic reassessment of the place of A.L. Rowse in the writing of British and Cornish history. Sadly, Rowse had known all along that—as in politics, with his attempts to root Labour in Cornwall, or in literature, with his determination to paint an insider's picture of Cornwall that ventured beyond the cosy nostalgia of the tourist trade—in his historical research and writing he had been out of step with his contemporaries. As a historian, he had tackled issues and suggested new methods long before the academic establishment was fully prepared to accept them, and yet was by turns forgotten or derided when at last these novelties were in vogue. As he had once put it, reflecting on his long life, 'I was before my time, caught betwixt and between'.[118]

Conclusion

'What Could I Not Have Done for Cornwall!'

'At the heart of Dr Rowse the embattled don there lives on a Cornish boy who throughout his inner lifetime never left his native land.' This was the assessment of Kathleen Raine in her review in *Country Life* of Rowse's *The Road to Oxford*: a collection of poems published in 1978. Cornwall was, she wrote, 'for A.L. Rowse at once a place on earth and a place of the imagination'. It was the little land that he 'describes with a master's art; place-names become a litany, the Road to Oxford is also the road of return to Cornwall'. Moreover, Rowse was 'a passionate man', Raine said. This was a passion observable in his poetry and in his insistence that '[k]nowing humans is a waste of time': this was 'a statement of defiance, half pride, half-loneliness thrown out long ago by that Cornish boy. . . in the face of the many obstacles with which the dead weight of incomprehension had threatened to destroy him'. But, Raine added, Rowse was also a man of intense relationships: 'there is in his friendships the same passionate perceptiveness as in his sense of the lie of the land'.[1]

As we have seen in this book, there is much in Raine's assessment that rings true, and it was a summing-up with which Rowse himself might have agreed.[2] She had identified many of the tensions that had underpinned his life: the escape to Oxford and yet the inexorable pull of Cornwall; the delights and disappointments of his academic career; the loneliness and defiance of a passionate man. Yet in her suggestion that Rowse's 'inner life' in Cornwall somehow compensated for his tortured existence as an 'embattled don'—as a place of solace, comfort and retreat—Raine had failed to appreciate that Cornwall too was part of the enduring embattlement: the underlying seat of the problem.

Having made good his escape from Cornwall to Oxford, Rowse did not return to Cornwall—either in his working life or in his retirement—with a sense that peace had been made at last or old anxieties resolved. Rather, he launched almost immediately into an extended political battle—with

Cornwall the battleground—in which he found himself in a crusade to enlighten and rescue a Cornish people who (he decided eventually) did not deserve or even want his attentions. Likewise, his autobiography, describing with unguarded intimacy his early life in Cornwall, was met with howls of disapproval in his native land: a self-righteous indignation that he considered typical of the Cornish Liberal-Nonconformity that he had learned to loathe. Buried within his autobiographical angst were anxieties about his family origins—his mother's promiscuity, his own paternity—which further complicated his relationship with Cornwall and accounted for a sexual ambivalence that he never quite resolved in his own mind.

When Cornwall let him down, as he saw it, Rowse turned to England for succour and inspiration. But—notwithstanding the Churchillian heroism of the war years—England at length also failed to live up to his expectations. Then it was to America that Rowse turned, a time of major reassessment in his life which led to the final severance of his emotional ties with contemporary England. His sojourns in America also kindled a renewed respect for his native Cornwall and its people: a regard which grew to unrestrained enthusiasm as he embraced the cause of the Cornish overseas. In his eventual retirement to Cornwall, he went further: espousing a Cornish nationalism that would set Cornwall free from the dead hand of English taxation.

But in this 'rehabilitation' Rowse's Cornishness became increasingly fierce, defiant, almost menacing: jealous of others who might assert Cornish credentials to rival his, and dismissive of alternative Cornish perspectives with which he did not agree. This combined with a waning academic reputation—where Rowse's increasingly outspoken and outrageous behaviour was derided and ridiculed—to further increase the sense of isolation in his final years at Trenarren. It was not until after his death that scholars began to appreciate the early, ground-breaking but hitherto largely overlooked contributions made by Rowse to the contemporary study of British history: to the 'new British historiography' with its emphasis on the disparate peoples and territories of the 'Atlantic Archipelago'. Here—after all and at last—Rowse was seen to have helped pioneer the construction of non-English approaches to the writing of British history, and to have carved out in that history a particular place for Cornwall and the Cornish.

For all his public insistence that Cornwall was 'the land of my content', Rowse knew that it was the source of so much of his torment. In a commentary on his time as a Labour candidate he offered an insight that stood as a wider assessment of his relationship with Cornwall. He had spent far too much time, he said, 'trying in vain to open the eyes of my own people in Cornwall, in my own home-town and countryside'. There had been much trauma. 'They never would listen', he complained, 'I went through Hell, one way and another; but it was my duty to do so.'[3]

There can be no doubt that Rowse's singular personality—coupled to the singular facts of his life—contributed much to this tortured relationship. But beneath it all was the acute discomfort of being neither one thing nor the other: not really English and yet no longer 'proper Cornish'. In acquiring all the affectations of an Oxford don, he was never fully accepted as 'one of us' by the English academic, literary and political Establishment; indeed, in his later years he was positively shunned. And yet, in shedding so completely all the indications of a working-class background, he threw away much of his Cornishness and distanced himself irretrievably from the society in which he had grown up. To this was added the wider ambiguity of the blurred boundary between Cornishness and Englishness—which Rowse felt acutely and sought, without success, to resolve—an explanation perhaps for his extreme vacillations between the two identities.

Rowse believed that Cornwall had failed him, but—paradoxical patriot to the last—he also felt, looking back on his life, that he could have done more for his Cornish people. Seeking, as ever, to shift the blame, he thought that if his wealth and resolve had not been sapped by the tax leviathan that was England, then he could have contributed more to his own little land. 'What could I not have done for Cornwall', he exclaimed in 1980, 'if I had not had my hard-earned savings confiscated so wastefully, purposelessly!'[4] In the end, however, Rowse decided that he had 'No Regrets' in life.[5] But there was also the sad admission that:

> Life has left its scars on me—
> Perhaps I should not allow
> That, but how could that not be,
> Beginning with questionable paternity,
> And hating to have been born
> Amid the alien corn
> Of a home without books, music, art,
> Or any promptings of the heart?[6]

Cornwall, then, or at least the Cornish working-class environment of Tregonissey and the Higher Quarter, was the 'alien corn' that had sown discontent throughout his long and varied life: the source, Rowse recognized, of his never to be relieved anguish.

Notes

1 'This Was the Land of My Content'

1   A.L. Rowse, *The Little Land of Cornwall*, Gloucester, 1986, repub. Redruth, n.d. (*c.*1992), p. 246.
2   See John Canning (ed.), *Macaulay's History of England*, London, 1988.
3   Rowse, 1986 & n.d (c1992), p. 250.
4   John McManners, 'Alfred Leslie Rowse, 1903–1997', in *Proceedings of the British Academy: Lectures and Memoirs*, Oxford, 105, 1999, 2000, p. 552.
5   Valerie Jacob, *Tregonissey to Trenarren: The Cornish Years of A.L. Rowse*, St Austell, 2001, p. 108.
6   Order of Service: *Memorial Service, Dr A.L. Rowse CH, Holy Trinity, St Austell Parish Church*, 4 December 1997.
7   A.L. Rowse, *A Life: Collected Poems*, Edinburgh, 1981, p. 272.
8   Rowse, 1981, p. 199.
9   Rowse, 1981, p. 173.
10 *Publisher's Circular and Bookseller's Record*, 5 December 1953.
11 Michael Williams, *My Cornwall*, Tintagel, 1973, pp. 1–2.
12 Ella Westland (ed.), *Cornwall: The Cultural Construction of Place*, Penzance, 1997, p. 1.
13 Henry Jenner, *A Handbook of the Cornish Language*, London, 1904.
14 Herbert S. Vaughan, *The British Road Book*, London, 1898, cited in Philip Payton, *A Vision of Cornwall*, Fowey, 2002, p. 50.
15 *Times Literary Supplement*, 2 December 1944.
16 *Oxford Magazine*, 9 June 1932.
17 A.L. Rowse, *A Cornish Childhood: Autobiography*, London, 1942.
18 Edwin Chirgwin, 'A Critical Essay on the Work of A.L. Rowse (Fellow of All Souls)', unpub. MS, n.d., Institute of Cornish Studies Collection, University of Exeter in Cornwall.
19 *Birmingham Post*, 21 May 1981.
20 *Cornish Review*, Spring 1949, p. 24.
21 A.L. Rowse, *Milton the Puritan: Portrait of a Mind*, London, 1977, p. 207.
22 A.L. Rowse, *Friends and Contemporaries*, London, 1989, p. 245.
23 Jacob, 2001.
24 John Hurst, 'Voice from a White Silence: The Manuscripts of Jack Clemo', in Philip Payton (ed.), *Cornish Studies: Three*, Exeter, 1995, pp. 125–143; John Hurst, 'A Poetry of Dark Sounds: The Manuscripts of Charles Causley', in Philip Payton (ed.), *Cornish Studies: Seven*, Exeter, 1999, pp. 147–164; John Hurst, 'Literature in Cornwall', in Philip Payton (ed.), *Cornwall Since the War: The Contemporary History of a European Region*, Redruth, 1993, pp. 292, 294.
25 Brenda Hull, 'Anne Treneer: A Biographical Sketch', in Patricia Moyer and Brenda Hull (eds.), *School House in the Wind: A Trilogy by Anne Treneer*, Exeter, 1998, p. 611.
26 Hurst, 1993, p. 292.
27 Alan M. Kent, *Literature in Cornwall: Continuity–Identity–Difference, 1000–2000*, Bristol, 2000, pp. 207–208.
28 Richard Ollard, *A Man of Contradictions: A Life of A.L. Rowse*, London, 1999, p. 1.
29 A.L. Rowse, *Tudor Cornwall*, London, 1941.
30 Richard Ollard (ed.), *The Diaries of A.L. Rowse*, London, 2003, dustcover notes.
31 McManners, 2000, p. 544.

32 McManners, 2000, p. 552.
33 Norman Davies, *The Isles*, London, 1999, p. v.
34 Davies, 1999, p. xxviii; A.L. Rowse, *Story of Britain*, London, 1979, repub. 1993.
35 Davies, 1999, pp. 524–525.
36 John Angarrack, *Breaking the Chains*, Camborne, 1999, pp. 39, 56.
37 *An Baner Kernewek/Cornish Banner*, 90, November 1997.
38 *Daily Telegraph*, 5 October 1997.
39 *An Baner Kernewek/Cornish Banner*, 90, November 1997.
40 *An Baner Kernewk/Cornish Banner*, 90, November 1997.
41 *An Baner Kernewek/Cornish Banner*, 90, November 1997.
42 *An Baner Kernewek/Cornish Banner*, 90, November 1997.
43 Judith Cook, *Daphne: A Portrait of Daphne du Maurier*, London, 1991, p. v.
44 *Cornish World*, 15, 1997/98.
45 Jacob, 2001, p. 111.
46 *An Baner Kernewek/Cornish Banner*, 114, November 2003. This 'A.L. Rowse Centenary Issue' included contributions on Rowse by Donald Adamson, Sidney Cauveren, Anne Cuneo, Pat Julian, Edna Milton, Raleigh Trevelyan, and James Whetter.
47 *Western Morning News*, 1 October 2002.
48 James Whetter, *Dr A.L. Rowse: Poet, Historian, Lover of Cornwall*, St Austell, 2003, p. 52.
49 *An Baner Kernewek/Cornish Banner*, 114, November 2003.
50 *An Baner Kernewek/Cornish Banner*, 115, February 2004.
51 Angarrack, 1999, pp. 47, 148, 187.
52 Angarrack, 1999, p. 47.
53 *Cornish History Network Newsletter*, 7, March 2000.
54 Claude Berry, *Portrait of Cornwall*, London, 1963, 2nd ed. 1971, pp. 119, 151.
55 A.L. Rowse, *The Cornish in America*, London, 1969.
56 Alan M. Kent, *The Hensbarrow Homilies*, Penzance, 2002, p. 42.
57 Rowse, 1969, p. 7.

2 'No Wonder I Preferred Life at All Souls'

1   A.L. Rowse, *A Cornish Childhood: Autobiography of a Cornishman*, London, 1942, pp. 16, 25.
2   Rowse, 1942, p. 124.
3   Rowse, 1942, p. 16.
4   A.L. Rowse, *A Cornishman at Oxford: The Education of a Cornishman*, London, 1965a, p. 91.
5   Exeter University Library (EUL) MS113/2 Journals and Notebooks/1/14, 7 April 1953.
6   Rowse, 1942, pp. 14–15.
7   Rowse, 1965a, p. 91.
8   Jack Clemo, 'The China Clay Country', in Michael Williams (ed.), *My Cornwall*, Tintagel, 1973, p. 45.
9   Jack Clemo, *The Marriage of a Rebel: A Mystical-Erotic Quest*, London, 1980, pp. 13, 32.
10 'Sufficiency', in *Penguin Modern Poets: 6*, London, 1964, p. 21.
11 A.L. Rowse, *A Life: Collected Poems*, Edinburgh, 1981, pp. 272–273.
12 Jack Clemo, *Confession of a Rebel*, London, 1949, p. 217.
13 EUL MS113/3 Correspondence/temp/Box89, Clemo to Rowse, 4 April 1948.
14 EUL MS113/3/Box89, Clemo to Rowse, 1 April 1948.
15 EUL MS113/3/Box89, Clemo to Rowse, 4 April 1948.
16 EUL MS113/3/Box89, Clemo to Rowse, 1 April 1948.
17 EUL MS113/3/Box89, Clemo to Rowse, 4 April 1948.
18 EUL MS113/3/Box89, Clemo to Rowse, 27 March 1950.
19 EUL MS113/3/Box89, Berry to Rowse, 2 October 1949; see also Chatto & Windus to Rowse, 2 May 1950.
20 EUL MS113/3 Correspondence/temp/Box188, Causley to Rowse, 13 April 1959.
21 A. L. Rowse, *A Man of the Thirties*, London, 1979, p. 35.
22 Rowse, 1942, p. 128.
23 Rowse, 1942, p. 129.
24 Rowse, 1942, p. 227.

25 EUL MS113/3 Correspondence/temp/Box30, Common to Rowse, 6 September n.d.
26 EUL MS113/3/temp/Box30, Common to Rowse, 21 October 1918.
27 EUL MS113/2 Journals and notebooks/5/9/Typescripts from American pocket books 1951–69, Los Angeles 1951.
28 *Spectator*, 2 August 1935.
29 EUL MS113/1/3 Press Cuttings/temp/Box35, unidentified issue *Books and Bookmen*.
30 *Vogue*, July 1980.
31 Rowse, 1942, p. 67.
32 Rowse, 1942, p. 201.
33 Rowse, 1942, p. 168.
34 Rowse, 1942, p. 219.
35 Rowse, 1979, p. 10.
36 EUL MS113/2 Journals and notebooks/1/5b, 8 March 1926; see also Richard Ollard, *The Diaries of A.L. Rowse*, London, 2003, p. 11.
37 EUL MS113/2/1/9, 12 June 1934; see also Ollard, 2003, p. 82.
38 EUL MS113/2/1/10b, 11 May 1938; see also Ollard, 2003, p. 105.
39 EUL MS113/2/ 1/10b, 6 February 1937; see also Ollard, 2003, pp. 96–97.
40 BBC 4 broadcast 'Transition and Triumph', published in *The Listener*, 10 September 1970.
41 A.L. Rowse, *Friends and Contemporaries*, London, 1989, pp. 245–246.
42 Rowse, 1965a, p. 39.
43 Rowse, 1965a, pp. 42–43.
44 Ollard, 2003, p. 388.
45 *Irish Times*, 23 January 1965.
46 A.L. Rowse, *Times, Persons, Places: Essays in Literature*, London, 1965b, pp. 1–2.
47 Rowse, 1965b, p. 5.
48 John McManners, 'Alfred Leslie Rowse, 1903–1997', in *Proceedings of the British Academy: Lectures and Memoirs*, 105, 1999, Oxford, 2000, pp. 537–538.
49 Rowse, 1942, p. 191.
50 Rowse, 1942, p. 125.
51 A.L. Rowse, 'Foreword', in Anon., *A Cornish Waif's Story*, n.p., 1956, pp. 9, 10, 11.
52 John Rowe, 'Cornish Mining in the 1920s', *An Baner Kernewek/Cornish Banner*, August 1986.
53 Rowe, August 1986.
54 J.A. Buckley, *A Miner's Tale: The Story of Howard Mankee*, Redruth, 1988, p. 33.
55 Philip Payton, *The Making of Modern Cornwall: Historical Experience and the Persistence of 'Difference'*, Redruth, 1992, p. 121.
56 Survey Committee, *Devon and Cornwall: A Preliminary Survey*, Exeter, 1947, p. 247.
57 Survey Committee, 1947, p. 244.
58 R.M. Barton, *A History of the Cornish China Clay Industry*, Truro, 1966, p. 172.
59 *Royal Cornwall Gazette*, 7 June 1922.
60 Rowse, 1965a, p. 21.
61 *Cornish Guardian*, May 1932.
62 Rowse, 1989, p. 245.
63 A.L. Rowse, *The Cornish in America*, London, 1969, p. 6.
64 Rowse, 1942, p. 106.
65 Rowse, 1942, p. 258.
66 Rowse, 1942, p. 214.
67 *Cornish Guardian*, 7 January 1937.
68 A.L. Rowse, *Quiller Couch: A Portrait of 'Q'*, London, 1988a, p. 244.
69 EUL MS113/2 Journals and notebooks/1/14, 12 June 1953.
70 Rowse, 1979, p. 127.
71 EUL MS113/2 Journals and notebooks/5/4, 20 June 1935.
72 Rowse, 1988a, p. 10.
73 Rowse, 1988a, p. 10.
74 A.L. Rowse, *A.L. Rowse's Cornwall*, London, 1988b, p. 6.
75 Rowse, 1942, p. 235.
76 Rowse, 1942, p. 277.

3 'You're No Rowse'

1   Andrew Motion, *Philip Larkin: A Writer's Life*, London, 1993, p. 404.
2   Cf. Larkin's 'This Be the Verse; see Motion, 1993, p. 373.
3   A.L. Rowse, *A Cornish Childhood: Autobiography of a Cornishman*, London, 1942, pp. 86–87.
4   Exeter University Library (EUL) MS113/2 Journals and notebooks/1/12 'Liber Amoris', 10 July 1944.
5   Rowse, 1942, p. 78.
6   EUL MS113/2 Journals and notebooks/1/27 'American Journal', 12 October 1965.
7   EUL MS113/2/1/5b, Last Day of October, 1925; see also Richard Ollard (ed.), *The Diaries of A.L. Rowse*, London, 2003, p. 9.
8   EUL MS113/2/5/3, Cornwall 1948.
9   EUL MS113/2/1/27, 12 October 1965.
10 Rowse, 1942, p. 77.
11 Rowse, 1942, p. 78.
12 A.L. Rowse, *A Man of the Thirties*, London, 1979, p. 120.
13 EUL MS113/2 Journals and notebooks/1/9, 18 November 1929; see also Ollard, 2003, p. 56.
14 EUL MS113/2/1/9, 18 November 1929; see also Ollard, 2003, pp. 56–57.
15 EUL MS113/2/1/9, 18 November 1929; see also Ollard, 2003, p. 57.
16 *Evening Standard*, 22 April 1977.
17 Rowse, 1979, p. 9.
18 EUL MS113/2 Journals and notebooks/1/28, 7 September 1967.
19 Rowse, 1979, p. 10.
20 EUL MS113/2 Journals and notebooks/5/3, 3 September 1951.
21 EUL MS113/2/1/14, 14 February 1953.
22 EUL MS113/2/1/14, 14 February 1953.
23 EUL MS113/2/1/14, 7 April 1953.
24 EUL MS113/2/1/14, 31 August 1953.
25 EUL MS113/2/1/14, 25 September 1953.
26 EUL MS113/2/1/14, 28 September 1953.
27 EUL MS113/3 Correspondence, Rowse to Sweet, 7 November 1953.
28 Rowse, 1979, p. 10.
29 EUL MS113/2 Journals and notebooks/1/27/'American Journal', 12 October 1965.
30 EUL MS113/2/1/27, 12 October 1965.
31 Rowse, 1942, p. 30.
32 Rowse, 1942, p. 29.
33 Rowse, 1942, p. 31.
34 Rowse, 1942, p. 188.
35 Rowse, 1942, p. 206.
36 Rowse, 1942, p. 217.
37 EUL MS113/2 Journals and notebooks/1/9, 5 March 1934; see also Ollard, 2003, pp. 81–82.
38 EUL MS113/2 Journals and notebooks/1/9, 5 March 1934; see also Ollard, 2003, p. 82.
39 EUL MS113/2/1/10b, 8 March 1937; see also Ollard, 2003, pp. 91–100.
40 Rowse, 1942, p. 80.
41 EUL MS113/2 Journals and notebooks/5/2, 3 May 1928.
42 EUL MS113/2/1/27, 12 October 1965.
43 EUL MS113/2/1/27, 12 October 1965.
44 A.L. Rowse, *A Cornishman at Oxford: The Education of a Cornishman*, London, 1965, p. 14.
45 Rowse, 1965, p. 17.
46 Rowse, 1965, pp. 258–259.
47 Rowse, 1965, p. 259.
48 EUL MS113/2/1/27, 12 October 1965.
49 EUL MS113/2/1/27, 12 October 1965.
50 *West Briton*, 29 December 1865.
51 A.L. Rowse, *The Cornish in America*, London, 1969, p. 352.
52 A.C. Todd, *The Cornish Miner in America*, Truro, 1967, p. 241.
53 Philip Payton, *The Cornish Overseas*, Fowey, 1999, pp. 333–338.

54 Rowse, 1969, p. 363.
55 EUL MS113/2 Journals and notebooks/1/27, 18 October 1965; see also Richard Ollard, *A Man of Contradictions: A Life of A.L. Rowse*, London, 1999, pp. 277–285—Ollard's reading of this complex, confused and much-amended set of entries is in places different from my own.
56 EUL MS113/2/1/27, 18 October 1965.
57 EUL MS113/2/1/14, 31 August 1953.
58 EUL MS113/3 Correspondence, Rowse to Sweet, 29 April 1965.
59 EUL MS113/3, Sweet to Rowse, 28 May 1965.
60 EUL MS113/2 Journals and notebooks/1/27, 12 October 1965.
61 EUL MS113/2/1/27, 12 October 1965.
62 EUL MS113/2/1/27, 12 October 1965.
63 EUL MS113/2/1/27, 12 October 1965.
64 EUL MS113/2/1/27, 12 October 1965.

4 'She Made Me Detest the Very Nature of Women'

1 A.L. Rowse, *Night at the Carn*, London, 1984, p. 8; A.L. Rowse, *Stories from Trenarren*, London, 1986a, p. 9.
2 A.L. Rowse, *A.L. Rowse's Cornwall*, London, 1988, p. 24.
3 Exeter Universitiy Library (EUL) MS113/2 Journals and notebooks/1/30, 8 September 1968.
4 A.L. Rowse, *A Man of the Thirties*, London, 1979, p. 55.
5 A.L. Rowse, *Tudor Cornwall: Portrait of a Society*, London, 1941, pp. 441, 446.
6 A.L. Rowse, *The Elizabethan Renaissance: The Life of a Society*, London, 1971, p. 142.
7 A.L. Rowse, *The Case Books of Simon Foreman: Sex and Society in Shakespeare's Age*, London, 1974, p. 9.
8 Rowse, 1971, p. 57.
9 A.L. Rowse, *A Cornish Childhood: Autobiography of a Cornishman*, London, 1942, p. 115.
10 Rowse, 1942, p. 247.
11 Rowse, 1942, p. 242.
12 A.L. Rowse, *A Cornishman at Oxford: The Education of a Cornishman*, London, 1965, pp. 63, 74.
13 This theme permeates A.L. Rowse, *Homosexuals in History: A Study of Ambivalence in Society, Literature and the Arts*, London, 1977.
14 Rowse, 1979, p. 120; my italics.
15 EUL MS113/3 Correspondence/1/ Rowse to Sweet, 7 November 1953.
16 EUL MS113/3/1/ Rowse to Sweet, 18 May 1965.
17 Rowse, 1979, p. 85.
18 EUL MS113/2 Journals and notebooks/5/2, 22 June 1934.
19 Rowse, 1971, p. 57.
20 EUL MS113/2 Journals and notebooks/5/2, 18 September 1930.
21 EUL MS113/2/12 'Liber Amoris', 11 June 1944.
22 EUL MS113/2/12, 11 June 1944, gloss dated 1974. Norman Scarfe went on to become a distinguished local historian.
23 EUL MS113/2/14, 21 December 1952.
24 Rowse, 1979, p. 42.
25 Rowse, 1979, p. 51.
26 *Economist*, 25 August 1975.
27 Charles Henderson (ed. A.L. Rowse and M.I. Henderson), *Essays in Cornish History*, Oxford, 1935, p. 80.
28 Charles Henderson (ed. G.H. Doble), *A History of the Parish of Constantine in Cornwall*, Truro, 1937, p. 3.
29 A.L. Rowse, *The Little Land of Cornwall*, Gloucester, 1986b, p. 293.
30 Henderson (ed. Rowse & Henderson), 1935, p. xvi.
31 Rowse, 1979, p. 16.
32 Rowse, 1979, p. 17.
33 Rowse, 1979, p. 16.
34 Rowse, 1979, p. 127.

35 Rowse, 1986b, p. 291.
36 EUL MS113/2 Journals and notebooks/5/4, 1934.
37 Henderson (ed. Rowse & Henderson), 1935, p. xviii; for a different version see Rowse, 1965, p. 197.
38 Henderson (ed. Rowse & Henderson), 1935, p. xviii.
39 Rowse, 1979, p. 16.
40 Rowse, 1979, p. 18.
41 Rowse, 1971, p. 16.
42 A.L. Rowse, *A Cornishman Abroad*, London, 1976, p. 190.
43 Rowse, 1976, p. 197.
44 Rowse, 1965, p. 38.
45 EUL MS113/2 Journals and notebooks/5/4, 8 July 1932.
46 EUL MS113/2/1/28, Trinity Sunday, 1967; see also Richard Ollard, *The Diaries of A.L. Rowse*, London, 2003, p. 407.
47 Royal Institution of Cornwall (RIC), Henderson MSS, 'A Journal of My Doings', 18 July 1925.
48 RIC Henderson MSS, 'A Journal', 2 October 1925.
49 RIC Henderson MSS, Letter from Maxse to Henderson, 8 October 1925.
50 RIC Henderson MSS, 'A Journal', 13 October 1925.
51 RIC Henderson MSS, 'A Journal', 17 December 1925.
52 EUL MS113/2 Notebooks and journals/1/28, Trinity Sunday 1967; see also Ollard, 2003, p. 408.
53 EUL MS113/2/1/14, 28 August 1954.
54 EUL MS113/2/1/28, Trinity Sunday 1967; see also Ollard, 2003, p. 409.
55 EUL MS113/2/1/14, 28 August 1954
56 EUL MS113/2/5/2, 26 August 1936: later gloss (undated).
57 EUL MS113/2/5/2, 26 August 1936: later gloss (undated).
58 EUL MS113/2/1/28, Trinity Sunday 1967; see also Ollard, 2003, p. 409.
59 EUL MS113/3 Correspondence/temp/Box 30, invitation to wedding of Mary Isobel Munro and Charles Henderson.
60 Henderson (ed. Rowse & Henderson), 1935, p. xxiv.
61 EUL MS113/2 Journals and notebooks/5/2, 22 July 1934.
62 EUL MS113/2/5/2, 22 July 1934.
63 A.L. Rowse, *Extempore Memorial (For C.H.)*, Oxford, 1933.
64 Rowse, 1941, p. 5.
65 Rowse, 1979, p. 16.
66 EUL MS113/2 Journals and notebooks/5/3, 1934.
67 EUL MS113/2/1/27, 29 April 1967.
68 EUL MS113/2/5/2, 26 August 1936.
69 EUL MS113/2/5/2, 23 April 1933: amended *c.* 1988.
70 EUL MS113/2/1/12, 22 December 1953.
71 EUL MS113/2/1/30, 21 August 1968.
72 EUL MS113/2/1/30, 8 September 1968.
73 A.L. Rowse, *Memories of Men and Women*, London, 1980, p. 179.
74 Rowse, 1980, pp. 180–181.
75 Rowse, 1980, p. 203.
76 Rowse, 1980, p. 203.
77 EUL MS113/2 Journals and notebooks/5/2, 22 June 1934.
78 Ollard, 2003, p. 351.
79 Richard Ollard, *A Man of Contradictions: A Life of A.L. Rowse*, London, 1999, pp. 87–88.
80 EUL MS113/3 Correspondence/1, Wedgwood to Rowse, 8 August 1946; Wedgwood to Rowse, 13 October 1945?; Wedgewood to Rowse, n.d.
81 EUL MS113/3/1, Wedgwood to Rowse, n.d.; Wedgwood to Rowse, n.d.; Wedgwood to Rowse, 25 October 1943.
82 EUL MS113/3/1, Wedgwood to Rowse, n.d.; Wedgwood to Rowse, 7 January 1957.
83 EUL MS113/3/1, Wedgwood to Rowse, n.d; Wedwood to Rowse, n.d.
84 EUL MS113/3/1, Wedgwood to Rowse, 16 July 1969; Wedgwood to Rowse, 20 April 1969.
85 A.L. Rowse, *Historians I Have Known*, London, 1995, p. 116.
86 A.L. Rowse, 'Bishop Thornborough: A Clerical Careerist', in Richard Ollard and Pamela

Tudor-Craig (eds), *For Veronica Wedgwood These: Studies in Seventeenth-century History*, London, 1986.
87 C.V. Wedgwood, *The Great Rebellion: The King's Peace, 1637–1641*, London, 1955, p. 13.
88 C.V. Wedgwood, *Seventeenth-Century English Literature*, London, 1950, p. 4.
89 Judith Cook, *Daphne: A Portrait of Daphne du Maurier*, London, 1991, p. 107.
90 EUL MS113/2 Journals and notebooks/1/14, 15 September 1953.
91 A.L. Rowse, *Friends and Contemporaries*, London, 1989, p. 274.
92 EUL MS113/1/3 Press Cuttings/temp/Box37, unidentified review in an American newspaper of Daphne du Maurier, *Vanishing Cornwall*, London, 1969.
93 Rowse, 1989, pp. 274, 278, 279, 281, 284.
94 Daphne du Maurier (ed Oriel Malet), *Letters from Menabilly: Portrait of a Friendship*, New York, 1992, p. 277.
95 EUL MS113/3 Correspondence/temp/Box 172, du Maurier to Rowse, 27 December 1983: gloss by Rowse.
96 EUL MS113/3 Correspondence/temp/Box 172, du Maurier to Rowse, 14 December 1982.
97 EUL MS113/3 Correspondence/temp/Box 172, du Maurier to Rowse, 14 December 1982.
98 EUL MS113/2 Journals and notebooks/1/28, 8 September 1967.
99 EUL MS113/2/1/28, 8 September 1967: see also Ollard, 2000, pp. 419–423; my reading varies from that of Ollard in several places. Both Cook, 1991, pp. 291–293, and Margaret Foster, *Daphne du Maurier*, London, 1993, pp. 289, 331–332, note Browning's infidelities and a drink-drive offence; the 'lower-class girl' at Fowey may have been the shop-girl 'Sixpence' whom Browning took sailing. For du Maurier's sexual ambivalence see Foster, 1993, pp. 419–420.
100 EUL MS113/2/1/28, 8 September 1967.
101 EUL MS113 Correspondence/1, Sweet to Rowse, 3 December 1935.
102 EUL MS113/1, Sweet to Annie Rowse, 1 November 1935.
103 EUL MS113/1, Rowse to Sweet, 26 November 1935.
104 EUL MS113/2 Journals and notebooks/1/10b, Whitsunday 1939; see also Ollard, 2003, pp. 119–120.
105 EUL MS113/1 Correspondence, Sweet to Rowse, n.d. *c.* December 1951.
106 EUL MS113/1, Rowse to Sweet, 28 December 1951.
107 EUL MS113/1, Berry to Rowse, 28 January 1952.
108 EUL MS113/1, Rowse to Sweet, 30 October 1968.
109 EUL MS113/1, Pounds to Rowse, 21 January 1969.
110 EUL MS113/1, Sweet to Rowse, 2 February 1975.
111 EUL MS113/1, Rowse to Sweet, 30 October 1968.
112 EUL MS113/1, Rowse to Sweet, 26 June 1975.

5 'A Deep Anxiety to Do His Best for Cornwall'

1 A.L. Rowse, *A Man of the Thirties*, London, 1979, p. 4.
2 Rowse, 1979, p. 4.
3 A.L. Rowse, *A Cornishman at Oxford: The Education of a Cornishman*, London, 1965, p. 95.
4 Rowse, 1965, pp. 95–96.
5 Rowse, 1965, p. 110.
6 For Rowse's assessment of this period, see Rowse, 1965, pp. 200–203.
7 For a general discussion of Cornish politics in this era, see Philip Payton, *The Making of Modern Cornwall: Historical Experience and the Persistence of 'Difference'*, Redruth, 1992, chapter 7 'The Politics of Paralysis'.
8 Rowse, 1979, p. 2.
9 Rowse, 1965, p. 21.
10 Exeter University Library (EUL) Rowse Collection MS113/2 Journals and notebooks/1/B, 10 January 1922; also see Richard Ollard, *The Diaries of A.L. Rowse*, London, 2003, p. 4.
11 Rowse, 1965, p. 174.
12 A.L. Rowse, *A Cornishman Abroad*, London, 1976, pp. 255–256.
13 A.L. Rowse, *The Use of History*, London, 1946, repub. 1963, p. 100.
14 Elizabeth Durbin, *New Jerusalems: The Labour Party and the Economics of Democratic Socialism*, London, 1985, p. 93.
15 Rowse, 1979, p. 32.

16 Rowse, 1979, p. 4.
17 A.L. Rowse, *Mr Keynes and the Labour Movement*, London, 1936, cover notes.
18 A.L. Rowse, *Politics and the Younger Generation*, London, 1931, pp. 81, 87.
19 Rowse, 1931, pp. 119–120.
20 Rowse, 1931, pp. 120, 204.
21 Rowse, 1931, p. 194.
22 Rowse, 1931, p. 211.
23 *Catholic Times*, 9 October 1931.
24 EUL MS113/2 Journals and notebooks/5/4, gloss on 1931.
25 *West Briton*, 1 August 1929; *Cornish Guardian*, 1 August 1929.
26 Rowse, 1979, p. 89.
27 EUL MS113/1/3 Press Cuttings/temp/Box33, Stone to Rowse, 4 August 1929.
28 EUL MS113/2 Journals and notebooks/5/2, 1930.
29 Christopher Cook, *The Age of Alignment: Electoral Politics in Britain, 1922–29*, London, 1975.
30 Stephen Koss, *Nonconformity in Modern British Politics*, London, 1975, p. 11.
31 Koss, 1975, pp. 8–9.
32 Garry Tregidga, *The Liberal Party in South West Britain Since 1918: Political Decline, Dormancy and Rebirth*, Exeter, 2000, p. 55.
33 Tregidga, 2000, p. 86.
34 See Payton, 1992, chapter 7.
35 *Cornish Guardian*, 30 January 1930.
36 *Western Morning News*, 30 October 1931.
37 EUL MS113/2 Journals and notebooks/5/4, gloss on 1931.
38 *Cornish Guardian*, 29 October 1931.
39 *West Briton*, 26 October 1931.
40 *Cornish Guardian*, 8 October 1931.
41 Cited in T.O. Lloyd, *Empire to Welfare State: English History 1906–1967*, Oxford, 1970, pp. 172–173.
42 Rowse, 1979, p. 176.
43 EUL MS113/2 Journals and notebooks/5/4, Thurs 22 n.d. 1931.
44 EUL MS113/1/3 Press Cuttings/temp/Unumbered Box, Maurice Petherick election leaflet dated 22 October 1931.
45 *Cornish Guardian*, 5 November 1931.
46 EUL MS113/2 Journals and notebooks/5/4, gloss on 1931.
47 EUL MS113/2 Journals and notebooks/5/4, gloss on 1931.
48 *Cornish Guardian*, 18 June 1931.
49 *Cornish Labour News*, August 1934.
50 *Cornish Guardian*, 28 June 1934.
51 *Cornish Labour News*, August 1934.
52 *Cornish Labour News*, August 1934.
53 *Cornish Guardian*, 17 January 1935.
54 See Garry Tregidga, 'Socialism and the Old Left: The Labour Party in Cornwall during the Inter-War Period', in Philip Payton (ed.), *Cornish Studies: Seven*, Exeter, 1999, pp. 85–89.
55 EUL MS113/3 Correspondence/1, Berry to Rowse, 17 November 1929.
56 EUL MS113/3/1, Berry to Rowse, 17 November 1929.
57 EUL MS113/3/1, Berry to Rowse, 9 March 1931.
58 *Cornish Labour News*, December 1932.
59 *Cornish Labour News*, December 1932; May 1935.
60 *Cornish Labour News*, October 1933.
61 *Cornish Labour News*, August 1933.
62 *Cornish Labour News*, December 1932.
63 *Old Cornwall*, Summer 1933.
64 Tregidga, 1999, pp. 87–89.
65 *Cornish Labour News*, May 1937.
66 *Cornish labour News*, November 1932.
67 EUL MS113/2 Journals and notebooks/5/2, 26 August 1936.
68 *Cornish Guardian*, 6 June 1935.
69 *Cornish Guardian*, 20 June 1935.

70   Ken Phillipps, *Catching Cornwall in Flight or the Bettermost Class of People*, St Austell, 1994, p. 59.
71   Rowse, 1979, pp. 89–90.
72   EUL MS113/2 Journals and notebooks/5/2, 22 June 1934.
73   EUL MS113/2/5/2, 22 June 1934.
74   EUL MS113/2/5/4, 1933.
75   *Cornish Guardian*, 30 May 1935.
76   *Western Morning News*, 28 May 1935.
77   *Falmouth Packet*, 2 August 1935.
78   *West Briton*, 6 June 1935.
79   *West Briton*, 18 November 1935.
80   *West Briton*, 9 January 1936.
81   Rowse, 1979, p. 95.
82   Rowse, 1979, p. 95.
83   *Cornish Guardian*, 8 November 1935.
84   *Cornish Labour News*, December 1935.
85   *West Briton*, 28 November 1935.
86   *West Briton*, 28 November 1935.
87   *West Briton*, 28 November 1935.
88   *West Briton*, 28 November 1935.
89   *Cornish Guardian*, 8 May 1936.
90   *Cornish Guardian*, 4 July 1938.
91   *Cornish Guardian*, 20 June 1935.
92   *Cornish Times*, 6 November 1936.
93   *Cornish Times*, 6 November 1936.
94   *Manchester Guardian*, 25 February 1938.
95   *News Chronicle*, 6 October 1938, 10 February 1939, 6 April 1939.
96   *Cornish Labour News*, April 1937.
97   *Cornish Labour News*, January 1939.
98   EUL MS113/2 Journals and notebooks/5/4, 1939.
99   *Cornish Guardian*, 31 March 1938.
100 *West Briton*, 28 April 1938; *Cornish Guardian*, 28 April 1938.
101 *West Briton*, 28 April 1938; *Cornish Guardian*, 28 April 1938.
102 *West Briton*, 6 October 1938.
103 *Western Morning* News, 22 March 1938.
104 Rowse, 1979, p. 5.
105 A.L. Rowse, *Friends and Contemporaries*, London, 1989, p. 177.
106 EUL MS113/1/3 Press Cuttings/temp/Unnumbered Box, unidentified *Cornish Guardian*, 1937.
107 *Western Morning News*, 17 March 1939.
108 *West Briton*, 2 February 1938.
109 EUL MS113/2 Journals and notebooks/5/2, 3 September 1939.
110 *Cornish Labour News*, November 1937.
111 Institute of Cornish Studies (ICS) Legonna Papers.
112 Rowse, 1979, p. 8.
113 *Western Morning News*, 11 November 1939; *Picture Post*, 2 November 1940; *The Times*, 3 March 1944.
114 EUL MS113/1 Journals and notebooks/5/2, Early 1936.
115 Rowse, 1979, p. 206.
116 A.L. Rowse, *The End of an Epoch: Reflections on Contemporary History*, London, 1945, p. 80.
117 *Royal Cornwall Gazette*, 22 July 1942.
118 *Cornish Guardian*, 23 July 1942.
119 EUL MS113/2 Journals and notebooks/5/2, 22 June 1934: later gloss.
120 *Cornish Times*, 28 August 1942.
121 *Western Morning News*, 1 July 1942.
122 Cited in *West Briton*, 24 June 1943.
123 Cited in *West Briton*, 24 June 1943.
124 Cited in *West Briton*, 24 June 1943.

125 *West Briton*, 24 June 1943.
126 Cited in *West Briton*, 24 June 1943.
127 EUL MS113/1/3 Press Cuttings/temp/Unnumbered Box, Shepherd to Rowse, 29 June 1943.
128 EUL MS113/1 Correspondence, Berry to Rowse, 26 June 1943.
129 EUL MS113/1, Berry to Rowse, 29 March 1945.

6   'Haunted by Cornwall'

1   A.L. Rowse, *Friends and Contemporaries*, London, 1969, p. 29.
2   Rowse, 1969, p. 29.
3   A.L. Rowse, *A Man of the Thirties*, London, 1979, pp. 54–55.
4   Rowse, 1979, p. 8.
5   *West Briton*, 24 June 1943.
6   Rowse, 1979, pp. 7–8
7   A.L. Rowse, *A Life: Collected Poems*, Edinburgh, 1981, p. 174.
8   Rowse, 1981, pp. 174–175.
9   Rowse, 1981, pp. 135–134.
10   Exeter University Library (EUL) Rowse Collection MS113/2 Journals and notebooks/5/2, 10 July 1945.
11   EUL MS113/3 Correspondence/1, Rowse to Sweet, 11 February? (*c*.1943/44).
12   *Western Morning News*, 6 February 1944.
13   *Western Morning News*, 6 February 1944.
14   *Western Morning News*, 8 February 1944.
15   EUL MS113/1 Journals and notebooks/5/2, 10 July 1945.
16   EUL MS113/1/5/2, 10 July 1945: later gloss. The book in question was A.L. Rowse, *The English Spirit: Essays in History and Literature*, London, 1944.
17   A.L. Rowse, *A Cornish Childhood: Autobiography of a Cornishman*, London, 1942.
18   Sydney Cauveren, *A.L. Rowse: A Bibliophile's Extensive Bibliography*, London, 2000, p. xvii.
19   Rowse, 1942, repub. 1975, back-cover notes.
20   *Brothers and Friends: The Diaries of Major Warren Hamilton Lewis 1895–1973*, London, 1982, p. 216, cited in Cauveren, 2000, p. 236.
21   S.M.B. Mais, *The Cornish Riviera*, London, 1928, 3rd edn 1934, p. 1.
22   Mais, 1938 & 1934, pp. 1–3.
23   *Cambridge Review*, 24 April 1943.
24   *Time and Tide*, 12 September 1942.
25   *Observer*, 19 July 1942.
26   EUL MS113/4 Press Cuttings/temp/unnumbered Box, letter dated 12 February 1944 enclosing MS from British Council to Jonathan Cape (publishers) regarding broadcast on Palestine Broadcasting Service, 12 July (1944?).
27   *Life and Letters Today*, August 1942; 'Bryher' may or may not have been the novelist (Annie) Winifred Ellerman.
28   *The Times*, 18 July 1942.
29   *Tatler*, 15 July 1942.
30   *Cornish Guardian*, 5 August 1942.
31   *Cornish Review*, Spring 1949, p. 28.
32   EUL MS113/1/3 Press Cuttings/temp/Box 53, letter from Rowse to Munro, 17 September 1988.
33   EUL MS 113/3 Correspondence/temp/Box 188, Causley to Rowse, 27 September 1946.
34   *Royal Cornwall Gazette*, 29 July 1942.
35   *Western Morning News*, 12 February 1944.
36   *Cornish Guardian*, 2 July 1942.
37   *Western Sunday Independent*, 5 July 1942.
38   *Cornish Guardian*, 25 June 1942.
39   *Cornish Guardian*, 25 June 1942.
40   Rowse, 1989, p. 54.
41   *Western Morning News*, 30 June 1942.
42   *Western Morning News*, 1 July 1942.
43   EUL MS113/1/3 Press Cuttings/temp/Box 35, unidentified *Western Sunday Independent*,

c. June 1943.
44 *Western Morning News*, 6 February 1944.
45 *West Briton*, 25 June 1942.
46 Brian Murdoch, *Cornish Literature*, Cambridge, 1993, p. 147.
47 P. Berresford Ellis, *The Cornish Language and its Literature*, London, 1974, pp. 163–165, 171; Margaret Perry, *The Heart of the Village: The Story of St Cleer School, 1877–1983*, Plymouth, 1992, p. 59.
48 Institute of Cornish Studies (ICS), Edwin Chirgwin, 'A Critical Essay on The Work of A.L. Rowse (Fellow of All Souls)', unpub. MS, n.d. *c.* 1942.
49 EUL MS113/2 Journals and notebooks/5/4, November 1946–47.
50 EUL MS113/2 /5/4, November 1946–47.
51 EUL MS113/1/12, 19 November 1948.
52 *Western Sunday Independent*, 5 July 1952.
53 EUL MS113/1 Journals and notebooks/2/14, 12 June 1953.

7   'Not Being English, Alas—But Hopelessly Cornish'
1 *New English Weekly*, 19 April 1945.
2 *New English Weekly*, 19 April 1945.
3 A.L. Rowse, *The Spirit of English History*, London, 1943, p. 5.
4 A.L. Rowse, *The English Spirit: Essays in History and Literature*, London, 1944.
5 Cited in Rowse, 1944, dustcover notes.
6 Exeter University Library (EUL) Rowse Collection MS113/1 Journals and notebooks/5/2, 10 July 1945.
7 Rowse, 1944, p. 1.
8 Rowse, 1944, p. 20.
9 Rowse, 1944, p. 21.
10 Rowse, 1944, pp. 21–22.
11 Rowse, 1944, p. 22.
12 *Evening Standard*, 29 November 1944.
13 *Sunday Dispatch*, 6 May 1945.
14 *Vogue*, July 1945.
15 A.L. Rowse, *Memories of Men and Women*, London, 1980, p. 1.
16 Rowse, 1980, p. 24.
17 Rowse, 1980, p. 1.
18 A.L. Rowse, *A Cornish Childhood: Autobiography of a Cornishman*, London, 1941, p. 61.
19 Rowse, 1944, p. v.
20 Rowse, 1944, p. v.
21 Rowse, 1944, p. v.
22 Rowse, 1944, p. 35.
23 Rowse, 1944, p. 31.
24 *Daily Dispatch*, 10 November 1945.
25 *Listener*, 22 October 1942.
26 Mark Stoyle, *West Britons: Cornish Identities and the Early Modern British State*, Exeter, 2002, p. 67.
27 Richard Carew, *Survey of Cornwall*, 1602, ed. F.E. Halliday, London, 1953, pp. 303–308.
28 Stoyle, 2002, p. 181.
29 Rowse, 1944, p. 48.
30 See Philip Payton, *A Vision of Cornwall*, Fowey, 2002, especially chapter 3.
31 A.K. Hamilton Jenkin, *The Cornish Miner*, 1927, repub. Newton Abbot, 1972, pp. 274–275.
32 A.L. Rowse, *The Early Churchills: An English Family*, London, 1956, p. 6.
33 Rowse, 1956, p. ix.
34 Rowse, 1956, p. v.
35 Rowse, 1956, p. ix.
36 Rowse, 1956, p. ix.
37 A.L. Rowse, *The Later Churchills*, London, 1958; A.L. Rowse, *The Churchills: The Story of A Family*, London, 1966.
38 Rowse, 1966, p. v.
39 Rowse, 1966, p. 49.

40 Rowse, 1966, pp. 45, 257.
41 Rowse, 1966, p. 90.
42 A.L. Rowse, *West Country Stories*, London, 1945, p. 29.
43 A.L. Rowse, *The West in English History*, London, 1949, pp. 5–6.
44 Rowse, 1949, p. 71.
45 Rowse, 1949, p. 72.
46 A.L. Rowse, *The Elizabethans and America*, London, 1959, p. 38.
47 *Western Morning News*, 29 May 1953.
48 EUL MS113/2 Journals and notebooks/1/14, 6 June 1953.
49 EUL MS113/2/1/4, 6 June 1953.
50 Rowse, 1966, p. 561.
51 A.L. Rowse, *An Elizabethan Garland*, London, 1954.
52 Rowse, 1954, p. 144.
53 Rowse, 1954, p. 144.
54 Rowse, 1954, p. 145.
55 Rowse, 1954, pp. 145–146.
56 Rowse, 1954, p. 147.
57 Rowse, 1954, p. 149.
58 Rowse, 1954, p. 152.
59 Rowse, 1954, pp. 154–155.
60 Rowse, 1954, p. 155.
61 Rowse, 1954, pp. 157, 158–159.
62 Rowse, 1954, p. 161.
63 EUL MS113/2 Journals and notebooks/1/19, 26 July 1958.
64 A.L. Rowse, *All Souls and Appeasement: A Contribution to Contemporary History*, London, 1961.
65 EUL MS113/3 Correspondence/1,Trevelyan to Rowse, 26 January 1950.
66 EUL MS113/3/1, Trevelyan to Rowse, 23 February 1950.
67 EUL MS113/3/1, Neale to Rowse, 25 November 1950.
68 EUL MS113/3/1, Neale to Rowse, 23 November 1950.
69 A.L. Rowse, *All Souls in My Time*, London, 1993, p. 167.
70 Rowse, 1993, p. 167.
71 EUL MS113/2 Journals and notebooks/1/14, Easter Monday 1954.
72 Rowse, 1993, p. 171.
73 EUL MS113/2 Journals and notebooks/1/14, 21 December 1952.
74 A.L. Rowse, *A Man of the Thirties*, London, 1979, p. 208.
75 EUL MS113/2 Journals and notebooks/1/14, 21 December 1952.
76 *Herald Tribune—Books*, 3 June 1962.
77 EUL MS113/2 Journals and notebooks/1/27, 14 January 1968.
78 *Sunday Telegraph Magazine*, 21 August 1977.
79 *Sunday Telegraph Magazine*, 21 August 1977.
80 A.L. Rowse, *William Shakespeare: A Biography*, London, 1963; A.L. Rowse, *My View of Shakespeare*, London, 1996.
81 *New Yorker*, 18 March 1974.
82 A.L. Rowse, *Eminent Elizabethans*, London, 1983, p. 1.
83 A.L. Rowse, *In Shakespeare's Land: A Journey Through the Landscape of Elizabethan England*, London, 1986, pp. 82, 90–91.
84 A.L. Rowse, *The Tower of London in the History of the Nation*, London, 1972; A.L. Rowse, *Oxford in the History of the Nation*, London, 1975; A.L. Rowse, *Heritage of Britain*, London, 1977; A.L. Rowse, *The Story of Britain*, London, 1979b.
85 For example, the publication in the United States of Rowse, 1966 (*The Churchills: The Story of A Family*), was greeted with numerous supportive reviews: *Morning Globe* (Boston, Mass.), 31 May 1967; *News and Courier* (Charleston, S.C.), 4 June 1967; *American* (Chicago, Ill.), 28 May 1967; *News* (Wilmington, Del.), 21 June 1967; *Times* (El Paso, Tex.), *Bestsellers* (Scranton, Pa.), 15 June 1967; *Wall Street Journal*, 20 June 1967; *Enterprise* (Beaumont, Tex.), 11 June 1967.
86 Rowse, 1954, pp. 129–130.
87 Rowse, 1954, p. 162.
88 Rowse, 1944, p. 36.

89 EUL MS113/2 Journals and notebooks/1/21 'American Journal', 19 November 1960; see also Richard Ollard (ed.), *The Diaries of A.L. Rowse*, London, 2003, p. 322.
90 Ollard, 2003, p. 381.

8 'The Biggest and Most Significant of Cornish Themes'

1 Exeter University Library (EUL) Rowse Collection MS113/2 Journals and notebooks/3/2 Pocket Notebooks 1970s–1980s, 15 November 1980.
2 A.L. Rowse, *All Souls in My Time*, London, 1993, p. 170.
3 Rowse, 1993, p. 171.
4 Rowse, 1993, p. 170.
5 EUL MS113/2 Journals and notebooks/27, 26 September 1965; see also Richard Ollard, *A Man of Contradictions: A Life of A.L. Rowse*, London, 1999, p. 213.
6 EUL MS113/2/1/15 Second American Journal 5 February 1956; see also Richard Ollard, *The Diaries of A.L. Rowse*, London, 2003, pp. 211–212.
7 EUL MS113/2/1/15, 5 February 1956; see also Ollard, 2003, p. 212.
8 A.L. Rowse, *Friends and Contemporaries*, London, 1989a, p. 121.
9 A.L. Rowse, *Historians I Have Known*, London, 1995, p. 88.
10 See Chapter 7, n. 85.
11 A.L. Rowse, *A Life: Collected Poems*, Edinburgh, 1981, p. 234.
12 *Sunday Times*, 23 December 1979; *House and Garden* (American edition), November 1987.
13 *Sunday Times*, 23 December 1979.
14 EUL MS113/2/3/2, 22 October 1974.
15 *New York Times Book Review*, 23 March 1969.
16 A.L. Rowse, *The Elizabethans and America*, London, 1959; A.L. Rowse, *The Cornish in America*, London, 1969.
17 Rowse, 1989, p. 121.
18 Rowse, 1969, p. vii.
19 Rowse, 1969, p. 9.
20 A.L. Rowse, *A Cornishman at Oxford: The Education of a Cornishman*, London, 1965, pp. 14–15.
21 C. Lewis Hind, *Days in Cornwall*, London, 2nd edn 1907, p. 352.
22 *West Briton*, 24 September 1896.
23 *Cornish Post*, 20 December 1906.
24 A.K. Hamilton Jenkin, *The Cornish Miner*, 1927, repub. Newton Abbot, 1972, p. 330.
25 A.L. Rowse, *A Cornish Childhood: Autobiography of a Cornishman*, London, 1942, p. 34.
26 Rowse, 1942, pp. 38–39.
27 Rowse, 1942, pp. 34–35.
28 A.L. Rowse, *A Cornishman Abroad*, London, 1976, p. 253.
29 A.L. Rowse, *A Man of the Thirties*, London, 1979, p. 119.
30 Rowse, 1979, p. 120.
31 Rowse, 1979, p. 120.
32 Rowse, 1942, p. 23.
33 Rowse, 1965, pp. 75–76.
34 A.L. Rowse, *The English Spirit: Essays in History and Literature*, London, 1944, p. 52.
35 Rowse, London, 1944, p. 52.
36 A.L. Rowse, *The Use of History*, London, 1946, repub. 1963, pp. 32–33.
37 EUL MS113/2 Journals and notebooks/2/21 American Journal, 1960.
38 EUL MS113/2/5/2, September 1966.
39 EUL MS113/2/5/2, September 1966.
40 EUL MS113/2/2/21, 1965.
41 Newton G. Thomas, *The Long Winter Ends*, London, 1941, p. 242.
42 EUL MS113/2 Journals and notebooks/2/21 American Journal, 1951.
43 *Listener*, 10 September 1970.
44 *Listener*, 10 September 1970; 'Empire State' is a slip of Rowse's (or an editor's) pen: it is the 'Empire Mine'.
45 Rowse, 1969.
46 John Pearce, *The Wesleys in Cornwall*, Truro, 1964, p. 27.
47 Rowse, 1969, pp. vii–viii.

48 Rowse, 1969, p. vii.
49 Rowse, 1969, p. vii.
50 Rowse, 1969, p. 8.
51 Rowse, 1969, p. 10.
52 John McManners, 'Alfred Leslie Rowse, 1903–1997', in *Proceedings of the British Academy: 105, 1999: Lectures and Memoirs*, Oxford, 2000, p. 552.
53 EUL MS113/3 Correspondence/1/Thomas to Rowse, n.d. *c.* 1967.
54 Rowse, 1969, pp. 30–33.
55 G. Pawley White, *A Handbook of Cornish Surnames*, Camborne, n.d. *c.* 1968.
56 EUL MS113/3 Correspondence/1/Harris to Rowse, 29 May 1967.
57 EUL MS 113/1/3 Press Cuttings/temp/Box 35, Letter: Nevins to Rowse, 13 February 1969.
58 *Western Morning News*, 12 September 1969.
59 EUL MS 113/3 Correspondence/temp/Box 188/Causley to Rowse, 28 July 1969.
60 *Times Literary Supplement*, 24 July 1969.
61 EUL MS 113/3 Correspondence/1/Todd to Rowse, 27 September 1969; see also Harris to Rowse, 1 October 1969.
62 EUL MS/113/3/1/Brogan to Rowse, 4 October 1969.
63 Glanmor Williams, 'A Prospect of Paradise? Wales and the United States,1776–1914', in Glanmor Williams (ed.), *Religion, Language and nationality in Wales*, Cardiff, 1979, p. 233.
64 Bob Reece, 'Writing about the Irish in Australia', in John O'Brien and Pauric Travers (eds), *The Irish Emigrant Experience in Australia*, Dublin, 1991, pp. 228–229.
65 Rowse, 1969, p. 113.
66 A.L. Rowse, *The Little Land of Cornwall*, Gloucester, 1986, p. 5.
67 EUL MS113/3 Correspondence/1/Todd to Rowse, 27 September 1969.
68 Roger Burt, *The British Lead Mining Industry*, Redruth, 1984, pp. 1–2.
69 R.W. Paul, *Mining Frontiers of the Far West, 1848–1880*, New York, 1963; for example, see Rowse, 1969, pp. 319, 348 and 381.
70 Sharron P. Schwartz, 'The Making of a Myth: Cornish Miners in the New World in the Early Nineteenth Century', in Philip Payton (ed.), *Cornish Studies: Nine*, Exeter, 2001.
71 Rowse, 1979, pp. 358–359.
72 See Philip Payton, *The Cornish Overseas*, Fowey, 1999.
73 *Birmingham Post*, 1 December 1979.
74 EUL MS113/1/2 Other MSS & TSS/temp/Box 134/Second Cornish Anthology.
75 Oswald Pryor, *Australia's Little Cornwall*, Adelaide, 1962.
76 South Australian State Archives (SAA), PRG96, Oswald Pryor Papers, Rowse to Pryor, 20 September 1950.
77 SAA PRG96, Berry to Pryor, 26 August 1950.
78 A.L. Rowse, *The Controversial Colensos*, Redruth, 1989b.
79 Rowse, 1969, pp. 6 and viii.
80 A.C. Todd, *The Cornish Miner in America*, Truro, 1967.
81 EUL MS113/3 Correspondence/1/Todd to Rowse, 11 January 1968.
82 EUL MS113/3/1/Todd to Rowse, 4 February 1968.
83 EUL MS113/3/1/Todd to Rowse, 16 March 1969.
84 A.C. Todd, *The Search For Silver: Cornish Miners in Mexico 1825–1948*, Padstow, 1977, p. viii.
85 EUL MS113/3 Correspondence/1/Todd to Rowse, 26 June 1972.
86 EUL MS113/3/1/Todd to Rowse, 24 June 1974.
87 EUL MS113/3/temp/Box 30/Rowse to Todd, 25 June 1974.
88 EUL MS113/3/1/Todd to Rowse, 25 March 1976.
89 EUL MS113/3/temp/Box 162, Wright (McKinney) to Rowse, 18 August 1966.
90 EUL MS113/3/1/Todd to Rowse, 23 December 1970.
91 EUL MS113/3/1/Todd to Rowse, 16 March 1974.
92 EUL MS113/3/1/Todd to Rowse, 30 June 1977; the immediate outcome of this work was Philip Payton, 'The Cornish in South Australia: Their Influence and Experience from Immigration to Assimilation, 1836–1936', unpub. PhD, University of Adelaide, 1978, and Philip Payton, *Pictorial History of Australia's Little Cornwall*, Adelaide, 1978.
93 Wilfrid Prest (ed.), *The Wakefield Companion to South Australian History*, Adelaide, 2001, p. 556; see SAA D6029/1–115(L), Letters written Home by Cornish Folk who emigrated to Australia in the nineteenth century, collected by John M. Tregenza; *Cornish Life*, June

1975; and EUL MS113/3 Correspondence/temp/Box 162/Wright (McKinney) to Rowse, 12 March 1971.
94 A.C. Todd with David James, *Ever Westward the Land*, Exeter, 1986.
95 EUL MS113/3 Correspondence/1/Todd to Rowse, 16 March 1969.
96 Sydney Cauveren, *A.L. Rowse: A Bibliophile's Extensive Bibliography*, London, 2000, p. xxxi.
97 EUL MS113/2 Journals and notebooks/30/9–13 August 1968.

9 'I Have Been "In Love" with Cornwall All My Life'

1 Richard Ollard, *The Diaries of A.L. Rowse*, London, 2003, p. 313.
2 A.L. Rowse, *Friends and Contemporaries*, London, 1989, p. 280.
3 *Old Cornwall*, 1:3, April 1926.
4 *Cornish Post*, 15 January 1938.
5 *Cornish Guardian*, 12 January 1939.
6 *West Briton*, 11 August 1941.
7 Claude Berry, *Cornwall*, London, 1948.
8 Exeter University Library (EUL)Rowse Collection MS113/3 Correspondence/1/Berry to Rowse, 8 August 1949.
9 EUL MS113/3/1/Nance to Rowse, 3 October 1953.
10 Institute of Cornish Studies Collection, Edwin Chrigwin, 'A Critical Essay on The Work of A.L. Rowse (Fellow of All Souls)', unpub. MS; A.L. Rowse, *Tudor Cornwall*, London, 1941, p. 24.
11 For an assessment of Revivalist influence in the Royal Institution of Cornwall in this period, see Philip Payton, 'Paralysis and Revival: The Reconstruction of Celtic-Catholic Cornwall, 1890–1945', in Ella Westland (ed.), *Cornwall: The Cultural Construction of Place*, Penzance, 1997, pp. 32–33.
12 EUL MS113/1/3 Press Cuttings/temp/Box 35/Letter: Douch to Rowse, 19 April 1973.
13 EUL MS113/1/3/temp/Box 52/Letter: Douch to Rowse, 10 May 1968.
14 Henry Jenner, *A Handbook of the Cornish Language*, London, 1904.
15 EUL MS113/2 Journals and notebooks/5/2/ 29 July 1929.
16 EUL MS113/2 /5/2/ 27 August 1945.
17 EUL MS113/2/5/3/ Easter 1949.
18 *Spectator*, 4 March 1938.
19 A.L. Rowse, *A Cornish Childhood: Autobiography of a Cornishman*, London, 1942, pp. 221–222.
20 *Western Morning News*, 17 December 1941.
21 See Trevelyan's review of *The England of Elizabeth*, London, 1950, in *Sunday Times*, c. December 1950.
22 *West Briton*, 5 March 1964.
23 EUL MS113/2 Journals and notebooks/5/11/1965.
24 EUL MS113/2/1/28/ 3 September 1967.
25 EUL MS113/2/5/11/1971.
26 EUL MS113/2/1/28/ 7 September 1968; encouraged by Rowse, P.A.S. Pool did go on to complete a full biography of William Borlase.
27 EUL MS113/2/1/28/ 7 September 1968.
28 *Irish Independent*, 8 July 1963.
29 *Irish Independent*, 8 July 1963.
30 *Irish Independent*, 4 July 1952.
31 EUL MS113/2 Journals and notebooks/1/14/ 20 December 1952.
32 *New Statesman*, 7 February 1953.
33 *Sunday Times*, 26 September 1976.
34 A.L. Rowse, 'Rudyard Kipling', *Kipling Journal*, March 1960.
35 Rowse, *Kipling Journal*, March 1960.
36 A.L. Rowse, *Portraits and Views: Literary and Historical*, London, 1979, p. 228.
37 Rowse, 1979, p. 155.
38 *Books and Bookmen*, November 1978.
39 Rowse, 1979, p. 223.
40 Rowse, 1979, pp. 228–229.
41 Rowse, 1979, p. 59.

42 *London Calling* (journal of the General Overseas Service), 2 May 1957. Rowse's talk was broadcast on the GOS.
43 *London Calling*, 2 May 1957.
44 EUL MS113/1/3 Press Cuttings/temp/Box 52, Unpub. MS 'Local and National History', n.d.
45 EUL MS113/1/3/temp/Box 52, Unpub. MS 'Local and National History', n.d..
46 See Dick Cole, Bernard Deacon and Garry Tregidga, *Mebyon Kernow and Cornish Nationalism*, Cardiff, 2003; see also Philip Payton, 'Territory and Identity', in Philip Payton (ed.), *Cornwall Since the War: The Contemporary History of a European Region*, Redruth, 1993.
47 *Guardian*, 5 December 1967.
48 *Cornish Nation*, 2:5, September 1971.
49 *Royal Commission on the Constitution*, Cmnd 5460, Report Vol. I, London, 1973, paras 221, 329, 1211.
50 A.L. Rowse, *The Little Land of Cornwall*, Gloucester, 1986, p. 298.
51 EUL MS113/1/3 Press Cuttings/temp/Box 33/Fragment of letter, Legonna to Rowse, n.d.
52 Llyfrgell Genedlaethol Cymru/National Library of Wales, Legonna Papers/7/4/Rowse to Legonna, n.d. *c.* 1944.
53 *Cornish Guardian*, 20 June 1968.
54 *Cornish Guardian*, 20 June 1968.
55 EUL MS113/2 Journals and notebooks/1/30, 28 December 1968.
56 *New York Times Book Review*, 23 March 1969.
57 Rowse, 1979, p. 148.
58 EUL MS 113/1/3 Newspaper Cuttings/temp/Box 37/unidentified American newspaper, dated 18 August 1967.
59 *New Cornwall*, 14:4 and 5, Winter 1966; see also Derek Williams, 'The Land of My Content: A.L. Rowse and Cornwall', *An Baner Kernewek/Cornish Banner*, November 2003.
60 Rowse, 1986, p. ix.
61 Rowse, 1986, p. 297.
62 Rowse, 1986, p. 297.
63 Rowse, 1986, pp. 299–301.
64 Rowse, 1986, p. 301.
65 EUL MS113/1/3 Newspaper Cuttings/temp/Box 53, pamphlet, *88th Annual Dinner of the London Cornish Association, 9 March 1974*.
66 Rowse, 1979, pp. 237–239.
67 Rowse, 1986, p. 297.
68 EUL MS113/2 Journals and notebooks/1/28, 16 April 1978.
69 A.L. Rowse, *Historians I Have Known*, London, 1995, p. 197.

10 'Marooned on My Headland'

1 James Whetter, *Dr A.L. Rowse: Poet, Historian, Lover of Cornwall—A Memoir*, St Austell, 2003, p. 51.
2 Exeter University Library (EUL) Rowse Collection MS113/1/3 Press Cuttings/temp/Box 33, 'My Delight' BBC Radio 4 MS, recorded 19 January 1978.
3 A.L. Rowse, *Cornish Place Rhymes: A Commemorative Volume*, Tiverton, 1997, pp. 7–8.
4 Rowse, 1997, pp. 52, 58, 60, 62, 63.
5 A.L. Rowse, *Peter: The White Cat of Trenarren*, London, 1974; A.L. Rowse, *A Quartet of Cornish Cats*, Redruth, 1992.
6 Rowse, 1974, dustcover notes.
7 Rowse, 1974, pp. 7–9.
8 Rowse, 1974, p. 37.
9 Rowse, 1992, p. 86.
10 Rowse, 1992, p. 115.
11 Rowse, 1992, p. 132.
12 A.L. Rowse, *The Little Land of Cornwall*, Gloucester, 1986a, p. 297.
13 EUL MS113/2 Journals and notebooks/1/30, 15 September 1968.
14 EUL MS113/2/1/27, 2 October 1965.
15 EUL MS113/2/3 Pocket Notebooks, 6 November 1982.

16 *Birmingham Post*, 21 May 1981.
17 Colin Wilson, *Poetry and Mysticism*, San Francisco, 1969, pp. 161–162, 182.
18 *Cornish Labour News*, January 1934; see also A.L. Rowse, *A Life: Collected Poems*, Edinburgh, 1981, p. 27.
19 Rowse, 1981, p. 293.
20 Rowse, 1981, p. 156.
21 Rowse, 1981, p. 302.
22 See Whetter, 2003; also James Whetter, *Cornwall in the Seventeenth Century: An Economic History of Cornwall*, Padstow, 1974, and James Whetter, *The Bodrugans: The History of a Cornish Medieval Knightly Family*, St Austell, 1995.
23 A.L. Rowse, *Tudor Cornwall: Portrait of a Society*, London, 1941, pp. 118–119.
24 EUL MS113/2 Journals and notebooks/1/30, 12 September 1968.
25 EUL MS113/2/1/38a, 24 April 1977.
26 EUL MS113/2/1/14, 15 September 1954.
27 EUL MS113/2/1/30, 12 September 1968.
28 EUL MS113/3 Correspondence/1, Trevelyan to Rowse, 15 June 1942.
29 EUL MS113/3/1, Trevelyan to Rowse, 17 February 1961.
30 EUL MS113/3/1, Trevelyan to Rowse, 8 August 1958.
31 EUL MS113/2 Journals and notebooks/1/14, 15 September 1954.
32 EUL MS113/2/5/11, USA 1960; see also F.E. Halliday, *A History of Cornwall*, London, 1959.
33 EUL MS113/3 Correspondence/1, Val Baker to Rowse, n.d.
34 EUL MS113/2/3 Pocket notebooks/3, 24 June 1982.
35 D.M. Thomas (ed.), *The Granite Kingdom: Poems of Cornwall*, Truro, 1970, p. 14.
36 EUL MS113/3 Correspondence/temp/Box 89, Treneer to Rowse, 23 February n.d.
37 EUL MS113/3/temp/Box89, Treneer to Rowse, April n.d.
38 Anne Treneer, *The Mercurial Chemist: A Life of Sir Humphry Davy*, London, 1963.
39 EUL MS 113/3 Correspondence/1, Harris to Rowse, 21 March 1973.
40 EUL MS113/3/1, Harris to Rowse, 24 May 1973.
41 EUL MS113/3/1, Harris to Rowse, 29 January 1975.
42 F.L. and Gladys Harris, *The Making of a Cornish Town: Torpoint and Neighbourhood through Two Hundred Years*, Redruth, 1976.
43 *Western Morning News*, 6 February 1959.
44 *Books and Bookmen*, February 1979.
45 James Mildren, introducing TSW television programme *A Cornish Childhood*, 1990.
46 Whetter, 2003, pp. 15, 21, 24.
47 Raleigh Trevelyan, *Sir Walter Raleigh*, London, 2002, p. xiii.
48 A.L. Rowse, *A.L. Rowse's Cornwall*, London, 1988a, p. 6.
49 A.L. Rowse, *Portraits and Views: Literary and Historical*, London, 1979, p. 95.
50 Bevis Hillier, *John Betjeman: New Fame, New Love*, London, 2002, pp. 477, 577; *Western Morning News*, 24 May 1957.
51 Hillier, 2002, pp. 477–478; John Betjeman, *First and Last Loves*, London, 1952.
52 Rowse, 1981, p. 1.
53 Cited in Hillier, 2002, p. 256.
54 EUL MS113/3 Correspondence/temp/Box 30, Betjeman to Rowse, 21 March 1967.
55 EUL MS113/3/temp/Box 30, Betjeman to Rowse, 22 May 1975; Betjeman to Rowse, 22 October 1977.
56 EUL MS113/3/temp/Box 30, Betjeman to Rowse, 1 September 1980.
57 EUL MS113/3/temp/Box 30, Betjeman to Rowse, n.d.; Betjeman to Rowse, 1960; Betjeman to Rowse, 1972.
58 EUL MS113/3/temp/Box 30, Betjeman to Rowse, 1 December 1971.
59 *Books and Bookmen*, September 1978.
60 Rowse, 1979, p. 90.
61 Rowse, 1979, p. 91.
62 Candida Lycett Green (ed.), *John Betjeman: Letters: Volume Two: 1951–1984*, London, 1995, p. 326 (Betjeman to Fallowell, 29 November 1966).
63 Hillier, 2002, p. 245.
64 EUL MS113/2 Journals and notebooks/5/3, 18 August 1956.
65 EUL MS113/3 Correspondence/temp/Box 30, Betjeman (Penelope) to Rowse, 12 July n.d.

66 John Betjeman and A.L. Rowse, *Victorian and Edwardian Cornwall from Old Photographs*, Batsford, 1974, p. i.
67 EUL MS113/3 Correspondence/temp/Box 30, 22 July 1974.
68 A.L. Rowse, *Memories and Glimpses*, London, 1986b, p. 477.
69 EUL MS113/3 Correspondence/temp/Box 30, 17 August 1978.
70 See EUL MS113/3/temp/Box 30, Cavendish to Rowse, 6 July 1983.
71 Rowse, 1986b, p. 502.
72 A.L. Rowse, *A Cornish Anthology*, London, 1968; A.L. Rowse, *The Cornish in America*, London, 1969; EUL MS113/1/2 Other MSS & TSS/temp/Box 134/Second Cornish Anthology.
73 A.L. Rowse, *Matthew Arnold: Poet and Prophet*, London, 1976, dustcover notes.
74 Rowse, 1976, p. 15.
75 Rowse, 1976, p. 12.
76 A.L. Rowse, *The Byrons and Trevanions*, London, 1978, pp. 2, 184.
77 Rowse, 1978, pp. v, 2.
78 A.L. Rowse, *Quiller Couch: A Portrait of Q*, London, 1988b, p. v.
79 Rowse, 1988b, dustcover notes.
80 Rowse, 1988b, p. 223.
81 A.L. Rowse, *Night at the Carn and Other Stories*, London, 1984, p. 7; A.L. Rowse, *Stories from Trenarren*, London, 1986c.
82 Rowse, 1986c, p. 9.
83 Rowse, 1984, p. 8.
84 Rowse, 1984, p. 9.
85 Rowse, 1984, pp. 40–46.
86 Rowse, 1984, pp. 47–54.
87 Rowse, 1986c, pp. 87–92.
88 Rowse, 1984, pp. 55–61.
89 Rowse, 1986c, pp. 27–38.
90 Rowse, 1986c, p. 62.
91 Rowse, 1986c,pp. 51–52.
92 Rowse, 1986c, pp. 83–84.
93 Rowse, 1986c, p. 111.
94 Rowse, 1986c, p. 64.
95 Rowse, 1984, pp. 175–176.
96 Rowse, 1986c, p. 102.
97 Rowse, 1986c, p. 94.
98 Geraint H. Jenkins, *The People's Historian: Professor Gwyn A. Williams, 1925–1995*, Aberystwyth, 1996, p. 1.
99 Jenkins, 1996, p. 5.
100 Deborah Gare, Geoffrey Bolton, Stuart Macintyre and Tom Stannage (eds), *The Fuss That Never Ended: The Life and Work of Geoffrey Blainey*, Melbourne, 2003, p. vii.
101 Robert Pascoe, *The Manufacture of Australian History*, Melbourne, 1979, p. 132.
102 *Spectator*, 24 February 1973.
103 *Sunday Independent* (Plymouth), 4 February 1973.
104 EUL MS113/2/3 Pocket notebooks/3, 1 November 1982.
105 EUL MS113/2/5 Manuscript Transcripts from Notebooks and Typescripts from notebooks/11, 24 February 1988.
106 *Evening Standard*, 19 November 1993.
107 *Evening Standard*, 29 January 1996.
108 EUL MS113/2/5 Manuscript Transcripts from Notebooks and Typescripts from notebooks/11, 24 February 1988.
109 Whetter, 2003, p. 39.
110 *Western Morning News*, 31 December 1996.
111 *Western Morning News*, 1 January 1997.
112 Donald Adamson, 'A.L. Rowse, Honoured Man', *An Baner Kernewek/Cornish Banner*, November 2003.
113 John McManners, 'Alfred Leslie Rowse, 1903–1997', in *Proceedings of the British Academy: 105, 1999, Lectures and Memoirs*, Oxford, 2000, pp. 544, 547.
114 David Loades, 'A.L. Rowse (1913 [sic]-1997)', *Renaissance Studies*, 12:2, 1998, pp.

318–321.
115 Christopher Haigh, 'Introduction', in A.L. Rowse, *The England of Elizabeth*, 2nd edn, London, 2003, pp. ix–xxxvi.
116 McManners, 2000, pp. 544–545.
117 *Daily Mail*, 22 October 1971.

11 'All the Island Peoples'

1 James Whetter, *Dr A.L. Rowse: Poet, Historian, Lover of Cornwall—A Memoir*, St Austell, 2003, p. 1.
2 *Royal Historical Society Newsletter*, Autumn 2003, p. 4.
3 *History Today*, May 2003.
4 Christopher Haigh, 'Introduction', in A.L. Rowse, *The England of Elizabeth*, 2nd edn, London, 2003, pp. ix–xxxvi.
5 Haigh, 2003, p. x.
6 See Mark Stoyle, 'Cornish Rebellions 1497–1648', *History Today*, May 1997; Mark Stoyle, *West Britons: Cornish Identities and the Early Modern British State*, Exeter, 2002a, pp. 3–4; Mark Stoyle, 'Re-discovering Difference: The Recent Historiography of Early Modern Cornwall', in Philip Payton (ed.), *Cornish Studies: Ten*, Exeter, 2002b; Philip Payton, *A Vision of Cornwall*, Fowey, 2002, chapter 5; Philip Payton, '"I was before my time, caught betwixt and between": A.L. Rowse and the Writing of British and Cornish History', in Philip Payton (ed.), *Cornish Studies: Eleven*, Exeter, 2003.
7 A.L. Rowse, *The Expansion of Elizabethan England*, London, 1955, p. 45.
8 See, for example, Brendan Bradshaw and John Morrill (eds), *The British Problem c1534–1707*, London, 1996, and Steven G. Ellis and Sarah Barber (eds), *Conquest and Union: Fashioning a British State 1485–1725*, London, 1995.
9 Helen Jewell, *The North–South Divide: The Origins of Northern Consciousness in England*, Manchester, 1994.
10 Stoyle, 2002a.
11 Geraint H. Jenkins, Review of Stoyle, 2002a, *History*, 88:2, 290, April 2003, pp. 314–315.
12 Norman Davies, *The Isles: A History*, London, 1999, p. 976.
13 Michael Portillo, 'Foreword', in A.L. Rowse, *The Expansion of Elizabethan England*, 2nd edn, London, 2003, p. xiii.
14 John Chynoweth, *Tudor Cornwall*, Stroud, 2002.
15 Nicholas Orme, Review of Chynoweth, 2002, *History*, 88:2, 292, October 2003, p. 687.
16 J.P.D. Cooper, *Propaganda and the Tudor State: Political Culture in the Westcountry*, Oxford, 2003.
17 Bernard Deacon, 'Propaganda and the Tudor State or Propaganda of the Tudor Historians?', in Payton, ed., 2003, p. 320.
18 Steven G. Ellis, 'Not Mere English: The British Perspective 1400–1650', *History Today*, December 1988.
19 Hugh Kearney, *The British Isles: A History of Four Nations*, Cambridge, 1989, p. 70.
20 Stoyle, May 1997.
21 Michael Hechter, *Internal Colonialism: The Celtic Fringe in British National Development 1536–1966*, London, 1975, p. 63; see also A.L. Rowse, 'Tudor Expansion: The Transition from Medieval to Modern History', *William and Mary Quarterly*, 3, XIV:3, July 1957, pp. 309–316.
22 Jim Bulpitt, *Territory and Power in the United Kingdom*, Manchester, 1983, pp. 37–44.
23 Amos C. Miller, *Sir Henry Killigrew: Elizabethan Soldier and Diplomat*, Leicester, 1963, pp. viii–ix.
24 Amos C. Miller, *Sir Richard Grenville of the Civil War*, Chichester, 1979, pp. x and 128–129.
25 Glen Burgess (ed.), *The New British History: Founding a Modern State 1603–1715*, London, 1999, p. 7.
26 A.L. Rowse, *The Spirit of English History*, London, 1943.
27 See Richard Ollard, *A Man of Contradictions: A Life of A.L. Rowse*, London, 1999, pp. 87, 174, 245–6, 269.
28 Steven G. Ellis, 'Tudor Northumberland: British History in an English County', in S.J. Connolly (ed.), *Kingdoms United? Great Britain and Ireland since 1500: Integration and Diversity*, London, 1999, pp. 29–42; Steven G. Ellis, 'The Tudor Borderlands, 1485–1603',

in John Morrill (ed.), *The Oxford Illustrated History of Tudor and Stuart Britain*, Oxford, 1996, pp. 53–73.
29 See Burgess, 1999, pp. 8–9; for a corroborating view, see Raphael Samuel, *Island Stories: Unravelling Britain—Theatres of Memory, Volume II*, London, 1998, pp. 25–7. The Pocock essays are: J.G.A. Pocock, 'British History: A Plea for a New Subject', *New Zealand Journal of History*, 8, 1974, reprinted in *Journal of Modern History*, 47, 1975, pp. 601–628, and J.G.A. Pocock, 'The Limits and Divisions of British History: In Search of the Unknown Subject', *American Historical Review*, 87, 1982, pp. 311–336.
30 Ellis, 1988; Kearney, 1989; Bradshaw and Morrill, 1996; Davies, 1999.
31 Burgess, 1999, pp. 8–9.
32 Pocock, 1975, p. 606.
33 Pocock, 1982, p. 312.
34 Carl Bridge and Kent Fedorowich (eds), *The British World: Diaspora, Culture and Identity*, London, 2003.
35 Rowse, 1955, p. 6.
36 Rowse, 1955, pp. 18–19, 22, 45, 60, 139.
37 Rowse, 1955, p. 18.
38 Exeter University Library (EUL) Rowse Collection MS113/1/3 Press Cuttings/temp/ Box 37, Confidential Report to the Warden of All Souls: 14 September 1944.
39 EUL MS113/3 Correspondence/1, Trevelyan to Rowse, 14 November 1955.
40 EUL MS113/3/1, Neale to Rowse, 12 June 1955.
41 S.T. Bindoff, J. Hurstfield and C.H. Williams (eds), *Elizabethan Government and Society: Essays Presented to Sir John Neale*, London, 1961, p. vi.
42 *New York Times Book Review*, 18 December 1955.
43 *Chattanooga Times*, 26 November 1955; *Hartford Court Magazine*, 25 December 1955.
44 *Hartford Court Magazine*, 25 December 1955.
45 *West Briton*, 17 November 1955.
46 *Time and Tide*, 8 October 1955.
47 A.L. Rowse, *Tudor Cornwall: Portrait of a Society*, London, 1941, p. 10.
48 Rowse, 1941, p. 9.
49 *Sunday Times*, 28 December 1941.
50 *Times Literary Supplement*, 27 September 1941.
51 A.L. Rowse, *The Use of History*, London, 1946, repub. 1971, p. 51.
52 A.L. Rowse, *On History*, London, 1927, pp. 30–31.
53 Rowse, 1927, pp. 36–37.
54 Jeremy Black and Donald M. MacRaild, *Studying History*, London, 1997, p. 109.
55 EUL MS113/1/3 Press Cuttings/temp/ Box 52, unpub. MS 'Local and National History'.
56 EUL MS113/1/3/temp/Box 52, unpub. MS 'Local'.
57 EUL MS113/1/3/temp/Box 52, unpub. MS 'Local'.
58 EUL MS113/1/3/temp/Box 52, unpub. MS 'Local'
59 EUL MS113/3 Correspondence/1, Hoskins to Rowse, n.d. *c.* 1960.
60 Cited in H.P.R Finberg and V.H.T. Tripp, *Local History: Objective and Pursuit*, Newton Abbot, 1967, p. 9.
61 A.L. Rowse, *The England of Elizabeth*, London, 1950, p. 48.
62 H.P.R. Finberg, *The Local Historian and His Theme: An Introductory Lecture Delivered at the University College of Leicester, 6 November 1952*, Leicester, 1965, repub. At http://www.bodley.ox.ac.uk/external/cross/finberg01.htm, 17 December 2003, p. 2; Finberg and Tripp, 1967, p. 9.
63 Charles Phythian-Adams, *Rethinking English Local History*, Leicester, 1987, pp. 12–13.
64 J.D. Marshall, *The Tyranny of the Discrete: A Discussion of the Problems of Local History in England*, Aldershot, 1997, p. 49.
65 Marshall, 1997, p. 105; here Marshall is echoing his J.D. Marshall, 'Proving Ground or the Creation of Regional Identity? The Origins and Problems of Regional History in Britain', in P. Swan and D. Foster (eds), *Essays in Regional and Local History*, Beverly, 1992, pp. 1–26.
66 Marshall, 1997, p. 107.
67 A.L. Rowse, *A Cornishman Abroad*, London, 1976, pp. 198–199.
68 A.L. Rowse, *A Man of the Thirties*, London, 1979a, pp. 127–128.
69 Rowse, 1979a, p. 16.

70 Rowse, 1976, p. 199.
71 EUL MS113/1/3 Press Cuttings/temp/Box 53, unpub. MS, 'Experiences with Manuscripts'.
72 Rowse, 1979a, p. 16.
73 Charles Henderson, *Essays in Cornish History*, Oxford, 1935, repub. Truro, 1963, eds A.L. Rowse and M.I. Henderson; Charles Henderson, *A History of the Parish of Constantine in Cornwall*, Truro, 1937, ed. G.H. Doble (the short title *History of Constantine* appears on the frontispiece).
74 *Spectator*, 4 March 1938.
75 A.L. Rowse, *St Austell: Church: Town: Parish*, St Austell, 1960.
76 John McManners, 'Alfred Leslie Rowse, 1903–1997' in *Proceedings of the British Academy:105, 1999, Lectures and Memoirs*, Oxford, 2000, p. 552.
77 Mary Coate, *Cornwall in the Great Civil War and Interregnum, 1642–1660*, Oxford, 1933, repub. Truro, 1963.
78 Rowse, 1979a, p. 111.
79 A.L. Rowse, *A Cornishman at Oxford: The Education of a Cornishman*, London, 1965, pp. 207–8, 315.
80 EUL MS 113/2/5 Manuscript transcripts from Notebooks and Typescripts from note-books/4, 1928; Ollard, 1999, p. 57.
81 Rowse, 1965, p. 315.
82 EUL MS113/3 Correspondence/1, Sweet to Rowse, n.d., later gloss by A.L. Rowse.
83 A.L. Rowse, 'Foreword', *History of Truro High School for Girls*, Truro, n.d., p. xii.
84 EUL, MS113/1/3 Press Cuttings/temp/Box 37, Clippings, *Devon and Cornwall Notes and Queries*, n.d. *c.* 1933.
85 Cited in A.L. Rowse, *West Country Stories*, London, 1945a, p. 148.
86 Cited in Rowse, 1945a, p. 129.
87 Rowse, 1945a, p. 129.
88 Coate, 1933 & 1963, p. 351.
89 Rowse, 1965, p. 157.
90 Rowse, 1941, p. 20.
91 Pocock, 1974, p. 6.
92 David Mathew, *The Celtic Peoples and Renaissance Europe: A Study of the Celtic and Spanish Influences on Elizabethan History*, London, 1933, pp. vii–viii.
93 Mathew, 1933, p. 306.
94 Rowse, 1941, p. 11.
95 A.L. Rowse, *The English Spirit: Essays in History and Literature*, London, 1944, p. 55.
96 Rowse, 1943, p. 12.
97 A.L. Rowse, *Froude the Historian: Victorian Man of Letters*, Gloucester, 1987, pp. 75–76, 78.
98 Rowse, 1946 & 71, p. 75.
99 A.L. Rowse, *William Shakespeare: A Biography*, London, 1963; A.L. Rowse, *My View of Shakespeare*, London, 1996. The estimation of sales is in Sydney Cauveren (ed.), *A.L. Rowse: A Bibliophile's Extensive Bibliography*, Folkstone, 2000, p. 18.
100 McManners, 2000, pp. 544, 548.
101 A.L. Rowse, *Story of Britain*, London, 1979b.
102 A.L. Rowse, *Court and Country: Studies in Tudor History*, Brighton, 1967.
103 A.L. Rowse, *Portraits and Views: Literary and Historical*, London, 1979c, pp. 125–126.
104 A.L. Rowse, *Historians I Have Known*, London, 1995, pp. 56, 57, 95, 101.
105 Rowse, 1979c, p. 116.
106 A.L. Rowse, *Discoveries and Reviews*, London, 1975, p. 163.
107 *Books and Bookmen*, July 1973.
108 David Underdown, *Revel, Riot and Rebellion*, Oxford, 1985.
109 A.L. Rowse, Review of Conrad Russell, *The Causes of the English Civil War*, London, 1990, in the *Telegraph*, cited at http://www.oup.co.uk/isbn/0-19-822141-X, 17 December 2003.
110 Mark Stoyle, *Loyalty and Locality: Popular Allegiance in Devon during the English Civil War*, Exeter, 1994.
111 Mark Stoyle, '"Sir Richard Grenville's Creatures": The New Cornish Tertia, 1644–46', in Philip Payton (ed.), *Cornish Studies: Four*, Exeter, 1996; although complaining that his eyesight was failing, Rowse readily undertook the reading of Stoyle's article as an external referee.

112 A.L. Rowse, 'Foreword', in Philip Payton, *Cornwall*, Fowey, 1996, p. v; repub. as *Cornwall—A History*, Fowey, 2004, p. vii.

113 A.L. Rowse, Review of Philip Payton, *The Making of Modern Cornwall: Historical Experience and the Persistence of 'Difference'*, Redruth, 1992, in *English Historical Review*, June 1995, p. 816.

114 *New York Times Book Review*, 23 March 1969.

115 EUL MS113/3 Correspondence/1, Nixon to Rowse, 16 May 1988.

116 Rowse, 1996.

117 Stoyle, 2002a, p. 4.

118 Rowse, 1979a, p. 181.

Conclusion: 'What Could I Not Have Done for Cornwall'

1   *Country Life*, 6 April 1978.

2   Rowse allowed part of Raine's review to be used for the dustcover notes for his collection *A Life: Collected Poems*, Edinburgh, 1981.

3   A.L. Rowse, *All Souls and Appeasement: A Contribution to Contemporary History*, London, 1961, p. 41.

4   A.L. Rowse, *Memories of Men and Women*, London, 1980, p. 112.

5   Rowse, 1981, p. 397.

6   Rowse, 1981, p. 394.

Further Reading

About A.L. Rowse

Sydney Cauveren, *A.L. Rowse: A Bibliophile's Extensive Bibliography*, London, 2000.

Valerie Jacob, *Tregonissey to Trenarren: The Cornish years of A.L. Rowse*, St Austell, 2001.

Richard Ollard, *A Man of Contradictions: A Life of A.L. Rowse*, London, 1999.

Richard Ollard, *The Diaries of A.L. Rowse*, London, 2003.

James Whetter, *Dr A.L. Rowse: Poet, Historian, Lover of Cornwall*, St Austell, 2003.

About Cornwall: General

Alan M. Kent, *Literature in Cornwall: Continuity–Identity–Difference, 1000–2000*, Bristol, 2000.

Philip Payton, *Cornwall—A History*, Fowey, 2004.

Ella Westland (ed.), *Cornwall: The Cultural Construction of Place*, Penzance, 1997.

About Early Modern Cornwall

Mark Stoyle, *West Britons: Cornish Identities and the Early Modern British State*, Exeter, 2002.

James Whetter, *Cornwall in the Seventeenth Century: An Economic History of Kernow*, Padstow, 1974, repub. St Austell, 2002.

About Later Modern and Contemporary Cornwall

Bernard Deacon, Dick Cole and Garry Tregidga, *Mebyon Kernow and Cornish Nationalism*, Cardiff, 2003.

Philip Payton, *The Making of Modern Cornwall: Historical Experience and the Persistence of 'Difference'*, Redruth, 1992.

Philip Payton (ed.), *Cornwall Since the War: The Contemporary History of A European Region*, Redruth, 1993.

Philip Payton, *A Vision of Cornwall*, Fowey, 2002.

John Rowe, *Cornwall in the Age of the Industrial Revolution*, Liverpool, 1953, repub. St Austell, 1993.

Garry Tregidga, *The Liberal Party in South-West Britain Since 1918: Political Decline, Dormancy and Rebirth*, Exeter, 2000.

About Cornwall's Great Emigration

Richard D. Dawe, *Cornish Pioneers in South Africa: 'Gold and Diamonds, Copper and Blood'*, St Austell, 1998.

Philip Payton, *The Cornish Miner in Australia: Cousin Jack Down Under*, Redruth, 1984.

Philip Payton, *The Cornish Farmer in Australia*, Redruth, 1987.

Philip Payton, *The Cornish Overseas: A History of Cornwall's 'Great Emigration'*, Fowey, 2005.

John Rowe, *The Hard-rock Men: Cornish Immigrants and the North American Mining Frontier*, Liverpool, 1974, repub. St Austell, 2004.

A.C. Todd, *The Cornish Miner in America*, Truro, 1967, repub. Spokane (USA), 1995.

A.C. Todd, *The Search for Silver: Cornish Miners in Mexico 1825–1978*, Padstow, 1977, repub. St Austell, 2002.

Principal Works by A.L. Rowse
Consulted in this Study

On History, London, 1927.
Politics and the Younger Generation, London, 1931.
Mr Keynes and the Labour Movement, London, 1936.
Sir Richard Grenville of the Revenge, London, 1939.
Tudor Cornwall: Portrait of a Society, London, 1941.
A Cornish Childhood: Autobiography of a Cornishman, London, 1942.
The Spirit of English History, London, 1943.
The English Spirit: Essays in History and Literature, London, 1944.
The End of an Epoch: Reflections on Contemporary History, London, 1945.
West Country Stories, London, 1945.
The Use of History, London, 1946.
The West in English History, London, 1949.
The England of Elizabeth, London, 1950.
An Elizabethan Garland, London, 1954.
The Expansion of Elizabethan England, London, 1955.
The Early Churchills: An English Family, London, 1956.
The Later Churchills, London, 1958.
The Elizabethans and America, London, 1959.
St Austell: Church: Town: Parish, St Austell, 1960.
All Souls and Appeasement: A Contribution to Contemporary History, London, 1961.
William Shakespeare: A Biography, London, 1963.
A Cornishman at Oxford: The Education of a Cornishman, London, 1965.
Times, Persons, Places: Essays in Literature, London, 1965.
The Churchills: The Story of a Family, London, 1966.
A Cornish Anthology, London, 1968.
The Cornish in America, London, 1969.
The Elizabethan Renaissance: The Life of a Society, London, 1971.
The Tower of London in the History of the Nation, London, 1972.
The Case Books of Simon Forman: Sex and Society in Shakespeare's Age, London, 1974.
The White Cat of Trenarren, London, 1974.

Victorian and Edwardian Cornwall from Old Photographs, London, 1974 (with John Betjeman).
Discoveries and Reviews, London, 1975.
Oxford in the History of the Nation, London, 1975.
A Cornishman Abroad, London, 1976.
Matthew Arnold: Poet and Prophet, London, 1976.
Heritage of Britain, London, 1977.
Homosexuals in History: A Study of Ambivalence in Society, London, 1977.
Milton the Puritan: Portrait of a Mind, London, 1977.
The Byrons and Trevanions, London, 1978.
A Man of the Thirties, London, 1979.
Portraits and Views: Literary and Historical, London, 1979.
Story of Britain, London, 1979.
Memories of Men and Women, London, 1980.
A Life: Collected Poems, Edinburgh, 1981.
Eminent Elizabethans, London, 1983.
Night at the Carn and Other Stories, London, 1984.
In Shakespeare's Land: A Journey Through the Landscape of Elizabethan England, London, 1986.
Memories and Glimpses, London, 1986.
Stories from Trenarren, London, 1986.
The Little Land of Cornwall, Gloucester, 1986.
Court and Country: Studies in Tudor History, Brighton, 1987.
Froude the Historian: Victorian Man of Letters, Gloucester, 1987.
A.L. Rowse's Cornwall, London, 1988.
Quiller Couch: A Portrait of 'Q', London, 1988.
Friends and Contemporaries, London, 1989.
The Controversial Colensos, Redruth, 1989.
A Quartet of Cornish Cats, Redruth, 1992.
All Souls in My Time, London, 1993.
Historians I Have Known, London, 1995.
My View of Shakespeare, London, 1996.
Cornish Place Rhymes: A Commemorative Volume, Tiverton, 1997.*

* Collected, edited and published after Rowse's death.

Index